Scotland's

AN AUTOBIOGRAPHY OF THE NATION

Century

Scotland's

AN AUTOBIOGRAPHY OF THE NATION

Century

COLIN BELL

HarperCollins*Publishers*

HarperCollins Publishers
PO Box, Glasgow G4 0NB

The HarperCollins website address is
www.**fire**and**water**.com

First published 1999

Reprint 10 9 8 7 6 5 4 3 2 1 0

ISBN 0 00 472225 6

A catalogue record for this book is available from the British Library

Printed and bound in Great Britain by The Bath Press

Contents

᭯

An Autobiography of the Nation

Acknowledgments

❦

This book began when Caroline Adam and Ken McQuarrie of BBC Scotland suggested to me that I might be interested in making a 26-part series for Radio Scotland to mark the Millennium – and then very generously left it to me to decide what form it should take. I am very grateful to them, since it has proved to be 18 months of fascination and discovery, shared with a quite splendid production team of Sharon Mair, Jonathan Rippon, Karen Murdoch and Hazel Marshall – and something like 300 Scots of widely ranging ages, origins and experiences, all of whom gave us their time and their trust, and many their hospitality too.

What I knew from the start was that neither I nor the audience wanted a series of lectures based on second-hand research, nor a view of this most exciting century concerned with the headlines of history – the stuff of Cabinet decisions, economic trends, expert overviews and scholarly interpretations. All that is of course important – but it is also available elsewhere. Instead, we chose to concentrate on actual lives as they have been lived: and whereas few of us have been involved in high politics or high finance, all of us have experienced families, homes, school, work, play, courtship, illness, getting and spending. The net was therefore cast widely, and although there are famous names among those selected for this book, that is only because we wanted to convey the astonishing diversity of Scotland, to hear the voices of those who kept servants as well as those who had been in service.

Almost as soon as we began, it became clear that the very nature of radio production meant we could only use a fraction of the material we were gathering. When someone talks freely about their life for half-an-hour or more, as most did, it seems shameful to use only short quotations as part of the sound-mosaic which the programmes offer. This book is the consequence of that realisation – too much too good to rest unheard in the archives. Sadly, even in book form, we could not possibly use anything more than a fraction – but on balance, I felt it better to select a minority to use at length, than offer little more than expanded sound-bites from them all.

As you will gather, although my name is on the jacket, in this case it represents not the author as parent, but more as midwife. And just as I wanted to hear the century in the voices of those who have lived it, I wanted as far as possible to see it as they saw it, not through the filter of official and professional images stored in museums and libraries. So my final thanks go to all those interviewees who gave up yet more of their time to trawl through their cupboards and attics to find pictures not just of the past, but their own past. I only hope that none of them has any cause to regret sharing their lives with me, with you, and with posterity.

Colin Bell
Balerno
1999

Photographic Credits

❦

All the images featured in this book have been kindly supplied from personal collections by the individuals in whose section each particular photograph appears, with the following exceptions:

Scottish Life Archive, © The Trustees of the National Museums of Scotland: pp. 11, 14, 19, 20, 21, 54, 98, 101, 110, 111, 117, 136, 168, 185, 190, 248.

The Herald & Evening Times Picture Library, © Scottish Media Newspapers: pp. 24, 25, 62, 95, 154, 159, 174 (top), 183, 237, 239, 255.

George Washington Wilson Photographic Archive, © Aberdeen University Library: p. 23

Camera Press London (Jessie Ann Matthew): p. 140

Aberdeen Evening Express: p. 12

PhotoExpress, Edinburgh: p. 171

Bainbridge, Belfast: p. 207

Cencrastus Magazine: p. 262

Introduction

In 1901, Scotland's population stood at 4,472,103, had been steadily rising, and was to continue to rise until sometime in the early 1960s. Since then, it has been in decline, and by 1991 stood at 4,962,152, down from a recorded peak of 5,228,963 in 1971. That's what the Census tells us, but it doesn't really tell us much more. It certainly doesn't mean we have undergone some new wave of Clearances in the second half of this century – Scots have always emigrated in search of success, just as others have joined us from choice or necessity.

The fact is, although we live longer, we marry later, and have far smaller families. In the early years of the century, women's life expectancy was around 47 years – and up to a third of that short lifetime would have been spent carrying and rearing children. Now, the life expectancy is 77, and the fertility rate has halved – so those women who do have children (and the overall average is now just two, when once even the most privileged averaged six) will only spend around 15 per cent of their lives mothering young children.

That is important, not only in itself, but for the perspective it offers on lives as they are lived, not as they are aggregated for official or historical purposes. Time and time again in interviews with women, I was reminded that far more people have real personal cause to celebrate the contraceptive pill, the washing machine, and indoor sanitation, than space travel, or even the computer. Relief from unremitting pregnancy, and domestic drudgery, has brought far more opportunity for happiness than has female suffrage, unquestionably desirable as was that goal.

It has also brought more married women into the labour market – since it was always the slavery of the wash-house and the kitchen which kept married women at home just as much as social prejudice or male insistence. Yet it would be wholly wrong to imagine that unmarried women didn't work until the recent past. At the beginning of the century, nearly 150,000 of them were domestic servants, doing other people's drudgery; 40,000 were working in

THE SERVANTS OF A TYPICAL MIDDLE-CLASS FAMILY, OBAN, 1910

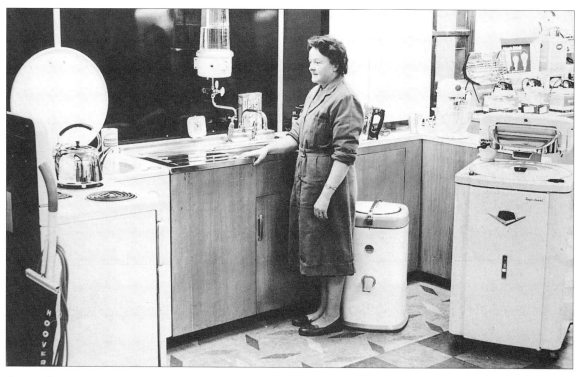

A WOMAN'S WORK IS NEVER DONE: THE 'IDEAL' KITCHEN OF 1959 WHERE GADGETRY WAS TO REPLACE DRUDGERY

agriculture; 200,000 in textiles, and as many as 20,000 up to their oxters in troughs of herring needing gutted. Which leads me to a point equally true for both sexes: what has changed, above all, in Scotland's working experience is the disappearance of the labour-intensive occupations. We may all know of particular local industries that have disappeared, from the herring in Wick to printing (and indeed paper-making) in Edinburgh, shale-oil in West Lothian to glasshouse tomatoes in Lanark, shipbuilding on the Clyde, jute in Dundee, the Navy and aluminium at Invergordon, coal throughout the Central Belt … but what *has* shrivelled on the broadest spectrum is hard, dirty, dangerous, manual labour. And if there is an up-side to the terrifying litany of Scotland's de-industrialisation – far more work now in hairdressing and public relations than in engineering – it is this: the cumulative total of great headline disasters like Gretna, the *Iolair*, *Piper Alpha* and Lockerbie, only amounts to about six years' regular daily toll from early 20th-century fishing and mining.

There are those who may still feel some curious, wistful regret that at the beginning of the century, only 0.9 per cent of the population worked in financial services, whereas now it is 9.0 per cent, while agriculture, forestry and fishing have plummeted from 12.0 per cent to 1.5 per cent. I suggest they turn to Matthew Sanderson and wonder which they'd rather their children did – a 'real' job down the pit – or stroked keys in a modern office?

Equally, although this book offers ample evidence that the National Health Service introduced in 1948 (and pioneered, we should not forget, by the Highlands & Islands Medical Service of 1913) ranks among the century's greatest improvements, a kind of collective amnesia has drawn a cloak over the plagues that once were with us every day. We quite rightly worry when *E-coli*, salmonella or meningitis strikes a dozen or two dozen victims, and seem to

SADLY, BY THE 1970S AND EARLY '80S, FOR MANY MEN, THE WORK WAS DONE, PARTICULARLY FOR THOSE IN SCOTLAND'S OLD INDUSTRIAL HEARTLANDS, NO MATTER HOW MUCH THEY FOUGHT TO DELAY THE INEVITABLE, AS HERE AT THE GARTCOSH STEELWORKS IN LANARKSHIRE.

have forgotten that for the first half of the century, Scottish children died in similar numbers every *day* from measles, scarlet fever, whooping cough and diphtheria. We may remember the scourge that was tuberculosis (and see Bill McLaren, p.61), but overlook the fact that in 1914, when TB took 7696, those four childhood killers accounted for 4516. The grim fact, appalling as it now seems, is that poverty alone could prevent a mother bringing in the doctor. For rather a long time in rather a lot of ailments, the doctor couldn't necessarily have done that much. Antibiotics are justly celebrated – but vaccines, prevention, matter just as much as cures. And we do now realise – thanks in part to the medical examinations of conscripts for two World Wars – that prevention isn't just a matter of jags. Diet and housing can stunt a life just as much as lack of appropriate medicine.

Sadly, that was a realisation – on which, in wartime and immediately post-wars, action was taken – which seems to have slipped way down the political agenda. The contrast between the children of the early century and the mid-century is very striking: so, unfortunately, is that between those of the Green Ration Book and those of today. Where once, public-sector homes, school milk and school dinners were seen as a common investment in the common good, they can now be presented as a reversion to the outdoor relief of the undeserving poor.

But then, every generation has its prevailing ideology, and all ideologists instinctively understand that to control the present, it is necessary to censor the past. If our politicians can no longer rely on the churches to exercise social control – and Scotland's religious observance has inexorably lessened in this century, to the point where the leaders of three different confessions told me that they could no longer attract enough vocations to staff their ministry –

then they will try to bring back family values. Which means, as it almost always has, bridle the lusts of the people.

For 70 years, from 1851 to 1921, the highest percentage of births out of wedlock – illegitimacy, as it was termed until only a few years ago – was recorded, not in the slums of Glasgow, Edinburgh or Dundee, but in Banff. In 1900, and still in 1930, bastardy was far higher in the rural North, North-East and Borders than the Scottish average. Without evidence, I surmise that the absence of access to contraception and illegal abortion is far more significant than the depth of religious commitment or social control. Only in recent years has the City of Dundee surpassed the illegitimacy rates of some North-Eastern parishes in the 1900s.

Of course, sex has many more competitors for our recreational time than once it had. This has been the century of the cinema, the radio, the television and unavoidable popular music. To all of which, the Scots have taken with enthusiasm – to the cost, perhaps, of traditional pleasures and tongues. The myth has it that Scots males, especially in the Central Belt, look only to the pub and the football ground for their entertainment: cinema attendances in the 1930s and 1940s, and, latterly, those at theatres, museums and galleries, suggest that this is not the case. And as for drink, the stern control between the First World War and Clayson can now be seen as a mere historic anomaly, when the interest of the temperance movement happened to coincide with those of the Ministry of Munitions.

It has also been the century of mobility. We may have lost much of the railway network which transformed lives in the 19th century, but many younger readers (those born after 1950,

IMPERIAL LOYALTY IN GAELIC-SPEAKING ROSS: SILVER JUBILEE CELEBRATIONS FOR QUEEN VICTORIA. THE BANNER READS 'LONG LIVE THE GREAT QUEEN OF BRITAIN'.

I realise I mean) will be amazed to discover there are those still living who had never gone from their island to the mainland of Scotland until adolescence, let alone to holiday in Spain. And personal mobility has been far surpassed by product mobility. The mobile grocer, even the Co-Op, never offered out-of-season vegetables (or hitherto unknown ones), and in the transition from the Divvy number to the Loyalty card, I think we have profited from a shift to consumer sovereignty (gullibility, in some cases) and away from supplier control. Refrigeration and the supermarket have, for many, taken yet more drudgery out of life: how nostalgically delightful that once there were a dozen specialist retailers to visit before the day's messages were complete. How exhausting to make all those pedestrian calls before going back to the blackleading, the water-boiling, the cooking, the ironing, and the shared bed in the shared room a stair-flight, or a garden path, from the nearest cludgie.

Oh, and by the way, very many of those 4,472,103 Scots registered in 1901 were happy to call themselves 'North Britons'. That is a change through which we're still living.

An Autobiography of the Nation

David Henderson

Farmer

Born 1890. Died 1998

David Henderson lived through the biggest decline in agricultural employment in our history. At the beginning of the century, it was our major industry, accounting, with forestry and fishing, for 12 per cent of the employed population, among them, 40,000 women. By 1991, that had fallen to 1.5 per cent, including just over 4000 women.

I left school between thirteen and fourteen years old, just at the beginning of the century. I never left the farming. When I started, I got no pay, just my food. I've had porridge for breakfast for one hundred and six years now. We got a choice when we were young, that was take it or want. Then we tried the want. We'd to eat a small turnip on the way to the school. That didna last long.

At the beginning, we grew wheat and oats. There was only wheat grown at that time after potatoes; we didn't think anything could grow but wheat sown in the autumn. It used to be twenty to thirty acres of wheat but now it's about three hundred acres. We sowed the barley and oats in the springtime and no matter how the weather was here, you could grow the best oats in Great Britain. There was oatmeal mills dotted all around the place at one time but they've gone now.

We had a drill which would work on the back of the traces on a pair of horses then – we would have done ten acres in a day. When I started work, if the land was too wet for the driller to be going, then they sowed by hand, which was a very hard job. We sow more grain now. Most of the grain now is sown in the autumn, barley, and quite an acreage of rape.

The coming in with the tractors was the biggest change, I think. When I come here in 1921 there was only three tractors in Kincardine-shire. I had one of them. My first tractor, a New International, cost £341, but there was the photograph of one I saw in the last few weeks – that was £56,000. A good pair of horses, well, the

THE OLD …

... AND THE NEW

price varied quite a lot, from time to time. About £100 each. They were Clydesdales – oh, they're wonderful animals, the horses. We missed the horses very much.

I started with three pair of horse and a tractor. If they ploughed an acre per day, a pair of horses, that was all they could do. This was hard land, more suitable for sowing in a short time with a tractor, compared with horses. Tractors can haul heavier implements and go faster and get the jobs done all quicker. Whereas for growing turrocks, with horses it's often too dry or they don't breer [germinate}.

Even when the tractors came, well, I don't think the manpower was cut down for some time after that. At the busiest time I had fourteen men. I've only three now. I had about four hundred acres. Now I've a thousand.

We raised Aberdeen Angus Cross and I went over to Orkney where they had very good ones at that time. That changed ... when they had to become attested [certified free from disease]. All the best Orkney cows were lost because the only cattle that were attested at that time was the dairy stock in the West of Scotland; farmers got a lot of subsidies in Orkney at that time and to carry on getting subsidies, they had to get the attested cattle from the West of Scotland but they were so different, the dairy breeds.

Farming and the Wars

During the 1914–18 War, a lot of our men were taken away, of course. We got soldiers in to do a lot of the work. First war, we'd very little food stuff: there was only wheat grown after the potato crop.

In the Second War, there was more government interference in what we grew. I was just ordered what to do at that time. We had to plough up when we didn't want to plough up. Some were surprised at the crops they could grow, and they kept growing them themselves but now the cereals are overgrown.

Farm workers

AN ANGUS FAMILY. C. EARLY 1900S

At the beginning of the century, an ordinary hind [a skilled farm worker] would earn a pound a week. In 1920, there was nobody got more than a pound a week. They often collected so much every fortnight or every month. In 1946, when I engaged the Thompson family, it was the whole family: the father and the mother, two sons and one daughter; the pay was £10 a week for the whole lot.

The married men, if they had a really hard master, often flitted [moved to another farm] every year. The single men they generally flitted every six months. They lived in bothies where I came from. They'd live there themselves. Brose, they ate, stirred with water and they'd have milk and meal and salt. There's not many bothies now.

Janet Adam Smith
Journalist

Born 1905

Early Life

I was born in Westbourne Gardens, Glasgow. My father, George Adam Smith, was then professor at the Free Church College in Glasgow and I was the sixth of seven children. We had a high house in Westbourne Gardens, looking onto communal gardens which were a great feature of our lives, what with our games and sports and so on. We had three servants including my beloved nanny, Bessie Crawford from the island of Arran.

In 1910, my father was appointed principal of the University of Aberdeen, and we moved away from Glasgow. We lived in the principal's house, Chanonry Lodge, a lovely house in Old Aberdeen which had an even better garden, huge with wonderful walls for climbing on, a tennis court and a big lawn in front of the house and lots of trees. We had one gardener though I don't know that he came every day. There was also a nanny for my sister and myself, but alas not my beloved Bessie because her parents didn't want her to come so far from Arran. So in all we had the nanny, and the cook, and a housemaid and a table maid.

In 1901, the Census recorded 146,788 indoor domestic servants, of whom 143,699 were women. Indeed, servants made up 5.7 per cent of the entire population of Edinburgh. (The second highest number were in Paisley.) Now, the census does not record them separately.

When my father was Moderator, we lived in another house because there wasn't then a Moderator's House; he was Moderator, not of the Church of Scotland as it is now, but of the United Free Church Assembly. There was a very nice minister friend of ours in Ballater, who would take us by train up Deeside on expeditions. Mr Walton, who was in Edinburgh at the Assembly, would show us the sights and one thing that was most exciting was to be taken into Princes Street Gardens and given these sliders – you know, wafers with ice cream in between. The Moderator then gave a series of breakfasts – this was in 1916 when austerity had begun – and we had porridge and cream. What I do remember is my father sending postcards when he did his Moderatorial tours. His tours were of Orkney and Shetland and the Outer Hebrides and he went out to the Army in France too. He would send us postcards from these so we were very aware of what was going on.

I began my schooling with a governess. We had a Swiss governess for some years who, along with my mother, taught me to read. Between the ages of about seven and ten, I had a governess who came for two hours every morning and taught everything really. I went then to Albyn Place School in Aberdeen till I was fourteen and then on to Cheltenham. My mother had been there as a girl and so had my next oldest sister Kathleen, so off I went away from Aberdeen.

A Privileged Life

We knew we had a privileged life in many ways. For one thing, we had one of the first telephones in Aberdeen in a private house – that was a great point of privilege, to be boasted about with friends, and we had electric light installed. But I think in general we realised we were very lucky. We had this lovely house and garden. I felt privileged being one of a large family because there was always something lively

ABERDEEN RAG FAIR, C. 1900

going on. We did plays and charades and games of all kinds and my elder brothers were very tolerant on the whole of their younger sisters.

But in Old Aberdeen one couldn't help but be conscious of people who lived a very different kind of life. At one end, beyond the cathedral, there was a lovely country house, Seton House, where lived the laird, Malcolm Hay and his family, who were great friends of ours. Their connections were more with county, where they had lots of friends among the other landed gentry. Malcolm was one of the last of the 'scholar lairds' and used to pass our house most days on his journey down to the university library. That was a slightly different world.

However, round at the back of us in Don Street there were big tenements and in the High Street of Old Aberdeen, as well as the shops like Maggie Forbes the dairy, MacWillie the grocer, and Mundy's the baker, there were various closes – one was called Wrights and Coopers Lane, another was called Waggerel's Close – and they were really pretty slummy. The old wifies would often emerge from them with their tartan shawls over their heads and their bad teeth. They would come into the High Street, which at that time also had handsome houses where professors and doctors lived, as a slightly alarming reminder that the world was not just for privileged people. My father used to walk daily to his office in Marischal College. We would often walk with him and it would take us up the Spittal and over the Gallowgate where there was plenty of evidence of lives lived on a less ample scale than ours.

The Great War

We had an uncle staying with us who had been a tea planter in India, a rather eccentric character who had raised a troop of horse from his tea estate to fight in the Boer War. He was tremendously agitated following the outbreak of war because he wanted to get into the army again although by this time he must have been well up into his forties. I don't think anyone was keen for this to happen but Uncle Bill's impatience and rushing to the post to see if call-up papers had arrived for him marked me very much.

ALICK ADAM SMITH (RIGHT), THE ONLY ONE OF JANET'S BROTHERS TO SURVIVE THE FIRST WORLD WAR, WITH HIS FATHER (CENTRE) AND US CHIEF JUSTICE TAFT DURING A VISIT TO THE WHITE HOUSE IN 1924

My eldest brother George, who was reading for the Bar in Edinburgh, was in the reserve of officers. He was called up by the Gordon Highlanders and went out to France. I remember it very vividly, and the sense of tension still more as the war went on. George was killed at Loos in September 1915 but for two or three days he'd been posted as missing. During these days I well remember my mother's gallant bearing and the anxiety in the house. I also recall her insistence that we younger children should not share too much in it, and her determination that we should not feel that, however awful the loss, all joy had gone out of life. Two years later my second brother, who had been in the Indian Army, was killed in East Africa. My third brother, Alick, was an officer, a subaltern in the Gordon Highlanders in France in the summer of 1918. That was a very tense time because you never knew what news there would be.

What I remember particularly is Armistice Night in 1918 because Alick was home on leave from France and he took my elder sisters Maisie and Kathleen and myself out to His Majesty's Theatre where a travelling opera company was doing Gounod's *Faust*. When it came to the Soldiers' Chorus, everybody sort of let go. It was just simply, 'here's the end of the war' and completely let go. My brother escorted us afterwards into Union Street to join the cheering crowds. I remember that we had great trouble in finding any kind of conveyance that could take us home, but it was a thrilling night.

Holidays on the Hills

We had our holidays, nearly always Easter holidays, on the island of Arran and as soon as we were able to trot up anything, we started climbing. It was scrambling rather than climbing on the Arran peaks at first. My brother George and his friends used to go off and do serious rock climbing but I always took it for granted that climbing was something that came naturally and that took one to lovely places.

Our inspirer and guide was my godfather, W. P. Kerr, later Professor of Poetry at Oxford, and he took us on all our first climbs. My father had been very active in his younger days in the Alps and in the Highlands, and he was an early member of the Scottish Mountaineering Club, but by this time he wasn't climbing so much. In fact, the poor man had to spend a good deal of his Easter holidays writing his books – I remember him toiling over Jeremiah while we set off with W. P.

My mother was always game for an expedition, and it was taken for granted that if girls wanted to go then, of course, they could go. There was no distinction that this was something that the boys did and the girls didn't do. My mother had climbed in the Alps in 1889 and there were plenty of her friends who enjoyed walking the hills of Scotland. Even if they weren't doing rock climbs and so on, it was regarded as an ordinary thing to do. I was quite surprised to find people who lived among the Highlands and never thought of climbing them. In climbing I had what you might call examples aplenty of women who climbed. The Ladies Scottish Climbing Club was founded when I was only two years old and its founder and first president, Mrs Inglis Clark, gave the Inglis Clark climbing hut on Ben Nevis, in memory of her son, also a climber, who was killed in the First War. The Inglis Clark name had been honoured in Scotland for a long time.

I started skiing under the auspices of the Secretary of the University, Harry Butchard, and my future brother-in-law George Thomson, who were both keen skiers in the Alps. Harry Butchard had a great idea that we should all go up to Braemar and ski one winter and I can't pretend that any skiing I've done in Scotland has been particularly enjoyable. It always seemed to involve a lot of trudging up wet snow on these boards that I don't think I was ever able quite to master there.

MORAY MACLAREN

An English Education A lot of girls from our part of the world had gone to Cheltenham – two from my own school had gone two years before I did. There must have been quite a strong connection with families in Aberdeen and Aberdeenshire and I'd heard so much about it. I was a great reader of school stories – I don't quite know if it was wanting to live out the fantasies of Angela Brazil but I always longed to go to boarding school. The thing that startles me in later life is how, having been a day girl in Aberdeen, taking the tram by myself, often escorting a younger sister or neighbours, coming back on a tram a bit late after play rehearsals, how I swallowed the whole business at Cheltenham of walking in crocodiles, never going out on my own, etc. I suppose I thought it was just a romantic part.

The teaching was on the whole very much better. For instance, at Albyn Place, I was taught Latin in a rather elementary way: we never did any Latin verse, any Latin poetry. When I was at Cheltenham, I was given special coaching by a mistress Jocelyn Toynbee who later on became a professor at Cambridge. I think it was a peak time for the quality of women's teaching because so few other professions were open to them; many who might have gone into the law or business or the civil service became teachers. For many graduates teaching was really the only option and we had first-quality teaching at Cheltenham which I greatly appreciated.

When I went to Oxford, there was no thought that I would have to be a teacher because I was lucky enough that my parents could afford to pay the fees, and I had a modest Exhibition as well, as a contribution towards them. Those who relied on what I think were called County Major Scholarships had to promise to teach, although during my time at Somerville, when the Higher Civil Service was opened to women, one Somervillian, Bay Kilroy, was in the first batch to be taken. The rules were altered so that County Major Scholarship people could opt for Civil Service and that's how Evelyn Sharp came not to be a teacher but the first woman to head a Civil Service department.

An Independent Life I think my wish to be independent, to earn my living and enjoy an independent life was stronger than my drive to do any particular thing. I had thought of the Civil Service following the example of Evelyn Sharp, but in those days you had to take so many papers. Each paper had a value of one hundred or two hundred marks and you had to take papers up to the value of some notional amount – 10,000, or something. People who'd read History or what was then called Modern Greats, and those who'd read Greats, I mean Classics, could accumulate the marks on subjects they'd done. But if you'd read English, as I did, you were very short of this. It would have meant cramming for a year or two in some other subject, to get the marks. I thought that would be rather a waste of time so I came home and had a very enjoyable year, learning to drive a car and learning rudimentary typing and shorthand. In those days, for graduates who didn't particularly want to teach and wanted to get into other jobs, it was pretty essential to have typing and shorthand.

So I came to London with a rather rudimentary qualification and got a job in the BBC, first of all in the Education section. My advice, given many times to young women who were hoping for a job in the BBC, was learn shorthand and typing. It's useful, but don't be too good at it; be very intelligent but don't be too good at typing. If you're too good at it, some man will clasp you to his bosom and never let you go.

If you're not too good at it but you are intelligent he will give you a glowing recommendation to move up.

I was given a job as sub-editor on *The Listener* when it started; I was pushed upstairs because my secretarial skills were not all that high. The assistant editor was Moray MacLaren; we became great friends and, in fact, I sometimes wonder how we ever did any work because we laughed such a lot. Moray was already, I think, in embryo a very keen Scottish Nationalist. It was only after he left *The Listener* and went up to the BBC in Edinburgh that I think he got to know the main figures of the Scottish literary renaissance. but it was through him that I got interested in Scottish literature in the 1920s. He wrote an extremely good book called *Return to Scotland* while he was still down in London, describing a walking trip he did across Scotland ending in Barra. He was a great friend of Compton MacKenzie too, so a lot of that trickled through. When I began, through my work in *The Listener*, to be really interested in contemporary poetry, it took in contemporary Scottish poetry. Some time later I gave some talks on BBC Scotland and was rebuked for my English accent!

Keeping the Aberdeen Connection

I've always enjoyed going back to Aberdeen, my younger sister lives there and I feel in a way I belong there. I was so young when we left Glasgow I had not had time to make all the connections and associations that I did in Aberdeen and so I've always enjoyed going back there. I'm always relieved to see that it doesn't seem to me to have changed as violently as many commentators felt with the coming of oil and so on. I mean obviously it has and on my visits it's just a superficial impression I get, but a lot does remain the same.

Alastair Dunnett
Journalist & Businessman

Born 1908 Died 1998

I was born in Kilmacolm, Renfrewshire, a very posh district, but we were on the wrong end of the rails. My mother had got back from Denver, Colorado in time to have me in Scotland so I've never a chance of being the President of the United States.

I went to school at Over Newton Public School in Glasgow. A chap whom I knew who was also there, when he went up for a commission in the Army he was asked what school he went to. 'Over Newton Public School,' he said. 'Damn good school,' said the Colonel, who was passing them in. I went to Hillhead after that.

We were in a dead end street and we were all experts at tanner ball. (In fact, when I was at the *Record*, I organised a tanner ball tournament.) It's a very handy size of a ball. You can stand on it and have the big boys floundering. When we got to Hillhead we had a very good team of keelie boys. With six of us we could outpace anyone in the playground. We had holidays in Cove in the Firth of Clyde, near Kilcreggan. That was wonderful. I learned to row boats and all that there.

The Lure of the Hot Metal

From very early on, I wanted to get into journalism. I had a rotten job in a bank but it was the only job I ever applied for and got. I sat an exam for it and was a promising accountant in the Commercial Bank which is now the Dome Restaurant in Edinburgh's George St. I had tried to get into journalism at that point and had failed, but about 1933 or '34, James Adam and I came to the conclusion we should be publishers. We published a tuppenny weekly for boys called *The Claymore* and that ran very successfully until the summertime – young people don't buy papers in the summertime – and we folded up. So we set out on another adventure: I suppose as a hopeful journalist I should have delivered papers but in fact I delivered milk instead. Sean Connery [also a milkman in an earlier existence] had a horse and cart – I had my own two feet in the slums of Glasgow but I've often laughed about it with Sean. I'm one of his trustees.

For my first newspaper job, I was headhunted for the *Daily Record*. Before that I'd been in charge of an extraordinary experiment by Outrams. They decided to publish, because they had spare presses in Aberdeen, a four-page supplement for *The Bulletin*. This was interleaved in the northern edition of *The Bulletin* which came up by train and the parcels were distributed up and down Deeside and all around. It was my first executive job. I was very happy and had a very happy time in Aberdeen – wonderful city.

Then I was headhunted by the *Record* and worked in Glasgow. My layouts in the north had attracted the attention of Clem Livingstone who was in charge. They asked me to be Art Editor which is nothing to do with art or editing: it's the picture chap. I then became Features Editor because there was no one else. I had said to Clem I think we should have a Features page with an article contributed from staff or outside and he said: 'Well, this is Friday, you start on Monday and you're running

28

it.' So I had to find six articles in addition to my pictures. This was still in the days of hot metal setting and if you wanted to put in a picture a stereo had to be made. I never experienced the paste-up pages. That was absolutely new to me. I was out of newspapers by that time.

People who weren't born then may say the pre-war period was safer, the tabloids now say there was less crime, but I wouldn't say so. There are stories now about how there's more sexual immorality and permissiveness, but I don't know. I don't think we were any worse than anybody else but we weren't an awful lot better. There was a tremendous amount of poverty and drugs and drinking meths and putting milk bottles over gas jets and filling it with gas, God knows. I've been in houses, slum houses which old Peter MacIntyre used to take me around, where you stepped over people with green faces drugged and lying there. We covered police courts, when the policeman would say, 'When I was called, Your Honour, to the scene the defendant was effing and c-ing.' I'm afraid that was of the essence.

The War

The war was a great occasion for me, if I may say so, because I worked all the time with Tom Johnston who was the Secretary of State. Tom was devoted to making sure that Scotland came well out of war. He had terrible bouts of course with Churchill and the Cabinet because it had been decided strategically that Scotland would manufacture nothing but they would store things. All the girls were taken down to England to work in munitions or whatever. I remember Tom coming back one day from the Cabinet and saying: 'If I don't get my way, Prime Minister, I'm going to tell the 51st Division after the war to bring their bloody bayonets hame wi' them.' He was a wonderful chap, he was terribly good. He saw the point and was very, very acute in finding the nub of the question.

After the war, Tom Johnston went off to do the Hydro Board which he had started during the war, amongst other things. I went back to the *Record* as Editor and that was my game. The *Record* then was a fairly scholarly paper – we had full pages of book reviews. We had a lot of excitement with comic strips of our own: Lauder, Willis and Gardnan – they were the three comic strips and they had some very good artists, beautiful drawings they made. One of them made Jack House a household name by developing his teeth which we all loved, you know. I hadn't thought of them as a beautifying or an attractive element.

Off to The Scotsman

In 1955 or '56, the Mirror Group took over the *Record* and it was the most unhappy six weeks of my life because I was abandoned by all my staff. They came to me and said: 'Alastair, I've got holidays to come' and off they trotted to get out of the trouble. I had no feature men left. I got on good terms with Hugh Cudlipp who liked haggis and neeps and I used to take him to the Royal Restaurant in West Nile Street. It was a very trying time – once we were in my conference room with two or three of the *Mirror* directors talking about the paper. I knew it was going to become the *Daily Record* or worse and I was called to the phone and it was Roy Thomson saying 'I'd like to see you.' I'd met him once or twice. I said 'How about lunch tomorrow?' So I went over to Edinburgh and he offered me *The Scotsman*. It was such a godsend because I decided never to leave Scotland, always to work in Scotland.

The Findlays, the former owners, had run down *The Scotsman* very badly. I met Findlay, the chief Findlay, six times and I never met him sober. I brought the

ALASTAIR DUNNETT WITH THE THEN-PRIME MINISTER, HAROLD WILSON, 1975

paper back from the dead, to be quite frank, I and the good team I found there. They were quite a good lot of people. I told Roy I wouldn't bring anyone new in for at least a year because I wanted to get to know the chaps and what they could do. We did very well. Circulation was hardly 50,000 and we brought it up to 80,000. I think the most we ever hit was about 100,000 under Eric Mackay, fifteen years ago, but it averages about 80,000.

Roy Thomson just left us alone to get on with it. His job was nothing to do with editing. He was always surprised that we had some other papers that didn't support the socialist view. They were all Tory papers under Lord Kemsley of course. He thought it very strange that editors weren't independent enough to be socialists in a socialist area, which Edinburgh was not. He was thinking purely in marketing terms: if you've got a working class, Labour-voting area, give them the paper that agrees with them. Roy always insisted he would spend any kind of money on plant and facilities, not on wages. It was your job to make it pay and you never could tell Roy anything carelessly because he never never forgot. But I was very fond of Roy. He set me free which was a great thing.

Dallas in Charlotte Square

Then, in the early '70s, Roy changed my life yet again: I became an oil tycoon. I was offered the job by one of his executives. He said: 'Roy wants to take an interest in North Sea oil. He'd like you to be president of the company' I thought, this is good, president of something – I was only chairman at that time of The Scotsman Group. In fact, I wasn't president, only chairman but that was a marvellous time. God knows the money we put into the Treasury and to Roy Thomson's family, hundreds of millions. Fantastic.

Gordon Wilson [later to be SNP leader] was going round saying it was Scotland's oil. I assumed it was Scotland's oil but I wasn't going around saying so. The Establishment moved in pretty quickly under Edmund Dell, who was a Cabinet minister, and they put the tax regime pretty stiffly on it but, nothing daunted, on we went.

They were wonderful chaps, these oil people – Texans and Californians. I got to like most of them. I had an office in Charlotte Square at this time with a good boardroom where most of the early meetings were held. These chaps, in Stetson hats and highheeled boots and dapper suits, came in at eight in the morning and took their jackets off and poured themselves coffee and they were hellish numerate. They were extraordinary people, very, very able. I think there had been a lot of spoils on the way but the ones who came through, by the time I was there, they were very good, and they were endlessly patient with a handless chap who just didn't know anything about anything.

Leisure Time

I used to go up to Arthur's Seat and back in the morning, with James Adam. We used to take a shinty ball and shinty sticks with us. We were founder members of the Edinburgh Camanachd Club. As for golf, well, everybody plays golf in Scotland. I can hit a golf ball always, left-handed or right-handed – I would always carry a number five corrie-fisted [left-handed] golf club in my bag.

I'm very hungry for the hills. I know them all very well and I'm terribly sorry I can't do it now. I never was a Munro-bagger, though. I thought that was a tiresome affair because you get some good hills in Edinburgh here. I remember two women teachers in Hutcheson's Grammar School in Glasgow. I remember them in the very early 1920s – they were Munro-baggers. With a new Munro they thought it was something for them to do. Women didn't take them seriously, men didn't take them seriously anyway. There's a chap, Hamish Haswell Smith, has just produced a marvellous book called *Scottish Islands*. When I reviewed the book, I said it's almost certain that there will be anchorage-baggers following that book – it's ideal for it.

Scottish Newspapers and Scottish Independence

People in Scotland have always remained loyal to their newspaper, whether it be *The Scotsman* or the *Herald* or the *Press & Journal*. They were well served by them. These were, I suppose, local papers. In metropolitan terms, they would be provincial papers, but they were good newspapers. We had people all over the world, often stringers of course, but they came through with stuff just as quick as anybody. I suppose the reason we flourished was just the sheer arrogance of the metropolitan mind. When the Festival started in Edinburgh we backed it right from the beginning. I wasn't there at the time, I was still in Glasgow but the last critics to come,if I recall, were the London ones. But there's an inbuilt patriotism, pride and style about Scotland still. I think this is a great place to live just now because Scotland's very exciting. The prospect of a new parliament of our own is very exciting. I've been on to that for a long time. In fact, we steered *The Scotsman* on to it. We were devolutionists, so to speak, from the very beginning.

There's some terribly good writing about the arts just now, some good criticism going. There's always been good criticism. I was successor to a staff man who had been fifty years at Stratford for the festival there, travelling down from Scotland to cover it and Glyndebourne and all these things. But we did our own thing and the Citizens' Theatre in Glasgow and the Traverse, we backed these to the hilt.

I think Scotland is more Scottish and more independent. In fact I hope to see Scotland absolutely independent. I've hoped for that for many a time but we worked up to it you know. We tried out everything in the way. I know Ireland very well, and they are making a wonderful job of it. The place is full of smart young chaps who wouldn't thank you for a job in London and they are very, very well trained and learning on the job.

David Daiches
Academic and Author

Born 1913

First Impressions

'This is Edinburgh, the capital of Scotland,' I remember my mother saying as the train drew into Waverley Station. I came to Edinburgh aged six when my father was appointed rabbi of the Jewish community here. I remember that journey very vividly: it was February 1919, a cold day and there were two horse cabs waiting for us. There were taxis in those days but for some reason they'd hired horse cabs. The President of the Jewish Community met us with a delegation and drove us to his house where we stayed for a few months before we found a house of our own. He was off to America so his house was empty. That was my first experience of Edinburgh. The house was in Lonsdale Terrace, right on the Meadows, which was to be my playground for years; our own house was on the other side of the Meadows, so the Meadows was always the centre of my childhood.

The myth of safer streets in earlier days is probably indestructible, but horses and horse-drawn vehicles presented their own dangers, killing 81 people in 1911, declining only to 36 by 1920, and 20 as late as 1935. And the beloved tram accounted for 24 in that same year. But also see Colin Morton, p. 74.

We played in the streets, we played in the Meadows, we went to Blackford Hill, we collected tadpoles in Dunsappie Loch; we were all over the place and nobody seemed to worry in those days. Nobody had cars in our street. If a car came into the street we all went to the window to look at it. I remember the old cable cars, before the electric trams came in. We used to go and peep through the middle rail and see the throbbing cable underneath. We weren't supposed to do this because it was dangerous, but we used to do it anyway and every now and again the cable broke and all the cars were stranded in the city until they repaired the cable. I remember my brother and I getting up early one morning and going to the top of Hope Park Terrace to see the first electric tramcar come up from the GPO to Newington. They'd already had electric trams in Leith, but they weren't in the city proper until sometime in the early 1920s.

There were still a lot of dray horses, carrying Leitch's Lemonade, and I remember them rumbling through the street. We used to run after them and cling to the back and get a free hurl. It was strictly improper and forbidden but we all did it. Those lumbering carthorses couldn't go fast anyway.

All our shopping was from local shops. We knew them all. My mother would ring Mrs Kerr the Fishmonger who served most of the Jewish community in those days, every morning and ask her what they'd landed that morning. 'I'll send the boy up with it' was always the response when my mother had decided what she'd want. There was always a boy with a bicycle, and a lot of things were delivered like that in those days.

My mother was 94 when she died. She remembered as a child in Liverpool, General Roberts coming back from the Boer War – the troops came back by sea to Liverpool. Everyone was given a holiday, and people lined the streets where he came riding on a white horse. I said to her, 'What was your impression of him?' and she said 'He was such a little man.'

Holidays

We went on holidays to Fife, always to Fife and mostly to Crail, where we went I think for seven years in succession, to the same house, at the corner of the Castle Walk. The old Fife Coast Express (which chugged along at about ten miles an hour) stopped at all the villages – Pittenweem, St Monans and all the others – and travelling on it, we

got to know all the fishing villages of Fife. I knew that coast like the back of my hand.

The great middle-class thing was to go to the seaside in August and places were classified according to income groups. You went to such-and-such a place if you were lower down the scale, and a little further up you went to another place and so on. Aberdour was lower down the scale than Crail. A lot of Glasgow people came to Crail, well-to-do, middle-class people. But the system of going as a family throughout the month of August, renting a house by the seaside, was pretty universal in those days; it's died out now – everyone goes to Spain or something like that.

Crail is part of my childhood, I loved it and I still have a great affection for it. It hasn't changed much.

Edinburgh's Jewish Community

At that time, the Jewish community numbered about 2,000 people, about four hundred families. The Jewish community first was established in 1816; there were individual Jews before then but the first community with a cemetery and a synagogue was established in 1816, but it was very small. It only grew with the influx of Eastern European immigrants following the pogroms of the late 19th century, mostly from Lithuania. People like Malcolm Rifkind's grandfather, for example, came over then. When my father came there were two groups of Jews in Edinburgh: there were what they called the Grune Yidden, the 'green Jews', the recent immigrants who still spoke Yiddish, and then there were the children of the old immigrants; these were educated at Edinburgh schools and were totally acclimatised to the city.

Then of course there was the marvellous Scots Yiddish which the Lithuanian immigrants developed in their encounters with their gentile customers. Most of them were pedlars, or 'trebblers' as they called it: they 'trebbled' or travelled on the railway line that no longer exists that went along the coast of Fife all the way up to Dundee with suitcases full of haberdashery to sell to the wives of fishermen in the little fishing villages. They went out early in the morning and came back in the evening and they acquired an extraordinary mixture of Scots and Yiddish which in fact isn't as odd as one might think because both have got Germanic backgrounds. There are many phrases, indeed whole sentences, which would be identical in Scots and Yiddish, for example, Goethe's alleged last words – 'mehr licht', 'more light' would be the same in Yiddish and in Scots and in German.

Many of the Lithuanian immigrants had wanted to go to America but they couldn't make it. Some got as far as Leith and settled in Edinburgh and a greater number got as far as Glasgow. The most extraordinary situation was that there was a rogue sea captain who took people to Dundee telling them it was New York, and landed them there – they really believed it was New York until they were disillusioned.

Originally the Jewish community were all around where the original synagogue was in Richmond Street, around Dumbiedykes way. As they prospered they tend to move out – Buccleuch Place became a favourite location. Number 33 Buccleuch Place had about four storeys, each of which was occupied by a well-known member of the Jewish community. It was known as *Drei und Dreizig* – '33' in Yiddish, and all around there there was a Jewish quarter. But if people prospered – some of them did, some of them didn't – then they tended to move out to the southside. Mr Stangel, the President of the community, who had a waterproof shop in Cockburn Street – he made a lot of money out of it, one of the few Edinburgh Jews who did make money, because we were not a rich community. He bought a house in Lauder Road, the first Jew to break out into the gentile southern suburbs. I was never aware of anyone who would have objected to having somebody Jewish arrive next door in a fashionable suburb.

The professional element in Edinburgh attracted those who wanted to be university teachers or doctors or lawyers but most Jews moved westward to Glasgow, which was the real Jewish city in terms of population. The Edinburgh community has dwindled now because it was never a commercial city like Glasgow. Glasgow was a magnet for Jews who wanted to get on.

Rabbi Daiches sets off from Edinburgh to visit Tel Aviv, 1924, flanked by his sons David (left) and Lionel

There were very few Jews anywhere else in Scotland. One or two settled in Inverness but there was never a synagogue there. There was a synagogue in Dundee; my father inaugurated one in 1921 although I don't think it exists now. I remember in the early 1930s meeting one Jew in the north-west Highlands who spoke only Gaelic and Yiddish, and had no English. But mostly they settled in Edinburgh and Glasgow.

Edinburgh Schooldays

People who were not bright, perhaps from poorer parts of town, may have regarded any type of protracted secondary education as not for the likes of them. They would have left school at the earliest opportunity. But there was a very generous provision by the Carnegie Foundation for bright working-class boys, and it was a meritocracy. If you were bright you could go right through university; there was funding, much more than there is today in a way.

There was a hierarchy of schools. There was of course Glenalmond and Fettes and then there were places like the Academy, which was socially higher up. George Watson's junior school had a very generous system of bursaries and if you were a bright boy, as I have to say I was, you won a bursary which meant you didn't pay fees – they actually gave you cash! Once it was seven pounds and ten shillings!

At Watson's, I achieved a modest competence in golf, which I rather liked. But you see, sports at school were always played on a Saturday, the Jewish Sabbath, so I was unable to participate and I got no experience or practice in sport at all. I was a good sprinter but I never in fact played rugger or any other sport, because it was on a Saturday.

We were a rugger-playing school. Soccer was regarded as a lower-class activity and nobody was very much interested in it. I don't remember any particular passion about Celtic or Hearts or anything like that among our sort of people – that was a working-class enthusiasm.

My father was totally uninterested in sports: the notion of people running around with a ball on a field seemed to him a terrible waste of time.

A Literary Life

I can't remember a time that I wasn't certain that literature was my vocation. I started writing poetry when I was about seven-years-old and I published my first poem when I was nine in *The Children's Newspaper*. BBC 2EH in Edinburgh – the old Edinburgh station which had a children's hour presided over by Auntie Molly – read out one of my poems when I was eleven.

By the time I was beginning to think about going to university, the Scots Renaissance of MacDiarmid and Grassic Gibbon had started. I graduated from Edinburgh in 1934 and then went to a number of universities all over the world, including Sussex and Cambridge; I was also at Cornell in America, for five years. After Edinburgh, I got a scholarship which took me to Oxford and then I got a fellowship at Balliol and then by an extraordinary coincidence I met Robert Hutchins who was the President of the University of Chicago, who'd just written a book called *The Higher Learning in America*. Hutchins was known as 'the boy president', he was only about thirty, but was a brilliant young man who wanted to totally revolutionise American higher education. A relative of his was a Rhodes Scholar at Oxford and we got to know each other. He introduced me to Hutchins, and Hutchins and I sat up all night talking about education. I was twenty-one or twenty-two and I'd just been appointed a Fellow of Balliol. He was terribly impressed that I'd read his book (which his relative had lent me). I think I was the only person in Britain who had read it because it had never been published in this country. Within two months I got a cable from Hutchins inviting me to go to the University of Chicago, which I did, with ambivalent feelings, but it was an adventure and it was exciting.

There was certainly an interest in Scottish literature in the USA and when they heard that I had come from Edinburgh I was asked by the University of Chicago to give a graduate seminar on Robert Burns. In fact, I gave the seminar on 18th-century Scottish literature and the Scottish Enlightenment. I gave the same seminar at Cornell and out of that my book on Robert Burns arose – which was first published in America. Professor Crane, the Head of the English Department at Chicago, who was a passionate lover of Robert Louis Stevenson, asked me next to give a graduate seminar on Stevenson. Imagine that happening at a Scottish university – it's unthinkable! And so that's where my knowledge of Stevenson developed because to prepare for a graduate seminar where you've really bright graduate students, you've really got to be pretty thorough. So I read all the works in chronological order and all the letters and all the subsidiary material that was available and then I wrote a book on Stevenson. So you see, my books on Burns and on Stevenson arose from my American and not my Scottish or English experience.

I always kept a base here. All the years I was in Sussex and Cambridge we had a flat in Edinburgh and came back every year, and of course the rest of my family stayed here. I always knew that I'd come back to Edinburgh eventually, even when I was in America. They had the excellent system there that if you teach through the summer session – you always got August off anyway – you got six months off the following year on full pay. So we always spent six months in Scotland every second year, all the time I was in America.

Wartime

The only time that I was away for any length of time was during the war. I served in the British Embassy in Washington; because I had the experience of working in America they wanted someone who had the gift of the gab and could talk to Americans. I came back two or three times. They flew me back to London in wartime and very nicely gave me a week's leave each time to spend with my family in Edinburgh. I remember coming back to Edinburgh for the first time after the war had started, noting the changes, and going round shopping with my mother to see how the rationing was working. I was a food expert: believe it or not, I wrote a pamphlet for the American public, for British Information Services, on the production and distribution of food in wartime Britain, which is regarded as a classic now.

Scottish Literature and National Identity

There's been a tremendous proliferation of talented Scottish writers: poets and novelists and short-story writers. There were a few in my time: of course there was McDiarmid who was the leader, and there were people like Norman McCaig who was two years ahead of me at university, and whom I knew from my first year at university; also, Archie Sutherland as he was then, who became Robert Garrioch or Geary, but there weren't many others. People like Violet Jacob were still alive when I was a student but MacDiarmid was well known and was a very controversial figure, and, of course, he liked controversy.

I heard MacDiarmid speak in the Edinburgh University Union in my last year at school and I was very much impressed by his extraordinary rhetoric and by the fact that his underpants were hanging out from over the tops of his trousers!

Hugh MacDiarmid

I think that in reading recent Scottish fiction, in particular, and reading the reviews and periodicals that come out, one is aware that there is a great deal of excitement going on in the literary world. I think probably this has something to do with changing political circumstances, but it's still true that though a bright Scottish novelist will have his first book published by, say, Canongate or some small Scottish press, his second book is almost always published in England, and until that habit is stopped there won't be a completely assured Scottish literary tradition flourishing.

At university, I was aware of the question of nationhood. I was aware of the National Party that was then being developed, and arguments about the Union. They were beginning to develop in the 1930s quite strongly and when I went to Oxford I found there was a group of Scots who were very self-consciously Scottish. Of course, Balliol was a 'Scottish' college and the Master, A.D. Lindsay, was a Glasgow Scot and so there was a strong Scottish tradition there. My first Immortal Memory at a Burns supper was in fact at Oxford – to mostly Scottish students.

I welcome the increasing interest in Scottish literature and in the distinctive features of Scottish social and cultural life, and I'm very much interested in the political implications of that interest. I wrote a book some years ago now called *Scotland and the Union*. I was trying to find out exactly what happened in 1707 and I got immensely interested in the early 18th century. I edited the works of Fletcher of Saltoun who opposed the Union, and I came to share the feeling that whether the Union was desirable or not, it was pushed through in a somewhat underhand manner. I think most people would agree on that issue. I got very interested in Walter Scott's view of the Union, which was curiously ambivalent. In *Tales of a Grandfather* which was written for his grandson, he tells the boy what a good thing it was that the two nations were now one and lived at peace, and yet, every now and again in his private letters and in his outbursts in his journal, he gives rise to quite the opposite sentiment.

That ambivalence is not uncommon. Boswell swithers the whole time. He was being proud of Scotland and the Scots, but he was deeply ashamed when he met a family from Fife in London who spoke Scots: 'Will ye hae some geel?' 'Oof aye,' he said. It was very common, that curious mixture. There was David Hume, a proud Scot who much preferred Paris to London and Edinburgh to both, but who nevertheless thought that Scots was a very corrupt dialect of English. Quite unhistorical, of course. I don't take that view.

I'm a great language man and I hate to see any language disappear. Every language is unique in its structure and its sounds and in its form. It carries a whole culture, a whole way of thinking and a whole way of looking at the world. Although I don't know Gaelic well, I did try to learn it once and I should hate to see it die out. As for Scots, there's an awful lot of artificial and fake Scots being written these days, which rather irks me. You see letters to *The Scotsman* occasionally, written in Scots that never was on sea or land, a sort of phonetic transcription of sort of street talk; if you did that to English you'd get a very strange language too.

In the 1920s, people were writing poetry in Scots, but I don't remember any Scots prose being written at all. I think this is a new development, because until there is a Scots prose, you can't really say that it is a literary language at the present time. The trouble is that Scots disappeared as a language of educated people, people who wrote books and were published, before the rise of the novel. So, the only way that Scots could get into fiction was as dialogue. There's some admirable dialogue in Walter Scott's works but he would never have dreamt of writing his actual narrative in Scots.

I think the 'Yes-Yes' vote about a Scots parliament gave an enormous boost to national Scottish feeling, I mean it was almost tangible; the number of parties I was invited to afterwards to celebrate the vote … There was no such feeling when I was a youngster. There was a tiny National Party and a great deal of 'wha's like us' and all that, but it wasn't channelled in a political direction at all.

Changing Times

Another thing which many people constantly allege is that morals have got worse, or alternatively more liberal, but it depends, of course, on what you mean by morals. I think there's much more of what they call permissiveness going on now among young people, and it's taken for granted that people have sex before marriage and all that. But in terms of morality in the wider sense, I think probably the years immediately after the First World War were at an all-time low. I remember the Meadows being full of drunks in the 1920s and people would go around throwing empty bottles about, and of course the poverty and squalor of the High Street in the early 1920s when there were children without shoes with rickets, and women with shawls coming out with bottles of gin from the back premises of pubs. It was a pretty sordid sight. On the other hand, I remember Rose Street as a student and of course it was the great street of pubs and The Abbotsford was one of the great gathering places of the poets. I don't remember it being rowdy or dangerous or rough. It was just a place where one gathered to drink. I don't remember – I may have had a very innocent eye.

In fact improved nutrition was not the main cause for the eradication of rickets: improved housing was. More windows and wider streets means more sunlight, and the body converts sunlight into Vitamin D at a far more effective rate than can be achieved by taking pills.

Though I deplore a lot of what is being done in Scottish architecture, like the horror that is the St James Centre or what the university did to George Square, nevertheless they have cleaned up the High Street, and the festering slums of the St Leonard's area and the High Street are no more. There's more *reported* crime but I doubt very much if there's actually more crime. In fact, there may well be less now.

Free orange juice and cod-liver oil brought the revolution. The barefoot children with rickets that I saw as a youngster in the High Street disappeared during the war and have never come back.

Probably the most palpable revolution in my lifetime is the enormous change in the role and status of women. My mother married at nineteen while her younger sisters all went into professions because the family lost its money. My mother's father was a furniture manufacturer in Liverpool and the factory went up in a blaze. He hadn't insured it, on the grounds that it was God's will that if it should burn it would burn. It was God's will and it did burn so the family lost its money just after my mother married and all her younger sisters – she was the eldest of five sisters – had to go out and work. They all got professional training: two became music teachers, one became a French teacher and oh, how my mother envied them! She was a gifted pianist and wanted to be a professional musician but in spite of a very good relationship with my father she was nevertheless frustrated because she didn't want to be just a housewife. She was so proud and pleased when my sister Sylvia did brilliantly in languages and became a professional university teacher of French. That's the kind of thing she always wanted to do.

One now takes it for granted that there's a woman Speaker at the House of Commons, and there's talk about a woman Moderator of the General Assembly. This would have been unthinkable in the 1920s and '30s.

Kenneth Roberton
Social Worker

Born 1913

Early Life

I was born in what was then Camphill Street, adjacent to Queens Park just off Pollokshaws Road, number five, at five o'clock in the morning on the 23rd of October. I've no vivid memory of it, although I undoubtedly was there.

My father was married when he was twenty-one and, in 1907 when he was only thirty-three, his first wife died. His mother actually died in his house in the very same week – it must have been a terrible, terrible time for him. He was a widower with six children and, it's apocryphal, but my story is that he ran out into the highway and shouted: 'A woman! A woman! I need a woman urgently!' However, it actually worked. He had employed a man called John Burkmeier, whose family lived in a tenement building not far from his office. The eldest daughter, Helen, was a woman of great dignity and compassion. She was at that time deeply religious in an orthodox manner and she was prevailed upon by her father and her elder brother to give up her job as a waitress in Glasgow and become housekeeper to young Roberton, who was in a state of utter despair – he had his business to run, he had his musical work to do, his heart was broken and he had six children to look after. Helen became his housekeeper and two years later, almost inevitably, they married. Then there were three more of us. So I call myself Opus Two, Number Three.

By then, my father had a dual occupation. He had started work in life as an apprentice funeral undertaker in the business owned by his father which was James Roberton and Son in Eglinton Street. My father had gone independent because the 'Son' was his elder brother who succeeded to the business and my father, at twenty-one, was the general manager of the funeral department of the Glasgow Tramway and Omnibus Company. In the course of time he came back into the family firm, but all the time he was developing his musical talent and interests, totally by self-education, and by the time I was born, he was undoubtedly both a funeral undertaker and a musician.

I was brought up in an extraordinary house. It was in the corner of a tenement building and had ten rooms and kitchen. It occupied two floors, a raised first floor and a semi-basement ,and had long, long passages in which we could roll jars to make what was called liquorice water. My father's music room was large enough that sectional rehearsals with forty-five sopranos could comfortably fit into the room and sing. It was a beautiful house and it looked straight into Queen's Park.

The 'Burns and Bible' Socialists

My father had been brought up in the Evangelical Union which is similar in tenets to the Congregational Church. My mother had moved from her native Presbyterianism to Wesley Methodism by conviction but together they, like many people at that time, moved away from an acceptance of the orthodox tenets and became socialists. The socialist movement was then burgeoning and it was far more than just a political philosophy: it was a whole philosophy of life and brotherhood and how you all lived with one another, and this seemed to them to be the true objective of true religion. So they became members of the Independent Labour Party

The polite pinks of the Socialist Sunday School are just one element in the mythology of Red Clydeside, alongside the women who ran the rent strikes, the shop-stewards of the yards and forges, and the municipal socialists whose first concern had been Irish Home Rule rather than revolution at home. For all the hagiography of John MacLean, Scotland's only successful revolutionary of the century was from Forth, not Clyde – but James Connolly ended up in front of a British firing squad in Dublin in 1916, not in the House of Lords, like Shinwell.

– active socialists. My father earlier had been the secretary of the Tradeston Conservative Association when he was a young and rising-up businessman and doing well.

We grew up knowing people like Ramsay MacDonald and Philip Snowden and George Lansbury and other leading figures in the socialist movement. Whenever they came to Glasgow they stayed with the Robertons. That was something I never understood except there was an astonishing air of hospitality about my mother. My mother was a miracle worker but I've never quite understood why it was assumed that it would be restful for these people to live in a house where there were nine children storming around but it was.

My parents became active in The Study Circle, which had been founded by Robert Shanks, who had originally been a Liberal. In essence it was a kind of socialist Quaker church, the declared aim of which was to study the social and political problems of the day in the light of the ethical teachings of Jesus. Many of the adherents of socialism in Glasgow at that time were, like Keir Hardie, 'Burns and Bible' socialists. They had emotional attachments to the old kirk, to Presbyterianism, but they had abandoned some of its tenets. Nevertheless, they thought that some coming together of minds in a worshipful way was appropriate, so the Study Circle met every Sunday morning at eleven a.m. At the meeting, there was an address, frequently given by some prominent speaker who had been there the night before for a Saturday dinner or was going to do a Sunday night meeting in the city, and they sang some secularist hymns. We attended the Sunday School.

Last year, when I did a memorial service for my brother, I was reflecting on how every Sunday morning, these three little boys left Camphill Church, which was the orthodox Established Church, and at the bottom of our drive we passed the United Free Church which believed in exactly the same God but believed that it must be united and free in worshipping him. We then passed the Church of the New Jerusalem and that was the same God also but you could only understand his mysterious ways if you were a Swedenborgian. We then passed the Synagogue which was also the same God but with some different emphases – did he have a son or didn't he have a son – and we then passed the Baptists where cleanliness was not only next to godliness but equivalent to it, more or less. And having passed all these we mounted a tram car which took us to the Study Circle where God was not really recognised. Jesus Christ as a man and a teacher and a philosopher and someone who gave something of infinite value to the world was recognised and in a sense he was the worship. It was the Socialist Church really of the city and quite a lot of the important ILP figures were attached to it.

Socialism in Glasgow at that time was very heavily tinged by Burns and the Bible. After all, what other nation had as its premier poet a man who was always preaching the brotherhood of man, who was an egalitarian and libertarian? And whatever one may think of the bigotry of Calvinism, at one time there was also the idea of universal education, of democratic control of the individual churches and of a national church. All these things fitted with the socialist ideals of that place and time – somebody once said that if the revolution was carried out by the Glasgow socialists the gutters would be running in tea.

Schooldays & Holidays

I went to to the local primary school first, Strathbungo Primary School, then after sitting what was called in those days 'the qualy' – really the 11-Plus – after that I went to Hutcheson's Grammar School. I expect I would have gone to one of the local secondary schools, Shawlands Academy or Queens Park, but a tradition had become established of all the Roberton boys going to what was known as 'Hutchy'.

During the General Strike, I walked to and from school every day as a matter of principle. I would not be seen on a scab-driven tramcar because my formative upbringing made me entirely on the side of the strikers, entirely on the side of the miners. It wasn't a long walk but it was two miles each way; for a boy of twelve it wasn't much but it was a quite deliberate act on my part. At Hutcheson's Grammar, the Roberton boys and no more than a handful of others were brought up Socialist while most of the others came from Conservative or Liberal family backgrounds and there were those with parents who were all for smashing the unions or driving the miners back underground. But I don't remember any animosity. We used to sit and discuss these things as the rain poured down in Crown Street at lunchtime. I would sit with Douglas Lilley and we would talk these things through and there was never any animosity. It was all tolerant acceptance of differences. We agreed to differ.

Holidays were of immense importance to us emotionally. In the beginning we were going to Whiting Bay on the island of Arran and had holidays on the Ayrshire coast. I have many happy memories of the Whiting Bay holidays. Coming back from Whiting Bay was a great experience: the whole of Glasgow was coming back at that time. There were middle-class families like us who somehow could afford to be on holiday for the whole month and there were lots of other families who were just on holiday for the Fair fortnight. The end of the Fair fortnight coincided with the end of the month so there were thousands and thousands of Glaswegians all trying to get home on the steamers. The old paddle steamers were beautiful. At each pier, family parties would swarm on to the steamer and the kids would look around to see if they could find a space for Mum and Dad. They could then go up to the bow of the ship or to the stern or to the engines – the engines were marvellous. There's family parties running around and they suddenly find a space: 'Mum! Dad! Here's a space!' So Mum and Dad got settled down with all the luggage in this space and just as they were relaxing, a little woman sitting beside turned to them and said: 'That's a coffin you're sitting on.' And this happened at pier after pier to these unfortunate mums and dads.

A Passion for Queens Park

I loved playing games, every kind of game. The merest sight of a ball to this day makes my feet itch. I want to do something with it in the way in which the great dribbling footballers did something with it. In my teens, my friend and I regarded ourselves as the real footballers. The others just kicked and rushed. We had ideas about the game, Dick and I. He was three years older than me and we used to go and watch the Queens Park team of that time. Before that I occasionally saw them, during what was known as the 'last twenty': twenty minutes from the end of the match the gates were opened to prepare for the exit of the crowds and kids could then swarm in for nothing so I'd seen quite a lot of last twenties. Then I was there for most home games for a period of time, following a very great Queens Park team, at Hampden.

They were good crowds. There would be ten or fifteen thousand people there to watch Queens Park because that team could compete with the best in the land. The team I followed was Harkness, Campbell and Wiseman, MacDonald, Gillespie and King, Crawford, Chalmers, McLelland, MacAlpine and Nicholson. Of that team, astonishingly six were all amateurs while six were full internationals. Now MacAlpine unfortunately had been born in Liverpool and by the rules of that time he couldn't play for Scotland but he unquestionably would. He was the most entertaining player in Scottish football. When Queens Park played a friendly with Liverpool he was offered – and this was about 1928 or 1929 – £10,000 to turn professional. But he didn't.

This was the twilight of amateurism and this was the last great Queens Park team. Harkness, Chalmers and Nicholson all turned professional; Harkness and Chalmers with Heart of Midlothian while Nicholson played for Rangers. That was the beginning of the drift away from Queens Park and we know where poor Queens Park are now. I look sadly every week to see them just managing to stay within the divisions, very near the bottom. Thereafter, Queens Park was just used as a showcase mainly by young players, as a stepping stone to professionalism. But that team was great. It was great fun because they did play like amateurs. When they ran out on Saturdays especially big Mutt MacAlpine, they looked like men out to enjoy themselves, to have fun.

The Orpheus Choir The Choir dominated the house – it came and went through the house like a tide – and not only the Choir, but many other people, who would sit down sometimes without anybody being invited. Invitations weren't necessary. The door was open and the people came in and sometimes they sat down with others; on a Sunday sometimes there were over twenty to tea. Looking back on it, I think that people in the Orpheus Circle, and the wider circle of my parents' friends, used to say after the Sunday mid-day dinner: 'What will we do this afternoon?' 'What are the options?' 'Well, you could go to the museum or you could do this, or you could go to the Robertons.' And they'd just turn up and open the door and shout 'Hello anybody in?' There were other functions of the choir which were performed in the house at that time – the annual re-examination of the members was held there. That was a pretty tense time. I can still hear: 'Will someone bring smelling salts. Janie Stewart has fainted.' She was a highly-strung lady was Janie.

I sang in the Choir for six years; it wasn't compulsory for the family but I was the last. I did it partly for companionship, I think. I was the last of the family left at home. Our family was greatly reduced by emigration. Cecil, Hugh, Arnold, Mamie and eventually John, five out of the nine went abroad to seek their livelihood because it was the only place that a livelihood could be got at that time. And then Alan went, so eventually I was left alone with my parents. My father had brought one member of the family, Arnold, into the family business. He used to sign himself 'Arnold M. Roberton, CA' and when he was asked what 'CA' stood for, he would say 'Chauffeur of Automobiles'. But Arnold was destined to be a rolling stone. That was in his nature and thereafter we all had found other ways of earning our living and no one was drawn into the family business. My father asked me at one time but it wasn't what I particularly wanted to do.

My father and I had a very warm companionship and he said to me one day, 'You must go to Gilbert and get some singing lessons.' Gilbert was a very revered family friend who was a prominent singing teacher. After I had had some singing lessons from Gilbert I was permitted to present myself for examination for admission to the Choir. I think he wanted me in so that we could travel to things together and so that when he had to go somewhere by car, he would have had a handy chauffeur.

Career Difficulties   It became my ambition to be a social worker. I was then a clerk in the office of the Canadian Pacific Railway Company in Glasgow, then known as the world's largest travel organisation while in the evenings I worked in a boys' club, preparing myself to become a full-time social worker if I could find the opportunity. In course of time there was an opening for a probation officer in Glasgow. I applied and was appointed by the Probation Committee. The appointment was subject to ratification by the Secretary of State for Scotland. Some time before, I had engaged in a rather bitter controversy with a man who was the Secretary of the Roman Catholic Archdiocese of Glasgow, concerning aspects of the Spanish Civil War. Within days of my provisional appointment, the Roman Catholic Church had lodged an objection to the appointment of this godless young man – they knew very little about me except that I had crossed swords with their secretary. Soon thereafter, the Presbyterian Church thought that if this young man really is godless and anti-Christ, we are failing in our Christian duty if we do not object as well. So they objected. At that time, there was in Glasgow a combined body of the other churches presided over by the Episcopalian bishop and they also discovered it was their Christian duty to oppose my appointment. None of them knew anything about me but that didn't matter and so they all opposed my appointment. The Secretary of State for Scotland or a senior official was then facing a dilemma. What do we do? Do we offend the entire religious establishment of Glasgow or do we thwart the ambition of one young man? They decided on the latter.

Two years later, I was an assistant warden of a hostel for difficult evacuees, and the probation authority in Glasgow attempted to appoint me once more and ran into exactly the same storm. I had a long interview with the bishop who was the chairman of this multiple churches committee. He said to me: 'We've made a terrible mistake. We've done a dreadful thing Mr Roberton. I can see that you want to be a probation officer, you have the qualities to be one and we must put this right. I shall therefore call my committee and we shall interview you.' So I was called to be interviewed and I stood outside a room which was not soundproof and I heard many things said about me which were untrue, which had no basis because they didn't know me. The secretary eventually came running out and said: 'Mr Roberton, I can't invite you in. The committee is refusing to see you.' I said: 'It's all right. I'll just go. I'm sorry for you and I'm sorry for it.' And that was the end of it.

At that time, I had just applied and been accepted for a job in Bristol. I became warden of a probationary hostel which I ran on certain principles which were established by people like Homer Lane and David Wills. The boys were all drawn into managing the community. What I was saying to them was, this is a small community, a microcosm of the world, and you've got to run it with me. I'm not going to tell you. I'm not going to make any rules. We'll all work out what rules are good for the community between us. At the end of the war (in which I was a conscientious objector), I withdrew from residential work because we had a child and my wife, although she was totally in sympathy intellectually, she was not temperamentally able for quite a difficult life.

A New Lease of Life   I was offered a job in London by the chairman of the music publishers, Kirwan's, who had been a close friend of my family for a number of years. Eventually I became the general manager. Then Kirwan's were taken over by an American corporation and many unpleasant things happened. One feared that there was an asset-stripping operation and an opportunity arose for me to withdraw, bringing with me most of my father's work which had been published by Kirwan and that was how I came to establish my own business. I was then living in Wendover and I had a large converted windmill and space for a business. So, like my grandfather before me, I set up on my own at fifty-seven.

Jack Firth
Artist & Teacher

Born 1917

I was born in Edinburgh and when I was a schoolboy, we lived in a tenement in Montgomery Street, off Leith Walk. We had no garden, so my playground was London Road Public Gardens or the Calton Hill. I played up there all the summer holidays usually with a pal or a couple of pals. We would come home and have something to eat at midday – it was called dinner then, not lunch – and then we'd go back up the Hill in the afternoon. You have to say that twice nowadays because people today look aghast when you say it – Calton Hill? We were never threatened by anybody or anything but it would now take an armed escort of SAS to get me up on Calton Hill after five o'clock at night because it seems to have been given over totally to all these perambulating males who go around and all the guys who bash them, if you get caught in the crossfire. I think there's a drug scene going on pretty heavily up there as well, I find that very sad; it's done away with one of the great delights of living in Edinburgh, to be able to go up there. It's a wonderful view.

We knew every nook and cranny of it when we were kids; there were places you could hide and where you could stage Custer's Last Stand on, attack the wagon train or the re-enact the Battle of Loos. There was a First World War tank up there of the Cambrai variety, the big rhomboidal shape, and it was parked on a piece of concrete just to the east of the Parthenon. It was well sealed up so you couldn't get inside it – we tried – and we used to play on that. There were various Peninsular War cannons sited all around the place, one of which I think is still there. It points over Princes Street and we used to sit on that and decimate the Scott Monument, in the immoral way that small boys have.

So many things are different now. In Nigel MacIsaac's famous little amateur film, *The Singing Street*, which is about children playing in the street – that was made in 1951 and they were still playing in the street then. Even

Jack Firth's father outside his tobacconists' shop at 7 South Clerk Street, Edinburgh, 1928

with all Councillor David Begg's efforts, very few children can play in the street today, not even in Princes Street. Kids nowadays, wherever they live whatever part of Edinburgh they live in, they can learn to ski, they can learn to sail, they can learn to horse ride, they can do all these things that we never even dreamt of. And skiing – people didn't ski in Scotland in my youth, nobody thought of it. Those that did went to Switzerland to ski so you had to be pretty wealthy. I was never abroad till I was in the Army.

I went to school at George Heriot's. I was a blue-eyed boy at school because they didn't have too many people doing art in a big way. I think I was three when I knew I wanted to be a painter. My family were totally supportive. My mother was a professional musician and was very happy about that. It was probably the only thing that I felt that I ever could do very well.

An Art Student's Life I trained at the Edinburgh College of Art. It was about a third of the size it is now. It's now a very large college. We operated out of the one building, behind the old fire station in Lauriston Place and the whole college was in there, all the four schools. They were grouped round the Sculpture Court and that was more or less the *Mare Nostrum* of our time and was the centre of the universe for us. Everything happened there, including your social life. You had the College Revel every year in those days, like the Chelsea Arts, and that was the big event of the year in the social calendar in Edinburgh.

Looking back on it, I think we were incredibly innocent. The idea that people go to an Art College to be wild Bohemians is rubbish. We had a very quiet student life, apart from things like the Revel. People thought you went mad at that, but it was really just a fancy dress ball. We didn't drink all that much, there wasn't a lot of that around. I didn't smoke until I was twenty-three as it happens, although other people did. I think we had a fairly cloistered life compared to students today.

In those days you never saw an anorak or duffel coat or jeans or anything like that – you dressed in flannels and a sports jacket. When I first went in my first year – I was just wearing the usual casual attire that I wore in those days – I remember seeing people walking about with smocks on. They looked as if they were about to form up and do 'Shepherds Hey', it looked very bucolic. I always said when I become a painting student here, I am going to buy a smock so that I will really feel like a painter. I bought one and I had it all the way through college. I used to wipe my brushes on the sleeve, in the crook of the elbow, everybody did this; occasionally you sat on a palette or something like that so you really had to have a smock on. I remember when I dispensed with it, I just stood it up in a corner near my locker!

We had no money at all. We had no student grants. Edinburgh College of Art was well endowed with bursaries from Andrew Grant's bequest; there were eight of these for entrance and there were also fellowships and things like that. I never had one and most of the people I know never had one. We didn't have government grants at all and the cost of materials was wild even in our day. Students today don't believe this but we painted on canvases because there wasn't any hardboard. A canvas and a stretcher cost a lot of money in our day. Students today are astonished because a stretcher and canvas are a luxury, especially for a student.

In our day you did a general course for two years, where you got a kind of taster of all the different schools in the college: design, sculpture, a bit of architecture (although not very much) and endless drawing. We drew and drew and drew. After the second year, and if you passed at that stage, you went into a third year and specialised in either drawing and painting or design or sculpture. I did two years of intensive drawing and painting, going on to a third year eventually. My training was as rigorous and as specialised as I think art training ever has been. Edinburgh had the reputation of being rigorous and maybe rigid even. The idea was to train people in the basics of the craft and let the development come later. So when we were students, we were not encouraged too much to experiment or to try and change the world by our art and we were certainly not encouraged to exhibit while we were students.

That's changed enormously. The Diploma Show in our day – it's a Degree Show today – was a non-selling show. Buying was really frowned upon. It did happen surreptitiously, and I know some very nice people, including professional artists, who bought from students to support them but they had to do it behind closed doors. Nowadays, the Degree Show is a selling show with big prices. Students now don't charge student prices, they charge professional prices.

In my year, 1935, there were twenty-four of us, twelve men and twelve women. By that stage it was acceptable for women to go to art college. In fact there used to be a society of women artists, it's now become SAAC. It was started by the father of Lily MacDougall, who was a very famous woman painter; she painted flower pieces all her life right into old age. It was started in order to give women a better chance in exhibitions. Women had always been put down in exhibitions and in the art world generally. The women artists that I knew when I was growing up as a student, artists like Penelope Beaton who taught me, they had a pretty rough ride up on the way to getting themselves established. They didn't cut a lot of ice with the old Academicians and people like that. Penelope was was sixty-six when the RSW elected her and seventy-two when she was made an Associate of the RSA; she never made it to full membership. I was lucky, I got into the RSW first time. The first exhibition that came round, I proudly put my full complement of five pictures up, and Penelope was at the opening and she came up and congratulated me and then she said: 'But you know you were bloody lucky. It took me five shots.' Anne Redpath got kicked out three times from selection for the RSW, so she never applied after that. She sent pictures into the exhibitions, but only after the management changed, once Adam Bruce Thompson and people like that took it over and it broadened out. Then she was quite happy to send pictures in. She said to me once: 'I will never give these old men a chance of rejecting me again.'

Making a living Anyone who ever goes in for art realises that it is fraught with hazards and it's always been like that. I was always intent on being a teacher. I think it's the missionary part of me. I wanted everybody to share what I enjoyed in art so I was very happy to teach. People occasionally taught because it was a way of making a living and it would enable them to paint. That was never my viewpoint but when you think about it, all the people who taught us and that's all the legends now, from Bill Gillies downwards, they were all teachers. Everybody had another job. There were very, very few people, even in pre-war days, making a living by painting alone – even those who did, with distinction, people like Sam Peploe, only made a reasonably comfortable living, they didn't make a fortune. In fact, most of the established professionals in my day didn't actually sell all that many paintings. It was almost a cause for celebration if they sold a painting.

In Edinburgh before the war there were only two commercial galleries. There was Aitken Dott's in Castle Street, and Doig Wilson & Wheatley in George Street. Other than that, there was the Royal Scottish Academy building which housed four annual exhibitions, a gallery in Shandwick Place called the New Gallery, which was the home of the very elite Society of Eight and one or two other groups who exhibited there over the years. They closed up in about 1939.

When I was a student, we didn't visit the two commercial galleries. We thought they were fairly august and probably catering for an elite clientele of reasonably wealthy collectors, which in a sense they were. I think we might have been welcome if we'd gone in but we didn't. We went to see what was happening in exhibitions like the SSA and occasionally the RSA. I don't remember ever going to the RSW when I was a student probably because it was a bit pedestrian in those days. But the SSA, yes, and we went mainly to see what our teachers did, people like Gillies, Maxwell, and Mactaggart.

Other than that, Edinburgh was a very sleepy scene as far as art's concerned. It had a National Gallery, of course, with a much smaller collection than now and much less fine. We did go there for study purposes, but it tended to have an aura of sanctity about it, it wasn't the kind of place where you felt the doors were wide open. In fact, although they were expertly and professionally run by wonderful curators from time to time, it wasn't until fairly recent times that Colin Thompson really came out to meet the public. He did it in a very discreet way but nevertheless, that's what he did and immediately the public awareness of the National Gallery and its treasures was greatly increased.

Before the war, Edinburgh's population were not enthusiastic buyers of pictures. It would be very unusual in the average middle-class house to find original works of art on the walls, though James Ritchie, who made *The Singing Street* with MacIsaac, has an enormous private collection. He's loaned a great section of it to the Gallery of Modern Art – two rooms full of Scottish Colourists, which formerly were housed in a small house in Kenmure Road in Corstorphine. He is a collector and out of a teacher's salary, he did that all his life. Nowadays, almost every house I go into has original works of art on the wall. Now, I'm aware that there are houses in Edinburgh where there's nothing on the walls, but for the great middle area of the population, buying pictures is something which is no longer unusual. Most people who buy pictures are not collectors, they just happen to like to have original works of art around the wall rather than Medici prints or Athena prints.

There was an explosion of art awareness on the part of the general public after the war. After those years of cultural starvation – the blackout and all that, galleries closed up, pictures removed to store – people really longed to get some kind of culture going again. The Arts Council started vigorously promoting art in a way they don't do now. They promoted exhibitions and bought pictures, they sponsored the arts in every possible way. Today they do nothing of that, they simply handle the finances and I think that's very regrettable. In Edinburgh we had the Scottish Committee of the Arts Council and a couple of very remarkable people ran that on a shoestring with minimal staff and enormous results. We also had the Festival in Edinburgh, which was a huge explosion of the arts in every direction, and for 10 to 15 years we had some of the biggest blockbusting exhibitions ever seen in Europe here. Those of us who lived through that period had the most fantastic art education. I will always be grateful for the Edinburgh Festival for that.

The Van Gogh exhibition of 1948 was the most stunning exhibition. I was teaching in Broughton High School and this was the first big exhibition to hit Britain after the war. It didn't come to Edinburgh. It went to Kelvingrove Art Gallery in Glasgow. I took five different parties of kids through to see it and went through myself over and above. It was totally stunning.

*An Unusual
Pastime for an
Artist?*

I was small for my age when I was at school which was a rugby-playing school and so I used to get trampled by every elephant in the team. So I became athletic. I played because you had to play or perish at Heriot's – you didn't have a choice. I wasn't really very interested in it. I boxed at Heriot's – that's at least something I could do against people of my own size. I continued to box for ten years, right through my student life, as well as in the Army and I also swam competitively.

It seems a long way from the stereotype of the art student, someone who's boxing and swimming, but actually the two things often go together, I've found. Apparently, Georges Braque was a boxer. It wasn't unusual to have people who were involved in one kind of occupation like the arts to be involved in boxing. Boxing before the war was an everyday sport, just as racing and football are now. Nowadays it's kind of politically incorrect to talk about boxing but nobody ever thought about that in the '20s, or the '30s. I was brought up in Montgomery Street which was the epicentre of the boxing world in Edinburgh. We had Sparta Boxing Club in Brunswick Street, in McDonald Row, and we had Leith Victoria where I was a member for a while. Up in Leith Street, where Lewis's is now, there was Charlie Cotter's Boxing Emporium. You went up there at the weekend and he would stick you in, and if he didn't know you he would stick you in with some young miner from Wallyford who would knock the living daylights out of you. If you came back for more then Charlie would say 'Yes, you'll do.' Sometimes if I walk up Leith Street I feel my nose is starting to bleed – it's a painful memory. But that was all going on then; there was at least one World Championship held a stone's throw from where I lived in the Industrial Hall in Annandale Street, it's now a garage.

*Scottish Identity and
the Scottish Art
Scene*

It may sound strange for somebody who was born and brought up in Edinburgh to say this, but I don't feel particularly Scottish. My parents didn't come from the mainland of Scotland at all – my mother's folk came from Shetland and my father's people came from Orkney and so they used to talk about going south to Thurso. I don't identify with Lowland Scots at all, I don't feel part of that and I've only got to go up to Wester Ross in to the Gaelic-speaking area and I feel totally foreign; I might be a Japanese with my camera. I'm delighted with the events that have taken place recently, that we're going to have a Scottish Parliament and I'm delighted that there is such a lot of attention being paid to Scottish art. This is commercial, of course – it's largely due to the fact that the Colourists fetch such huge prices at auction now that everybody down in the south, in England and in London in particular, has latched on to this. If you're a Scottish painter then you're the flavour of the month, even if you're no good. You see advertisements in the art magazines 'Six Scottish Painters' and you look down and you've never seen any of them before. But this is latching on to the Scottish thing and of course it works and if people are buying that way, if they just want to buy a good investment or if they want to buy the flavour of the month then that's what they get.

I think primarily in terms of my own subject area, there have been vast changes in public awareness. In Edinburgh we've got nearly thirty galleries now and, as I said earlier, a lot of people buy pictures. I don't know how well the galleries all do but they seem to do reasonably well. I suspect that in some ways they perhaps do rather better than the people who exhibit in them. I know it's a hard struggle to own a gallery and to keep it – the need for a constant supply of new exhibitions. Some of our gallery owners are fantastic, having a show about roughly once a month and often with more than one artist in it. I'm full of admiration for them and I deal with quite a few of them, they're all friends and I don't have any complaints at all about them. But I find also that the public awareness extends to supporting things like lectures in the National Gallery, there are lunchtime lectures now every week in one or other of the free galleries. There's the Portrait Gallery on Monday, the Gallery of Modern Art on the Wednesday and the National Gallery on the Thursday or the Friday and you'll get, most of the time, fifty people at these half-hour lunchtime lectures. I was in the Portrait Gallery when there was a lecture on Nigel MacIsaac's painting of Willa Muir – a painting that never sees the light of day because it's in the store, which is sad. It was a wonderful lecture all about the painting and the painter and the lady in the portrait and there were about fifty people there, all very appreciative, and I thought that was great.

I think we've developed an eye over the last couple of generations. There's been an awful lot of art education going on in a quiet way. I spent sixteen years doing Arts Council lectures and I travelled all over Scotland and found myself in places like Ardrossan and Inverness, in Galashiels, Glenrothes – always there was an audience, anxious to hear more about painting. I did courses of lectures for the Fine Arts department in the University here in the extra-mural department. Again I'd do a course of ten lectures, that's quite a lot and you would get people who would come and sit through the whole lot, without falling asleep.

Joe Pieri
Chip-shop Owner

Born 1919

Coming to Scotland

I was born in a little hilltop village in Tuscany called Barga, of a peasant family. My father was a peasant – he tilled the land. In common with thousands of other Italian families my parents had to emigrate to find work. Italy in those days was a very, very poor country, almost Third World by today's standards, and the only way an energetic young man could provide for himself and his family was to emigrate.

The great agency for helping immigrants in those days was the Church. You went to your local priest and the Church, having contacts world-wide, suggested to my father that there was a place called Glasgow in the north of Great Britain, where one or two Italian families had set down roots, that there was work to be had there with Italians, and would he like to go there? And, yes, what kind of work? Well, any kind of work as long as you can use your hands.

It's quite a remarkable thing: there are two Italian villages which have seeded Italian immigration in Scotland. One is Barga and one is Piccanisco in the south. Probably at the end of the last century, one or two families would have come here, one or two families from Piccanisco. As they began to prosper, they would send to their respective villages for manpower to come and help them in their businesses. Presumably, that's why the two masses of population in the west of Scotland, at least until about twenty-five years ago, all came from Barga and Piccanisco. If you go to Barga now you speak English and everyone speaks English – it could be with an American accent, South American accent, German accent, but everyone speaks English because everyone's been abroad.

More than one or two families – some 4000 Italians came to Scotland in the 1890s, largely from Barga, but they were outnumbered among the foreign-born in 1901 by 10,737 Russians and only just exceeded the 3232 Germans. If that seems odd, remember that Europe in 1900 looked rather different on political maps – and many of those Russians and Germans were in fact Jews from the modern Poland and the Baltic States.

I was one year old when my family came here. Obviously, I don't remember much about it – my memories go back to when I was about four or five. We grew up apart from the society around us. My parents spoke very broken English so they were detached, they didn't mix with the population. Italians didn't live in a closely knit community. There were possibly a few hundred families widely separated, and for myself and my brother – I had an elder brother – life was very dichotomous: outside you would speak English and you'd go to school with your Scottish schoolmates; back home you would be Italian. A foot in one culture and a foot in the other. You never really felt part of either. The Jesuits say that if you take a child up to the age of seven, that is that child formed for the rest of his life. Really, you never forget, no matter how old you get – and I'm nearly eighty now – you never forget the dichotomy of your childhood.

In school, you were different. Remember, the horizons of the general population in those days was very limited. No one had been abroad. The average person went to Saltcoats for a day or Queens Park. But someone coming from Italy, someone whose parents spoke with a peculiar accent, you were immediately classified as different. We were 'wee tallies' or 'dirty wee tallies', you know, so you had to fight. The funny thing was that in those days religion was very very polarised. You may think that there is a religious divide today but in those days it was even greater. I went to a Catholic school, St Mungo's. And the funny thing was at school, they'd call you a 'dirty wee tally' and you had to fight. Then when you left school, you had to stand shoulder to shoulder with your enemies of the playground because you'd get stopped in the street, you'd get gangs coming up shouting, 'Are you a Billy, a Dan or an Old Tin Can?' So I was both a Tally and a Tim, I kicked with both feet.

The religious divide exists in this country in a way in which it does not exist in others. People in Italy and in Spain throw up their hands in astonishment when they hear of what's happening in Northern Ireland or when I tell them about the religious divides with Celtic and Rangers. Incomprehensible – why? I think a religious divide is something which is peculiar to Scotland and I think the northern part of the United Kingdom.

I was brought up in the Gorbals – Cumberland Street, Crown Street. I think it's now demolished, thank God. It wasn't the most salubrious of areas but, strangely enough, in retrospect you were better living in those areas because there is a certain affinity in the working classes. This may sound old-fashioned socialism. The working class of Glasgow respected other workers and they saw that Italians were hard working – they'd work 14, 16 hours a day and that gave you self-respect. 'They're good hard-working people,' they'd say, and they would treat you quite nicely. Whereas the middle-class snobs, if you want to call them that, looked down their nose if you were an Italian. So life wasn't really so bad, because I think I would rather have grown up where I did grow up in the Gorbals than have grown up in those days in Kelvinside or Bearsden – although Bearsden didn't exist then.

Fish and Chips

My father came over here as a fish fryer in a fish-and-chip shop which stood on a vacant piece of ground where the Greens Playhouse used to be. Three pounds a week, I think, was the wage, and he saved up a few shillings every week because the dream of every immigrant is to have

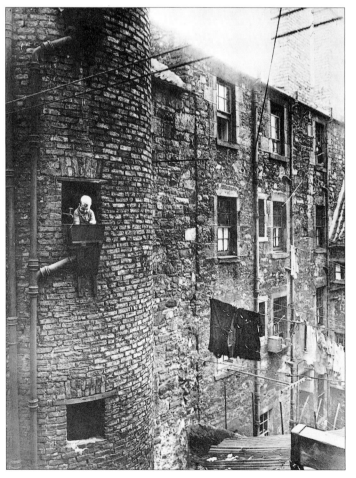

A Glasgow tenement in the 1930s: 'not the most salubrious of areas'

a place of your own – especially the Italians, Italians are very individualistic; they don't like working for people. They don't like government. The idea of every immigrant was 'I'll have a place of my own, a wee shop, cafe or fish-and-chip shop or whatever.' So he saved up a few bob and by the time I was six he had a wee fish-and-chip of his own in Crown Street, and I remember coming back from school – I went to St Francis, just a few hundred yards away – and I'd have my tea, which consisted of a pie supper, underneath the counter. To this day, I have a vision of my father and mother serving customers. I can see their legs walking up and down, and hear the sizzle as the chips went in to the hot fat and the ringing of the cash register.

The strange thing is that fish and chips *per se*, does not exist in Italy. You get what's called *fritto misto*. As far as I can understand, fish and chips originated with Greeks in London. The Italians took it up here, possibly because you required practically no capital. In the days before town planning, all you did was get a bricklayer and he put you down a few bricks with an oven in the middle of it. You got a couple of huge frying pans which you moved over the coal fire, you put up a wooden counter and you were in business.

A Divided Community

In the early days, there were only a few hundred Italian families. Then as time progressed and we came into the late '20s and early '30s, Italian communities began to grow. The Italian government – which by that time was a fascist government – had opened up the *Casa del Fascio* in Park Circus, a magnificent building which originally belonged to the tobacco barons of Glasgow, and they made that an Italian social club. Some of us would go there on a Sunday and meet other Italians of your own age. Some of us were not encouraged to go because there was a great split in the Italian community about fascism. Many were actively pro-fascist, but others were not. So even in those days in the Italian community, there was a split: those who supported Mussolini and those who did not. We have more of a cohesion in the Italian community now, with the Scots-Italian golf club and the various Italian dances, than we ever had in those days. Now we've got very prominent members of the Scots-Italian community as role-models, like the sculptor, Paolozzi. The interesting thing about Paolozzi is that his father was killed in the *Arandora Star*, the ship that was torpedoed at the beginning of the war.

Internment

At the start of the Second World War, Churchill decided that all theoretical aliens, however much they might have fled fascism, should be interned. I was arrested the very same night war broke out. My brother was in the British Army. I had never bothered to take out British nationality. In retrospect, I didn't feel British. Again, at the age of seven, your character is formed. You don't get called 'dirty wee tally' for eighteen years and then start wearing a Union Jack. Anyhow, I was arrested. After a month I finished up in Canada. By merest of chances I escaped the *Arandora Star* which sailed a few hours before ours did.

I always remember that our camp leader was a fellow called George Martines who was a Cambridge-educated Italian. And we had in our camp a fellow called Mario Paoli who came from a town called Moscow in Ayrshire, and he spoke broad Scots. I had to act as an interpreter between Mario Paoli's Scots and George Martines' Cambridge English because they couldn't understand one another. They couldn't even communicate in Italian because Mario Paoli couldn't speak Italian. The amazing thing was that there were two hundred and fifty civilian internees in our camp in Canada and I think only a third of us actually spoke Italian.

In the camp we had five fishermen from Ischia which is a little island near Naples; they had been picked up the night war broke out by a British submarine which surfaced, came out of a fog bank and came upon this little fishing vessel. Now he must've been a very humane man, the captain of that submarine, because he could've sunk them without trace and that would be that. But he sank the boat and took them prisoner on his submarine. He took them to Gibraltar, from Gibraltar they came to Liverpool, and finally to Canada with us on our ship. Well, you could be talking to someone from the Middle Ages – they didn't have a clue. A cinema, one of these 16mm soldier cinemas, came to the camp once a week. They couldn't comprehend the two-dimensional image on the screen, they'd go behind the screen to see if there was anything behind it. They were of average intelligence but yet they could not comprehend, so backward were they. I used to translate letters for a little friend of mine who came from Sicily, and he was illiterate. He would have me write to the parish priest where he came from, the parish priest would read the letters to his parents and he would write back. Terribly backward.

Back to Normal

I spent three-and-a-half years in Canada and had a very easy war. Compared to some, it was a piece of cake. When I returned to Glasgow, I worked in the shop. It was expected in those days that a boy follow in his father's footsteps. If you were a shipyard worker, you went to the shipyards; if you were a miner, you went to the mines; if you were the son of a fish-and-chip man, you went into fish and chips. No complaints about that because it gave you a certain amount of individuality. You were your own boss and it was a lucrative business.

The bulk of my friends were Scots lads and we used to go to football – Celtic and Rangers matches. Outside, I would say I was as Scots as the next one. My accent I suppose doesn't betray my Italian heritage, and the same was true in those days. I used to play golf, I loved playing golf. I used to play on the corporation courses because finances didn't permit joining a club, plus the fact I doubt very much whether any golf course would've accepted anyone with an Italian surname. It's a fact of life, that even though you had the wherewithal, you'd never have thought of applying for membership of Douglas Park or Haggs Castle. Strangely enough, that changed after the war. When you might have expected that Italy having fought against Britain, that the populace at large would have been bitter against the Italians, I found the reverse. When I came back from Canada I was quite apprehensive; here I've been an enemy alien for three-and-a-half years behind barbed wire – what am I going to find when I get back? What is the attitude of the people going to be? I found that the attitudes had changed. People were very friendly – soldiers coming back from Italy would say, 'Oh, you're Italian – do you know such and such a village? I fought here and I met a family there and this family helped me escape from a German camp, and the people were so nice.' And suddenly they seemed to be genuinely interested and attached to Italians in a way that hadn't been true before the war. So the war seemed to be a great catharsis.

A Change in Attitude

All I wanted to do was play golf, earn money, sell as many fish and chips as I could and go out with the girls, although you had to be careful because your mother would bring out the poker if she thought you were going out with a Scots girl. It was expected of you that you married your own kind, which is only natural. I finished up marrying a Scottish girl, Mary Cameron, and after a while she became the apple of my mother's eye. Though at first her family thought the same about me as my family thought about me going with a Scots girl. My mother would throw up her hands and roll her eyes and bring down all kinds of maledictions on these 'wanton Scottish girls'. And my wife's people would say 'He's all right – but an Italian? My God!'

Attitudes have changed enormously. I've got four children and they're all very well up now, but I used to ask them did the fact of their having an Italian surname in any way impede them socially, or did they find anything at all as a drawback because of having an Italian name? And they looked at me blankly. No, things have changed. The possession of an Italian name now doesn't ostracise you as it possibly once did. It's an established part of Scottish life, like Conti, Tom Conti, the actor. Oh yes, we're now well integrated. It's only old codgers like myself that still feel maybe slightly apart because of the indoctrination we had when we were children.

Some of the second generation Italians now, they're ersatz Italians, you know. They go and see *The Godfather* – suddenly, ah! This must be how Italians act. So they clap one another on the shoulders and you know, it makes me laugh. But I strongly suspect that there are still people in the Italian-Scots community who'd prefer their children married within the community – they like to keep the line pure, as it were, as I'm quite sure some Scots do, too. Although, mark you, I've watched the English abroad and they feel themselves slightly superior to other races. They do feel that the natives should learn English and the Englishman has no business in learning Spanish or Italian. So I would imagine that an Englishman wouldn't like his daughter to marry an Italian. How would you feel if your daughter brought home a black man? How would you feel if your daughter brought home an Italian?

I go back to Italy regularly for holidays. I have a daughter married there. She teaches English at the University of Pisa. I've got two grandchildren, so we go over frequently. When I arrive there they say 'Ah, il vecchio Scozzese' – 'the old Scotsman's arrived'. And when I'm here: 'Oh yeah, here's the Tally.' I love Italy, I love to visit it, its beautiful countryside, the cities, the art, the music. Italy is probably the only country in the world you cannot generalise about. There are many Italies: Italy of the North, Central Italy and Italy of the South, which is a disaster, absolute disaster. But the way of life in Italy I find intensely irritating. There's no social cohesion, there's no sense of social responsibility – it'd drive you crazy, more because of the fact that I'm one of them and I speak Italian. So I come back here and – despite the weather – enjoy it. Italy to me is an amazing place because they have a very high standard of living – everyone's flying about in Fiats and sporting mobile phones and gold watches and how do they do it? We used to go to Italy and we were the rich relations. I remember just before war broke out, we would go and visit Italy and we would take parcels of old clothes which were greeted with open arms by our families, because they literally had nothing. Now when I go over I feel the poor relation, they're the wealthy ones.

A Wider World   What has impressed me most is the unification that has come about amongst peoples, because of travel, because of the electronic revolution, even within the past twenty-five or thirty years. You know, I remember one of the great things in our business was the English–Scottish football match. The English team would come to Hampden and when they came up, hordes of English supporters would come with them. One of our shops was situated near the Central Station and these strange people would come off the train and no one could understand their accent. What language are they talking? They were English and yet we couldn't understand them. Now we understand them because of television and because of cinema – you can understand a Yorkshire accent, but in those days you could not. In the same way that who could understand an American accent before the advent of the talkies? People are more European now in a way that they never were. Younger generations don't have the same racial animosities if you want to call it that – national animosities – which existed when I was a boy. I find a great levelling of culture, a greater understanding. Education has widened immensely. There is still the residue of bigotry and insularism, but I think the progress, the curve, is steadily upwards.

Bill McLaren
Teacher & Rugby Commentator

Born 1923

I was born in Hawick in the Borders. We stayed in a council house in Weensland Road: three up and two down. We were a lucky family in the respect that we were lower middle class, and my father had a motorbike which was a great emblem in those days. We were comfortable and happy. I had two sisters who kept me along the paths of righteousness.

Rugby was the number one religion in Hawick – I was brought up in a rugby background, so even as a boy of five, six, seven, and eight, I knew through my father and his factory friends about the great Scottish players of the day. The 1920s were halcyon times for Scotland – the likes of J.P.S. MacPherson and Simmers and Nelson and Waddell and John Bannerman. They were household names to me so, purely from the point of view of rugby, you couldn't really have had a better background. Although my father came from the west, from Bonhill in Dunbartonshire, he very quickly became a rugby convert. He was a factory manager in the local Braemar knitwear factory, then called Innes Hendersons, and through him I developed a great love of rugby and golf.

School Days

I went to primary school at Trinity School first of all. Our headmaster was one Robert Burns who had lost both legs in the First World War and who was a fierce man at his best but for whom we had a tremendous love and respect. He had a lot to do with my early upbringing. Then I was at Hawick High School for five years. I took my Leaving Certificate there and surprised both my mathematics and my French teacher by squeezing through with fifty-one per cent in each and getting the Certificate. Eventually I finished up as a teacher of Physical Education.

I enjoyed playing rugby at school. I never reached my potential in the classroom. I had an ongoing battle with E. Vera B. Fisher who was our French mistress, a short, stocky lady with no great sense of humour. Unfortunately, we had a French lesson in the period before we went out to rugby in the Wednesday afternoons. I always had the feeling that Miss Fisher, with whom I didn't get on too well, partly because my knowledge of French was so disappointing to her, kept us late so that we lost five or ten minutes of our rugby and I always held that against her. However, when I covered the first Scotland–France game, I was able to ask Jacques Foreau, the French coach, if he'd slept well, if he'd eaten well, and so, to some extent, I was quite grateful to E. Vera B. Fisher.

However, we did have a mathematics teacher called William Redpath and he was a lovely man. We called him Gandhi because he had a facial resemblance to the Mahatma. I remember him saying to me: 'You know, William, there's not much point in you taking your Higher mathematics. It's an absolute waste of pen and paper.' And I remember when I got fifty-one per cent and actually passed, he did have the goodness to come and say: 'You completely surprised me, William.' So that was school for me.

I left school just before the outbreak of war. I'd be fifteen or sixteen, in 1939 and I can remember as a boy – it was a Sunday morning, Neville Chamberlain told the world that we were at war – and I remember a feeling, not of fear but of concern. My mother and my father were there and they reflected the general sadness at the whole business, and that's one little spell that I remember distinctly and vividly, that speech by Neville Chamberlain.

I got a job for a little while before being called up. In the Army, they tended to ask what regiment was your father in, so I said, 'Well, he was in the Royal Artillery.' I finished up in the Fifth Medium Regiment Royal Artillery. I served in Italy, in the Italian campaign for about three years and was away for four years altogether and then after the war, came back and got settled into what I hoped would be a long career in physical education.

I took a training course and went to college in Aberdeen. They squeezed a three-year course into about fourteen or fifteen months because of the need for teachers and I had a lovely time up in Aberdeen. I played for Aberdeenshire – that was an experience in itself. In one game, one of the fellows thought he saw a stone on the pitch and he went to pick it out and we dug out a boulder about three feet wide and two feet across and that was the kind of experience with Aberdeenshire. But I had a great time up there. In those days Aberdeen Grammar School FP were the great side in Scotland, I remember playing for Aberdeenshire against them and we lost 49–0. I don't think we touched the ball in the entire game, but a lovely experience.

I'd always wanted to be a games teacher, maybe just because I loved sport. As a boy, I used to enact sports matches and competitions. I used to play fictional golf shots around the house and imitate the great golfers of the day. I had a big ledger in which I wrote up stories of great golf matches, great athletics contests, and all the rest of it. I've still got that manual and every match and every contest has been laboriously written in and reported. So clearly (a) there was a great love of sport and (b) a great desire to communicate my love of sport to whoever or whatever.

Love at First Sight

I went to one dance which was very distinctive and memorable for me. I'd been demobbed and all my friends were still away, so I took my sister to the pictures and on the way back she said, 'Look I've got a ticket for a dance and I don't really want to go. Would you not like to pop in? You might meet some of your old friends.' The dance was in the Hawick Town Hall and the band was Oscar Rabin and his Orchestra, the great dance band at the time. But I walked into the main town hall and looked straight across the hall and there was a gorgeous creature in white, all in white, and I remember thinking at the time, what a smart-looking girl. I'd never seen her before, I had no idea who she was and I went across and asked for the next dance, which was a tango. That was Betty Hill, as she was known then, and we've been married for fifty years. So don't tell me there isn't love at first sight because that is exactly how it happened. Probably the most sensible thing I've done in my life was to go into that dance in the town hall.

I'm no expert tango dancer. Indeed, for fifty years, Bet really has made me look like a good dancer because she's brilliant, she's wonderful. We were just dancing the other night at the Scottish scrum half, Andrew Nichol's wedding to Janet. It was one of these crowded floors, with the dance floor about ten feet by ten feet and about three hundred people dancing on it and I just thought to myself, you know, Gorgeous, you actually make me look like Fred Astaire.

A Severe Setback

I trained in Aberdeen and then looked for a job near home again. I was lucky – I went for an interview with the Roxburgh Education Committee, as it was then, and I was appointed as a visiting teacher, around five or six schools, two in the country. But unfortunately, after I'd been teaching only about a couple of months – I played in a game against Glasgow Academicals and tackled Russell Bruce, the Scottish internationalist. He says I never tackled him in my life, but I tackled him this time, about the only time, and I could hardly get up after the tackle. I had some awful bouts of coughing and felt run down. I thought that being on such an intensive physical education course, maybe I'd done too much. My doctor said, 'Oh, I think you've probably been doing too much. I would pass you for a life insurance.' But a week later, I went back and got an X-ray and found out that I had a big hole in my left lung, pulmonary tuberculosis – not that I knew what it was, all I knew was that I was feeling ill and not right at all. Dr William Murray who was the Superintendent of East Fortune Sanatorium came to see me in Hawick and he was appalled that I'd actually been playing rugby – I could have had a haemorrhage in the middle of the rugby field. He said I would be in bed for four years in East Fortune. So that was it at twenty-four. Of course, I was also told I would never play rugby again because tuberculosis was a recurring disease, and you had to be desperately careful. Things like colds, flus, bronchitis and other -itises could cause all kinds of problems.

Antibiotics, particularly the combination treatment pioneered in Scotland by Sir John Crofton, transformed the prospects of the tubercular. But steadily improving diet, hygiene, housing and diagnosis (by mass radiography units, for example) had already make significant inroads. In 1914, 7696 Scots died of 'consumption' or TB; in 1926, 4861; in 1935, 3646, and in 1951, 2179.

In East Fortune Sanatorium there were two doctors, a Dr Murray and a Dr Biaje, who were wonderful guys and whom I remember with great affection and gratitude. Not long after I was in East Fortune, they discovered a new drug called streptomycin, which was a great boon and blessing in so far as tuberculosis was concerned. Six of us in the ward were asked if we would be, in a sense, guinea pigs, because it was comparatively untried. I'd lost about three stones and I would have taken anything at the time. With me, it worked right away and I remember Dr Biaje coming in and standing at the bottom of the bed with two X-rays held up: one, the original X-ray with the hole in it and one showing how the hole was filling up. And he just used to shake his head. I was told later by Dr Murray that my X-rays had gone all over Europe because it was a miracle cure. Instead of being in bed for four years, I was an up-patient in about thirteen months and I was out in nineteen months with a complete cure. Although it was a terrible blow to not be able to play rugby again, I was just so fortunate that that worked with me. Two of the other lads had miliary tuberculosis and they died, but thereafter, streptomycin played such a part in helping to cut down the incidence of tuberculosis. It does concern me that it seems to be on the move again in the west of Scotland and elsewhere.

I went back as a PE teacher and I taught for over thirty years or so, always round about Hawick – good hard work but thoroughly enjoyable. You get regular checkups for years and years afterwards. One aspect of the treatment which shocked me a little bit was when I was called along one evening to the surgery and laid out and asked to bare my tummy. Dr Biaje was standing with a needle about four inches long and I said to him, 'What are you going to do with that?' and he said: 'I'm going to stick it into your tummy.' I said, 'You're kidding,' and 'Oh no,' he says, and he did, and the curious thing was, you were asked to puff your tummy out and he just threw it like a dart and in it went and the idea was to get it in underneath the diaphragm and they pumped air in through it. The diaphragm lifted and so it lifted the lung and therefore rested the diseased part of the lung. We got a couple of these every week for about eight or ten years. I've still got the little indents near my belly button. When I think of the first time: you'd think it would be very painful, and the first one was like a harpoon but in your mind you got used to it. We used to troop up there every Friday, three or four of us in the ward and get this dart business in our tummies – an extraordinary affair.

Another thing was called a frenic crush. The idea was to crush the frenic nerve which runs across the front of the scapula. The doctor had to make an incision and then dig in with a pair of pincers and get the nerve and when they crushed it, it whipped the diaphragm up. You leapt off the board and landed hopefully safely with this thing crushed and this was another way of resting the lung. When you look back on it now it seemed crazy, but it worked. I'll never forget the gratitude I felt when I got out of East Fortune Sanatorium.

Children Then and Now

Over my time as a teacher, I never had a lot of problems with children. Obviously, there were great ranges of ability, and it was important to encourage the ones who struggled as much as possible. But I think the whole idea was to try to make it fun, and not to be too concerned if they couldn't achieve what they had sought out to achieve in the way of physical ability. Children were so funny. One little girl, about eight years old, at Burnfoot School came up one morning and she said, 'Mr McLaren, my mother saw you on the television and she says you wear a wig.' So I

GETTING THEM YOUNG:
BILL MACLAREN, 1982

said, 'That's actually wrong, dear, and so to prove it, then just feel it.' Well, she took my hair and she almost pulled the scalp off. I'll never forget that wee girl. Of course, it was a delight when youngsters achieved something that they didn't think they were capable of doing and I think that gave you as much pleasure as anything. The great worry was danger, and I was maybe pretty strict as a disciplinarian because I just felt that we couldn't afford to have anybody acting the goat. They had to be thinking about what they were doing and playing the game as it were. We got through pretty well on that. I had thirty-odd years which were a great thrill because I'd always wanted to do it.

Over the years, I think children probably got fitter and stronger. Certainly that's been the whole modern trend. But in the olden days, we did so many things that kept us fit. I can remember as a boy playing all kinds of games. We had girds, yon iron hoops with the handles on them and we used to have races up and down the main road because there was so little traffic on it. We used to play with yon knucklers, yon little coloured bools and you used to knuckle them and you had to knock out as many as you could from the circle to beat your opponent.

I can remember as a boy of seven, eight and nine and ten, going down to the pitch which was about 100 yards from our front door, it was like a great big circular cricket pitch really, and we used to organise our own games. We used to organise hockey with our fathers' walking sticks, and I remember once my father's walking-stick head came off and what a job I had getting it stuck back on, petrified lest it fell off when he got it back again.

We did other more devious things like attaching a bit of thread to somebody's front-door knocker and reeling it out and going behind a bush and pulling on it so the knocker went. They came out to the front door and there would be nobody there, which amused us tremendously. It didn't amuse the people. There was a kind of variety of what was permissible and what was downright infuriating, but we worked hard at our games whereas nowadays everything's laid on. What I found in teaching, and more recently at the end of my teaching experience, children had lost the art of listening. In my own time as a schoolboy we only had the radio and if you didn't listen carefully, you missed everything. But nowadays with television, they just need to see the pictures in a sense and so to some extent, I felt they'd lost that art of listening. You really had to work to get them back to concentrating on what you were saying.

The Changing Face of Rugby

As an old codger, one of the old fashioned breed, I think rugby has changed for the worse because I remember the game as it was – really, the greatest team game in the world. First of all there was intense loyalty to either club or town or old school. I love to see Gala men playing for Gala, Hawick men playing for Hawick. That was the rugby that I knew. There was a wonderful feeling of sportsmanship, nothing like the cheating that there is nowadays. And at the end of games, opponents were friends. I was just reading about in the history of Hawick Rugby Club – each player had to take down two bottles of beer, one for his immediate opponent and one for himself. That was their after-game entertainment back in the 1920s and '30s.

Rugby Union really was meant to be a break from the daily grind, it was meant to be a bit of fun. Now it's *become* the daily grind. Professional players are now playing, training, thinking about or doing something in rugby every day of the week.

Although I loved the game I wouldn't have fancied that. You trained on Tuesdays and Thursdays, played on the Saturdays and the rest of the week was your own – if you wanted to go a run over the hills to keep fit you could do it. On the other hand there's no doubt players are stronger, they're fitter. Even our grandsons who are playing for Scottish schools, when we have them down to Gullane for some golf and I say, 'What would you like to drink with your meal?', expecting the older one to say a pint of lager. 'Iced water please.' 'What do you want iced water for?' Dieticians tell them iced water. Boys now are channelled in a sense. Skill-wise and fitness-wise that's great. I say it goes a bit far when you can't have a pint of shandy. But I suppose part of rugby's tradition was about having a beer and a chat, and so I think the game has lost a lot in the way of spirit, sportsmanship. Nobody in my day would ever have dared question a decision, for instance, by Jock Allan of Melrose. 'We'll have nane o' that here.' I can hear him now. Nowadays they tend to intimidate referees and they question their decisions a lot – in my day you would never have thought about doing any such thing.

A Borders Obsession   Initially, the Borderers tried football and rugby and they decided on rugby football because, as they said at the time, it was manlier and more congenial to the Border nature. That meant simply that the Borderers were a bunch of tough louts. They'd been pinching cattle from the English for years and years, warring and all the rest of it, so they were used to that kind of competition. They embraced rugby football delightedly and were regarded by the city fellows as being rather uncouth and rough. I remember hearing about the first city referee who was sent to down to referee a Borders rugby match. He got back home and his friends asked, 'How did you get on?' 'Get on?' he says, 'It's not a referee those people need, it's a missionary.' The cities took a while to catch up with that kind of approach to rugby football in the Borders. Certainly, my own boyhood was all about rugby football; you heard about Rangers and Hearts and all the rest but rugby was the religion.

It also has always struck me that the Borders player is at some disadvantage in that if he has a bad game, on the Monday at the factory or on the estate, there will be five thousand critics waiting to tell him how badly he played. Once we played for Hawick at the Melrose Sevens, we met Kelso in the first round and we lost. George Hook and I were walking along the High Street that night – we didn't see the fellow, we only heard the voice: 'You wint tae hing up yir boots, ye auld pair.' That kind of criticism showed you just what the Borders player has to go through whereas the city player who has a bad game can disappear into the night, anonymous. You run the gauntlet of the High Street if you've been beaten as a Hawick player, especially in Hawick where they've been weaned on success over many years and they don't take defeat kindly at all.

As far as Scotland is concerned, as a small country we have to accept that there will be long hungers and that our successes will come in short bursts. When I first started commentating in the '50s, I actually did commentary in a lot of matches which were part of that series where Scotland lost seventeen internationals in a row – seventeen internationals in a row! You can imagine how difficult it was to make that exciting and interesting for listeners as it was then radio. So we have to accept that that will be the case. But when success does come along, the whole nation shares in it and rejoices. The greatest day that I can remember in Scottish rugby was in our last Grand Slam in 1990. England came up here having slaughtered everybody else, magnificent side, big, powerful, fast, heavier, stronger, faster and all the odds against the Scots, and yet they won 13–7. That was when David Sole walked the team onto the field. They said that was the first time that had been done. Not true. As a boy I remember in 1935 when the South of Scotland played New Zealand at Mansfield Park, my home town. I was sitting in the enclosure with my father and I remember Jack Manchester of Otago, the New Zealand captain, with a black scrum cap on, walking his team on the field and he held the ball in one hand like an orange. I've still got that vivid memory of fifteen great muckle black louts coming out there with this thing leading them and they walked out like prophets of doom. Curiously enough the South played a wonderful game against them – I think they lost 11–8. Wonderful day but I can always remember those fifteen black figures coming out the dressing room.

A Local Delicacy

Hawick Balls have been made for years and years, a little mint sweet and done up in a lovely tartan tin. They're greatly prized, especially by people from overseas; I got to like them and I took one or two down to my matches, a tin here and a tin there. Once, I offered Gareth Edwards one and he got a taste for them. Whenever I landed up at the Angel Hotel in Cardiff with the Welsh team, I always heard this sing-song voice, 'Hey, Bill, you got any o' they Hawick Balls?' he would shout out and so I had to take down a tin. Actually, he's owing me about £10 or £12 for those tins, never got it from him. In any case, Gareth was then quoted in one of the national newspapers about Hawick Balls and they became part and parcel of my rugby experience. I gave one to David Campesie, the Australian wing and I said, 'Now David, that'll put a yard on your speed,' and he held it up and said: 'Will I pass a bleeding drug test with this inside me?' I remember once a Fijian manager brought a Fijian Seven to Gala; it was when Fiji and Canada were invited to play in Gala Sevens. I went down to see them train for identification purposes and I gave the manager a tin of Hawick balls just to welcome him to the Borders. You'd have thought I'd given him a gold chain or something, he was simply delighted. Yeah, Hawick Balls have become part and parcel of my rugby story. They used to be made by the Hill family in Hawick. I knew all the Hill family and David was a pupil of mine. Now they're being made over in Greenock to a secret recipe which has been kept secret for a hundred years. I got a few tins the other day and I must say they've done a good job with them. They're very like the original Hawick Balls. I think Gareth Edwards will like them.

Matthew Sanderson
Miner

Born 1924

I was born in New Cumnock, just quarter of a mile up from Burnfoot at Dalmellington Road – I've been in the village all my life.

Most of the miners walked to work in those days. In the early morning there was certain men you could tell by their walk going up past. One was lame, one wore clogs, and you knew these. Then there were some that were smokers and as young boys you collected cigarette cards, so some of the miners that were friends of my older brother would fling the packet with the cigarette cards into the house and when you was going to the school they was lying on the steps of the house. You gathered these cards – it was photographs at that time – the 'Gay Cavalier' was one, and 'Mother and Son', a horse with a foal. You kept them until you had a full set. You'd maybe swap them if you had two the same and somebody at school had one you wanted. I don't know whether it was fifty you had to collect or not but you sent them away and got a picture back about eighteen inches by fifteen inches. They hung on the wall in the house.

There was a hen cray near us and some of the men that was unable to eat their piece – not because they weren't feeling well, but because they were working too hard – they used to fling their slice of bread over to the hens and there'd be about fifty hens all fighting for the sandwich.

I just enjoyed the carefree life with no worries. We never missed a meal. Our dad was a miner but there was always a meal on the table. When you came out of school in the summer, you'd be swimming, say, in the River Nith, things like that, and maybe a picnic on the Afton was a favourite. I cannae pinpoint any definite thing that I was overjoyed with, I just enjoyed life – you was young and you was healthy and you was carefree.

I enjoyed school through and through. I wisnae at the top of the class but I got through without failing. I got what was known as the Lower Leaving Certificate, in all my subjects. The last three years, if you were leaving at fourteen to work, it was three nine-month classes, whereas for the Higher Leaving Certificate, those going on to Cumnock or beyond, it was three one-year classes.

Off to the Mine

I left school when I was fourteen, to the mining industry. My first year was in a surface job. There was a job known as 'crawpitting' – the coal was tipped from the hutches and went along a belt about three feet wide. The sides of the belt were at knee height, so you had leant against it with your knees and you had to fling dirt from the coal so that the customers were getting a reasonable clean coal. So I was in that for a year, in different surface or pithead jobs. And then after a year, down the pit.

An odd person maybe stayed in the pithead but nine out of ten, it was pithead for roughly about a year and then you'd be down the pit. I went with my elder brother down to a job. I did ask the manager of the pit at the time if there was a tradesman's job available but the answer was just a kind of abrupt 'no' – ken, it was no talk. So it was sweat of the brow. When I started down the pit it was on stonework. The seam I was sent to with my brother was two feet three high only, and we started on the afternoon shift. The men took the coal out afore in advance the full length of the face so therefore we had to create a road you could walk in, so we had to take four feet off the roof and pack it into the sides, creating a road. Nowadays they call them gait roads but that word wisnae used when I was a young man.

Day-to-day Work   You would walk half a mile to the coalface, to the main coal seam. But they worked two smaller seams and I was in the smallest of these two – a half a mile walk to get to your work. You had hand drills, there was no electric borers – a 'rickety' was the name used in New Cumnock for the hand drill. Some of the strata of rocks was very hard, and this coal seam that was in the first two feet was easier brought down, the surplus came down when you knocked the supports out. But this white sandstone rock was very difficult to penetrate and when you complained your arm was sore, you were just told to use the other arm.

In the bit I was in, the coal was just hand-filled into hutches which went out the level to the bottom of an incline and then it was direct haulage. Direct haulage then feeded on to another haulage, which went at walking pace roughly, maybe a quarter of a mile or so to the main mine to the surface. In the inclines down the pit the rope was maybe just less than half an inch thick, maybe take three hutches at a time. Whereas the rope going to the main mine to the surface was a big heavy rope, about the thickness of your wrist. There'd maybe be fifty hutches hanging, a single tub say every thirty yards, roughly. There was a man at the top of the main mine that took the chains off and just turned round and put the chain on the empty hutch. Everything was continuous, as long as there was a supply of full hutches, everything was continuous.

Most of the people who worked at the pit came from the same village. There was odd ones come up from Cumnock, but that would be the only village they came from to here. The pits had shut in earlier years in Cumnock, so they either came here or they went to Auchinleck. Everybody knew everybody and everybody's family.

Quite often it was hard, abrasive talk but it wisnae abrasive talk with malice. It maybe appeared to the rest of the world not to be friendly but it was friendly. When you're only talking to other New Cumnock people, you're not sitting in an office or where you would have to speak what you would term 'TV English'; you're only local. I seem to be bad for that: when I'm away on holidays I've sometimes difficulty in being understood, and I know at that time I think I'm no speaking local, I'm speaking my best English. I'll maybe say, 'Two cups of coffee, please, and two cakes,' and I've to say it again, and yet I thought I was saying it in reasonable English. But I think that's the reason, because we're all just in a manual sweat-on-the-brow job. I ken what you'd be told if you spoke nice English shouting down to your fellow worker.

Everybody knew everybody else. In those days your graith or tools, you left them at the side of the road just, and they was always there when you went back. But as the years went on and we came up to the '40s and '50s, we'd to bore a hole in the handles o' wir tools and shove a bar through and put a small padlock on to try and keep them secure, but even then there was somebody that would break the padlock. There was quite a lot of misuse in later years. Maybe we lost the fear of being kicked oot the pit. See, in early days you'd to watch and no' offend the mine owners, and you'd hear your father and grandfather talking about offending and saying 'putting your sticks in the cairt'. That meant, ken, that you was getting hunted to other work, and you should be blacklisted here and you maybe couldnae get other work and you'd come to poverty then.

Nationalisation changed quite a bit, I think due to a kind of minimum wage, brought oot a guid lot of laziness I think. That's my opinion just, but I think there was a wee bit slackness. With a guaranteed wage, you knew you were not going home bare, whereas when you flung a hutch and putting a pin on, then you was dependent on filling your tubs to get your wage.

One of the benefits of nationalisation that came about after the war when there was a big demand for coal was that the union was able to force through certain upgradings. But when you get upgradings, you depend on the integrity of the workman to pull his weight. One or two didn't pull their weight. And they got away with it, but not on rated work. Where there was mechanisation, the rated work went out, but there was still rated work in my village, for there was very little mechanisation. It was long wall-faces and then there was known as 'strippers': in other words, the coal was undercut. You would bore a hole if it was required and blast a seam and quite often they could take the rest of it with just the pick and shovel into the conveyors. So where it was rated work, more or less everyone pulled their weight.

An Underground Disaster

It was September 1950, and at that time, I was the shotfirer for the district. In Auchshinnoch, it was mainly solid drivages, that's places about twelve feet wide and about six or seven feet high. There was this brescoal as they called it, which could be worked out with the pick, holed out just like a machine undercutting, but it always took one or two shots to break it down, and the same with the stronger splint coal on the bottom. So I was a shotfirer. That Thursday about half past seven – I don't know the name of the young boy running the chain for the hutches, but he came down with the information that we'd to leave the district immediately and go for the surface via the return – the pit bottom was flooding. There was no urgency, ken, he didnae come running doon shouting, and dropping wir tools and away. The tools were put to the side quite peacefully and we all walked away as a district, maybe about twenty men making for the surface. And at a certain point, we had to start dipping downhill. But we couldn't go, the road was full of this sludge. It didn't look or smell like peat, just kind of sludge. Ken it wisnae flapping aboot like semi-liquid, it was stationary. This would be maybe an hour or two after the initial in-rush, so everything was stationary. But there was no road through; one of the plays I watched, that was the title, *No Road Through*. We realised within a quarter or half an hour that there was no road through anywhere, that we was trapped in.

It didnae gie me a churn up in the belly or anything like that, it was just accepted, and we just all retreated back to a central point. We was told later that the instruction that we got was wrong, we should have been told to go to this central point, and not to go making for the surface, but the word we got was definite: go to the surface as the pit bottom is flooding.

No one had thought of trying the phone, assuming the cables would be pulled apart with the force of this in-rush. I mention it in a wee booklet I wrote: this workman just says, 'Is the phone not working?' and us being a wee bit offhand, just kind of dismissed it as being a foolish question, but the man asked again and someone says, 'Well, if you think it could be working, you try it.' He tried the phone and it was working. That was the start of a wee bit order and instructions as to how to proceed. We all knew we were near to Bank Six, another mine which had been closed for about ten or twelve years, but we didn't know there'd be a road to it. There was a twenty-four-foot barrier left between it just to prevent ony water or gas from going the wrong way. We got instructions to reduce that twenty-four feet and leave two or three feet only, until the rescue had seen that there was a road to it and if it was possible to have a rest there. But the last two or three feet actually blew or fell through. I suppose it was from a wee bit of increase in pressure on our side, plus the coal would be loose.

We had a wee bit of a sing-song when the hole was made through because we was expecting to be walking out in a short time, but it didnae turn out that way. The Bank Six mine had been stopped for years and it was always a gassy mine. The methane came up to us, plus I suppose the loss of pressure, our own methane would come out our strata. There was miles of strata in Auchshinnoch, bare coal strata, due to this 'stoopin roon' method they called it. So we had a wee bit of a sing-song, but the singing stopped abruptly when the gas came up. At that point there were a hundred and sixteen of us. It's not a lot for a full mine, but it's a hundred and sixteen men that were trapped in.

Next, the rescue raid [a preliminary party] came up through with a box of sand. The rescue raid must've been sent up to check that the road was clear on the other side. But they didn't speak to us. They came up into our presence and they observed, and they turned and walked away. There wasn't one took the mouthpiece out of their mouth to speak. It was a silent visit which caused one or two sarcastic remarks, ken, that they might have spoken to us. That was one of the things that happened that I remember quite well. I suppose we were that relieved to get oot, I don't think we questioned it. It might not be known aboot apart from the a hundred and sixteen men that were there, that they hadnae spoke. I heard later that their instruction was to go to the top of the main road down to this barrier, and they had only come out to have a look round, they hadn't come out with any instructions or orders, so maybe that was the reason they didn't speak.

A Mr Dave Pack got a lot of paper talk at the time: he was a local man that was in a white-collared job, he came up through. He were supposed to have got word that we was a wee bit unstable, that we was threatening to run out. So he came up through, promising to be with us and that if we didn't get out, he wouldn't get out. That was the first wee feeling of peril I had, when he made his first statement. And he'd begun to tell us about the build-up of who was headlining in the paper and different brigades, different parts of Cumnock and the tremendous effort being put into it. Which I agree was happening. But then, well everybody's no' the same, and I don't mean panicking, but there's some people talk more than others. One man said 'We don't want to hear all this – just tell us when are we going to get out,' and they said, 'We are quite hopeful of making a rescue.' The words are still crystal clear in my mind. That was the first pang of fear I had in my belly, when he made that statement. They say if you can't give good news, don't give bad news. So I thought that was bad news: 'We are still hopeful', which means that there must have been a no-hope side to it.

I'm not too sure of how long we'd been underground at this point, I do know that it was into the early hours of Sunday morning when the final men went oot. There was still about twelve or thirteen left when I left. They worked it in from the oldest and youngest to finish at the twenty-five-year group, they counted that the most fit and stable type. I suppose the older men would have more maturity but then they wouldn't have the same, maybe, stamina. So when I left there was still about a dozen to come out and the gas then would be getting quite dense, but there was no record of it, unless the brigades were taking a record of it, because the safety lamp had been put out when it was approaching the two and a half. There's a danger with these safety lamps – although they record gas, if they're in gas continuously then it's the same as you boiling a kettle on the gas – the gas heats the gauze and if it's full the gauze could turn red hot, so that would let the flame through. So the lamps were put out as a precautionary method.

We had to go out with just an escort, because they couldnae maintain this chain, it would be too long, so the brigade men would come up, and a list of names and the order we was to go out had been drawn up. My deputy was a wee bit older and he asked me if would I take the names just to relieve him. So these names were all compiled into a big sheet and as I say, working in from the oldest and the youngest to the twenty-five. There'd be a wee bit of alteration maybe on the list where there was two brothers, or I think there was three brothers in one of the families; they wouldn't all wait to their stick turn. To begin with, the brigade man just showed you how it was, it was just a mouthpiece your lips came over, this big flange and your teeth bite onto two prongs that came out. The brigade man himself turned on the wee knob and the three of you left with the brigade man. And you walked, it was roughly a half-mile. That half-mile wasn't all in gas but we had the salvers on for the full half-mile. When I say not all in gas, there was that maybe three or four or five per cent where we left, but you could still have walked without oxygen at that point. You needed it as you went down through the old bank workings.

It had never dawned on me until I actually left, and then it flashed through my mind, 'Will everyone have made it or will there be any bodies on the road?' Happily, that never came aboot. Once we got through there was an advanced first-aid post where it was the local doctor and the local first-aid captain of Auchshinnoch, working at the instruction of the doctor. I got three breaths of the cylinder because my head was thumping. I think maybe I had run out of oxygen, because I had an extra couple of hundred yerds to walk. I don't blame the brigade man because we on the inside should have had the roads definitely marked so that you couldnae stray. Well, we strayed, the brigade man went past – it was a sloped road down to the barrier, and the brigade man took us past this road. There was three of us and one of the men told him that we'd gone past it, but the brigade man just shook his heid, and ken, 'stay with me'. This same man said no, he wasn't going another step, and he turned and went back up. We followed through the barrier hole, that was a hole just about two feet square for twenty-four feet. Then it was a downhill and my head started swimming. I realised my knees was going to buckle so I just stopped and put my head down and the brigade man just looked at me. I think maybe I was going out of oxygen because he just swiped this mouthpiece off me and he shoved a haun ablow my oxter and says 'move' and he propelled me doon and within a hunner yerds, there was the two lights, that was the advance fresh air base. But my head was thumping so when I said this to the doctor he just pointed to the floor and says 'down there'. Everything was blunt – 'down there!' and he looked at the senior first aid man, Mr Wilson, and he says, 'Give him three, John' and he just put this mask over. I took three big breaths and my head cleared. There was nae hangover, it cleared it just immediately. Then he just says 'on yer way' and you started walking.

There was quite a crowd at the surface, although you didn't feel like looking aboot ye or anything like that. I remember somebody coming forward and, again, their hand in at your oxter and after walking up, you felt a wee bit of a sham, ken getting assistance this thirty or forty yards to the back door. Anyway, it was all done with the best of helping us out.

Thirteen people lost their lives. Eleven in the initial burst-through and two that were trapped that couldnae be approached. They would maybe have lived for, they reckon, about ten days. Just with no hope. I was actually at the recovery of their bodies. I knew them: everyone in New Cumnock knows everyone else, especially when you're at a working age. They was twenty-one-hundred feet away from where they had worked, down this south bog drivage and they would have been cold and exhausted and they just lay down but their boots were off. As if they'd went to bed, their boots was lying at the side and they was lying just tight together, dead. And there was no odour or smell whatever, until we attempted to roll them onto screencloths and then the skin broke and then there was terrific pong. If you're walking through a wood or anything and I smell this smell, I'll know it's human flesh rotting.

We got more than a couple of days off, it was quite a wee while. I'll say at least a month. You went up to the doctor and I don't know what he wrote on the line, ken. Then we started again. Nearly all the a hundred and sixteen all started back down Auchshinnoch. I continued there the rest of my working days. I retired through redundancy at fifty-eight years of age. So that was still seven and a half years to go.

Changed Days in
New Cumnock

The likes of a Friday nicht, we'll say roughly at least the half of a village are no' teetotal, so you'd go down to some of the local bars and they'd be stowed to the door on a Friday and on a Saturday. I'm no' talking noo about alcoholics – mostly beer drinkers. And there'd be some always liked their feet against the counter. I don't think you get that nowadays but there used to be a sawdust trough in them working areas. That was because, like I was, a lot of chesty old miners and it was a bit for them to spit into, this sawdust trough, which run alongside the bottom of the bar. And there'd be a separate room set aside for men that liked to play at cards – I don't know what games they played, I was never involved in the card-playing. And another big room that was known as the singers' room – a big round table in it. But if you went in there, it was expected that you would sing. And it was the same song every week because everyone had their own favourite song that they was able to sing with gusto, ken, it was their song. You'd have been looked at if you'd tried to have sung somebody else's song. I suppose maybe there was a wee bit joy at having survived the week – you was hale and you had your pocket money. I used to go in for a pint myself, but I reckoned about two or three at the most, but there was some of the older men would tell me about having eight or nine pints at what they called the 'first house'. This was on a Sunday – having eight or nine pints then and eight or nine in the evening, it's an awful lot of beer when you think of it going through your system but it was the procedure.

Then there was a lively church membership too, ken, of the three main churches. There was always a lively open-air meeting up at the Connel Park Rose from the Baptist Church. I stayed just halfway up here and some of them you could hear quarter of a mile away. But there was never anyone ever protested; it was looked for – a lot of people, even if they wasnae church men, would enjoy it. Ken, it was no' just preaching, it was singing and different things. There's still an open-air meeting in the summertime but it's not the same attendance; last year there was a protest, someone asked them to stop 'cos he couldnae hear his TV. You'd never have got that in the '30s or '40s. The church attendance is also doon. These days there'd be a part church every Sunday morning, but that's generally I think all over Scotland. One of the things you get noo is noises at night: we went to wir beds maybe tennish to be rested for getting up at five in the morning. Young men noo don't need to get up at five, so they're maybe parading the streets in wee crowds and making noise till maybe one and two in the morning which didn't happen when I was a miner. That's one of the big changes. I cannae really say ony mair apairt from it's quite obvious there's no' the same work for the young men. That's a pity. There is no deep mines in New Cumnock left – I think there's only one left in Scotland. The last deep pit shut in New Cumnock in the '60s but I couldn't put a definite date on it. I'm no' saying it's a pity the pits have shut; that's never a pity, but it's the alternative means of employment that's lacking. But I think it's the same all over the country when you read your newspaper and hear your news – unemployment's a big worry.

I'm not sad to see the pits go, no. Although I was out maybe seven years early, I was needing out. My chest was giving me trouble, ken, I've got what you call chronic airways obstruction. The consultant tells me I've got sixty degrees loss of function, which is quite a big loss. Especially like this spring, I had a bad time. I got a lung infection, so if you've already less than hauf your lung working and you get an infection, you can surmise the distress you can be in and I was in a distressed state for a week or two. But I don't think onybody'll miss pits apart from the fact that everybody had a wage.

Colin Morton
Architect & Theatre-designer
Born 1925

Maxwelltown

I was born on the outskirts of Dumfries in Maxwelltown; at that time it was separate from Dumfries, though it was subsequently amalgamated. Maxwelltown was an early council scheme that had just been built. My father was an architect surveyor and had worked on the Maxwelltown scheme so he was in line to get one of the houses.

The houses were high-quality. They were terraced with an arched opening to get access to the back greens. Our house had two bedrooms, a bathroom and boxroom upstairs; downstairs it had a large lounge, a press under the stair, a kitchen-cum-scullery, and a big pantry. The heating was by coal fire in the living room, and that was all. It heated the hot water in a back boiler. It was right on the edge of the town, and behind us were fields so we'd plenty of open space.

Mainly professional or semi-professional people lived there – we had excise officers, bankers. My next-door neighbour for instance had a bicycle shop with motorbikes – Grant & Irving it was called. Mr Irving lived next door and Grant, in fact, at that time was quite famous because he built the 'Flying Flea', a very small aircraft with a motorbike engine in it, which he used to fly around the area; it had a wingspan of about ten feet. Two doors up from us lived Alec Graeme, who became a quite famous cartoonist.

There were three housing schemes in Maxwelltown. Ours seemed to be a scheme in which had a better class of tenant. Then there was another one, the Traquair scheme, which was a lesser class and then there was a poorer-class one at Sandside. Whether that was done purposely or not, I'm not quite sure. There may have been some deliberate decision to have respectable people in one set of houses and the less respectable elsewhere. I would honestly go a bit further: when the poorer people started to come in, there was a lot of, not discontent, but a lot of people not pleased that the scheme was not keeping its end up in terms of tenants. I'm quite sure of that. I remember as a boy, we were warned that there were children that we might get scabs off if we played with them.

School Days

I went to Dumfries Academy Primary School and Secondary School. Dumfries Academy was a fee-paying school, but I don't think it was any better than other schools in the area; professional people sent their children to the Academy. I spent my whole school life there. They were building the new school then so we had classes in halls and big houses while the school was being re-built. We wore a uniform – a maroon blazer, grey shorts, grey stockings with maroon tops.

It wasn't particularly snobby. It wasn't like a Glasgow private school. We mixed quite well. If you were particularly clever at one of the lower schools, you could actually move up at the Control time. Or you could move out of the Academy if you failed your Control and you went to the High School, you weren't allowed to carry into the Senior Secondary. It tended to be more snobby, maybe, in the Primary

School. Passing the Control was a worry: there were certain better-class friends, who were in your classroom and when you got to P5, P6, they were sent to a boarding school before the Control and taken out of the system.

A Boyhood in Dumfries

Our house backed onto countryside and immediately over the hedge there was a football pitch, so we played very much on this, what we called the 'playing field'. Beyond the playing field was open countryside for miles, and that you roamed. In your summer holidays, you tended very often to help with the hay in the adjoining farm and things like that.

It may seem perverse of Colin to have managed to get himself knocked down in rural Dumfries in those distant days when everyone believes it was safe to play in the street. It wasn't – either perverse, or safe. Motors killed 747 people in Scotland in 1930, 555 in 1935 – and only 383 in 1997. There are, of course, far more vehicles making far more journeys – but pedestrians and drivers expect each other, roads are better signed, lit and engineered, and much traffic is segregated onto motorways.

Our parents didn't particularly worry if we roamed the countryside, though they worried slightly about me because I was very accident-prone, from my early life right through 'till I was about nine or ten. Even in those days, in the 1930s, I was knocked down twice by motor cars, once by a grocer's van – Johnston the grocer's van, in fact, who were our next-door neighbours then – and once by a car, a farmer from Lockerbie, and dragged about eighty yards under the car. Then I was blown up with a gas oven, strangely enough. My mother had smelt gas up the stairs and shouted to me to check it. I came in, opened the oven door, the whole thing exploded and I got my face burnt. And I also lost the top of my finger in a gate being smashed shut. What strikes me about all this, looking back on it, was that in every case the doctor came and treated me. He came in every day when my face was covered for something like six weeks – he didn't take me to the Infirmary. The only time I was in the Infirmary in all my accidents, in fact, was when he wasn't available and he arrived about half an hour after I'd been taken away, with splints and bandages and everything. You were treated at home then, rather than going into the Infirmary, which of course is the reverse of today.

We used to have holidays in Kirkintilloch, where my mother came from. We had relatives there, and we usually went to stay with my cousin Isa. My grandfather was a blacksmith in Kirkintilloch and had a big blacksmith's shop. In fact, it could take six Clydesdales [horses] at a time, my mother used to say. They also built carriages and my mother's brothers wanted my grandfather to build a carriage, put an engine into it and run a bus to Glasgow and back. But my grandfather said they were new-fangled and wouldn't last. The boys later emigrated to New Zealand and they were among the first settlers in New Zealand.

I had an older brother, a younger brother and a younger sister. My mother had to look after the house, look after my father, get us all off to school. She had to do all the washing and cleaning herself, and look after the dogs. My father bred wire-haired terriers and took them to dog shows, at which there was usually a children's section and I was usually dressed up in some fancy dress. And I took Rex 'cos he was the one that was most amiable of the three he had.

Wartime Memories

I think we were quite isolated from the war. It meant two things as far as we were concerned: there was an influx of troops and sometimes they were billeted on us or the neighbours. Not on us so much because we actually had evacuees. We had a family from the Gorbals in Glasgow and it was difficult. We had fleas and impetigo and things like this in the house and it worried my mother no end. Maybe I shouldn't say this, but eventually she said they had to do something about it so they packed their bags and went home, and we all breathed a sigh of relief. Then they met the priest halfway to the station and he said they were ungrateful and sent them back. So we had them for another two months! Then we had air force officers billeted on us. Really it was only one Air Force officer, Stanley Jones. He was the MP for North Wales in fact, and he was killed in a plane coming back from the Isle of Man. This was while he was staying with us.

I was in the ATC to start with and the air force was going to be my life. I was actually in the Borough ATC, not the school ATC which hadn't started then. In the summer I used to get passes and go out to the local aerodrome. I'd be fourteen then, and I used to get navigational flights up to Wick and 'round Wick and back down the coast and to Stranraer – four-hour flights at a time. I built up quite a lot of hours and then I had an accident playing football. My ear was damaged, and when I went for my medical, they said 'Grade Four' and I was never called up.

I played a lot of football, for the ATC in fact. Queen of the South were heroes to us. I was quite friendly with a lad whose father was a director. When we went out at Hallowe'en he got his Queen of the South stockings and we went out as Queen of the South players. I can remember to this day in fact, my piece of poem that I said:

The whistle blew, the game was o'er
The good old Queens had won once more
The football world sat up and gazed
And said now how was this team raised
Scouts and spies from near and far
Came rushing down by train and car
To see if they could only guess
The secret of the Babes' success
They all ran home and yelled 'We're beat
The whole darn team eats Yardley's meat!'

Yardley's Butchers, 37 English Street, Dumfries. It was an advert in one of the papers, and I can still remember it to this day.

To University – and Back

There was never any pressure on any of us in the family to do anything. My father said to me when I was leaving school, 'Well, what are you going to do?' And I said, 'Well, I'd quite like to be a gym teacher,' 'cos I was a good footballer and a gym champion. He said, 'Well, the difficulty is that when you get to thirty-five or forty, you're going to be finished. What will you do then? Just sit out and watch other people doing it?' So, I thought, right, I'll go in for architecture. I went to Glasgow School of Architecture, which was housed in the then Technical College – now Strathclyde University, and the School of Art.

I ate in the refectory of the college, because I went home to Kirkintilloch – that was during my first three years. We also went to a place called Easy Eats in Buchanan Street, in which we got fried leg of rabbit and chips for about one and ninepence. And there was a pub in Queen Street which you could go to and you got a brawn sandwich for fourpence and a cup of soup for sixpence.

Apart from my studies, there weren't lots of parties – but I do remember the very first post-war Charities Day, and that was a real party. I was out subsequently on other charities days, but the first one after the war was really something in that the public accepted you and were pleased about it. On that day I can remember filling twelve cans with money – and that wasn't unusual. They collected an enormous amount of money. Subsequently, the public weren't so sure about you, but the first post-war one was very exciting.

We had to do a year's apprenticeship, but I actually did it in the middle of my course. When we started you could do it in four summers – a year – but they stopped that. I did a summer and they decided that wasn't going to count, so I stayed on in that office for a year and then went back to college. During that year I was handling quite big work – Carntyne Industrial Estate, for one, and I was being paid seven and thruppence a week.

When I finished I got slightly trapped. I was twenty-four the summer I finished and I went home and was looking for a job. At that time my mother took ill. She was taken into hospital for a serious operation, but I was never ever told what it was, but I can guess now it was a 'ladies' thing'. I don't know to this day what my mother's operation was and that's the truth. We were brought up in that kind of household. It wasn't strict – it was a very free household, but we were very shy in terms of inter-relations, I would say. You wouldn't talk in the family about the deepest emotions, or questions about sex. I think the first time I went out with a girl to the pictures, my mother said 'What are you doing tonight?' and I said, 'Oh, I'm going to the pictures. Can I have money?' And she said, 'Yes – and you'll need another one and ninepence.' So she knew. And that was the first that I knew that she knew.

Anyway, when my mother was ill, I knew the surgeon, so I went to her and said 'How long will it be before my mother's all right?' She said, 'Well, she'll be pretty bad for a year, or eighteen months.' So I decided to stay in Dumfries for a year – and I'm still here! I worked with my father because there was a certain amount of work at that time. We were doing all of Annan Town Council's postwar work – we built over a thousand houses in Annan, post-war. We did all the creamery work at Lockerbie and Sanquhar for Northern Wholesale Dairies. We did all the McGeorge's Hosiery Factory work, and individual houses so it wasn't too bad.

The Theatre: a Lasting Interest

I was on holiday at Kirkintilloch when I first went to the theatre and saw a ballet. That was my first attraction to theatre, the lighting and the costumes and the effects. When I went back to Dumfries, one of my friends said 'why not come down to the theatre?' so we went down and helped with a show that the theatre club put on in St Mary's Church Hall. We helped a couple of times with the show and at the following annual general meeting, Herbert Milne who was headmaster at the High School, then suggested that we convert our studio into a little theatre. (He had been at the little theatre in St Andrews – the Byre Theatre as it was then – which I subsequently saw and it was a byre: you went upstairs, outside stairs, and you went into what was something like a Nissen Hut, and there was the stage at the end.) So over the summer we converted this building which had been a children's primary school built in the 1880s. It had then become a band hall and then a small factory where they sewed up jumpers from the main factory.

The stage we had was portable so we fitted it in and adjusted it. It was seventeen feet square and the wings were only eighteen inches. There was only three feet from your knees to the stage, and it was only one foot eight inches high. It ramped back and at the back there were four rows of passion seats, or double seats, which we got from an old picture house in Lochmaben. We had three rows of stackable metal chairs – we cleared them away for working space when the shows weren't on. We put on everything there: from *Mourning Becomes Electra* to Shakespeare – everything. The standard was very high.

When we started we only had two hundred members, and this little place held ninety-six. It became so popular that within two years, we had six hundred members, and so we had to play for a week, hoping for absenteeism, playing on a Sunday as well. After three years and we had six hundred on the waiting list and six hundred members. We formed the Little Theatre in 1952, and we were in that building for about five years. By that time the Town Council were taking it over to knock it down for road widening. Just about a hundred yards along the street, there was the old Theatre Royal cinema. It wasn't the 'good' cinema, it was the local scratch, the bughouse, as it was called.

It was where cinema actually started in Dumfries. You could trace the cinema coming down the years. For the shows you had moving pictures which they had on two big rollers. They would roll the scenery, for example, as they rowed on the stage, as they went up the Amazon. And when that ended, they closed the curtains and somebody came on – an entertainer – while they changed all the rollers again. Then they brought in silent pictures, and then singing pictures. A local gentleman, Pat Cooney, who was a joiner to trade, was a great singer. They'd singing pictures and it was actually him singing behind the screen while the actor was opening and shutting his mouth in the actual film.

The Theatre Royal had come on the market because television was killing off the local cinema. There was a public committee set up, which I was on – to buy it for the town, but it faded away. So three of us went to have a look at it and its condition was not bad. There was only one bit of dry rot in, so the solicitor for the three of us trotted off to Glasgow and it was bought in 1960 for something like £1800.

An Appreciative Audience

There was a very lively audience for theatre in Dumfries. It was a very steady, very faithful audience. Same night, same seats. Monday, Tuesday sometimes you had empty seats but on Wednesday, Thursday, Friday, and Saturday, it was always full. The standard of shows that we were putting on was very good. When you had your own stage and could work on it for a month, rather than moving to a place and doing it in two nights, it made a tremendous difference just having your own place and knowing where you're standing. The director knew what he could do and us stage designers knew what we could do. So the standard raised to a very high standard in my opinion. There was not a single full-timer or paid person. I think the standard was so good because over the years a lot of people had been learning bits about the theatre, with the result we had a lot of skill. When we were doing six shows a year then I was designing six sets, so I was getting well practised at it.

We also ran a Friday night film society, which we projected ourselves. Usually between each of our productions, we had a professional travelling production and we ran a pantomime as well. The year could've been filled better, to tell you the truth, if we'd had better rehearsal space and better stage-building space. If we'd had that we could've let the theatre out more, but that was, and still is, one of the difficulties. The cost of shows was the other thing: when we started off with Scottish Opera it would cost £600 whereas the last time it was £2000. Now when you've only got two hundred seats and the Arts Council grants were getting tighter and tighter for that kind of work, it wasn't practical to bring them. Though we never had Arts Council grants for ourselves, we did have Arts Council grants towards travelling productions. Scottish Opera Go Round came once a year and sometimes an English company would come up. We'd get the Citizens and TAG [Theatre About Glasgow], and companies like the Perth Rep. But eventually it became very hard. The Arts Council would tell you to apply early so you'd apply early and they'd say 'Oh, there's no use applying 'till October – that's when the grants are decided.' So you'd apply again in October and they'd say 'All the money was allocated in August.' It was hard.

They like good drama in Dumfries. We did everything from *The Glass Menagerie, Johnny Gibbet,* down to the heavies – *Mourning Becomes Electra, Parts One, Two and Three.* The audience is almost all professional people, schoolteachers and things like that, and a certain amount of old dears, but they don't like too much comedy. They like something serious. I think if you're going to the theatre regularly, if it's flippant, you start to get tired of it.

In retrospect

If I had a choice again, I'm not sure that I'd have gone into the theatre full-time, because I saw so much of the professional theatre. It's such an unstable way of living – you don't know where your next meal's coming from, you don't know where you're sleeping that next night. I'd a lot of friends in professional theatre, and I don't think they'd a settled life. I don't think they got down to doing something very positive, because you're in a play, or you're working a play, you're lighting a play, and then you're on to lighting another play, and there's no connection between the two. I think if you're working in a rep company and you're doing all the work and you know what your lighting people can do for your stage and how the actors will act on it, then I think that's when you get the best. I did many, many, many stages. And I knew what the effect was going to be, I knew what the producer would do with what I was doing.

It's more fun doing the stage, than building a house, if the truth be told. But as I say there's not the security in the theatre. There was quite a number of our people went professional – one in particular, Julie McArthy, was never out of the West End – but you still don't know where your next job's coming from. But I liked working in the theatre and if I'd been associated with a theatre, rather than a company, I'd have been at my happiest. The stages we did and the sort of production that we put on was considered to be professional by many professionals, and by many critics.

I don't regret coming back to Dumfries, but when I was twenty-four I was going to conquer the world. Instead, I stayed and went into the family business and all that it means. I've known Dumfries for seventy years and the thing that I notice most, or to some way regret most, is the modern town. When I was a kid it was a treat to go over the town every Saturday night with my mother, and we got sixpence to spend in Woolworth's. The town was jammed with people. Now there's nobody in the High Street. Previously, you went to one shop for one thing and one shop to another, and you knew the grocers here and the butcher there. Now you just go to the Safeways and go home, and that's it. It's a lonelier town than it was. And the traffic – it has to some extent not ruined it, but when the traffic was there, there was hustle bustle, but now there's no traffic and it's sort of dead. There's no life, no enthusiasm, and that's the biggest change that I see. It's the biggest thing that I regret.

Eric Malcolm

Engineer

Born 1925

Cromarty
Schooldays

I was born in Cromarty and grew up here until I went away to Glasgow University in 1941. I went to school when I was four. My mother died when I was four so I was put into the school – that was easy, Father being the headmaster at Cromarty School. It was difficult, my father being headmaster. He was quite severe with me and I don't think there was any special treatment that I got, not from him anyway, maybe from some of the other teachers, I don't know. But he was very even-handed.

On the whole, I enjoyed school. The teachers were very good and it was a very stable teaching staff: they were there for years and years and years. Now teachers come and teachers go. The local school now is primary only. Children are bussed away at the age of eleven and the headmistress doesn't even stay in the town, she comes in. The schoolhouse is deserted, the bank house is deserted, so many people that used to be integral to the life of the town don't exist any more.

In those days you could carry on at the local school until school-leaving age – we carried on there 'till the third year of the secondary education and then so many left. About half the pupils just left and went to work, locally or went away to work, or joined the Navy or the Merchant Navy. If you wanted to carry on to Higher Education to get a Senior Leaving Certificate, you went to Fortrose Academy ten miles away. The boys cycled every morning ten miles to school and every night ten Highland miles home. There was only four of us that cycled. It took an hour and ten minutes, depending on the wind. The girls took the bus but the boys took the bike. You didn't get home until after five and by the time that you'd eaten, it was after six o'clock. You had your homework to do and you'd better get your head down because

THE FLEET ENTERING THE
CROMARTY FIRTH, C. 1910

you were away in the morning – at times I'd be on the road at ten to eight, cycling away.

We played the usual football up in the parkie. Most of our games were connected, as far as I was concerned, with the harbour. There was always activity at the harbour, little boats to row about in, 'helping' the fishermen, climbing the rocks along at the Soutars. This was when I was about nine or ten. The only strange game we played was called Smoogly – I think it means smuggling, we called it Smoogly. That was on the dark winter evenings – two teams, and you picked each team and one team guarded the den and the other team scattered themselves round the town. Then you'd to try to capture the den and the other team tried to catch you, and if you caught one of the opposing team you'd to hold onto him while you said, 'Smoogly smoogly smoogly, neem neem neem.' Then he was dead and out of the game. We would play that on the links; the lighthouse shone over the links out to sea and we knew exactly when the flash was going to come and then we'd lie down and when it was dark, we would run another ten yards. Och, it was all stupid, but it was good fun too.

Life in Cromarty

Cromarty's unusual in as much as it's at the end of the road. There's no through traffic here and we were very isolated. Back in the 1930s, and even until quite recently, we were very much self-contained. We had our own tradesmen, our own shops. We got our shoes repaired locally, had our own chemist, two banks, two butchers, even a wee hospital of our own – there's none of these things now. We don't even have a garage, you can't get petrol. There used to be two petrol pumps – all gone. One bank a couple of days a week. Hospital's gone, shoe repairers have gone, no tailors, no barber. It's sad, but it's progress in a way.

We were allowed out to wander at night; even now, this is one of the few places where people don't lock their doors. Kids come on holiday, wander about and they're not in any trouble, so far. Our grandsons come up from Aberdeen and when they were wee, they were so surprised that everybody said, 'Hello, good morning' to them. After a few day,s they're saying, 'Hello, good morning.' Then they go back to Aberdeen and they get taken aback when they get stony stares from the locals. It's a funny wee place.

Cromarty was the base for the travelling shops. The midnight grocers went out from here to the countryside, round the farms and round the little villages. Our main provisions came in by sea. The coal boat came in, a hundred tonnes at a time and put in the store here. The coal was distributed throughout half the Black Isle. Now our coal comes in on a lorry twice a week, and is delivered a bag at a time to you. The whole system of living in Cromarty has reversed. It was a little fishing town with little fishing boats. The fishing has gone, we didn't move with the times. We didn't go in for the bigger fishing boats in time and the fishing industry died, and in the last war, we had so many young men lost at sea that the whole thing just petered out completely.

Young Scots now have it a lot easier in some ways, but it's very confusing; it must be very difficult to grow up now. There are so many distractions, so many temptations that we didn't have. We were very unsophisticated. We had concerts in the hall and we thought they were great. People now would just laugh at them because they're used to seeing very sophisticated stuff on the telly. We had a picture show at the cinema every Saturday night. I can remember one or two: *All Quiet on*

CROMARTY HARBOUR, C. 1910 [TOP] WHEN THE NAVY WAS ITS MAIN CUSTOMER AND AGAIN IN 1989 [BOTTOM] FROM A SIMILAR VIEWPOINT WHEN THE OIL COMPANIES PROVIDED MUCH OF THE BUSINESS

the Western Front. There were a lot of Westerns. But there was one, I'm sure it was called *Tell England* and it was about the First World War and Gallipoli, the Dardanelles; I've told people about this *Tell England* and nobody else seems to have seen this film – only me! These brothers came down from Beauly – they only had one projector and between reels when they were winding it up, it was mayhem in the hall. Sometimes they would forget to put on a reel and things were in the wrong order and people that were killed and bumped off in reel one appeared again – we thought this was marvellous. There was one lady I was talking to who went away to

Edinburgh to be a nurse; she went to the cinema and said it was very dull, not half the fun it was in Cromarty.

In those days nearly everybody went to church. Now it's completely the reverse, hardly anybody goes to church. There were two congregations here: the United Free, and the Parish Church and they both had a good turnout. They were self-sufficient: they could send funds off to headquarters and had no trouble about keeping the minister going. The two congregations united – Scottish church history's terrible. The United Free Church rejoined the Church of Scotland in 1929, so we had two Church of Scotland congregations here, so the powers that be, the presbyteries, said that's too many, so we united in 1934 – one church, and it would be pretty near full. We had interesting ministers. Again, we weren't very sophisticated, and we listened to them; they were men of wisdom and they were listened to.

The town declined: before the war it had an eight hundred and thirty-odd population. In the late 1950s and '60s, it went down to five hundred. It was really in danger of becoming a ghost town completely. There was nothing for people to do and they drifted away and it was all old people. The Kessock Bridge has certainly rejuvenated the place – younger families and young people have come in. They're good earners, working in Inverness in quite well-paid employment and they commute long distance – they go to Inverness and further every day to work, which was unheard of before. The Nigg [oil] industry, that's good for them too.

You can just look out the window here and you can see the oil construction yard. I don't mind that myself; you can't live off the scenery alone. It's a bit unsightly right enough and my big worry with it is that it's like all the other industries that rise and fall. Brown and Root, and Wimpey, were the people who started up, crossed their heart they would reinstate it all, take it all away. It would be reinstated and perfectly good and they were even going to have a sinking fund that would be put to this use. I bet you ten-a-penny that when that place is finished, it'll just rot away like

CROMARTY'S FUTURE ARRIVES, 1974

everything else. The structures in the North Sea, they were all to be removed; now they say, 'well it's a bit difficult to remove them,
so we'll cut them off so far below the sea,' and that's your lot. They're going to get away with it. It's a disgrace; they should have to come all away because the fishermen have lost a lot of their sea room to do their job and they're just not going to get the chance to have a good sea bed again, so that's sad. I don't mind industry in the Highlands, but we could do with a bit more feeling than we're doing it just now.

To Glasgow and University

I'd been to Glasgow twice before – down at the Empire Exhibition and one other time. The Empire Exhibition was magic. It really was well built. Nowadays you see Expo '96 or something like that and you can tell these are temporary buildings just knocked up for the occasion. The buildings in the Empire Exhibition were very high standard, especially the amusement park, and the Scenic Railway. We had the giraffe-necked woman and Hugh Miller, the great Cromarty stonemason – they had his mallet on show and they'd the old Clachan with the Highland wifie doing her spinning wheel act – it was marvellous.

I think I just always had a bent for maths or engineering, so I went to Glasgow University to study civil engineering. After the fifth year at Fortrose, I got enough subjects in the leaving certificate to be accepted for university, so I didn't do a sixth year – I was away at sixteen. It was a bit bewildering right enough, but I was the youngest of the family and I took over digs that my brother had been in. He'd been called up – this was 1941 and he was off in the Army. I was made welcome in his old digs by the landlady and I was well looked after.

It was a four-year course but it was a sandwich course: your winter months from September to April at University and then the summer months you had to go to a company for practical experience – a county surveyor or a drawing-office consulting engineer or a contractor. The first year I came back and did my practical at the county surveyor's in Inverness. But the war was on. The second year, the Government Ministry of Labour had decided that they wanted more cannon fodder so we didn't get a break. We had a week's holiday at Easter, a week's holiday in the autumn, but we did the third year in what would've been the second-year holidays and we did the fourth year immediately afterwards so we did it in two-and-a-half years. We did the same course work and I sat my final exams at the age of eighteen and got a first-class honours degree! You couldn't do that now, no.

In our final year, we were called up. We were given a War Office Selection Board exam, and some of us were chosen for the services, some of us were chosen for civilian work like the establishment at Farnborough, and so on. I was called up to the Army five days after graduating, did basic training and got commissioned after six months and then went away to the Far East and fiddled around there 'till 1947.

We were demobbed from the Army in rotation. I knew that my demob was due quite shortly and that Glasgow University had what they called an Appointments Bureau. It was a kind of labour exchange for old graduates. I wrote to them and asked if there was any job going connected with the hydroelectric schemes – I wanted to come back and do something for the Highlands particularly. They wrote back that there was this company who had a vacancy so I just joined that company and for the next thirty-odd years I wandered about. I was out in the field, as they call it, for the first twenty years and then in the office in Edinburgh for another seven or eight years.

Early Days of the
Hydro Board

The Hydro-electric Board was formed during the war, and it was a tremendous act of faith. The man behind it was Tom Johnston, who was the Secretary of State. He was a man of vision: he had this board set up and they started work immediately after the war. There had been hydroelectric schemes before that – Cromarty got its electric power from about 1935 from Loch Luichart. It came in here in poles and most of the sizeable townships in the north had electricity before the war, but it was only after the war that it was developed. The engineers, the chief engineers and all the staff of the Board itself, as well as the contractors, were very much aware that it was pioneering work that they were doing. It was almost like being in the Army. A lot of the workers were displaced people from the continent – Poles and Hungarians and Ukrainians who couldn't go back home – and quite a lot of them lived in camps set up as far up the glens as they could get. It was a tremendous source of employment: hundreds and hundreds of people on the schemes. Nowadays they can do it with a fairly small human and a huge mechanical input. There was no mechanical diggers then, just a few steam cranes to begin with and it was all hard work for the locals. Now these boards are all very comfortable and full of regulations. When there's a power cut and you ring up to ask when the power's coming on, they won't tell you until you give your name, address and postcode. But this is a complete change of attitude from the pioneering days. People like Sir Edward McColl and Mr Lawrie, the two chief engineers, they were great chaps altogether and it was quite inspiring to work for them. Mind you, I was young.

I was out on the field. I worked for a contractor – my job was putting up the steel tower lines from the power stations to the collecting points for the grid. Fifty, sixty miles at a time, from Pitlochry, Tummel Bridge right through to Falkirk. Up from Glen Quoich and Glengarry down to Fort Augustus, and in Argyll on the Shira Scheme from the top of Loch Fyne right down to Carradale – sixty-six miles of steel towers and it was great. You had to get on your feet and get up the hills with your theodolite and survey it all. You see tower lines going through the countryside and think, 'Nothing to it, it's just like Meccano sets' – it's nothing of the kind, it has to be very well thought out. These towers, there's not a surplus kilogram of steel in them, they're all working to a very tough design. The clearance from the ground, the span, and the various levels have all to be calculated. You'll get lots of power cuts still in the winter, but not because the steel towers fall down, it's usually the poles!

The hardest part of the job was just getting through the peat bogs and getting the material to site. Nowadays, they use helicopters; we had no helicopters and a lot of it was manpower. Before my day, it was actually horsepower. We had special tractors, caterpillar tractors with specially wide tracks – two foot six inches wide – dragging sledges along with the sand and ballast and steelwork and insulators and other accessories. We'd to drive roads sometimes, but on the peat bogs we just had to get across the best way we could. Some of the men lived in tents up on the site; in the summertime they'd hardly come down at all. We lived in a caravan, even after we were married, and just towed it around, a couple of years here, a couple of years there.

It was only latterly, at the time of the Cruachan Scheme in the early 1960s, that we used helicopters for the first time, getting across the area above Loch Katrine where the Glasgow water supply was. We weren't allowed to cut up the heather in case we polluted the water supply. They were poor little helicopters. Nowadays, you can get huge lifts made by helicopters; these were little Bell helicopters and most of the ones we used only could take up three hundredweights. We'd a special big brute of a machine – it would take eleven hundredweights – that would come up specially from Cambridge now and then. But that was the way it was done, everything had to be broken down into small amounts and taken up just a little bit at a time. The Hydro Board themselves paid us the extra cost of this as an experiment, to see how it would be done. We took up about eight hundred tonnes of stuff on helicopters, but before that there was no cheap way up, it was all sweat of the brow.

Once the work was completed, the impact on the community was enormous. The bigger towns had had their own supply even during the years before the war. But the small places like Drumnadrochit, Invermoriston and Invergarry, up the glens at Dalmally and these places ... it was paraffin lamps, and we used to trim the wick and light the Tilley lamp when it got dark and take your little lamp to bed with you so it was a complete and utter change. Things like electric cookers and vacuum cleaners and kettles and so on – marvellous! You didn't have to get up in the small hours of the morning again to light the stove to get hot water, or cook on ovens or ranges in the summertime in the heat. It brought a complete change of life.

Over the thirty years that I worked, from the days that I started until I finished, I would say the biggest change was the end of drudgery for the housewife for a start. Smoky fires that wouldn't draw, going out to cut the blinking wood to get for the kindlers, wood for the fire, cutting peats – they're all things of the past. Instant light, instant heat: it's just taken a lot of the drudgery out of life. And when the Hydro Board was formed, they gave free connection to anybody. Didn't matter where you were, away up the glen ... a pole line and a little transformer and there was your power. That lasted for quite a few years and then gradually it became 'oh, this is a bit expensive' and then you'd to pay a proportion, then a bigger and bigger proportion. Nowadays, if you live in a remote place or even a semi-remote place, to get a connection costs the earth, thousands and thousands of pounds before they put it in. This is why I say the fathers of the Hydro-electric Board were really pioneers and very far-seeing people.

The schemes dried up, slowed down. More and more objectors – you could hardly get a scheme passed now. Most of the big catchment areas are now tapped, there's not many left. The only thing they can do now would be with what they call pump storage schemes, like Cruachan. There are one or two ideal places for pump storage schemes but you'll never get them past Scottish Natural Heritage and the various objectors. It's a whole new type of renewable energy, that's the thing again about the Hydro Board resource – it's clean, no pollution, every time it rains, it fills the dam up, it's all renewable. The wind farms and the sea power, that's where the next lot of pioneering engineers have to come and attend to.

Scotland's Power in the Future

Scotland's a very strange country in that it doesn't exploit its natural resources. We have one of the best areas in the world for getting energy from the sea. There's been one or two attempts, like the attempt up near Dounreay a couple of years ago but it came unstuck. People laugh at these nodding ducks and odd things like that but there is a tremendous power to be gained from the sea and it's there for the taking. There's one wind farm quite visible from Cromarty, at Evanton: over twenty windmills right along the skyline. Some people object to them, but the locals don't.

The thing is, the power produced by the hydroelectric schemes, is not really anything like what's required to run our infrastructure now. So they have to have Hunterston or Torness and so on, oil-fired, gas-fired power stations are going ten-a-penny just now. But these will stop and they do pollute. I think the nuclear industry's very much in disgrace now, I don't see much more of that developing. So I'm sure that wind power and sea power is where future power should come from.

Irene Livingstone
Police Officer

Born 1925

Childhood

I was born in Partick, Glasgow. My father was an inspector in Central Station and my mother, who came from Carnoustie, became the first woman guard in the railway during the First World War. That was her war work and that's where she met my father – they married in the February of '24. We stayed in a flat at 789 Dumbarton Road, and then we moved round to Victoria Park Drive South, beside the park gates, and then to a large terraced house in St Vincent Crescent.

I went to school at Balshagray to begin with, then Kent Road School and then Woodside. At school I was into everything – I was in the netball team, I was being coached by the Scottish women's hockey team as a goalkeeper – I rode cycles, I played tennis, I swam, I did just about everything.

We played the usual ball games and skipping rope, but mostly we went up to the park and played tennis or putting, and hopscotch of course – the usual things with children. By and large we didn't tear around a lot. In those days, fortunately, it was very safe to allow children to go out and play or walk the short distances to school. It was world headlines if a child was molested in any way. I know that as a youngster – I was sixteen – and one of my friends used the word pregnant and we thought this was terribly, terribly forward. Everybody in that condition was 'in an interesting condition' in those days. I think today's children have lost their innocence because we were still playing with dolls when youngsters of today are going to discos and that kind of thing. I wasn't allowed to go to dance halls. That wasn't the proper thing to do. And you didn't go out unless you had an escort. That was a very rigid discipline. This was all during the war.

Wartime Glasgow

With the number of troops in the town, Glasgow was quite a swinging city in those days but I wasn't allowed to go out. I had to be in at half past nine when my father was on night shift, to make sure that I was home safely. And even out on a date with one of my schoolfriends, it was half past nine on the dot, or I wasn't allowed to go out again.

I remember listening to the radio, a big Echo radio. That was about the only thing you had at home, of course, and most people either played an instrument or sang or went to dancing classes. Otherwise, it was the cinema or the theatre, with girlfriends, mostly. Cinema was a very popular entertainment during the war. The Wilson Barrett Company used to come regularly and then of course, there was *The Five Past Eight Show* and the various musicals and things. I used to go regularly to the theatre. Of course, it was a very dressy-up affair before the war – I remember my aunts dressing up in their evening dresses to go to the theatre.

In those days, you had a lot of homework at school and when the war came, the junior school was evacuated and we were left with one subject, one hour a day. The older boys were leaving and joining the forces and I decided that I was never going to get through the year with one hour a day, so I left and started work as an office girl, and progressed from that to typist and went to night school, to do shorthand; I was sitting in Hamilton Crescent School at night school when the bomb landed down at Partick and we were all duly blown off our seats and spent the night in the shelter. Then from working in Barr & Strouds, I moved to Wickmans in Hillington.

How the Other Half Lived

At the end of the war I went to America – I was quite interested in seeing how the other half lived. And I had a feeling that one day I'd end up as a police officer, and so I was quite anxious to get as much experience of life as possible. My uncle sent the necessary papers and I emigrated to live with him, for just about three years. The first thing that I noticed in the streets was the electric lights – it was so light with all these bulbs burning even during the day, and after the wartime restrictions it was quite something.

I worked in an office for a few weeks when I first went out, and then I became a secretary to the Superintendent of Schools in Dearborn, Michigan, and the Superintendent was sacked for failing to put £200,000 through the books. I was asked if I would take on the administrative duties of the Superintendent and so for six months, until they were able to engage a new one, I was acting Schools Superintendent. We had two kindergarten schools in the area because we were out in the sticks, and we had to bus seven hundred pupils to about nine different schools in Dearborn. It was very interesting and it was marvellous experience. One time when I 'phoned up to order school supplies the voice at the other end of the 'phone, after I'd given the order, said 'Pardon me, ma'am?' So I repeated what I'd said – 'Pardon me ma'am?' and I repeated what I'd said, and this went on for about six times until I was speaking through my teeth, and eventually an apology came. They said 'terribly sorry, ma'am but we've been passing the 'phone round the office – you've got such a cute accent.' And a large bunch of flowers and a box of chocolates were duly delivered with the order.

A Family Tradition

I always felt that I was going to end up in the police service one way or the other. The only other ambition I had during the war was to get into the forces, into nursing. At school, when I said I was going to leave, the headmaster was doing his best to persuade me to stay on because I thought I might become a physical instructress and I was into all the games and gymnastics. I was part of a team doing gymnastic displays for the Scottish teachers at one time in Jordanhill, and I was very keen on it. But no, I felt that the police force was where I belonged.

There's a family joke that I did my first undercover job when I was in my pram in 1926. My father was designated to keep the mail trains running from the Central, and of course during the strike in the May the pickets were all out, and my mother brought a change of clothing and food for my father, and walked from Balshagray Avenue all the way up to the Central Station with the food and the clothing under the pram and me sitting on top, and she duly pushed her way through the pickets – so that was my first plainclothes job.

My grandfather had been in the Metropolitan when he was seventeen. His first job down there was to keep the rats off the dead bodies, and had tales of being in the Metropolitan and later on in Edinburgh city. I had another relative via my grandmother in the Partick police apparently. My brother was in the police for a short time, so a police career seemed to be inevitable. I was interested in the wide variety of jobs that the policewoman had to do.

So in 1951, when I came back from America, I was interviewed and accepted for the Glasgow force, but at that time they only had twenty-eight women and there was a waiting list of twenty. The only time there was a vacancy was when a woman retired or got married. So they couldn't tell you when there was likely to be a vacancy. I was asked if I would go to a county force, and I wasn't terribly keen because I'd come home to nurse my mother who was due to go into hospital. However, after twiddling my thumbs for a month, I just couldn't stand doing nothing and so I said yes, and I was sent to Ayr Burgh, starting in the June of '51. That was the last plainclothes police force in Scotland. They had never had a uniform.

You must remember that the men in the higher ranks had probably joined way back in the 1920s when women had just been appointed in Glasgow – the first two were only appointed in 1919, and they weren't attested as police officers until 1924 when they were given the power of arrest – and weren't terribly keen on women joining. It was a man's job, so when I joined it was a case of patrolling in plainclothes and typing up statements for the CID, and making enquiries about women and children and missing persons, and taking statements for indecency cases. When we went into uniform it was quite something. We were something of a celebrity in town and the local photographers would follow us round the streets taking photographs. I remember walking up the High Street, passing a woman with a little boy of about five, and the little boy said 'Whit's that?' and the mother said 'That's a polisman's wummin – now you behave yourself or she'll take you away.'

As I say, we were quite something in those days but when we got into uniform – and I was a lot smaller than I am now, with 34-inch hips – you can appreciate there wasn't much space in a straight skirt which was quite long. I had been out with the CID boys – there had been a complaint of an assault on a child down a railway embankment, and of course when we got to the locus the boys had all louped over the dyke and gone, and I was left standing trying to move in this long, thin skirt. So when I had to go in and do my twirl in front of the chief constable, to see how I liked the uniform, I didn't dare to tell him I tried to climb a dyke in the new uniform so I said, 'Well, it wouldn't be

Irene and a colleague patrol in Ayr in September 1952 – the first day they were allowed on the streets in uniform

much use for chasing someone up the High Street', and he said 'Miss Livingstone, you're not supposed to chase people up the High Street, remember, you're a lady.'

We were very well looked after and very well protected. But we were useful where they felt a woman was required: a little boy was murdered in the racecourse and the boys were going out and getting the statements, and bringing them in and we sat and typed them up – a copy for the chief and copy for the CID. As a result of the publicity people were coming forward from way back and telling of things that had happened in their childhood. One was a fellow who had been indecently assaulted by a man. He had never told anyone before and he came and reported this in case it had any bearing on the case; I typed up his statement and sent it away and the chief constable was appalled that I should have to type such a statement. And I mean it was a lot milder than some of the statements that we'd dealt with, with rapes or abortions or anything else, but the poor detective officer who'd handed in the statement had to come in and apologise. He was threatened with being put back in uniform on the street. The idea was that, as a lady, I wouldn't know about homosexual behaviour.

There plainly was child abuse at the time, but people were much less open about it. I think it's been going on since time began, but I think it wasn't to the same extent. Nowadays there is so much sex and violence portrayed on television and in books and magazines, it's talked about, and youngsters seem to be growing up in this environment that they use words and phrases and they have knowledge that we never had. In fact I was in my thirties, I think, when a youngster of about thirteen enlightened me about a certain form of contraception.

But the men were very helpful. They went to training schools, of course – if you wanted to know something you asked them. At that time the women didn't go to training school – it wasn't considered ladylike in the force. Training had only started for women in 1947. In 1952, the Chief decided, as I say, that we would come into the 20th century and get into uniform, and then because of domestic circumstances, I had to move back to Glasgow and that's when I joined the City of Glasgow, starting off in headquarters.

Life in the Glasgow Force

In those days, in the middle 1950s, when I transferred to Glasgow it was the first big intake of women and they brought on sixteen extra uniformed policewomen to bring the total from twenty eight up to forty four. It enabled them to send two uniformed girls to each of the divisions. There were six girls on each of the two shifts at headquarters at Central, and with those six girls we managed to cover ports and escorts and patrol, and later on the parking shifts, the early shift and the afternoon shift. We also were able to have one girl on night shift to cover the whole of the city of Glasgow to take statements. One policewoman. You based yourself at headquarters, and when a division required a policewoman to come and take statements and see if someone had to be medically examined, take productions, they sent a car for you and you were taken to that division. When someone else wanted you they 'phoned headquarters and were told that you were at such-and-such division. They then 'phoned that division and said that they'd send a car, and a car was waiting for you to transport – this is how you could go on all night.

It was only when they started to bring on extra women that they had enough women to send to the divisions, that they in turn could take care of the women in their own shifts, in their own divisions. You earned your pay in those days – after you were finished your entire night's work and had all the statements typed out and sent to the various divisions ready for the CID women in the morning, you then had to sit and write out a resumé of what you had done during the night for the superintendent or the chief inspector in the morning.

Glasgow had a much bigger force and had policewomen doing much more in the way of police work than I had done previously in the Burgh – the men were much more able to accept women in the job. But again you had the older men, the senior men, some of whom had joined in the '20s and '30s. When I first went to the Marine Division the superintendent there didn't know what he had two CID women for, so what was he going to do with two uniformed girls? He didn't want us, and he made that perfectly plain. I suppose the modern term would be 'male chauvinist'.

Our duties at that time – we patrolled from Granville Street to Holland Street in Sauchiehall Street. It took all of seven minutes, and we had to patrol up and down and up and down, so much so that the shopkeepers came out and asked us if we were looking for something. The fact that we were in uniform was a spectacle in itself, I suppose. That was Mondays, Wednesdays and Fridays. Tuesdays, Thursdays and Saturdays – Byres Road. Of course in those days, you only had one day off a week. Up one side, down the other, reverse it and go up and down. Report back to the office for our break – we got three-quarters of an hour break – report with the chief inspector, officer on duty at the bar, and check with him on the way out – make sure it was three-quarters of an hour on the dot. Back to up and down Byres Road. We were supposed to help anybody that asked us the way, asked us directions or something, or somebody passed us some lost property or something like that. But the chief inspector just didn't want us to do anything. He was quite determined that we were extra baggage and we weren't needed. And then came the day when we were asked to do a school crossing on a pedestrian crossing, a zebra crossing. Now we had directed the traffic in the centre of town but he sent two of us to the crossing, supervised by a male sergeant, to see children across.

But the men were very good. They were very keen to give us jobs to help them out. When Billy Graham came to the Kelvin Hall, and the hundreds of people went there, hundreds left their Bibles, their gloves, their umbrellas, their coats; all this had to be collected the following morning in the last big prison van – they were huge – and taken back to the office and catalogued. Now the boys at the bar were supposed to do this, and so they asked us if we would help and we were delighted. It was a change from going up and down Byres Road or going Granville Street to Holland Street. We duly checked out with the officer on duty as per instructions from the divisional boss, round the back of the Marine and in the back door and snuck in the corridor, and the boys brought us in, locked us in the casualty surgeon's room, took away the keys just on the off-chance that the superintendent be looking for an aspirin or something. We were left in there to write out the tags and catalogue all the missing properties so that they could be taken to headquarter's lost property department. These are the little things that were sent to try us.

Being of the disposition that I am, if a shopkeeper in Byres Road had rushed out and said 'I'm so glad to see you because there's this shoplifter', we dealt with it, took them to the nearest box and 'phoned. In those days we had no radios, and so we went to the nearest box and 'phoned in and did what we had to do. We did as much in the way of police work that we possibly could, we got a row for it at times. There was an indecent call reported I remember, there were no CID women on duty, so a colleague and I went out and took the statements from the woman and filed them. It came to the notice of the superintendent who informed the officer on duty to bring me in and ask me on whose instructions had I taken this statement. I was informed that I was not to take statements unless I was particularly asked. But having said that, the CID boss, Detective Chief Inspector Johnstone, he used policewomen at every opportunity and we would do a lot of undercover jobs, plainclothes jobs. He would take us out on enquiries, murder enquiries, serious assaults, and we got a lot of experience that way.

The majority of bosses were only too delighted to have the women in the divisions. The work gradually built up until we were doing everything and the jobs were all open. Equal pay came along, and that didn't meet with too many hurrahs from the men at the time. That was 1960s, and the odd one or two – and I do hasten to add, the odd one or two – would turn round and tell you that you were just in the job to find a man, and they had a wife and four children to look after and they didn't approve of this equal pay business at all. In vain we would try to say, well, we're doing work of equal value and that's what we're being paid for. I remember one in particular saying, 'Right, you can search the men at the bar and you can run across the roofs and catch the housebreakers then.' And I said, 'Well, do you search the women at the bar when they come in?' He said, 'No', and I said, 'Well what makes you think we're going to search the men at the bar?' There was the odd one or two who thought they were God's gift to women, but I don't think any policewoman worth their salt would take long to put them back in their place. I think the younger generation are more aware that women are part and parcel of the job.

Training

When I went to Glasgow they threw up their hands in horror to discover that I'd almost three years' service and had never been to initial training. So I joined the girls who were brought on – the twelve in the first class – three were brought on later to make up the sixteen. I joined them for their three months' initial training. Normally someone transferring from another force would just have done a couple of weeks on the Glasgow by-laws, but because I hadn't been to school, I went through the first three months.

For physical training, we learned the 'come along holds' as they were called, because we didn't have batons and we didn't have handcuffs – it was a case of arresting someone by laying hands on them, and most of them came quite willingly. In thirty years I only had two who didn't wish to come when I asked them to come. One was six foot two or three, he was mentally retarded and he was drunk, so that was a bit of a struggle, and the other one was a woman who was under the influence of LSD. She was in a dance hall and we had to go in and collect her and she was raging mad, and five gentlemen, civilians, offered to help and each took a leg and a limb and it took five of them to get her into the van.

This was just at the beginning of drugs becoming a major part of the job, when I was in Headquarters in the 1960s. I was on Court Duty the day that they had the first raid on a house in the West End and they brought in these zombies, is all you could call them, they were completely and utterly stoned. Such was the interest, the corridors leading to the cells were full of police and probation officers to see this chain of people walking past. The drug office was beside our policewomen's department at one time and you would see them coming in, young women. I remember one – she was only twenty three – she came in to speak and she had a daughter who was out at the Castlemilk Home at the time; she was going to get the daughter back, because she was going to stop the drugs tomorrow – it was always tomorrow. I remember her arm, it was pock-marked with broken needles and lumps and things – a terrible mess – but it was always going to be tomorrow. She used to buy little presents and things to take up to her daughter. She was dead before she was twenty-four I used to think that was so sad – youngsters using drugs, doing it to themselves.

Before that it was glue-sniffing with the youngsters. We had occasions to deal with them and that was horrendous too, to see children under the influence of those things. Not knowing what it was going to do to their body and what was going to happen in the future as a result of what they were doing to their bodies, with drugs and LSD and glue-sniffing, and they were quite wild under the glue; it was very sad.

On the Beat When I was in Central division and we eventually got extra staff on night shift, we could walk round Glasgow in perfect safety, and in fact it was quite a joy to walk around Glasgow at night. After the last bus had gone the next people you'd see would be the reporters coming from the *Glasgow Herald* office in Buchanan Street when they put the paper to bed and then the next people you would see were the women cleaners coming to the offices around about half past five in the morning.

There were gangs in the East End and there was no doubt the odd bottle fight and knife fight, but after the gangs of the '30s and '40s, when the razor gangs were given very harsh sentences, that sort of died down. Then gradually these youngsters, who I suppose through boredom formed gangs and had fights, but they were dealt with by the men in the divisions themselves. If there was anything on the town then you would have the men in cars dealing with it. We wouldn't be dealing with it on patrol, because in those days we didn't have walkie talkies and we had to watch for the light flashing on a box.

You had to know where all the police boxes were in the town, and where all the telephones were attached to lamp standards and things – police ones. If you were needed, the lights flashed, and if you saw a light flashing on top of a police box you would go there and find out if it was for you or a beat police officer or whatever. If you were on patrol duty, you called in on duty at the boxes to the girls on the switchboard and they took a note of your number, that you were on duty. Likewise, when off duty you went to the police box and you called off duty, and again your number was noted and scored off to show that there wasn't a police officer missing, lying assaulted in an alleyway somewhere.

The police box at St Enoch Square was the largest box. I remember one occasion when they decided to try and find out how many police officers could get in there, and my colleague and I ended up on a shelf, but that's another story. One night going off duty, the police box in St Enoch Square was there, one side of the subway and then on the other side, just a few feet away was the men's toilet. The buses left from just facing that, and there was an old drunk sitting on the pavement and some of the boys were going down to the toilets before they would go on a bus to go home, and other boys were coming out of the police box. And this old drunk was watching this parade going down the stairs and coming out the police box, and he said '...is there a so-and-so basement in that so-and-so box?' If you arrested someone you took them to a police box and 'phoned in and the van arrived. And on occasions I remember being left holding a dog when the van arrived to take away a drunk, and the fellow had had a dog. They took the drunk into the van and I said 'What about the dog?' And they said 'Sorry, Sarge – the van's just been washed,' and away they went and left me to walk along Argyle Street in the Trongate with a dog on a bit of rope. Which was a bit better than my colleague, 'cos she was landed with a horse and cart because the driver was drunk when they took the horse and cart and left her.

When the first walkie talkies came in, there was a receiving set and a talking set, and so you had one or the other and your neighbour, as we called our colleagues, had the other. So one could hear what was going on and the other had to speak into it. Then, eventually, of course you had the one item.

In the '60s or '70s, the baton was wrapped in tissue paper, and the handcuffs were also wrapped in tissue paper and they were handed back still wrapped in the tissue paper. When they decided to give us batons we said, 'Well, where are we going to keep them?' because our uniforms didn't have the place for them and they decided they would give us a baton pocket. They put baton pockets into the skirts without enlarging the skirts in any way, so there was this stupid bulge that looked like an extra leg hanging down at the side, and so they got short shrift, it was put back in the drawer and that's where it stayed. I never drew my baton.

Trousers came in in the '60s when the girls were doing parking duties, and in those days if you came across a car that was illegally parked, you had to stand over it for the entire time until the owner came back. No such thing as a parking ticket in those days, much as we would have loved them. So you could stand there for hours in the miserable wet and one girl eventually collapsed, threatened with pneumonia, and so it was decided that we could have slacks and that would be a bit warmer. But the order was that no slacks had to be worn inside the police building. So when you came in the slacks had to come off. One of the girls, I remember, very cutely got over that by wearing her slacks underneath her skirt. When she came into the office all she had to do was take off her slacks and she was dressed for the office. These things sound very funny and peculiar when you look back on it but it was accepted in those days.

Coping with Disaster   The Ibrox disaster was a dreadful day. It was appalling to see the grief. I was late-shift duty sergeant at the policewoman's department that day and I got a 'phone call to say there had been a major incident at Ibrox. There were a large number of casualties and that relatives would probably be coming in – would I house them in the courtroom and have the girls see about tea or anything like that for them? Once I'd done that, I was then directed to go to the mortuary and take charge there. And one of my recollections was of seeing a man in the corner, outside the courtroom, in the foetal position, too shocked to move. Then the mortuary – there weren't enough trays for the bodies so they were laid out on the mortuary floor covered with plastic. And the one woman who was killed was in the side room – they'd separated her in the side room. As people came in they were shown... they gave us a description of what the person was wearing when they last saw them and we had the clothes in bags

*A NURSE FROM THE
SOUTHERN GENERAL
HOSPITAL RUSHES TO
IBROX STADIUM TO TEND
TO THE INJURED*

and tabulated, and we showed them clothes to see if they could identify the clothes, and then we took them through to identify the bodies. That was a dreadful, dreadful night. I was on duty for thirteen hours that night and the men, too, they had come back with blood on their uniforms where they had been helping to try and resuscitate the victims. It was quite dreadful.

You knew part of your job was to deal with anything that came along. I remember one of my probationers, she had to deal with a street accident and it was between a motorcyclist and his pillion passenger and a bus, and people don't seem to realise that someone has to clean up after these things. She attended to the accident and then she was cleaning up and sweeping, and realised she was sweeping up fingers. She went into a bus, sat down and was sick. We're human. You try your best but it's very difficult at times and, as you're told at the beginning, you're not to get emotionally involved in your job and that the ratepayers don't pay the rates to see a police officer sitting weeping – they expect help and so help you have to give.

There was no such thing as counselling. It was very difficult when one of your colleagues was killed or there was an accident involving a child or something; there was a gloom descended on the office. It was very hard and there were tears, but to the public you had to bring the shutter down and attend to what you had to do.

*Promotion and
Discrimination*

There was a great deal of favouritism towards male promotions because the jobs were nearly all supervised by male officers. But gradually throughout the years... the first woman to attain the rank of inspector in Scotland was Jean Molloy, who was one of the first policewomen in Glasgow; she was promoted sergeant and then inspector, I think, in 1945, and she was the very first. And Miss Grey, who had transferred up from an English force in 1932, she became sergeant. When I had started in Glasgow Miss Grey had become Chief Inspector and there was Mrs Beattie who was an

Inspector – at the time of us joining I think there were six sergeants. The women themselves, for example in the CID, didn't become Detective Constables until 1962, but from this period on, from the '50s onwards, more women were being brought on and more women were being promoted, until finally Miss Grey retired as Superintendent in 1961 and was appointed as the first Assistant HMI of women. It was a gradual process: up until 1968, when the marriage ban was lifted, only single women and widows were recruited into the police service, and you could only either retire from the force or marry out of it.

Things were being added to our work all the time; women were gradually being put into departments which before were no-go areas because they were jumping-off places for promotion for the men: the fraud squads; the special branches, the dog branch, the mounted branch. Patrol cars, that was the first one really to have the women in, I think, and much to the men's annoyance, the girls came out tops in examinations – one of my girls got ninety-nine per cent in her written exam and that didn't go down too well with some of the men when you think of how they think of women drivers. But I think it was up to about a hundred and seventy-two women in the '70s in Glasgow: they gradually moved into all these different branches and consequently were being accepted. To begin with, with the policewomen's department, the women who were promoted were promoted to supervise women, but gradually of course they were brought into shifts. In 1975 we were declared no longer policewomen, we were police officers, and in that way we were integrated into the job.

There were several circulars from the Home Office and various places about women shouldn't be allowed to dictate to men and order men around but gradually that has gone. A woman could finally give orders to a man.

I think the fact that women are accepted now is the biggest change between 1950 and 1980, when I retired. I hate to see macho types in the job; I don't think they do the job any credit. The first women in the job were ladies, and as a result of the work that they did, and the dedication that they showed to the job, those of us who followed on were accepted. It's been a gradual build-up; there are those who want to be as tough and as vociferous in the language as the men, and I don't like to see that because I think that we were much more respected for doing the job that we were doing than if we had tried to act like a man.

Thomas Winning
Catholic Clergyman

Born 1925

I was born in a little town called Wishaw, near its bigger brother, Motherwell, in Lanarkshire. I went to the local Catholic primary school and then Our Lady's High School in Motherwell. Apart from school, we played football. There was a fair field beside us so we would have football in the evenings. When I was about fourteen I took up golf. One of my uncles was quite a keen golfer and I got a small set of clubs and became a member of the Wishaw Golf Club. But the Clydeside was right on our doorstep and there was no question of us being city boys, we were country boys. The parish would also probably have taken up some of my time, taking part in plays or operas in the parish.

We were just ordinary kids and played as they do today, even in spite of many of the dangers. After school we would often go out to play or just be with one another. There were about six or eight boys in the neighbourhood. We got up to all the tricks that boys get up to, especially on dark nights when you kicked doors and so on but no one ever really worried about us. We would be in by times and maybe do your homework and get to bed but I don't remember any occasions when our parents were really anxious about us being out. In a place like Wishaw during the Depression there wasn't a great deal of motor traffic, practically none in fact. My uncle had a business near Lanark and to me, he seemed pretty well off. He had a lovely car and now and again, he would take us out for a run, to the seaside or something.

We didn't have holidays – on one occasion I said to my mother, 'Why can't we have holidays like the people next door?' They went to Portobello for a week every year, and my mother said 'Well, if you would like to eat margarine every day instead of butter, I'll take you a holiday.' So that finished me. My first holiday was with my family after I became a priest. I would be about twenty-four and we went to Ireland for a week. That was my very first holiday. As part of my college training, one year was spent in North West London in a college there. The whole college from Glasgow went down. That was the only time I left the country until I went to Rome as a student for the priesthood.

Finding a Vocation

I was very very much involved in the parish life – I was in the choir, I was an altar boy. When I was about thirteen years of age, I plucked up courage and spoke one day to the parish priest. I hadn't said anything to anyone at home, but he, quite honestly, didn't have a very good experience in his junior seminary days. The food wasn't to his liking and I don't think he ever went back, although he taught for about twenty years in another seminary in Glasgow. But he didn't like the idea of my leaving at that particular age, in case I had the same experiences he'd had. He said, 'You stay on at school until you get your Highers and then we'll see about it.' So I just more or less put it out of my mind for the next four years. When I got my

Highers, he was still in our parish and he made the arrangements then. I told him and spoke to my parents and off I went.

My parents were pleased, I think, but they never exerted any influence, any pressure. They were good practising Catholics and, in those days at least, there was a kind of feeling that it would be a great blessing on the family if one of their boys became a priest. I was the only boy, my sister and myself were the family. So they were pleased without going cock-a-hoop about it.

After my Highers, I went off to St Mary's College, Blair's in 1942. I began my studies for the priesthood with two years' philosophy in Aberdeen. I began my studies halfway through the war. Actually, I was only seventeen when I went off to college, but one of my friends at home was amongst the first batch of conscripts in 1938 – he was twenty-one. A lot of our students felt that, in a time of war, fit young men should not be studying for the priesthood, but should be away fighting. There was a rule that if you had expressed your intention of becoming a priest or taking Holy Orders before the war, then you would be exempt unless you wanted to go yourself, spontaneously; as I had done this then that was accepted. But many of my contemporaries had to go off, some of the boys in my year who were not within that category had to go for four or five years.

A Strong and Loving Family

My family was originally Irish, but a long way back, 1855 or so. My mother was born in this country. I think both my grandfathers were born in this country so the Irish connection would really go back about 150 years. After the Famine [1846–47], I think, both my mother's and my father's families came from Ireland. We were aware of the distinction between Catholics and Protestants in the west of Scotland: I think of making my way to the local Catholic primary school in the morning there was one particular area which was a bit dangerous. But that was about all. We had Catholic and Protestant neighbours and the boys and girls, we played together and so

A COMMON SIGHT DURING THE DEPRESSION OF THE '30s

on. Now and again round about the Twelfth of July you heard strange tunes but we got on pretty well.

My father was a working man: he'd been in the mines, and he'd been in the trenches for four years during the First World War as a fairly young man. He went to America round about 1919 to see if he could get any work, stayed for about five years, came back, married my mother and got a job locally. He worked in Stewarts & Lloyd's, who had a big tube works in Flemington in Motherwell, till it closed in the early '30s. They invited him to go to Corby but he didn't want to break up the home and from then until about the war he was unemployed. Not from the lack of searching for work – he wasn't a lazy man. Looking back, he seemed to have a fair share of equilibrium and balance so that he didn't really get uptight about the lack of a job. He was on the Labour Exchange, the Means Test. They were paid by the government, by the Means Test, thirty shillings a week, for husband and wife and two shillings each for the children, and sometimes when we wanted something that was unreasonable, we were reminded about this. Then one of my uncles suggested that to pass the time he might make sweets and get a hobby and he took it up in a very big way, to the extent of buying machinery for making sweets and learning to make so many others. He sold the sweets to the local shops and very popular they were. He was a bit conscientious and he thought, how much am I allowed to make over and above the Bru money, and he was told four shillings a week you can make without losing any money. So he carried on like that till shortly before the war. Then he retrained as a fitter and got a job in Glasgow till he retired.

My mother was purely a mother and a housewife, though she threatened to go and get a job and leave us to come home by ourselves or to come into an empty house. She was the youngest of a very big family and she had an old aunt whom she used to look after, about quarter of a mile away. She helped another aunt who was working to look after the home and so on but apart from looking after us she was at home. She never really expressed any frustration that she could herself have gone and done something else. I think the world has changed so much – if you look at the '30s and '40s, people were different. The vast majority of women who were at home seemed to enjoy being there and had a lot of hard work to do. There were no washing machines, no great facilities at home. There were coal fires and so on. My mother all in all had a pretty tough life in the sense of really working hard at it.

Four people on thirty bob a week was hard, but I found she was a good manager. We never went around with the backside out of our trousers. Neither my sister nor myself would have admitted that we were poor but I think it was because the mother made such a good job of managing in the home that we were like that. We were well fed and we weren't neglected in any way. When you look back on those days, you really feel very proud that you had such a good father and mother.

Hugh Johnstone
Miner & Musician

Born 1925

Early Life and Education

I was born in 61 Craigmark, that's a village, old mining rows about two miles from the village of Dalmellington. The living was primitive, in a way. Each row had its communal wash-house where each family would take its turn on certain days for washing. The clothes poles, that was a communal thing too. Summer time we ran about with our bare feet. When I was three, we moved to 59 Burnton where there was electric light, inside toilet, that sort of thing. It was from there that I went to the school. We had to make the mile-and-a-half walk from the school, which was in Dalmellington in the centre of the village. I went with my older sister and an older brother.

I liked the school. There was various things I was good at. Writing was one. Some of the teachers were local, like Miss Chrissie Thompson and Miss Agnes Hill who become Mrs Campbell – her husband was killed in the first year of the war. He was Lieutenant Sandy Campbell and he was killed in the bomb disposal in London. Some of them that didn't come from local lived locally, like Miss Morrison who lived with an aunt of mine out at Gordon House on the Cumnock Road. Miss Drysdale from Girvan stayed in the village with people called Smith; their father was a tailor in the village. The headmaster came from Newmills in Ayrshire. He could get a train from Newmills to Ayr and then from Ayr to Dalmellington. That train picked up pupils at Patna and Waterside and it arrived in Dalmellington at ten to nine and left at four-fifteen to take them back.

The teachers become very much a part of the local community and there were highlight days in the village: the Sunday school trip which the band were involved in – the children were all assembled in the church green and they would march behind the band to the station and go to wherever: Prestwick, Ayr or Girvan, to the seaside. The other highlight day was the school sports day organised by the school staff. There again the band got involved. At the end of the sports day there was a square roped off on the football field and, in the evening, the climax was a display of Scottish country dancing and the band provided the music. We rehearsed for that for probably six weeks prior to the event. Oh, aye, I have great memories of the school.

When we were at the school, our latter two or three year, during the summer holidays, the farmer was always looking for somebody for thinning the turnips. It was all hand-done – picking tatties, forking hay; the hay was all cut by horse-drawn reaper. We were living in a country area, it wasnae unknown to us and hard work was nothing to us.

Off to the Pit

I left school on Easter Friday at twelve o'clock and I walked from there to the pit and I asked the gaffer in the pithead for a job. I got the third degree: who was my father, who was my mother, who is this, who is the next thing and he said. 'Right, there's a job for you. Start tomorrow morning at 6 o'clock.' I was fourteen that day. I got home and I said to my mother, 'I've got a job', 'Where?', 'At the pit.' I was the

second youngest of a large family and she didn't want me to go to the pit but the deal had been done. She sent me into the Co-operative to get a pair of dungarees and at five o'clock the next morning I was wakened and at twenty past, off I went to work at the pit. Six o'clock in the morning, Monday to Friday, we worked from seven o'clock to quarter past three. And you got a fifteen-minute break from ten o'clock to quarter past; on Saturday it was six o'clock to half past two.

I can remember my first day. The place was only half a mile from the road where we lived. I remember walking up the stairs into the screes where they picked the dirt out of the coal. The coal came down in these revolving metal tables and you picked the dirt out and that was the first job I had. A man standing at the top of the step had a wooden leg, Johnny Givens was his name, and he says, 'Are you sterting to work here, son?' and I said, 'Aye'. 'Right,' he said, 'you're to come wi' me.' He was watching for me coming. I can well remember that.

The pit was the only industry in the village, in the valley really – the Upper Doune Valley was dependent on the extraction of coal from the various pits. There were eleven pits within a radius of five mile. Now I had so long in the screes, as we call the screening plant, and then I had about three month in the wood yard and then I was sent up the brae. The pit was right up at the top of the hill. I had about three months there. The day before I was fifteen the pithead gaffer came out and said to me – it was a Saturday – he says, 'You're going down the pit on Monday.' They gave you a hard hat, similar to what you'd see about building sites now, but smaller because it had to hold a carbide lamp, a naked flame lamp. And on the Monday, I went down the pit with my older brother.

My first wages was nineteen shillings and a penny, for a week's work. I'd go down the pit with my older brother, Adam, and then later I had spells with my brother Quentin who's in Canada. You shuffled about with different people, doing different things. In the early stages you were doing what we called being a 'putter'. There were maybe about four or five fellows older than us and they would shove the tubs. The roads were probably only four feet high and five feet wide and it was steep, up into the coal faces from the lies. I'm talking about well underground, it took about fifty minutes to walk into where we worked and my first job was as a putter. You would maybe be a putter to three different drawers – drawers were the fellas who

PULLING HUTCHES TO THE PIT BOTTOM, 1933; CHALMERSTON NUMBER 6 PIT, DALMELLINGTON

filled the hutches. Now because it was steep, you had to give a hand to hold these hutches back down these headings, as we called them. Eventually I become a drawer and then there's somebody gi'en you a hand. I did that until I was about twenty-one and then I'd a spell in the night shift and the back shift, and then I went into the face line tae work, hewing the coal.

At the Coal Face

We'd had hard graft in the pit. It was brutal. In the early days at No. 7 Chalmerston, we worked in a seam for three years during the war. It was a good seam of coal, it burnt away to about two percent ash, quality house coal, but the coal was only eighteen inches high and the water was running in on top of us. Added to that there were rats all over the place. They used to say that rats wouldnae venture into the face lines but they did; when you fired a shot in the coal and bring a shovel out, there was a dead rat. There were two fellas died at that time with the disease off the rats, Weil's Disease. They took them to the hospital on the Monday and one died on the Friday night, Jock MacFarlane, and Tommy Winning died on the Saturday morning. One of the things that we were all affected with probably had nothing to do with the rats – the doctor at the time said it was the lime in the water. We were bruised and cut all over – eighteen inches, you can imagine, you were crawling about just like human ants.

To work, you just lay on your side. One of my brothers was the blacksmith at the pit; he shortened everything, the shaft of our shovel, the handle of the boring machine, so that we could operate that sort of thing. I would shove the hutch down the road, for instance, and my brother would be up the face line which was only eighteen inches plus three inches the cut, they'd put an undercut in what we'd call daugh, this saft mealie stuff at the bottom of the coal and they'd put an undercut about four feet in this wi' an Anderson Boyce coal-cutting machine made in Motherwell. We would have a wooden box, about fifteen inches broad and a foot and a half long wi' a rope on either end. He would pull the box up and put the coal in it, and I would pull it doon and empty it into the hatch. At that time, we got two and thruppence a ton. He had to buy his own gelignite for blasting the coal down, he'd to pay for his pick blades being sharpened and he'd to pay me from that. Now he was married wi' two of a family and he'd go home wi' ten shillings and I got nine shillings. That was the worst time in my life in the pit.

Factory Work

That went on until 1948, and we got married. Jenny comes from Galston. There were no houses available at the time so I got a transfer to the pit in Mauchline. We got a house and an attic which was three floors up the stairs from where Jenny's family lived in Galston, in Gas Lane. By about 1950, my brother-in-law, who worked in a lace factory in Darvel, got me a job. That went very well. It was a totally different environment from working in the pit.

They were a different breed of people that worked in the factory. There were a camaraderie in the pit that was totally different. Anyway, in 1952, the apartheid situation had developed in South Africa and a lot of the lace factories lost their South African markets and we were put into working a week and idle a week. The week I was not working in the lace factory, I went to work on a farm between Darvel and Strathaven and dug tatties. Around this time, I come back home around the New Year time, to see my folks. As I stepped off the bus in the village I met my old pit manager and he says, 'Whit are you doin' these days?' and I said, 'We're working a week and idle a week.' He says: 'Right, come back here on Monday and go to Number Seven Pennywheeny. There's a new pit which had just been sunk, 125 fathoms doon into the rich seams of coal and tell the manager, William Dryburgh, I said he's to give you a job.' I said to Jenny, 'Right, I've to go back hame' and within three weeks we had a house here, because housing was plentiful. I came back to work in the pits; my last twenty-odd years I was working on constant night shift. I operated one of these coal-cutting machines that put the undercut on the coal. That lasted until 1969. All this time I was involved with the band.

War Memories You could see the war was coming, right from '38 with the actions of the German war machine, Czechoslovakia, threatening France and then the invasion of Poland. I remember coming up the pit that day and the men that were coming doon were saying that the Germans had invaded Poland. At that time, before the war started, any young men when they arrived at the age of nineteen and six months were taken away. It was called the militia, they wore their own clothes, they were given a tunic, but they were the first conscripts for national service. When the war broke out they were put into army uniform. Now a lot of these fellas never came back; they lost their life in the beachhead at Dunkirk: Freddy Galloway, Jock Hamilton, wee Jock Robertson, just young men. There was a government legislation called the Essential Works Order – if you were off your work for three days you'd tae go in front of a board tae answer why. There was no respite.

Rationing affected everybody. Probably in heavy industry it affected people more because we would go away to the pit wi' five slices o' breed in a metal box. Now how oor mithers catered for that we don't know, because the rationing was so extreme on the food line. The clothes line, you only had a certain amount of coupons. You made the boots last as long as you could. As the war went on, wir boots, the soles become inferior, we used to say they were soled wi' laminated broon paper. They didnae seem to last as long as you were forcin' these tubs up steep gradients, working in wet conditions.

Food – normally we'd come home tae a dinner, but on a Saturday we always come home to what we liked, a tea dinner which was fried. For three weeks in Dalmellington there was no butcher meat, no stuff had come into the butcher's shops. I came hame and what was sat doon in front of me was a plate o' porridge and I've disliked porridge to this day. I detest the stuff. In the latter part of the war, the government legislated that heavy industry were a deserving cause. In the pits we were allocated a piece or a lunch box, which was made by the Co-operative and you could buy that at the pit and that didnae inflict intae your normal rations. That's how we survived.

It was difficult for everyone with the rationing of clothes. Prior to the war it was always customary that a fella's trousers had a turn-up. Here they called it the Dalmellington fold, it was famous locally, wi' the local tailor. With rationing, the folds were no more. Of course you tried all the tricks of the day to get the tailor to – 'I'll gie you an extra coupon if you put an extra fold in oor troosers.' Now, it's commonplace, you'd never give them a thought.

Wartime Holidays

The first year doon the pit, you got no holiday pay, we'd no money and we sat for a week because it was idle time – we were just wearyin' for the Monday coming to go back to work. The next year it was the same. By the winter of '43, eight of us decided, we're going a holiday next year. Where were we going? Somebody suggested Morecambe. During the winter, we started to save up tins of, normally, tomatoes – they were in supply, it wasnae in the ration so we gathered up these. How were we gonnae get there? We decided we'd bike it. We come up the pit on the Friday o' the Glasgow Fair holidays, had wir dinner, met in the railway station and off we set at five o'clock. We biked all through the night and arrived in Morecambe at half past eight the next morning. Biked all the way. We'd sent two tents on two days before. The camping site was Regents Road; you went over a railway bridge, and the field was on the right-hand side. The man there allocated us wir tents, we put up the tents and we fell asleep. We woke between two and three in the blazing sun and that was it. We had a great holiday. On the Saturday night, we were walking back up into the camping site, and four of us that were in the band were whistling a march called *Punchinella*. Fellas over in the site heard us and they shouted over, 'Hello! Do youse play in a band?' 'Aye, we play in a band. Do you play in a band?' 'Aye.' 'Where do you come from?' 'Oh, we from Dalmellington. Where do you come from?' 'We come from Douglas Water in Lanarkshire.' They had biked it too. We palled up wi' these fellas and we'd a great week. Now wan o' these chaps left the pit, Jack Farrington's his name, he left the pit at age twenty-one and went into the police force and he finished up as the superintendent of police for Motherwell and Wishaw. He's now living in Hamilton but he and I still keep contact. We still keep talking about that venture to Morecambe in 1943.

The second year, some of us decided we'd go back. A local fella, Hunter Smith and I were on a tandem. We decided we would venture down further and there were no road signs – all the road signs during the war were taken away – so we landed up at Chester. On the way back two days later, it was coming evening and we'd had enough. We put the bike over this fence, put up the wee bivvy tent and slept. Between five and six in the morning there was somebody probing this tent wi' a stick, I look out and see this big army officer with a big walrus moustache and a cane and he'd a sergeant major with him and I said, 'Whit ye wantin'?' 'Whit am I wantin'?' he says. 'Get your bloody tent over that fence and get out of here!' I said, 'Where are we?' He says, 'Where are ye? Ye're in Britain. Now get over that fence.' We got doon that tent in a hurry. We were just moving away and this old man was walking down the road pushing a bike, and he says, 'Oh, aye that's Haydock Race Course. It's been taken over by the army.' So we were in army territory, could have been German spies. We landed back at Morecambe in the tent and we were biking home. On the Saturday night we biked so far, again slept in a tent behind a dyke, and got home on the Sunday. The Monday morning, five o'clock we were away at our work again. So that was the war years. Difficult time for everybody, for the fellas that were taken away for the Forces. We thought we were bad, but they were worse.

Life in the Band

When I left the school, my father said to me, 'Right you've left school noo, you're working, you've got to get involved in something. What aboot getting involved wi' the band?' There were four of us who all had started work at the same time, we stood at the door of the band room, which was an old wooden hut wi' a corrugated iron roof. The band cam oot and they were nearly all old men – we said we want to join the band, so this one got a cornet, next one got a cornet, next one got a cornet and then I got a euphonium. The fella that was taking the band explained to us what to do, gave us this wee sheet of paper with some music on it which we didnae understand and he said, 'Right go away home, just blow the instrument and come back here next week.' He was very good and eventually he gave us individual tuition.

By 1941, a lot of the older players had left the band and it was down to about eight or ten players – three adults and the rest of us were young teenagers. But we encouraged ones working along wi' us to come into the band, and gradually the band built itself up. By the end of the war the band was at a full complement of twenty-five players. We've got a photograph in the band hall of the day the war finished. We were alerted by radio that when the war was declared to be finished, there would be a national holiday. The Home Guard in every village and town organised a Gala Day and of course, the band played at it that day and there was a photograph taken.

I know the names of everyone from 1901 to the present day who have been in the band, and all the photographs. The earliest photograph we've got is 1870. The band master at that time was William Saddler, from Wanlockhead, and he was given a house in the old schoolhouse, a job and a remuneration. Back in those days the band would play at various concerts and parades; in the Saturday afternoons they played in the village green and the people danced to it. By 1888, Saddler advised the band that they required someone more capable because the contesting scene was looming up. The band advertised in the *Band Press* and they appointed a man called Albert A. Carr from Barnsley in Yorkshire For two years, he came here once a month and do an extended weekend rehearsal. By 1890 he came to live in Dalmellington and the band were able to give him a house, Pool Cottage, round by what's now the Dalmellington Inn.

The band was maintained by public subscription by the villagers and Carr got that house and a job at the new pit. Number Two Pennywheeny had been sunk 120 fathoms down to three seams of coal. By 1897 the band was doing very well. In 1897 they got an invitation to go to Carlisle to play at a competition commemorating Queen Victoria's diamond jubilee. The villagers were so elated at this happening to their band that they had public subscriptions round the village and they bought him a commemoration sword which I have. He did a lot of hand writing and we have hand written scores that he did at that time. By 1910 Carr was becoming older and he felt the band needed a change, so the band appointed a man called Bob Thompson.

DALMELLINGTON SILVER BAND, 1922

Thompson got a job in the pithead in Number Two Pennywheeny and a remuneration to handle the band. But with the First World War, again there was fellows taken away to the war. He'd just got the thing back on its feet after the war when there was the 1921 strike. That was demoralising. After the strike, there was a government scheme where miners got quite large rises, the Sankey Bonus Scheme. The band were able to raise sufficient funds to re-equip the band in 1922 with new uniforms and new instruments. Thompson started to generate the band into a contesting unit, and they competed at Hamilton at the Scottish championships in 1925. Then Thompson died suddenly in September 1927.

William Oughton, the man that got the job, arrived from Brandon in County Durham on the twenty-third of December 1927 and was due to start work on Christmas Day. Christmas Day was a working day in those days, right up even into my time in the pit. Ben Yates was one of the committee, he was designated to go and take him to his work, so he went at six o'clock in the morning, knocked the door and an old man came out and Ben says, 'I'm Ben Yates and I've been designated by the band committee to take you to work.' Oughton says, 'Work? I am an Englishman. I don't work on Christmas Day.' Anyway, William Dalrymple, the general manager, was sympathetic to the situation and he started his work on the Monday. During Oughton's time, the band did very well. His two young boys became players in the band, as time went on and they did their first broadcast on radio in 1930 for the BBC.

In the depressed times in the 1930s, there was no work here and the band were unable to pay the band master's salary so Mr Oughton left to go to Kendal. His young son, Cecil, although he'd been trained in the brass band, had joined up with a dance band, Nat Gonella's. At the time, Gonella had a very prominent dance band, big-band style, and Cecil went to play with him. Gonella did things like Satchmo, played the trumpet and sang the items. His wife, Stella Moyer, sang with the band. Cecil Oughton actually ran away from home to join this band. He became a superb

DALMELLINGTON BAND PLAYERS PLAYING CAROLS DURING THE WAR-TIME BLACKOUT, 1944

trumpet player but he was called up for the Royal Artillery, not for the band but the regular forces. He was killed in the beach-head in Normandy in 1944.

In 1947 the father had retired from work and he come back to Dalmellington, and the band started contesting with him again. By the mid-1950s we were broadcasting again with the BBC, two times a year was normal practice for Scottish bands. Broadcasts were live on a Friday evening after the six o'clock news. They did these in Studio One in Glasgow – the Scottish Home Service. It wasnae until my time with the band in the '60s and '70s that we did national radio programmes. During the '60s you could get a brass band in any one of the BBC regions. At some part of the day there would be a band on. It's gone now.

In 1961 we lost our old band master and I was asked to take over the band. By 1967 I had trained the band up and we had won the Scottish Second Section Championship in the Usher Hall in Edinburgh, which moved us up into the top section. Next year, the Scottish Championship was at Bo'ness, it was Beethoven's Eighth Symphony we played and we were fifth that day. The next year the Scottish Championship was in the Carnegie place in Dunfermline, and we won the championships – the top accolade of banding in Scotland, the first time that had come to an Ayrshire band. That opened doors in all directions, one of the first was an invite to the Edinburgh Festival in August. We'd also qualified the band to play at the Miners National Championships in Blackpool and we went there in September and took second prize to Grimethorpe Colliery, the band that was featured in that film *Brassed Off.* Then more radio broadcasts and by 1972, television. In '76 we won the Scottish Championship and again in '78. During these years we were making trips to the Albert Hall in London to play in the national finals.

Because of radio and television, the band become not only known throughout Britain, it became internationally known because we did a radio programme for BBC World Service. One weekend we were playing at Prestwick and after the programme this fella spoke to me: he'd been oot in Brazil working and he'd heard a programme we did. We did a lot of work for the BBC at that time and it was an excellent shop-window for the band. And not only for the band – the village became known as well. 1964 was the centenary of the band – we brought back as many of the old former players as we could find and we had a big celebration in the community centre.

What Future for the Band?

When the pits closed here in 1980, that left a void in the village; prior to that all the players in the band worked in some capacity: some worked underground, some were tradesmen, engineers, joiners, electricians and such like. The void that was left, it just decimated the village really. A lot of people moved away to find work. That was the difficult time for the band. It took us probably about ten years to rejuvenate; all we were doing was holding ground, we're only holding ground just. But by 1992, with the process that I had started back in the late '60s of teaching younger players, things had become more stable. The band started to come back up again and since 1993, it has more or less taken on the mantle it had in the late '60s and through the early '80s. Our band's in the top section, we're doing well contest-wise and we play all over the place.

The band gets involved in all sorts of functions as it has done throughout its lifetime. The band did the local concerts, they would do church services, there was a Sunday school trip. People danced to the band in the village green, not only in Dalmellington but the village green at Craigmarket, the miners' rows two miles out the village. When I was conducting the band during the '60s, on a good summer night, we started practising at six o'clock because they were all working in the pit and were home by three o'clock. On a band-practice night, they'd just take their instrument and a chair and go and sit in the middle of the street somewhere. We'd sit down and we'd play a programme for a couple of hours. In no time, a mass of people appears and maybe the next night, we'd come out here and the next night we'd go somewhere else. If a car came down they'd just reverse and go away out the road. They got to know. We'd play in the square and people passing through the square would stop.

We still have a lot of involvement in the community. Five years ago, one of the fellas in the band who's now the band president, started a patron scheme whereby people in the village can pay a £10 patronage per year. We put on two concerts a year, one in May and one just prior to Christmas. We call them Patrons' Concerts and we bring something added to the band: we've had Bill McCue, Peter Morrison, a pipe band, all sorts of things. Jenny's in a Women's Committee in the village and at these concerts they give the people a cup of tea and they get home baking and such like. At Christmas, the community centre was bulging at the sides; I had to send a couple of guys from the band to bring down more chairs. It's become popular and raises money for the band. Four or five times a year we send all the patrons a newsletter, to keep them informed about where the band has gone, what the young ones are doing. The council in South Ayrshire – Ayr, Troon and Prestwick – they'll phone up and we can turn the band out just like that and we'll play for all sorts of functions. Bert contacts local businesses and they pay a business patronage. They give what they like – £20, £50, £100 – and it all adds up. In February 1997, we applied for a lottery grant and were successful. We had been allocated a grant of £60,000, but we had to raise £15,000 in this village. By the end of May we had raised the money. With the patron scheme we let the people know what we're doing and the people respond to that. Proof of this was the fact that we raised that amount of money in such a short time. It amazed me, but it happened.

Phyllis Herriot
Saleswoman & Councillor

Born 1926

I was born in a part of Edinburgh which was very much slum property, in East Thomas Street. It had the sobriquet of 'Chinatown'. We never found out why this name was given. There was a song from one of the films going round the area 'Oh Chinatown, my Chinatown'. But it really was just a nickname for the street and it didn't really mean anything. It was streets of single houses, rooms and kitchens, some of them with outside toilets, some with their inside toilet, and the old gas lighting. We were one of the smaller families with mother and father and five children. The norm was the tens and twelves. That would be in a room and kitchen, so life was really just trying to survive.

In the kitchen would be the bed that the mother and father slept in. There would be the kitchen range, and the sink, and table and chairs. Usually there was a wee fender in front of the fireplace where the wee ones could sit, and a wee bed closet. There would be the bedroom – my mum had two beds for the size of her family, but in some, it would be practically bunk beds or beds all over. A small percentage of families really were unable to cope, as present day, but there was others again who were amazing, because they kept their family and homes neat and clean. The 'buggy van' came for some of the families who really were inadequate and unable to cope – no money coming in, unemployment and no real ability to look after all these children. It was very sad. The children were taken away from time to time but returned again, which was good because there was this feeling in the whole street, the whole community were involved in this. We wanted them back, they were

our friends, our playmates. It was a time of a lot of hunger, unemployment, but it was a time of pulling together.

The whole area was a slum. Later on, the council house programme started and then you got families moving out – the bigger families were going to better housing. That became quite an accolade to be able to get a council house. My mother didn't get one until after the war started – we moved to a council house with three bedrooms. By that time, my two brothers had gone away to the Forces, one sister was married, the other sister was in the ATS, so here we were, ranging around this three-bedroom house, my mum, dad and I for a lot of the time.

My dad was one of the lucky ones, he had a job. He worked as a labourer on the roads. That was a set wage coming in. My mother would go to the baker's and she would be cleaning out the baker's shop in the early morning. When she had to go to the local wash-house, we youngsters met her with a wee pram to help bring the washing home again. You helped with dishes. You only had coal fires then so people had turns. It was mainly the girls who helped around the house. I'd get mad. It was only the girls that were supposed to do this. The men had different jobs, the windows and things like that, but you were brought up that there was traditional girls' work and boys didn't do that. Things have changed for the better.

There was no such thing as a sliced loaf – that was a big innovation later on. At home we were very well looked after because my mum came from the country area outside Edinburgh and her relatives supplied us well with vegetables and things. There was always big healthy soup pots on the old range and inside the wee oven, there was bread puddings and rice puddings. I hated sago, mind you. Everything you got, it was, 'It's good for you and there's starving ...' and I got really fed up hearing about the starving millions in China. I thought: 'I wish my mother would give the sago to some of these poor wee starving bairns and no' make me eat it.' I think most children were pretty well fed. If there was an undernourished child they usually were

Dinner hour at an Edinburgh school, c. 1914

spotted in the school. There was no such thing as the National Health Service in our days.

There was a lot of campaigning for the NHS before it came in. And it would be by people like my mother. I was amazed because I didn't know – she told me later on – that she had gone to suffragettes' meetings before I was born, and I thought, 'Gosh, what an amazing wee lady', coming in from the country, leaving school early, one of about twelve children. She brought us up on Burns, and we were experts on Burns. She sang to us, and enacted plays because in Tranent it was the old Byre Players that came round. So in the middle of helping her peel the potatoes, we would get a scene from *East Lynne*, you know, 'Gone, gone and never called me mother.' Very dramatic. And the wee daft poems that she had. She must have absolutely soaked up knowledge and again there were a lot of mums like that, that really passed on so much to their children.

In the close, you had to take turns with the stair; you would have been put out if you didn't do that sort of thing. And we were lucky, we had the inside toilets so that wasn't a problem but the outside ones would have to be cleaned, because there was always the threat of the Sanitary, you know, 'I'll send for the Sanitary.' I live in a tenement now and I see it all around me that younger people don't have that commitment to do it, to look after the fabric of where they live.

I remember as a wee one, I had a wee brush and I was sent to sweep outside the stair. Then the lorry came round and the big hydrant was turned on and it washed all the street, and, of course, we were jumping about like mad, we were all washed as well. But you did help. You went messages, you were really trained by your parents that if any older person in the street wanted you to go for the messages you would go, and you would not hang around looking for ha'pennies or pennies back. We were very much brought up to respect the older people in the community and help them where you could. There was a blind man lived at the foot of our street and we had the responsibility, different children, just to make sure that the street was cleared for him, and if there were any impediments you would take him down and tell him. You were brought up really in a much more caring atmosphere, although there was a lot of savagery about but it didn't really affect, I don't think, young people's lives.

Children played outside because there wasn't cars going up and down the streets. There was carts with horses, for the coal merchant and this sort of thing but mainly, the children played out. The boys played with their tops and the girls with their diabolos. You had the peever beds where you played on the pavement and chalked them, and the skipping rope time. You played a lot of singing games outside, the ring games, 'The Farmer's in his Den', the guessing games about film stars' names or the Minister's Cat. The boys went into the stairs and played with cards. The girls had their scraps and dressed their dolls. It was funny how the seasons came for games – the weather had a lot to do with it. We played hide-and-seek games and you chased all over the world. Later, we got on to roller skates, and you roller skated everywhere. When I see the kids on their skateboards, I think, 'Gosh, we were just the same.' Just up everybody's nose. The streets were safer for us to go out and play, but you were brought in for the curfew, and you didn't wander too far afield.

It was a mixed community, different religions and things, but that didn't matter. Our community centres really in essence were the churches and you went to everybody's church. You went to the Band of Hope at the Baptist Church, you went to baptisms there. You went to the Episcopal Church and you went to a German church for Kinder Spiels, they called it. You joined the Salvation Army, you joined the Carrubbers Close Mission – this is where children went. You got 'saved' every so often by the Salvation Army and you got three ha'pence so there were queues to be saved. Then you went to your own local church but you went to Midnight Mass at a Catholic church if your friends were Catholic. There just wasn't this feeling of 'them and us'. We were all in it together.

The Co-op

One-stop shopping for food is now the norm; but as late as 1959, the Classified Directory had five columns of Fruiterers and Greengrocers, almost three of Fishmongers and seven of Butchers'. The 1959 Classified Directory had no heading for Supermarkets.

The big thing in your life was the store. The local Co-op was the place where you bought everything. Still, today, I was asking some people, 'Do you still remember your mother's store number?' and everybody does. 75351. It was etched on your memory, that. You went to the wee sort of groups for children that the store ran, the Circle and all that, and your mother joined the guilds. The dividend time was so wonderful. You chummed your mother for the dividend and she took you for a cup of tea and a bun up to the restaurant. Oh, you were all mesmerised with this excitement and the buzz. And the store was always very good – my dad wouldn't go to buy shoes or shirts or anything so they would give my mother two and three pairs of everything and then you, as the wee one, had to rush back with the ones he didn't want. We were mesmerised when they put the payment money into one of those balls and it went to the cashier away up through that wee railway thing they had all round. What if it disappears and that's all my mum's money in there? And the store book. I was told you got babies on the store book so I kept rushing in with this store book in the hope that there would be this small sister or brother but it never appeared.

Death & the Community

When you helped with the ironing, there were the different drawers in the chest of drawers, the drawers that you put the towels in and the sheets in. In one drawer was this beautiful white sheet and I always wondered why we were always using more used-up sheets and why we never touched that one. I used to say to my mum: 'There's a nice big sheet.' 'Leave that alone,' she said. It wasn't until I was a bit older that she told me that that was the funeral sheet that was loaned out because the coffins of whoever was dead were brought to the house. The neighbours helped out taking children and things and then the body was laid out in the bedroom and this was the sheet that was under the coffin. There was a great emphasis on giving proper respect to somebody, but also being respectable by having this. People didn't have all that wherewithal, so this sheet went the rounds – it was laundered and kept and it wasn't used for any other purpose. Again, I suppose that's part of the unity of the community, that you knew which person would be helping out with what. Then all the men in the street went round to the Easter Road cemetery with the cortege. The women didn't go there. The women stayed at home. They would help with making the funeral tea, but the men followed the cortege. Everywhere you went along the street, everybody stopped still as it passed and the men took their hats off. We all knew each other in the community and a death was such a tragedy. If it was a young person's death, everybody was so upset. Somebody used to go round and collect money; there wasn't a lot of money about but they would collect a few coppers to get flowers for the funeral, and also maybe to give the widow, who didn't have anything, a wee bit to help through this time.

*Before and After the
National Health
Service*

My mother came from a country area and actually knew so much of herbal medicine. My dad came from Lancashire, from Bolton. He was invalided out the Army during the '14–'18 war and they met when he was sent up here to a hospital to be cured. I remember one of her friends kept saying, 'Your mother really is a white witch.' If somebody was ill, they'd send for somebody like my mum; if the baby had a croup then they knew how to deal with it. My mother knew just which types of herbs or flowers to use. Bread poultices were all the thing, but when you think of it, the Red Indians also knew about that – the source of penicillin from bread mould, foxglove or digitalis and that sort of thing. They knew it all just from the fact that they had imbibed it in the sort of country lore. We were a very fortunate wee family, having my mum there, and I wish I'd taken more notice and written things down. You've really lost out on somebody who had a lot of wisdom.

We were well dosed in all the herbal remedies, but she also was very keen that our health should be properly looked after. Every Monday night, my brother and I, who were the wee ones, accompanied her up a few streets away to where a Friendly Society had their office. She paid four pence each for my dad and herself, and tuppence each for each of the children, five of us, so that was ten pence. Out of a labourer's wage, that was a lot of money but she believed in it. That meant that we could call on a doctor on the list of the Friendly Society. Only about two families in our whole street could do that because money just wasn't there. It really was very important that a health service was established because otherwise people couldn't afford a fee to bring a doctor in.

When I was born, the doctor had to come because my mother was very ill and I was born prematurely; two people were very ill in the street, the other family who could call in the doctor and myself, and the doctor had to make the decision to be there. 1926, of course, was the year of the big strike so my father had come out in support of the miners and lost his job in consequence, but he was there to help because the district nurses came in to look after my mother and to look after this wee tiny baby. But if we hadn't been able to have a doctor, there was nowhere else for my mother to go, unless they could have got her into one of the charity hospitals.

The infant mortality rate was very, very high. I remember a wee friend in Prestonfield, Mary Findlay, she's one hundred years old now, so she survived. She said when she was young and her mother had a big family, my mother sat at the bed of a wee one and worried whether this wee one would live or die, just trying to do everything she could to help, but Mary's mother couldn't have called in medical help because she did not have the money to pay. There must have been a lot of families who went through a lot of suffering and pain and knew they had lost a child because they didn't have the wherewithal.

The district nurses were sent in by the doctors, usually. The schools could refer children. I think they watched very carefully if there was any kind of diseases like scarlet fever that could be catching in a population. My brother was in Liberton Hospital and they took me in as a suspect; I didn't have it but I thought: 'Ooh, horrible.' If there was any kind of contagious disease in any way then children were moved, but it was usually found out by the schools or the parents.

When the NHS came in, that was absolutely marvellous. People were hoping and campaigning for it but they just didn't expect it, particularly after a war. Britain was in a pretty rocky state and we had to rebuild; rationing was still on and here we are, we had a government that had the foresight and the courage to bring in a Health Service. It led the world, and it changed a lot of thinking in a lot of countries, which was good. It was just one of the best things that ever happened. Then, they had better housing which was a big thing – people working in local government knew that unless they got rid of the old slums and brought in decent housing then what was the point even in having a Health Service? You weren't going to keep your population very healthy.

School and Work

We went to the local school at Leith Walk. When the 11-Plus came, this really got me so angry – and I think it shaped a lot of my feelings in life later – you had the exams and then you went on to whichever school was designated. There were three of us in our class that were sent to the Broughton High School in McDonald Road, where you got a bursary to go, to pay for books and things like that. The rest of the children went to the Junior Secondary Modern School at Norton Park, and a lot of them made a better success in life, and here's to them. But it was wrong, I thought it was so wrong. I lost all my school chums. They were being singled out as one thing and you were being singled out to another, and that was really very unfair. I fought all my days for decent comprehensive education. While not saying that people with abilities shouldn't be given opportunities and help, there was no point in labelling children in any way at that early age and I was so very angry at what had happened.

I thought I was going to go on to university. My mother was so keen, she was going to go out and get a job and keep me at school. There was arguments at home, because my father at that time thought that education really was a bit wasted on women, girls, because they would just get a job, get married. Up until then, and I could see his reasoning, women didn't really work when they were married. The war changed all that. But I left school when I was fifteen. My father forever afterwards kept apologising to me but it was too late then. I remember Willie Ross, who was the Secretary of State saying: 'Do you know, I owe the fact that I could go on to become a teacher and go on to higher education to my sisters, who took jobs in laundries or shops or something to keep Willie at school because the boy of the family was the one who was to get the education.' I felt that was wrong. His sisters were every bit as bright and intelligent and should have been given an opportunity, but there wasn't the money to do it. It was such an unfair, unjust practice and it was people like my mother that inveighed against it. That made me battle that I was going to make sure, while I'm not in any big feminist camp, to make sure that girls had every bit. We were brought up with that, that you had a sense of justice and you fought for it.

In 1911, just 5.3 per cent of Scotland's married women were in paid employment. By 1991, it was 60.4 per cent.

I went to work when I was fifteen. I got a job in an office in a printing company, and then from there I went on to a manufacturing chemist, when I was about seventeen. There were jobs, of course, where girls weren't even thought of, engineering and those sort of things. There were set designated jobs, you had shops, offices, this sort of thing, but you weren't going to do the jobs that women take for granted now, that they can do and are proving themselves very good at.

The war had started and at nights we had to take our turn watching for enemy aircraft. What we would have done, I don't know. We were firewatchers. My mother was a full-time ARP warden. Everyone had their gas masks and you had everything inside that gas mask case *except* your gas mask. You had your comb, you had your lipstick, you had everything, but the gas mask was left at home. My mum would go berserk. Just at the start of the war, I was evacuated with the school to the Borders, and we stuck that out for a few months and then that was enough. We came back home. At the time, the family was moving to Piercehill and I thought, 'Gosh, if I hadn't come home, would they have vanished out of my life?' Anyway, that was quite an experience because you were living a different style of life again. But going back to work, I thought, my brothers had joined, one had been called up by the Territorials, the other had joined the Air Force and one sister joined the ATS and I thought, I'm joining something. But because I was with a manufacturing chemist that made drugs and bandages and all that sort of thing, you were classed as an essential. I was in an office but you were in essential war work so you weren't allowed to go. And I thought, 'Here again, it's because I'm a girl' but it wasn't really. That lasted quite a long time.

I went to the Gas Board, to the showrooms in the Gas Board and I was there for thirty years, 'man and boy', but that was a good experience. We had to be very well trained, and we were told then we had to give a service: it was service and sales, not sales and service. You met a wide range of people and you were really interested in what your job was. You were promoted in jobs then if you were capable and if you were there a long time. Then the seniority got you promotion. When it came to my time for promotion, I had been very capable, but the boss said that he couldn't promote me because I was a woman. I got so angry at that. Nowadays you would have gone to a tribunal but then there was no such thing. I was the Trade Union representative and I fought that case. I asked why women weren't being promoted and really got things started, and they had to start showing figures that women were being given promotions.

Then I went and joined the council as a councillor. I was on the social work committee and on education – I fought the battle there – and on transport, again because that was so important. I'm retired from all that now, but in the pensioner's movement – concessionary travel and all this sort of thing is so, so important to the elderly and to people with disabilities, as well as the rest of the community. We battle about the low rate of pensions here, about the lowest in Europe, so we're still battling.

Entertainments and Holidays

The cinemas were the big thing, everybody went to the cinema, but my parents also liked the live theatre, and they liked the old-time music halls. Edinburgh had a couple of those. They thoroughly enjoyed that way of life. We had all our entertainment in the churches and if we were in plays or anything like that, your mother and your father always came to see you.

We were a fantastic reading family, we had books and the music, because my mother loved singing, music in every way, and you were brought up to appreciate that type of thing. And then travel: they took us everywhere. I liked going on the trains, on excursions. There was the ferries, across to Fife or Rosyth. There wasn't the buses so much then, but there was the trams – you went everywhere on the tram cars. We got around a lot, I think, because of my mother's itchy feet mainly. It opened your mind up: there wasn't just Chinatown and East Summer Street, there was all this much bigger world.

Because we were linked to this doctor, she put our names down to go a holiday every year and we went to Fife, to Kelty and Kinross. It was usually mining families that took the children in for, I imagine, very small amounts. My mum talked to the other mums in the street and they brought their children's names forward and we all went. There wasn't a lot of money, but on the odd occasion, we went down to see

Granny in Bolton. My Granny Taylor lived in the mill houses so my aunties there worked in the big cotton mills, and you were taken along there to see that way of life and to see the sort of different moors round Lancashire. There were Lancashire witches so my mother might have been looking them out. We were made so welcome. We went to Tranent every other weekend to my mum's relatives. You stayed there during the summer, and my brother would go and help to pick the strawberries. I always thought the things my brother did was absolutely marvellous: delivering papers, picking strawberries and coming home with a sore neck, and it was always 'when will I get to do that'.

So we had a very varied type of life but nobody would ever have thought of going abroad then. There just wasn't that sort of money. The big dream that everybody had then was winning the football pools. Now, of course, we've replaced that with the lottery, with millions and millions of pounds. But again it's the dreams that people all lived on, that this was going to change life from the struggles, because the 1930s were a big struggle up to the war, up to our families growing up and getting work and really having better opportunities for things.

A Century of Change

The biggest changes I've seen would be the housing set-up, better housing being brought in, equal wages and equal opportunities for women, the fact that transport has modernised and is a lot better, the types of equipment and entertainment in the home. The first radio we ever got was the old battery type. You were sent to get this old battery recharged and you mustn't spill it, you were told, or the world would collapse. We didn't have phones in our homes. These are just part of the everyday life now but they were looked upon as fantastic luxuries. I think of my mother being able to sit with a video and watch her favourite film again and again if she wanted to. She would wonder what all this was about.

Although it was a good place to be when I was growing up, the home has become a much more comfortable place for everybody to be within: pressing the button for the washing machine instead of having to use the kitchen sink, or go up to the wash-house. It was a harder way of life but very happy in lots of ways and very fulfilling. I don't think I'd want it all back again though.

There are great strides ahead to be made but I'm a wee bit worried about all the computer systems; we have been gifted one for the pensioners and I've got to take a course. I was better with the old pounds, shilling and pennies than with the decimal pounds and pence and I'll probably be better without this. But again you've got to move. These have opened up all types of opportunities for children.

Then there's the fact that we've been at peace for so many years. I know it's been fraught with problems, we saw the terrible ravages that war made on families and nations; I had a dad who was wounded in the '14–'18 war and saw the effects of that, then having lost a brother in the next war, to have seen the effects of what that did. To know that people are striving very hard for peace and the fact that there are so many people who are battling and fighting to keep the environment and to protect nature and wildlife – I'm very very keen on that.

But I think one of the biggest things to us was the National Health Service – that really did make a complete difference to everybody's life. I worry about the whole set-up now, about what they're going to do with benefits and things. I still think we're a very rich country and we should be thinking a bit more and helping people to get a better way of life, a fuller, richer life, and I'm not very happy about some of the things that are being advocated. I think there's going to have to be a lot more thinking. I worry about single mums, about the people with handicaps, I particularly worry about the elderly. So we don't sit back complacently; there's a lot to do. But a lot of good things have happened.

I think we've got to march forward. We can't go back and nobody really wants to. You learn from the past but you live for the future. Live in the present but plan for the future and hopefully make it better for the youngsters who will come after.

Edith Macarthur
Actress

Born 1926

Early Life

I was born in Ardrossan in Ayrshire. I'm a child of the '20s. My mother was born in Old Cumnock, a very small village in Ayrshire and my father was a civil engineer for ICI; he was connected with Ardeer and was doing something with the Water Board. Before their marriage, my mother had worked in the post office in Largs, which is where they met.

I was born in a home that I look at now and think, 'Oh, I would quite like to have that house,': I think it was their first married home, two rooms on the top floor of Arran Place looking across to Arran. When I was about three, we moved to Saltcoats, to a council house. It was awfully respectable and new, like new housing estates are now, and it was really considered rather ritzy. It was where Saltcoats stopped at that time, up at the top of the town and then after that it was country. Mummy would take us up for walks in the country, up the High Road going to what's now Stevenston, I suppose, with my younger brother who was pushed in a pram.

Kerr Avenue in Saltcoats was where I would be a little five-, seven-year-old child running around playing with the children next door, in the street. This is one of the immense differences that I see now – we always played outside. There was no such thing as radio or television, and games were played outside. Anyway, Saltcoats was a seaside town too, and we were down at the beach or else we were in woods – and we climbed trees and played on the beach or in the country.

The girls all tended to do girlie games like skipping ropes and running around in circles and jumping up and down and hide-and-seek and things. The boys were always doing Cowboys and Indians. At the foot of the garden at the house, there was a little garden hut, and that became 'Pine Creek Ranch'. I had two younger brothers. John was about three years younger than me, and Donald was three years younger than that, but John was the tough guy and he was always the leader of the party: he was always the sheriff or something and they'd always be doing these gun noises – 'ch, ch' – all playing round Pine Creek Ranch. But we'd be kind of doing civilised things like skipping – all these terribly complicated skipping steps that you had to learn to do.

Looking back on it I suppose sometimes my parents worried – I used to wander away a great deal when I was very little. Apparently I was quite well known in the local police stations and the cry went up, 'Edith Macarthur's lost again' and I would be collected, having walked all the way down into Saltcoats, climbed over the railway passenger bridge – which is still there – and gone down to the shore with my tricycle, and I'd be brought back. Or else I'd go walking along the country road. I once took my little brother, who was then a baby in his pram, and I was found in Stevenston, the next town. I'd taken John for a walk to Stevenston because that's what mummy did, you see. So I did these sort of things. I don't think things ever occurred to you. It's one of the great, great differences I notice just now with the problem about children. I mean we walked to school, to Saltcoats Public School, and you walked along Argyll Road to go there. I suppose it was between a mile and a couple of miles or something, which was nothing because you knew that your parents had done much, much longer distances walking. Walking was the way one got about. But there was no traffic on the roads, nobody had cars except terribly rich people who didn't really live round about where we lived. One does remember the absolute safety, and the kind of innocence of life then; there was no thought of any danger happening to a child then, or to anybody.

Then we moved back to Ardrossan to a new house, because the family were now getting a little bigger. It was 1939 and we moved in three weeks before war was declared. It was a proper house with a garden at the front and a huge garden with a wood at the bottom at the back, and you could see the sea from the back. It was just wonderful and I always remember that very well. That's still the family home: one brother married and the other's remained a bachelor like me; it's now his house and I still go there. But it's very different now; it's a place of abject despair. I wouldn't go if my brother didn't still live there. But it was then a very attractive, quiet place – rather select, I think was the phrase for it. Far from the way it is now, alas.

You got loads of sweets. Well, before the war you could get sweets, but during wartime ,of course, you didn't get any. When aunts or uncles came to visit, you would get pennies when they went away; the object of the exercise was not the quality of the sweets, which weren't very interesting – I can't remember chocolate oddly enough, so I suppose chocolate must have been more than tuppence – but to get the sweet that you got the most of for a ha'penny or a penny. You got enormous bags of sweets for a penny. I remember things like Lavender Cushions and Rosebuds and Ogle Pogle Eyes. I was trapped in a Latin class once with an Ogle Pogle Eye in my mouth. We had a wonderful Latin teacher, Polly Wilson, and she was a bit beady and obviously knew everything that was going on. Of course the minute I had this huge gobstopper in my mouth which literally made your cheek bulge out, she asked me a terribly complicated question, in Latin of course, and that was a hundred lines. How I thought I'd get away with it I'll never know, but I was given it and I ate it.

School holidays seemed endless. I was lucky, I had two lots of grandparents who lived country lives although very different country lives.

EDITH WITH HER PARENTS AT ROADSIDE COTTAGE, HER GRANDMOTHER'S HOUSE IN OLD CUMNOCK

My father came from a long line of sheep farmers and so the holidays were on his farm and to this day, I absolutely love farms. He farmed in Argyll. This in itself was a huge adventure because you went by bus to Largs and then to Gourock, and got the paddle boat to Blairmore. Or we went to my mother's parents, who lived in a tiny cottage called Roadside Cottage, covered in ivy and honeysuckle in Old Cumnock, which was quite a long way from what was then still a village of Cumnock. That again was an adventure: two buses and then quite a long walk. The bus deposited you at a fork in the road and then you'd to walk down this quiet country road to come to Roadside Cottage, which had no electricity and an outside toilet which had two seats. I remember the great adventure: which seat to choose. Never gave a thought to who cleaned the thing out. There was a wonderful wild garden with gooseberry bushes and orchards and apple trees. You had to go down with Sanny (which was what we called my step-grandfather because my grandmother had married twice) to a well about quarter of a mile down the country road from Roadside Cottage and draw buckets of water, which were then brought up and kept in the scullery. By the back door there was a huge water butt and that's where my mother and her one sister – my aunt was born in 1898 and my mother in 1900 – and were brought up washing in rainwater. My mother always attributed her lovely skin to the fact that she was brought up washed in rainwater.

Nothing too odd about outside sanitation. As late as 1965, a Scottish Office survey found that 200,000 homes (about one-eighth of the total stock) still didn't have an indoor WC. And 430,000 still had no hot-water supply to bath or sink.

Life During the War

During the war, life changed unbelievably in Ardrossan. For a start, the holiday theatre called the Beach Pavilion became a chart and chronometer depot because Ardrossan was used as a refuelling base and where ships got new charts and things. There were barrage balloons. The beach which we had played on – and I could swim practically as soon as I could walk, because you lived by the beach – was covered in coils of barbed wire. There were strange posts that stuck up for years after the war, which I think they were anti-tank things, which were kind of metal rods in concrete stuck up out of the sea.

I left school, having sat my Highers just before the end of term, because the rector read out a notice one morning that people with very neat handwriting who could draw tiny things were required by the Admiralty to help to mend charts at the Beach Pavilion; so I applied. You had to get your parents' permission and I went and was drawing these amendments on charts in the Beach Pavilion. Working in the chart depot was my first experience of meeting other kinds of strange exciting people – you usually just met people in your family and their friends and your schoolmates' friends and all that.

We'd be still going on holidays to the farm in Argyllshire. There was one little working paddle steamer, *The Marchioness of Lorne*. The other paddle boats were all in service and painted battleship grey, of course. But they had their names all blotted out and boards along their sides to protect them from Hitler.

One time a German plane did get over 'cos we could see the glow in the sky over Glasgow and you knew that they were being pulverised. But we were blissfully free of everything. During the war, my father became a bomb-disposal expert and he was always tinkering around with bits of things ticking in his underwear drawers. When you helped with the ironing, you'd be putting things away and you'd open a drawer and there'd be little bits of things, all whirring around and ticking, and he was playing with these bombs. But I remember him going away one night and not seeing him for three days, because I think most of the work was underground, under the sand dunes at Ardeer. We heard afterwards that the Germans were desperate to find Ardeer and bomb it to bits. I suppose the west coast was being prepared for that, and also I suppose because that coastline was a shelter for boats in the war.

Dramatic Leanings   I remember being still in primary school and writing an essay about what we wanted to be – you know how you were always asked to write essays on 'The Life of a Christmas Tree After Christmas' and 'I am a Penny' or things like that, and after holidays 'What did you do in the school holidays'. I wrote that I wanted to be an actress; this idea must've come from a book that I'd read. I remember it because it was the best essay in the class, and to my undying mortification, it was read out, to the derision of the rest of the class, you see, because it had stately phrases in it like 'the cries of bravo as the curtain falls' – so obviously I'd pinched it from a book. But that made me shut up about wanting to go on stage because this was a ludicrous thing, obviously. Even when I got to secondary school, in Ardrossan Academy – after Form 4 you see you could choose to do something, to get your Highers – I suppose it was geared to what you were going to be. In those days, if you were a girl in Ardrossan, you got married or you were a teacher, or a nurse ,or a secretary in an office. Whatever it was, it had to be terribly respectable, you see. There was no drama school and I hadn't really thought, I think, that seriously during those schooldays that that's what it would entail.

I'd never been to see a play in the theatre. I've a faint feeling that we were taken to see a Shakespearean production in a school – all I remember about that was the rabble and the noise and I hated it all. We were taken to the pantomime once when I was teenager, which was a huge adventure because it meant going on trains and everything. It was at the Alhambra in Glasgow and I think that's when I probably saw Will Fyfe and Harry Gordon. I remember them being just wonderful. But the first play that I consciously went to see, I was eighteen. By this time, I had left school; I'd taken my Highers in music and I was carrying on with my studies at the College of Music in Glasgow, which to me was the Athenaeum. There was no drama school, although I think by that time I had a hankering what I really wanted to do was go on the stage and be an actress. But the nearest I could get to it was music, which was my other passion. I was given my rail fare exactly and two shillings for a businessman's lunch or something – at Miss Cranston's Tearoom or one of those kind of respectable little restaurants – and I got permission to stay and see a film in Glasgow, which was an adventure. But my parents had to know what train I was coming back on, and I decided I was going to see a play in the Citizens' Theatre in Glasgow. I'd never been to the Citizens' Theatre and people I knew were talking about it, but the main reason was that it was a play starring Sybil Thorndike. She and Edith Evans were the two great, great actresses in Britain. It was Sybil Thorndike and her husband Lewis Casson in a play by J.B. Priestley called *The Linden Tree*. That was my first conscious memory of being really grown up, seeing a play.

I was a pretty undistinguished music student, but I think by that time, I really very much wanted to be an actress, except that I couldn't think how. The only way to do it, as I could see it, was to go to London and get a scholarship into RADA. Of course, my father would never have heard of that. His attitude to my wanting to go on the stage was, 'How do you think you're going to earn your living play-acting?'

He didn't really come round to it until I actually really did begin to earn my living a little bit at it.

At that time all the communities in Scotland had their own amateur dramatic companies and the Ardrossan and Saltcoats Players company was very famous. The director was Jamieson Clark, who was a professional actor. They did a play each season at the Countess Cinema in Saltcoats. Jamieson Clark cast me in *Pygmalion* as Mrs Ainsford Hill, so I was the youngest member of the company, playing one of the old character parts. Jimmy Clark was very understanding and didn't laugh at me, which was wonderful. I owe him a great deal and but for him I might never have managed to be on the stage. At that time I was eighteen; I was so painfully shy and the idea of joining a dramatic company, I thought, I absolutely can't. How do you tally that with this desperate desire to go on the stage? About a year or so after, I did two or three plays, things like *Quiet Weekend*, charming, wartime plays. It's funny, isn't it, how comedy always becomes the antidote to war?

EDITH AS MRS MANNINGHAM, WITH RIKKI FULTON AS MR MANNINGHAM IN THE ARDROSSAN & SALTCOATS PLAYERS' 1948 PRODUCTION, 'GASLIGHT'.

From Amateur to Professional

It was difficult, and painful to make the switch and become a professional. Again, I owe great thanks to Jamieson Clark. I did a play called *The Light of Heart* by Emlyn Williams. It was beautifully cast and it was one of those productions that worked – a lovely part for me. After its three days' run at the Countess Cinema in Saltcoats, Jimmy knew the Popplewells who ran the Gaiety in Ayr, and *The Light of Heart* went on for a week in the Gaiety Theatre in Ayr. That was the first professional theatre that I'd played in, and Jimmy Clark, bless him, got marvellous people to come and see it. He got James Crampsie who was then the Head of Drama Broadcasting in radio; this was pre-television days, and radio was very important.

Before the war I can only really remember English things like *In Town Tonight* and Henry Hall's *Guest Night* – wonderful. I remember these from the radio. I can remember the march that started *In Town Tonight* – an Eric Coates march, *The Knightsbridge March* – and they said, 'Once again we halt the roar of London's traffic... to bring you some of the interesting people who are *In Town Tonight*.' Or Henry Hall saying 'Good evening ladies and gentlemen. This is Henry Hall speaking and tonight is my *Guest Night*.'

Since 1946, there was the Home Programme and we got programmes like *The McFlannels* and regional things, things Scottish, the Scottish Home Service. During the war, I remember tuning into American Forces Network which was wonderful, because they had wonderful classical concerts on a Sunday afternoon on the AFN, and it was all from America; they had the film stars doing plays and you could recognise all your favourite film stars' voices. But the Scottish programmes I really only register after the war.

Jimmy Clark had got Robert Kemp to come to see me. He had spoken to Wilson Barrett about me and I got a letter inviting me to an interview with Wilson Barrett. I went to see him – it must've been in the Alhambra in Glasgow where they were playing. I remember him being very kind. I was terrified but I could see that he was just being kind to this very Scots-spoken, hick, country girl, you see, and explained to me that his company was already fully cast and he had to cast professional actors but if I was still determined to be an actress to write to him in a year's time. A year went by and I wrote again, to get a very kind reply, again saying that his company was cast and that I had to understand that he had to take professional actors. For years, while I was in the Wilson Barrett Company, I used to think about this awful passionate letter that I wrote: 'How did one ever become a professional actress?' The minute it was posted I wanted to have it back again, I was so embarrassed by it.

A short while afterwards I got a script with a request to come and read the part of Mary in a play called *Musical Chairs* for the producer, Robert Gaston at the Lyceum Theatre in Edinburgh. I got this part – and it was just to be this one engagement – two weeks' rehearsal, two weeks' playing, some months ahead. This was ecstasy, and then, my heaven was made: I was in a summer job and my mother

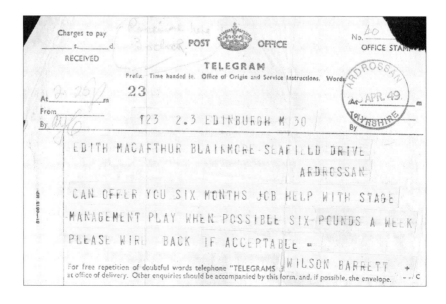

phoned to say a telegram had come for me and 'Shall I open it?' She read it over the phone to me: 'Can offer you job – ASM – six pounds per week, summer season. Do you accept?' Mummy wired back 'yes' and that's how I got into the Wilson Barrett Company, I started as an assistant stage manager and I spent three years in stage management. I remember the first year I cried a lot because I was very lonely; it was a whole new world to me. I hadn't been away from home really in that way before – living in digs. Sometimes it was strange and it's hard work being an acting ASM: you were the first in the theatre and the last out and you were where the buck stopped when you were the newest ASM. It was hard, but it was wonderful. You called everybody 'Mr' and 'Miss', and there was no tannoy system in those days, you went round the dressing rooms and knocked on people's doors and said 'Half an hour Miss DeLys' – there was a wonderful old actress called Kitty DeLys in the company.

People smoked a lot and there was always this wonderful bit of business – all plays had coffee tables with cigarette lighters on them and an ASM's job was to see that they all worked. Matchboxes had to be arranged with a match discreetly sticking out so that the actor could get at it quickly. All the tricks, yes.

Six pounds a week – it was riches. Of course, you had to pay your digs, but all your meals were provided by your landlady for between two to three pounds a week. They were terribly ritzy digs if you had to pay three pounds a week and that left you three pounds, of which you gave some home and out of the rest you had to buy the clothes that you needed. I think the men had to provide one dinner suit and one lounge suit and shirts and everything. As a girl, you were expected to provide a coat and a day dress and an evening dress. You had to make do and mend a lot.

You went to other peoples' digs and you had cups of tea. Coffee was really quite new, and you had coffee breaks. It was a world without drugs and, by and large, without drink. I think some of the actors drank beer sometimes, but girls didn't go to pubs. You absolutely did not go into pubs at all. Well I didn't. I was very hesitant about going into pubs. You would do it if you had a lot of people with you and there was always one section, the saloon bit, where people could sit. But never, ever, ever alone. Of course, to this day I would faintly hesitate about going into a pub by myself.

A Changing World   Television was coming in and striking a lot of the repertory companies very hard because, of course, people were staying at home. Bill Barrett decided to take that opportunity to retire. My first job after that was to Perth Rep. By that time I'd come up through the company and I was playing nice parts. My first job in Perth was a principal boy in the pantomime. It was *Cinderella* and I was Prince Charming. I stayed for a year, finishing with the following Christmas pantomime which was *Mother Goose*. I was working also at theatres like the Gateway. I was broadcasting quite a bit and then there was the Citizens' Theatre in Glasgow – Duncan MacCrae and Fulton Mackay and Annette Crosbie, Johnny Grieve and Ian Cuthbertson were all then the young actors in the Citizens' Theatre Company.

Wilson Barrett was basically an English company and this was one of the reasons I think that I was very lucky, that Barrett took me on. Never having had any drama school background, I didn't know what RP [received pronunciation] was, I just knew that I had to speak an English that was the same as the people spoke in the films that I saw and the other plays that I was then seeing. People always wax lyrical about *Brief Encounter* and I did too when I saw it first, but you know how often they show it on television now and it just makes me fall down: 'Terribly, terribly, frightfully' all sort of like that. I just think it's so funny now, not that we spoke that way when we did English plays, but of course Bill Barrett did a lot of the plays that had been West End successes; these were then released for repertory companies' use and so there were a lot of these sophisticated plays and also Terence Rattigan plays. People forget that Wilson Barrett also did classics. The first Shakespeare I ever did was *The Merchant of Venice*. Barrett did a lot of Scottish plays too. He did Barrie and plays like *Lady From Edinburgh*. We did have quite a spectrum of things, but by and large, it was an English company, so my accent had to be ironed out quite a bit. I was always very self-conscious. I was living in London for about twenty years, and by this time grown up a bit more, and chameleon-like, was beginning to speak just that way, the voice that I was hearing all round about me all the time.

It's one of the great changes – a regional accent is *de rigueur* just now. It is fatal really to have a posh London accent, a posh way of speaking, which is interesting. Recently, they've been showing *Brideshead Revisited* again on television and to play all these sort of parts, you need actors who can do the accent and a lot of young actors now can't because it's just not in their nature – they think of it as a funny voice. Really, the great stress now is on doing regional things in a regional way.

The position of women in the theatre has also changed up to a point. You didn't really fight awfully much about money; you were grateful for the money you got. But there was an awareness that men actors were paid more than women actors. This seemed a bit unfair, but you didn't do too much about it, although I think Equity did do an awful lot to get a minimum established. But the attitude was always – and I think to an extent there's still a case for argument today – that plays are generally biased more in favour of men than of women. Soap operas have kind of emancipated women an awful lot because the most interesting parts seem mostly to be for women in soap operas. But for the theatre, even nowadays, there is almost too much stress on the violence of men and it somehow has become such a violent, ugly age, compared with my memories of youth and growing up. There was no violence, no drugs, no drink. Sex was something that was whispered about, but in a funny way it gave a kind of, well I suppose romance is a kind of sentimental word to use, but there was a kind of innocence. There was a sense of wonderment that has gone, a kind of wonder of discovering things that was just so exciting, and I think that's gone. I can't see that coming back. Well, nothing comes back. Everything is excitement in its own time and I'm an old lady being nostalgic now.

Jimmy Halliday
Historian & Politician

Born 1927

I was born in Wemyss Bay. My father was a gardener and my mother was in domestic service: she was a table maid in Skelmorlie from about 1915. She came from Tarbolton. Like half of Skelmorlie, my father's father had come up from Lockerbie with the Caledonian Railway, so my father was born in Wemyss Bay as well. Some people were employed on the railway, but practically everyone else, if they weren't in shop assisting or something like that, was in private domestic service. It was then the commonest single source of employment in Wemyss Bay. Their employers were in business and finance; most of them travelled up to Glasgow on business. The overall landowner was Lord Inverclyde, Burns' laird's successor. I suppose he was fourth generation – sufficiently aristocratic by that time.

Their houses weren't holiday homes, these were very much their main homes, and of course they had staff to match. To me, *Upstairs Downstairs* was just the life I recalled. It wasn't fiction at all, it was what I'd seen. We lived in a cottage which, I think, was older than the big hoose. But it was by then the gardener's cottage, and had been a gardener's cottage in the 1841 Census. So there has been a presence there for quite some time. The Bay was feu'd off to the Glasgow business people. Kirkmond Finlay, the famous ex-Lord Provost of Glasgow, was one of the residents of Wemyss Bay at one time – not in my time, I hasten to add.

It was a very plainly divided community, totally, but amiably. By and large they were good employers, they were paternalist. There was one old lady whom I recall very vaguely who was a nurse in a family locally. I think the last child that she nursed was by then 57 or something like that, but they had sustained her in what was originally a dowerhouse for the family, and this old buddy and her companion were living in it. They had the better qualities that one likes to think existed in the *noblesse oblige* sector of society. In the '30s, it seemed that these people weren't dependent on their investment incomes, or indeed their earned incomes in the city, in Glasgow.

YOUNG JIMMY AT TARBOLTON IN 1929

None of this was dramatically changed by the slump, as far as I saw. Thinking of them: one, for example, was a glass merchant. What happened to his business I just wouldn't know. Then there was my father's employer of the time who was the widow of Dubs of the North British Loco. Next door was a stockbroker who lived with his mother. What I do remember vividly was the terror among people like my father and others about getting thrown idle, even though there was no immediate threat – but hanging over the whole caboodle of them was this fear. One of our closest friends actually was made idle, and for a time he and his wife lived in what was the harness room in another of the big houses before they found a place, and he took to jobbing gardening in West Kilbride.

I think I was around three when I first started to wonder why the world should be ordered thus. It wasn't that I heard anything – my mother was conformist and loyal and defererential. A very clever woman, but absolutely on the side of her betters. And there was a difference between the people that came from the same background as we did 'along the Bay', as was talked about. The children of those who were in private service were brought up on the pattern of their employers. I used to tell my mother that she was like those plantation servants who worked indoors; she could've stepped out of *Gone With The Wind* in that regard quite easily. But the frightening thing is that they had a degree of good behaviour and cleanliness and all sorts of things which you didn't find among those who were not in private service. So it had its merits.

The gardener's cottage had much better accommodation than vast numbers of people were enjoying elsewhere in Central Scotland at the time. Just five miles up the road was Greenock – there was a name to freeze the bones of those of us living along the Bay, because there were nameless things in Greenock. When I went to secondary school in Greenock, of course, I found some of them.

A Life by the Water   Our play had largely to do with the sea. There was a family of four boys who were playmates, and another two singleton boys along the shore. The four-boy family had a rowing boat, and we spent a lot of the time tying up under the pier and dodging the paddle wheels of the Rothesay and Millport steamers and fishing. One day all of us we lost our clothes because there was a cruiser on trial and the waves washed away our clothes at the water's edge. We skipped about the rocks and we sailed boats on the ponds and the rocks and when all else failed we just walked about on the water, playing at being paddle boats.

Our families must have gone through moments of terror – we went off one day out of sight of the community and nobody knew where we were. We were in good hands, as there was a boy who was at least ten who was in charge of the boat, but there were three mothers watching on the shore as this crowd arrived back. My mother was very quick to worry and how she put up with it I do not know. Just off the rocks was where one steamer, the *Viper*, went down and she was so deep there was no point in even trying to see what had happened. There's a real deep channel out there and we were ploughtering about on the top of it.

Education and Conflicting Values   I started school in 1932. We were all from the cottages and servants' quarters. We were never very sure where the businessmen's children went to – England, I think. There were one or two exotics: somebody at Edinburgh Academy or something like that. The young of the owners just disappeared and reappeared on holidays. But there were no children of the gentry in residence.

I'm sure some felt that education was not for those like myself, or that perhaps I was getting above myself. Thoughts like that would always exist, then and now. I mean, bless me, the Government are just discovering that boys do not do all sorts of things well because no decent fellow will work hard in the class. That was always the way of it and the clever child was always liable to be getting a right good kicking in the corner of the playground, just by definition. The power in the playground lies with those who can fight best. That is the ultimate arbiter of human relationships, certainly at that age, and some people are never fully civilised out of it. But I was never aware of any snash like that, largely because I wasn't alone. Three of us from my qualifying class went to the High School, and there were others who went to the Academy, which was fee-paying but also had probably higher standards.

For some time I hoped and expected to go to university, and then become a teacher. I think my mother just took it for granted that if it was in her power to bring this about, that this was what was going to happen. My father was perfectly happy to go along with this. It was a very good example of how, in the average Scottish – what used to be called 'respectable' – working-class home, it was the woman who set the tone. If the man got the right woman the whole family soared and he with it; and conversely, of course.

It's maybe a modern myth that the dominie used to hold a position of great respect in Scottish society. I think my contemporaries respected teachers in a kind of a sense but I never told anybody that I wanted to become a teacher because I was embarrassed. The fact that practically everybody except me seemed to regard teachers with contempt was disturbing but it didn't make me change my mind – that was what I wanted to do.

I was enormously happy at school. This was one of the reasons I suppose why I wanted to be a teacher, because I admired the teachers that I had. The man who taught me English, Dewar Robb, I reckon was one of the best teachers that God ever put breath in. I think James Currie's autobiography mentions him. As a young teacher he taught in Paisley Grammar and then he became principal teacher of English in Greenock – superb, superb man. And the man who taught history had disciples and spear carriers all over the country, generation upon generation. And these were only the two that had the greatest influence on me.

The maths teacher failed hopelessly to teach me maths but that wasn't his fault. The blame, if there is blame, lay with another member of his staff much earlier on in the course. No one ever told me what Algebra was; no-one ever told me what an equation was. I always remember an exam which said, 'Form equations from the following,' and, as I say, no-one had ever told me what an equation was, so how was I to do this? When I sat the Highers, I was summoned on the grounds that I had done something very peculiar: I had got ninety-something in Geometry and Trigonometry, and I think twelve in Algebra. How had this happened? This was all very dreadful and there was great frothing. I have always reckoned that intellectually, the closest relative of history is Euclidean Geometry. Not a lot of people have ever thought about that. Logic, logic, logic.

We moved in 1937, just before the Coronation. I helped to erect the Coronation bonfire and we went back down to see it but by that time we'd moved two and a half miles up the road to Inverkip. I lost immediate touch with Wemyss Bay at that point. I was still going back on the bus down to Skelmorlie School for my last year but what I saw of the Bay was coming close to destruction. For a start, they concreted the foreshore and the First Army did all its training there before they went off to North Africa. The actual physical appearance of the Bay was altered beyond redemption. The grassy patches were chewed up by tank tracks. All along the road from there right away up to Gourock and beyond, and under all the overhanging cliffs and trees, there were lorries parked – and I mean real, big, Ford lorries and Bedfords – this was the transport for the invasion. To this day I feel vaguely surprised that there's nothing like that parked there. I still think of this as the norm – there should be lorries there, just as in the streets of Greenock there should be debris.

As a young boy, I wasn't very enthusiastic about the whole idea of there being a war. My father had had the worst war of any man that I ever encountered. During the Great War, he landed not once, but twice at Gallipoli. He came back in time to be wounded on the first day of the Somme. When he recovered from that they sent him to Salonica where he got malaria. As well as playing at steamers we all played at 'the war', and it was the Great War, of course, against the Jerries, and so on. And we were afraid – we got it through our pores, our parents were so visibly afraid. Most of the men that I knew as a boy had been injured in some way in the war. The postman – the father of those four boys I was speaking of – had lost a hand. The insurance man who came round weekly had only x percent use of his lungs because he'd been gassed. The gardener next door – he came to work next to the place where my father worked; they spotted one another across the wall and discovered the last time they had seen one another was in the Struna Valley, north of Salonica. And he was emaciated. So it was something that we didn't look forward to.

I remember that Sunday just after Chamberlain's broadcast, a plane flew over. I said simply, 'There's a plane, I wonder if this is it starting.' I didn't mean anything, I didn't mean either enthusiasm or fear or anything else, My father, whose nerves were run ragged by what had happened that morning, rounded on me and gave me an absolute keel-hauling with his tongue: I wasn't to start this, and we're going to have to be quiet about it, and none of this panic was supposed to happen. The reason he went on at such a length was because he was on the verge of panic himself.

We were still on the West Coast at the time of the Blitz at Clydebank. The first bombs that fell anywhere on the Clyde were part of a stick which started on the moors, about half a mile above our house, straddled our house and finished up in the Ardgowan Estate policies. The rumour afterwards was the plane was brought down at Port Bannatyne but whether there was any truth in that, I don't know. But I can remember that night when I was lying on the verge of sleep, and all of a sudden it must have hit the same rock as the foundations of the house were on, because what a wallop it gave. That was just for starters. In March was Clydebank and that, of course, was a real noise and light. There was a gun battery at the Cloch, just behind us, and I think most of the noise was coming from it, actually.

Then Greenock: of course, that's only four miles away across the hill and that was really quite colourful. I went back to see how my pal was getting on in the street and it was quite a mess. By that time I was in the third year at school in Greenock. Loyal to the nth – I'd been well brought up you see – I went back to see if the school was functioning and got a lift up in a lorry. I walked up Dunlop Street in Greenock and discovered that the school had been gutted by two landmines, one on each side. I was reminded of it when I watched Neil Armstrong landing on the Moon. What I saw on the television on that occasion was what I remembered seeing on the streets of Greenock. Your feet squeaked on a strange mixture of powdered glass and soot as you walked along; they squeak-, squeak-, squeaked. The cream of the jest that day was the bombers hit a distillery and two sugar refineries, and of course the stuff just ran burning down the gutters. I walked down Anne Street which was still burning, with burning beams across the road and so on. There were a group of women standing with shawls round their heads – it was like something out of Yeats – and there they were, loudly denouncing Churchill and demanding peace. That's one of the things I recall most vividly. It didn't appear in the official documentation after.

At school, nearly all the boys were in the ATC; the Air Cadets was their favourite. I didn't join anything other than the Scouts, because the last bus left Greenock at eight o' clock. But everyone else joined; the expectation was that of course they would all go and, indeed, one by one the years ahead of ours went. It was taken for granted this would happen. I think I was the second-youngest in my year group, so there were others who were being enlisted at seventeen-and-a-half, and then my time came to sign on. The question then was, what do you do? By that time, if you waited for call-up, as you were more or less obliged to do, the State wanted to choose where to send you rather than give you the choice.

All those who were waiting for call-up were going to be sent to Burma. Now the average Scottish summer I find tedious and exhausting enough, and the thought of Burma did not appeal one little bit, nor for that matter did the Japanese. So I thought the clever thing to do, and where my own wishes had gone anyway, was to enlist in the Navy – but you weren't allowed to do that unless you knew somebody. By that time my father's employers had naval and shipyard connections and I was interviewed by a chap who had been the second-in-command on *Repulse*. He changed ships, fortunately, just in time, and he advised me how to go about it – who to see and what to say, and so on. In due course, I was accepted for the Navy. I was sent back to finish the time at school and then started at Glasgow University. I'd sat the bursary competition and there was some arrangement that anyone who had done that commendable thing and sat the Glasgow Bursary Competition was allowed to complete their first year at the university and then they were whipped away. It's the kind of thing that would create riots in the street nowadays. Some went straight from school, and some did this. I was finishing my first year at university, but by that time I had injured my spine. Instead of ending up in the Navy, I didn't serve: I ended up two and a half years in plaster.

I had been doing things as you were supposed to do of course, in between times. I worked in the boat pool in Greenock on the crash boats. As the name suggests, the job of the crash boats was supposedly to go out and pick up people who had ditched in the sea. Most of our time was spent ferrying people hither and yon to places like Ardentinny from the Albert Harbour in Greenock. Then in the summer just before, I'd been physically ill at ease, I was very quickly tired and had a rotten pain in the back. I was working on the *Queen Mary II* as an assistant purser – it was a great job. But there was one or two occasions where I cracked my spine nastily. I don't know what the sequence of events was, but the upshot was that I developed tuberculosis in the spine. At that time the only treatment was to keep your fingers crossed and lie prone and motionless as far as you possibly could. I used to eat soup off my chest at parties to show how it could be done – I can still do it. After that two-and-a-half year gap, I took my degree in History and started teacher-training at Jordanhill in 1952.

A budding Scottish Nationalist

I remember one of the sort of upper members of Wemyss Bay society, a very nice lady, stopped me – I think I was four – and asked me what I'd been reading. At this time I'd been reading *Tales of a Grandfather*, with pictures, which I got for a birthday present and was enormously attached to. And I launched into a denunciation of the English and she said, 'Oh, Jim, don't you know I'm English?' To which I made no reply but internally I thought, 'So what?' Didn't cause me to alter what I had just said. I have no idea why I was aware of Scotland; again, it wasn't at home, it wasn't internal, it wasn't school. It just seemed to me, as it has seemed to me from that day to this, that it is an obvious piece of justice, right and proper, and that's all that I felt was required.

At school, there was a sort of brief flurry in my last year when they started a debating society. One of the people who was organising things in other schools in Greenock was John L. Kinloch, the organiser of the Clan Scotland youth group. He taught in Greenock Academy but he was known in the town. The fifth and sixth year pupils would be invited along to some hall in Greenock and Hector McNeil, the MP for Greenock, would be there. We would have debates and discussions, and I found myself uttering the nationalist cause. I got books: I had Boyd Orr's book, Bowie's, some of Alexander McEwan's, *Thistle and the Rose*. The books were a kind of standby and you referred to them; to be honest, they also were a kind of badge. You carried them around with you, it was a declaration that this was how your mind was working. I joined the Scottish National Party once I was eligible at 16. People used to say, 'Why did you join?' and I'd say, 'Because I was old enough to be allowed to.' That was all that was required. I kept in touch with it through the columns of the *Scots Independent*, which I read in Greenock Public Library without purchase.

At that time, it was thought kind of cranky to be in the SNP, though at school it didn't arise, possibly because of Kinloch's activities. In the Academy, because they were from the better-off sector of society, the fact that he was an influential and a well-regarded teacher in the school and generations of school pupils had come up that way possibly had taken the edge off the ridicule throughout the middle class of the town. You didn't have that same sort of attitude to the same extent as you might have expected. None of my contemporaries shared sympathy, but equally nobody ever ridiculed me in a really hostile fashion. They pulled my leg about it, but that's different; you knew it didn't matter. When I started work – first of all in Ayrshire and then in Lanarkshire – I suppose the saving grace was that you were not seen as a menace.

Early days of the Movement

In the late '30s, early '40s, there must have been some element which didn't look too fondly and indulgently on Scots Nationalism and thought we genuinely were threatening. Douglas Young had refused to be conscripted as a conscientious objector, Arthur Donaldson had been whipped up under 18B and put inside just in case he was taking German gold. But I was probably too young to encounter it quite at that point. Even in later years I would not have taken the view that Young did, or still less the view that Arthur Donaldson did, looking for neutrality. As far as I was concerned – then and today – I take the view that neutrality is something where you see no moral difference between the conflicting sides. And anyone who could see no moral difference between the sides in 1939 has got a lot to learn. So I would have taken the view that I suppose brought tolerance for me and others, the attitude of people like John McCormick and those who went with him. Now the odd thing was you see that people who took a wiser view of the war were also taking a strangely less strict party view in politics and I had no sympathy with McCormick's line in that regard. [Former SNP Chairman McCormick believed the party should not fight elections but should seek all-party support for independence.] But he and those who sided with him tended to have what I believe was a much wiser attitude towards the war, and possibly this, as I say, earned tolerance from the patriots.

In the immediate post-war period the national movement itself was often labelled romantic. I never really found myself in such an argument, I'd just grin and let it pass. Some of the duller romantics in the movement you never clapped eyes on, and I didn't meet any of the worst 'Tir-nan-Og-eries'. The people that I encountered were fairly matter of fact characters. All the people I was associating with shared the hostile estimate of those people who got the movement a bad name. And in later years I always took the view that if someone was destructive of the party's best prospects, if they were even an electoral liability then they should be encouraged, or even pushed, to either hide or resign.

Robert McIntyre was a key individual in that he provided a link with the past, although I think the link with the pre-war party can be misjudged. I think you're wiser to look on 1945 as a completely new beginning because the people who'd been in the party before had by that time either gone into the Covenant or into the wilderness, or had changed their opinions. McIntyre remembered something, even though he hadn't been in the party as a youth, and it was he who provided it with something approaching a stability of ideas. [McIntyre overhauled and improved SNP organisation in the 1930s and '40s, and became the party's first MP in 1945.] While I don't say that he would necessarily win medals and prizes as a dramatic political philosopher or anything like that, as a practical guide to what national party ought to be bending its energies toward, then he's the man who provided it.

It's only since Arthur Donaldson died and people have started writing about him that I've understood as much as I now do about him. I didn't know him all that well because he was on the other side of the country. Part of the party's problem was that it was led by people who had their living to earn. I remember in the time of my early days in the chair, if I was going to a meeting I had to go on a bus, or more likely several buses. Since I get travel sick on buses, nearly every outing to the sticks was fraught; but we had to do it, it was the only way you could get round. And I was just a young teacher. Arthur was still running the newspaper in Forfar, so there was no cadre of leadership at all. It wasn't until Billy Wolfe came along and was willing to give of his time instead of earning his living, that helped us. When Arthur retired, that helped and then gradually others came in, but it's only when you have got the modern creation of full-time professionals, elected persons, salaried by the State, that the party has soared onwards and upwards.

A great many people in that situation will believe that this is somehow testimony to their excellence. So it may be, but equally it is testimony to what time

*It was not until the
General Election of
1964 that the SNP
vote moved to the left
of the decimal point
– at just 2.4 per
cent. By 1966, it had
doubled to 5 per cent
and by 1970 more
than doubled again
to 11.4 per cent. Since
1967, the SNP has
always been
represented in the
House of Commons.*

has brought and what the general rise has made possible. But you needed people to do the work and you needed people to have leisure to do the work, and that's what we didn't have. We weren't able to grow in the Highlands because there was no one there to take the initiative. The Liberals were given a free hand to get in there, ditto in the Borders. I remember Murdo Young and myself trying to organise a branch in Buckhaven and it was a logistic feat of buses and so on. Going up to Crieff where Gordon Boyd was trying to start a branch ... two people turned up – Gordon and the hall keeper. And that had been a two-and-a-half hour bus journey from Glasgow to try and start the branch. That was the level of it. People just did not consider it a possibility. So, rather than ridicule of romanticism and folly and so on, people just weren't interested.

*The Turning Point:
1967*

I know that there's a great temptation to feel that somehow or other the movement came along with a trump card and all was well. I think the people did it themselves. I suppose what we did was keep this thing tick-, tick-, ticking away. In moments of irritation the public looked and they saw us still sitting there saying, 'We told you so'. And we're going to go on telling you so, until you tumble to the possibilities. They tottered from one economic crisis to another and one disappointment to another, and also the old-fashioned traditionalists began dying off, whatever party or loyalty they had. Youngsters maybe hadn't paid much attention to the nationalist argument, and maybe hadn't been terribly convinced, but they knew it was there. They knew it was ongoing, and I think circumstances, like the economic fiascos of the British economy, and the British state, got them interested. That's why I think in Hamilton, in 1967, we got them at precisely the right moment, that the memory of Tory economic failure was still reasonably fresh in the mind, just as the Labour Party was tottering into yet another economic ditch. [The SNP won an important by-election victory in Hamilton in 1967.] And at that precise moment they got them at Hamilton and of course after Hamilton things were never quite the same again. That was the beginning of thirty-one consecutive years of there always being an SNP member in the House of Commons.

And, of course, Donald Stewart taking the seat in the Western Isles in 1970 – that was interesting. Things like that, you see, were happening quite apart from whatever the central party organisation was trying – you had individuals like Donald, who was a local representative. The Party, the movement, was happy to have him as a representative. He was happy, he wasn't beholden to them, he didn't have to get their permission to do things, they were fortunate to have something like that happening. I mean, Donald made the SNP a present of that seat. Little doubt about that.

Old Haunts, New roots

When you retire, you should stay where you are. People in Dundee love to retire up Glen Esk and places like that. I always think of Alastair MacLean's stories about how his father died in the ambulance on the way from Ardnamurchan to Fort William. I think if you retire up a glen, the chances are that you're going to – well, to live to regret it maybe isn't quite the right way of putting it … I used to say that I would retire to a lodge at the gate of Ninewells Hospital, that seemed to me a very sensible thing. I used to tell this as a funny joke and people would sort of smile vaguely – until, of course, I went through an experience that made it no longer a joke at all. And one of the things that keeps me in Dundee is the fact that the medical facilities here are rather better than average and certainly an awful lot better than some of the things that you hear about in the West of Scotland.

The only reasonable alternative to staying put is to go back to your childhood home. I might have been tempted to go back to the West. Every time I go through, it's like the old legend of Antaeus, who liked to touch the earth once in a while and that sustained him again. It's ridiculous, but I have to go, even in the car, just take the car out for an afternoon and go down the Greenock Road. As I head south from Glasgow past the airport, when I see the water at Langbank, I feel restored. I can turn back to Dundee, refreshed. It's the water that does it, the Firth, the estuary. The Tay lacks what the Clyde has got in terms of scenery. It's better than the Forth, but none the less it's not the Clyde. I've got no contacts any longer with Greenock. I've been in Dundee since '67 and I've no relatives or friends on visiting terms actually in Greenock or down the Clyde Coast. So if I go back I go back just as a guest or a visitor.

Lord Cameron of Lochbroom
Advocate, Politician & Judge

Born 1931

I was born in Edinburgh, Walker Street, in a nursing home. My parents were living in Dublin Street, just at the very bottom of the New Town. Father had been at the Bar for some six years. He was still a junior, working as an advocate depute part-time then for Ramsay MacDonald's National Government.

I started school first of all in what would have been a nursery school called St Aurans, which was in Drummond Place, and then at the age of five went straight to the Academy. It was taken for granted that I go there, in part because Father had been there as well. It was close by and I suppose in those days that part of Edinburgh was very largely professional and the children, or boys rather, all went to the Academy. Their sisters went to St George's, even in those days.

When I was about one and a half, we moved to Gloucester Place; my recollections are of having a cook and a nanny, certainly after my sister was born, three years after me. We had a New Town flat which was ground floor, below was the basement, or the 'area' as it was known, where the live-in cook and nanny were. There was a door in between the basement and the ground floor where my parents and my sister and myself lived.

The area steps was the means whereby the messages were delivered; the Newhaven fishwife and generally any person calling with goods would go there. The coal cellars were down below. The front door was the way in which visitors, proper visitors, came to the house. It's all changed now. It must have been changing a great deal, as even my father would agree, between the First and Second World Wars. It had become slightly less formal but Edinburgh was still very formal. I've been told by my stepmother when she came up from London just after the war, that she found Edinburgh society much more formal than that she'd known down south.

Both my parents were extremely musical and I can remember as a child being taken to concerts in the Usher Hall. Father also painted, and again, I suppose you

A FISH MERCHANT SELLING FISH FROM HIS CART

*DRESS WAS FORMAL EVEN
WHEN PARENTS WENT
SHOPPING IN THE EARLY
1930S*

*DRESS WAS FORMAL EVEN
WHEN PARENTS WENT
SHOPPING IN THE EARLY
1930S*

get imbued with a liking for certain pictures. He collected a bit, more particularly just after the war, and the house began to be filled with paintings. As a kind of osmosis I enjoyed music and I enjoyed going to picture galleries. Just by chance, I'm involved with buildings and architecture through the Cockburn Association. I was obviously aware of things such as classical architecture from school, having been a classicist, but I think probably only it's in the last twenty years that I have been much more conscious of architecture as a separate idiom of art.

As a boy, walking to and from the Academy, the keelies would taunt us. We had what would now be called gang fights in which we faced up to the massed troops of India Place or Drumacre Street; in fact, one lived cheek-by-jowl with those communities and thought nothing of it.

I didn't see my parents all that much. They were fairly busy and we had a nanny. The great family occasion was in fact Sunday lunch and we would all eat together then although I don't think he spoke to me about cases – I wasn't interested. I was much more interested in the kind of pursuits which he had outside, which often involved the sea and sailing and we did a lot of that either on holiday on the West Coast or he sailed on the Firth of Forth a lot.

He had his own boat, indeed two. One was a yacht and one was a motor boat and just before the war, I remember going on two occasions across to Lochgoil for the summer holidays. The yacht and the motor boat were brought across and moored outside the house taken by my parents for the holidays – going across, packing up with the maid, the wicker workbaskets going on ahead: it was extraordinary.

We had a car of our own then, I remember it being bought, the last one we had before the war from the garage, the Eastern Motor Company, in George Street, a Wolseley Sixteen. The smell of leather comes to me even now. Though not unusual in the New Town, in Edinburgh as a whole there would have been very few cars. I can remember as children being allowed to go off on our own up to play in the Gardens. Admittedly, Nanny might sometimes take us but certainly in the wartime the streets were, of course, absolutely empty and we just roamed around almost at will.

War Memories

When war broke out, I felt fury: we were on holiday and my father had said that if I was able to swim, I think it was something like thirty strokes, then I'd be able to have my own sailing dinghy. I had just achieved that at the end of August 1939 and that man Hitler ruined everything, so he was my enemy from a very early time in the war.

Edinburgh was going to be a military target, or so it was thought, so my parents arranged with a great friend of theirs at the Bar whose parents had a house just outside Ayr. My sister and I were evacuated there for a year. It was thought that the German aircraft weren't able to get that far. We went to school there and that was a wonderful year, watching the Clyde and the *Queen Elizabeth* going up and down on her sea trials and the like; and Anson aircraft going out from Prestwick.

We came back, and I went back to the Academy, just in time for the Clydebank bombing. I can remember the bombers going overhead. And I used to go out next day and try and look for shrapnel. It was a great thing. The school had a system whereby if the air-raid warning had sounded and if the all clear didn't been given before a certain time in the night, then the school didn't start until say ten o'clock. So you got an extra lie-in because you'd been in the shelter all night.

A Lawyer's Life in Edinburgh

I was fairly conscious of my father being an advocate early on because until he took silk [became a King's Counsel], which was 1935, he had at least one devil [an assistant lawyer] in the house. In those days, of course, each advocate, if he lived in the Quarter [that part of the New Town where most of the legal offices were] used his house as his chambers and, therefore, there were people calling for consultations; latterly, I was letting them in so I got to know a lot of the solicitors quite well.

In those days, like everybody else's, my father's practice was fairly general, probably with more civil than criminal work. But there was no legal aid and you just took what work there was. He was, I would say, in English terms, a common lawyer. There were far fewer judges, far fewer advocates. There were probably in those days about a hundred and twenty to a hundred and thirty practising advocates; there were then still fifteen judges. Just to show the concentration of lawyers in the New Town, in India Street, at the bottom of our street, there were, before the war, five judges living up the street, all of whom I can remember in one way or the other.

I did National Service before going to university, which was very good for me because it took me away from Edinburgh for two years. First of all down south, then for a short period, I went to the Far East, and then the last year down at Portsmouth. I didn't actually want to live and work in England. I'd seen a little bit of school friends round about London, and it was too large so I came back here to read law, keeping again my options open between being a solicitor, as my grandfather had been, and an advocate as my father was. By sort of a gradual progression the Bar was attractive, you were your own master. I had been two years as an apprentice in a law office and I didn't particularly enjoy that. So I decided to go to the Bar where I would have certain assistance anyway from knowing a number of solicitors.

I don't think I can claim that there was any higher motive for becoming a lawyer at all. It just appeared to me to be a kind of life which I'd enjoy. I'd enjoyed a bit of public speaking. Intellectually, there was a certain attraction in that kind of use of words and employment of language in court and, to a certain extent, the rough and tumble I quite enjoyed, more so than the arid side of the lawyer's life, as I saw it, as a solicitor.

Changes in Law Practice

By the middle 1950s, the practice of the law was changing – probably those who were in the law would be more conscious of the changes. Civil legal aid had made a little bit of a difference, criminal legal aid didn't come in until the late '50s. More obvious was the kind of loosening of the formality of society that was about; those who'd been away during the war came back, and it was a much more informal atmosphere in the law, even just in matters of dress. I can remember my father going off to court in the '30s wearing a tail coat, striped trousers, a black silk hat and wing collar. Now in the '50s, he still had the wing collar but it was a black jacket and waistcoat and striped trousers and a Homburg; it was in small ways like that that the whole thing was changing. People were beginning not even to stay in the Quarter. They were going outside and only having chambers for consultations in the Quarter itself.

I completed while we still had capital punishment on the statutes. I never took part in a case in which a capital murder was involved. I suppose the only one I was conscious of, the year before I was called, was in fact Peter Manuel. Father presided over the trial, and I think I'm conscious then that it must have been an ordeal to sentence someone to death, although in that case, the particular individual was perhaps one whom you were less sorry to see go that way than many others.

As far as the 'not proven' verdict is concerned, I'm perfectly content with it; I think it's a verdict with which we're familiar. Although there are obvious cases which have created a great deal of public discussion, in the end of the day, the jury know what the choice is, which is between guilt and innocence. Once that decision is taken then the question of what form of acquittal is one for those who've chosen that particular verdict and being satisfied that guilt has not been proved.

One change that has taken place within my professional lifetime is the gradual increase in the number of women not only in the Faculty [of Advocates] but also, finally, with Hazel Aaronson (Lady Cosgrove). When I was called I can remember about three: Margaret Kidd of course, Isabel Sinclair was another and one or two others I can think of – Hayley Hatterson – but they were very few and far between and when I look round at the bar now as they appear before me. It's been very good for the Faculty; certainly, when I was in Crown Office ,the proportion of women to men was growing really very rapidly. That's ten years ago but they were getting to the point of between thirty and forty per cent.

The Faculty itself doubled, if not trebled, after the war and certainly, in relation to crime, there's been an enormous increase in the workload. I can think, for instance, of just reading lists for a Glasgow circuit in the early 1950s which would mean two judges going over for a week once a month or something of that order. Obviously, it depended on how long the cases lasted but now we are running four, occasionally five, courts over there throughout the year.

It might just be that the CID is spectacularly better than it was, but I think one reason for the increase in workload is, of course, the issue of drugs which are involved in a very substantial proportion of the cases. Another is that people are prepared to report matters of sexual abuse, which involves everything from rape to lewd and libidinous conduct, in a way which they probably wouldn't have done before. It's reflected in a sense in divorce actions where cruelty actions suddenly became much more common in the latter part of the time that I did divorce work because people were beginning to be able to say that I'm not going to put up with that kind of conduct.

On the civil side there have been enormous changes but that's been in part an

*In 1900, just 142
individuals in
Scotland sued for
divorce; in 1991,
12,400.*

exchange of work. Divorce, when I started, was quite an important part of a civil practice and indeed the court sat on a Saturday morning to deal with undefended divorces. So that when the Calcutta Cup match [the annual Scotland vs England rugby match, played biennially in Edinburgh] was being played, a country solicitor suddenly found that he had clients who had an absolute desire to be divorced that particular day and that they must come along and sit behind counsel and assist. That went, and then reparation in personal injury work, that used to be a civil jury trial but has receded, although it's come back a little. The great proportion of work now is of the kind which was probably unheard of when I started at the Bar: judicial review, the supervision of administrative decision-making by the Executive.

One of the qualities which was expected of you as an entrant to the Faculty when we joined was the obligation to serve the public. The Latin phrase was *pro bono publico* which meant that you were expected to appear for nothing for those who couldn't afford to pay. There were those who appeared in the civil and more particularly in those days, the criminal courts, for no fee. I think they received expenses from the Crown but that was expected of you as being part of your obligation to society as a member of the Faculty of Advocates. In some ways, perhaps, that has been slightly eroded, now that we're paid for everything that is done, except on a speculative fee basis.

One of my father's pronouncements was of some significance in the whole development of women's rights in society – the existence of rape within marriage. In other respects the law respected the marriage bed. For instance, even now, spouses are not compellable witnesses against the other partner, although they can give evidence,

if they are willing and prepared to do so, and must do so, of course, if the offence concerns them. But otherwise the law still respects, as it were, the marriage bed and its secrets. I think my father took the view that if you looked at the proper definition of rape, then the fact that the parties were married should not be a bar. In the particular case, he recognised there were decisions which said while the parties were living together, you couldn't have rape but he said that if they were separated that was different. Later, an Appeal Court decision redefined the whole matter and said rape was possible even while the parties were living together.

LIKE FATHER, LIKE SON

The Lord Advocate Appointment

Undoubtedly my greatest challenge was being Lord Advocate. I'd been in Crown Office as an advocate depute for three years and was about to leave and go back to ordinary practice when I was invited to take the appointment. I found that a fascinating four years, being thrown into a completely different milieu, a sort of parliament I find again both fascinating and exasperating – fascinating just to see just how in fact government worked from the inside. I'd watched it from the outside in the law, law reform and the like, but you understand a bit more of how the system works when you get inside it. I regard myself as being extraordinarily fortunate to have held that appointment.

The Scots Law System

What we have evolved is a system which has recognised the rights of the individual, a system in the criminal law in a very sort of individual way. The issue, for instance, of corroboration is a very important part of our criminal law, as is the issue of time limits, although that in a sense has had to take into account the problems of time and space in court work. These are native institutions and have been with us for something like two centuries. I think, too, the system of courts, with the district, sheriff and superior courts again is one which is individual. It can't bear comparison immediately with any other system. The adversarial system is one which we're relatively comfortable with, although it's not unusual because it is in common law countries generally. I know there are critics of it but if you go to countries which have the inquisitorial system, then they have equal critics as to the problems which occur there, more particularly regarding delays. In the last ten, fifteen or twenty years, people in the law and outside it have started looking to other countries to see other ways and means of solving problems which can be adopted here. It's a two-way process, of course.

Changes in Edinburgh

I think the changes I've seen in Edinburgh have been the disappearance within the New Town of offices and the return of some of those houses to residential use. The big change has been in the Old Town, certainly within my knowledge. The expansion of Edinburgh which I find amazing when I look back and think of walking along Queensferry Road beside my nanny who was pushing a pram with my sister in it; you'd get as far as Orchard Brae, go across the road and on the other side of the road going out there was a horse trough. If you looked over the wall, which I was just able to do if I stood on a particular milestone, there were fields below you. All that is covered and yet that was within three-quarters of a mile of the centre of Edinburgh. Of course, the other thing is just simply the issue of traffic and the form of transport. No steam engines, no trains, no trams – it's a poorer place.

Donnie Nelson
Printer

Born 1932

I was born at 95 George Street, Stranraer – that was the family home at the time. My mother was an old-fashioned housewife: she stayed at home, looked after the kids. My father was a fisherman. The fishing at that time had more or less gone defunct in Stranraer so he tended to get jobs here and where he could, helping to unload the occasional cargo boat that came in at the West Pier. Previously it had been herring fishing which in the last century had been very good in Loch Ryan and around the local coastline but the herring seemed to have deserted the normal fishing banks. Old photographs show that at one time many fishing boats came from much further afield and unloaded their catches in Stranraer. I think the last set of photographs which I have seen showed that 1910, 1911 there were tremendous herring catches in Stranraer. After that it died away. There was very little fishing done except for the local markets.

WHITE FISH AUCTION, STRANRAER

We stayed in an old tenement house: a small shop in below, central doorway and my grandmother had one half of the house upstairs and my mother and father had the other half. We shared attic bedrooms. Accommodation was tight. I had one sister at that particular time and my grandmother and an unmarried daughter who lived with her as well as my mother and father but we squeezed in. It was a very happy household.

We had electricity in the house. It must have been introduced shortly after I was born because I can recall in the old bedrooms we still had gas lighting. I can remember discovering as a child that, while gas mantles were objects of curiosity, you did not poke your fingers at them. Expensive game. We had an outside toilet and a wash-house, relics again of Victorian days but I can recall my mother doing the family washing in this outside wash-house in an old boiler which had to be lit every Monday morning.

Schooling and the War

I went to St Joseph's School in Stranraer. I had quite a hectic schooling, actually, because I had not long started the school when the war broke out. To further complicate matters, St Joseph's was a very old Victorian school – built around 1872 – and at 1939 the education authority and the Diocese of Galloway, which had owned the school, had come to an agreement that the school would be rebuilt. Between finishing school in the May or June at '39 and going back to school again in the August, Mr Hitler stepped in and we discovered that St Mildred's Hall, the church hall, had been grabbed by the government. So we found ourselves squeezed in to what was Stranraer's answer to a nightclub. It was known as the Ritz in Dalrymple Street. I quite liked school, despite the fact that I was at about seven different schools before I eventually became a senior, finishing at Stranraer High School. This was because of these wartime moves. Half-day schooling suited us very well.

Father was away to the Navy. He went away about a fortnight before war was declared because he'd been in the RNVR (Royal Naval Volunteer Reserve). This meant I was growing up at a time with no male influence in the house at all. School having finished at four o'clock, I'd arrive home maybe about half past six or even seven o'clock – because there was so much happening around, because of wartime days – to be threatened what would happen when Father came home on leave. Army camps were going up all over the place, things were changing at Stranraer Harbour and there was so much to do and to see – it was an exciting time for a schoolboy.

I can recall when the military railway was being built between Stranraer and Cairnryan to serve the huge military port, number two port, that was being built at Cairnryan. We used to rush out after school and we actually helped the squaddies, the fellows in the Royal Pioneer Corps who were building the railway embankments and bridges. Some of the brickwork is still standing, which possibly says more for their overseeing of the work than my actual bricklaying. We used to have our tea with these Army fellows. This was right on the edge of town, it was a huge transit camp because at that time, more or less all the army traffic passing to Northern Ireland went via Stranraer and Larne.

The Black Art

It was simply taken for granted that on school-leaving age, which at that time was fifteen, I would simply get a job and that would be it. There was no question of anything beyond senior-secondary education; that was for people who had plenty of money. I left school quite abruptly because I had just heard that there was a job going in Stranraer which took my fancy. The job was apprentice printer – the black art. I asked for it, got it, went to school the next day and told the register teacher that I would be leaving at the end of the week.

It was a small jobbing firm that I served my apprenticeship with and really everyone who served an apprenticeship there became what was known as a twicer – you were a compositor but you also were a machine minder. You did everything: finishing off jobs, stitching, bookbinding and things like that. At that particular

DONNIE AT THE 'FREE PRESS' PRINTING WORKS IN *1965*

place, it was handsetting. If we had a big job on we used to use the good offices of the local newspaper for whom I later worked. They would set up heavy stuff for us, Linotypes they had then. I can still read it all upside down, it's a habit never forgotten.

It was a seven-year apprenticeship then. I then went on to do two years' National Service then back to the printing. I eventually shifted to another firm in Stranraer, the local newspaper, and I worked with them for the next, almost forty years. When I first came to work with the old *Free Press*, as we call the local newspaper, there had been three Linotype machines and a Miehle for printing the newspaper on, and two or three other, smaller printing machines. In 1974 they decided to shift, to modernise, and they built a completely new printing works just about fifty yards away on St Andrews Street. We left the hot metal, we left the handsetting, the stones, the Linotypes, all these were left behind and we walked into a brand new place. One week the old paper was printed as it had been for donkey's years and the following week it was web-offset.

It was very well planned. Along with two of the other younger fellows, I did a couple of weeks in Llandudno Junction working with the *North Wales Weekly News* on their printing machines. It had been decided that I would shift entirely on to the printing side and other people were sent on retraining courses, to change from the old Linotype keyboards to the new set-up producing bromides. We all were retrained with a lot of help, it must be said, from people who were supplying new machinery, etc. One week, as I say, it was done the old way, the next week we just produced a first newspaper in the new building. There were no jobs lost at all. We found something for everyone to do.

In the event, I finished up doing paste-up, and also graphic work in the camera room. That was where I finished my time with the *Free Press*, in the camera room, making PMTs, photo-mechanical transfers, copying, enlarging, reducing. Plates as well, we also made the plates. In addition to that I also did a wee bit of writing on the side for the paper.

Courtings and Weddings

We tended to meet girls at youth clubs. When you actually met someone you liked it was a case of inviting them to accompany you to the local picture house. That was really all that there was to do apart from walks, plenty of good walks around Stranraer. That was it really. It was the days before teenagers found pubs, you might say. There was quite a bit of dancing that went on. It just so happened that I was born with two left feet so I didn't tend to frequent dances terribly much. We'd go occasionally with some of my friends but we discovered, my wife and I, that we enjoyed long walks together. We went occasionally, as I say, to the pictures, but mostly walking. If you walked together for a while it was expected that naturally you would get married. Weddings then were a big occasion, they tended to be quite a family affair, but never getting out of hand.

In the course of my writings for the local newspaper I followed up the story of a wedding that was not all that quiet and I managed to get a hold of one or two people who had been there or had seen the aftermath of the incident. I was probably about five or six years old when it happened. There was a group of houses right in the centre of old Stranraer, known as the Pretty Mill. It tended to be a small community on its own, just off Dalrymple Street. They had originally been built as workers' houses and there had been an old mill beside them. They went right back to the 1840s and '50s and were pretty derelict. In fact, it was places such as that that led to Stranraer's first commitment to building council houses. As quite often happened with poorer families at that time, the wedding took place in one of the church manses: the minister would marry them in his home and they then went back to either the bride's house or the groom's parents and would have a family reception with a few friends invited. This particular party had been held in the upstairs part of the house and the house was so rotten and so damp that with too many people crowded in, when some folk had between dances leaned against the wall, the back wall of the house fell out.

I can remember one local doctor showing me rather proudly round his garden many years ago and we came across an old zinc tub filled with flowers and I knew him well enough to say to him, jocularly, you could have got a better flower container than that. 'No, no,' he says, 'that has pride of place in my garden because when I came here as a young doctor I was so appalled at the conditions in the Pretty Mill.' He says, 'I was one of those who begged and pleaded with councillors, "For God's sake, get a housing programme of some kind going," and that is from one of the old houses in the Pretty Mill, when they were pulled down, when the people were finally moved out towards the end of the 1930s.'

Local Politics

I was probably still in my teens when I became a Youth Club representative on a sort of forum which they had covering the whole of Wigtownshire. In later years just after I was married I was asked if I would serve on a local area education sub-committee which dealt with schools in Stranraer. We made not the heaviest of decisions, we didn't hire and fire teaching staff – we hired janitors, we gave permission for schools to be used for other purposes. Then at the time of the first re-organisation [of local government in Scotland] in 1974, I was one of the founder members of Stranraer Community Council. I'd also been involved in the Children's Panel at that particular time and later on was asked to stand for the District Council. Then I became a magistrate and so I had to give up the Children's Panel.

I was unfortunate enough to take over as Housing Convenor at a time when it was obvious to everyone in local government that the government of the day had decided that more resources should be made from local sources and I inherited a fairly good stock of town council and county council houses. But our housing support grant had been cut for a few years before that. Eventually it was shaved away to nothing, so we depended more and more on the sales of council houses, which, of course, meant that you had a reducing stock for rental yourself. When I first took over as Housing Convenor, we still had a substantial housing support grant and when my term of office came to an end with the last [local government] reorganisation in 1996 we had no housing support grant at all. We did indeed have an idea which was floated at that time, that we would set up a local housing association ourselves which would have access to government funding and Scottish housing funds which we didn't get to as a council. We thought that we made out a pretty good case for it but unfortunately, the tenants voted otherwise. Being a democratic lot, we agreed that the tenants should have the final say. Maybe they didn't like the councillors who were their landlords, but they certainly didn't like the idea of someone unknown.

Changing Roles

My wife went back to work after our children were born. She continued working after she was married which I think was the thin end of the wedge which had come in in the thirties. Round about the 1930s, younger women did tend to keep on working after they were married but it was still the case at that particular time that if a family came along that was the work finished. But by the time my family had been completed my wife got the offer of a part-time job to fill in for people taking holidays. After a few weeks at that she said, 'I've been asked if I'll do it permanently.' That was it. This was becoming more and more the case: women were going back to work, when the kids were at school and older people, grannies, were still available to look after them when they came home from school.

I was not at all happy to begin with. I can remember saying to my wife – I really like to think that I left the decision to her – I said, 'It's up to you, if you think you can cope then fine, let's do it'. I very quickly learned to appreciate the difference an extra income made. Stranraer was never a place for paying particularly high wages and unemployment was at a fairly high level and kept steadily at that. An extra wage coming in made a tremendous difference. Of course, we fully appreciated it when the boys grew up and they wanted to go on to something better than their parents had done, and it helped to fund their further education.

Local Pastimes

Probably angling is the biggest sport so far as participation is concerned – sea anglers and freshwater fishermen are very thick on the ground here. Football runs a very close second, I would say: there's plenty of boys' leagues, local leagues, amateurs, and then there's Stranraer Football Club itself. I was never a good footballer but certainly I've got a great regard for the game and I've been writing about the local team now for nigh on forty years. I must admit that I'm a Stranraer man through and through.

Curling is also tremendously popular here. At one time it used to be a game mostly confined to the rural people, the farmers and the farm workers, but the building of the curling rink at North West Castle, which has produced European and world champions, has introduced many other youngsters to the sport and it is a much more widespread sport now. Golf, of course, has its devotees. There are some very fine golf courses locally. Of other games peculiar to this area, the only one that I can think of which has disappeared now is quoits. It used to be a very keen area for quoits – or 'kiting', as they said locally. I have never actually seen quoits being played. By the time I was growing up it had more or less gone out of existence, although I believe it was still played here and there, particularly in the eastern end of Galloway.

I remember speaking to a fellow one time who described very vividly to me his memories of a curling tournament at Wigtown and the 'kiting rink', as he called it, was down beside the river. He described how they came from Ayrshire; there was even one or two from across the border because, he said, the money was good – maybe £300 or £400 resting on the result of this tournament. He says they finished about four o'clock in the morning, people lighting torches so that they could finish the match. A lot of money.

Speech and Dialect

The way that children in Stranraer spoke forty or fifty years ago was very different. In the classroom it had to be proper English, but in the playground it was just the way you wanted to be, same as the rest of the kids. In this corner of the world we tend to be labelled 'Galloway Irish'. I'm never very sure whether that refers to the number of Irish people who came here in the Hungry Forties of the last century and settled down and didnae go any further or whether it was a reference to our speech. I do know that over the years quite often people have mistaken me for Irish. One time in London I was asked, 'What part of Derry are you from?' It was as close as that.

Years ago, when I was doing National Service, four of us were coming home on leave from Lyneham in the West Country and we travelled as far as London together. We had managed to get our leave passes early, settled down in the train in Swindon after a jar or two at a local and there was an old boy sitting in the carriage. It turned out that he was a local from Swindon, Irish originally. He got speaking to us and he remarked to Mike, one of the number of us, 'Ye havenae far to go,' and Mike said, 'No, I live in London.' And he said 'Yeah, you live about Highbury.' Mike said, 'That's right, right next door to Arsenal's ground,' and the old fellow claimed that he had been studying dialects, twangs all his days. He then turned round to Ray and he pinpointed him very accurately as County Durham. So the third member of the quartet, Big Ginger, said to him, 'How about me?' 'Oh, you're not quite Glasgow,' he says, 'perhaps Lanarkshire, further into Lanarkshire.' Well, Ginger came from High Blantyre. Ginger then turned round to him and said, 'Well, what about Donnie here?' He says, 'He's frae the Clye Hole.' Now 'the Clye Hole' is a purely local expression in Stranraer referring to what is more properly Agnew Crescent and Seuchan Street, an area to the west of the old centre of the town. And it turned out that this ancient fellow had worked in Stranraer during the First World War, and he said it was such a distinctive twang he never forgot it.

Pat McCormick
Shopworker & Trade Union Official

Born 1933

I was the eldest of a big family. My father worked in the shipyards and my mother was looking after the household duties and the big family. We lived in a tenement in Greenock, in a room and kitchen with an outside toilet. Conditions were deplorable, quite honestly, when one looks back on it now. It was a tenement with three balconies, with fifty houses on each balcony so there was a hundred and fifty houses in total. But there was a camaraderie among the neighbours then that's sadly disappeared.

First Job

I went to school in Greenock – a primary school which was nearby where I lived and then to the High School from twelve. I left school at fifteen. I wanted to be a joiner, actually, and I went round all the shipyards because that was the biggest employer of labour in these days. Although they all took my name, nothing came up, so I started work in the Co-operative as a van boy from the age of fifteen, delivering rolls on a housing estate in Greenock. I started at six o'clock in the morning and I finished at two in the afternoon. I had to be up at half past four 'cos I had about a forty-minute walk from where I lived to pick up the van at the Co-operative depot. So it was quite a long day but I didn't think much of it in these days.

I got paid one pound, nineteen shillings and sixpence, which was a good wage, at that particular time for a fifteen-year-old. And, of course, I made more than that actually in tips from customers. Some people were very, very generous. Indeed, one customer used to give me five shillings a week, which was absolutely amazing. I always remember her name for the reasons of the sizeable tip that I got every week. Her and her husband worked and she had four boys who were all working and I used to leave in four loaves and half a dozen cakes every Monday, Wednesday and Friday. When I went to collect the money on the Saturday, she gave me five shillings' tip.

I'd take my wages home in an unopened packet for my mother; I didn't have to look for pocket money because my tips, believe it or not, exceeded my two pounds a week salary, so I was able to help out by giving her proceeds of the tips. I was a keen cyclist and I went camping and I bought a bike, of course, and it was the pride of my life. And a tent – I'd been in the Boy Scouts and I'd a yearn for camping and I continued in that. I had gramophone records and a radiogram in those days, so my money went just as I think teenagers now spend their money on CD discs. I'd buy Top of the Pops in these days – all the ones in the Top Twenty and things like that. There was a Top Twenty every Sunday night from eleven 'till midnight on Radio Luxembourg, and it used to give you the number one right through to the top twenty – Dennis Lotis, Lita Rosa, Ted Heath and his Band, Dickie Valentine – they were all Top of the Pops in these days. We listened to the radio a lot, because we didn't have television then of course.

In 1948 or '49, shops were much smaller and you had the grocer's, the baker's, the butcher's, the greengrocer's, the footwear shop, the hardware shop, and customers went round all the shops to do their shopping. In those days, most people didn't have a car and the shops were more convenient to the housing population in the tenement properties for that reason. People like my mother, with large families and without cars, had to go their messages every day, very often twice a day, if they forgot something in the afternoon for my father coming home for his tea. Usually it was me, being the oldest of the family, that nipped down to the shops to pick up whatever had been forgotten. We'd have corned beef, beans and chips. Chips were pretty well the basis of most meals, which when one looks back now, I wonder how I still survive. It was a struggle for my mother to look after us all and she did a wonderful job when one looks back, but the meals were pretty plain and basic. There were two reasons for this – one, there was rationing, and the other was the finance, of course. My father was a labourer in the shipyards, and it was a struggle.

When I came near sixteen, I was desperate to get into a trade, but when I saw I wasn't being successful at that, I moved then into the shop to work. I stayed there until I did my National Service at eighteen – I went into the RAF. When I came out at twenty, I went back into the shop and became a branch manager at the age of twenty-six. During that period, I was active in my trade union, USDAW, where I was the branch secretary. When I became a manager, my full-time official asked why didn't I apply for a job in USDAW as a full-time official. I did, and I left the Co-operative shop at the age of thirty-two, to become a full-time official with USDAW.

Innovations and Changes

Over those years, shopping had begun to change and the Co-op itself changed. In the shop that I was manager of, we were asked to take in a frozen food cabinet, as it was called then. This was an entirely new venture. We got fish and chips – that was the main diet in those days – and the fish and chips was packed in a cardboard container but it was like a newspaper. We got in frozen dairy-cream sponges and things like that. There was customer resistance to this: 'Oh, if it's frozen it can't be fresh.' In fact, we were thinking on taking it out because it certainly wasn't paying. It was about twelve months before customers started to purchase the things in sufficient numbers to make it economical. Of course, there wasn't the same advertising because it was something new at that time, and that didn't help us promote the sales. It took quite a long while for that particular side of the grocery business to pick up. When one goes into a supermarket now and sees the amount of refrigerated products that are on sale, there's a tremendous difference.

A large grocery store in these days employed about forty people and that was a big, big shop. The average grocery shop employed from ten to twenty people. But there were many of them but now, sadly, they've all disappeared. You have one superstore in the town centre, or in many instances, out of town, because most people have cars now. The other change of course is that you have one-stop shopping now, you go into the supermarket and buy everything. Whereas when I first left school you had to go into about a dozen shops to collect the things that you can now collect under one roof.

When I left school, your tea break was in the back shop. You picked up some cases and that was your seat. No such thing as a canteen, because obviously the shops weren't big enough to accommodate that. Standards of hygiene were deplorable too, mainly because there was no refrigeration in the shops. They used to bone their own ham: you got the side of the pig in, boned it, rolled it and just put it up. Those who were around in those days, if they think back, they can recall seeing a shelf in the grocer's shop window, with all the ham up there, with the price on it and usually quite a number of flies flying around too.

You could go into the local butchers or fishmongers or whatever and get something on the slate, especially in the Co-op. The Co-op were the pioneers of credit – a large number of customers got their groceries marked on the slate as it were, and came in on the Friday evening or Saturday morning, paid their weekly bill and then immediately, the groceries they ordered they got on credit. I suppose you could say they were always in your debt. When it came to paying out the dividends of course, that was a way of recouping back that debt, and I must say as a manager, I used to have some problems in trying to get people to understand that the week when we were taking stock and the dividend was being paid out, I couldn't give them tick or put it on the slate on that particular week, until the Wednesday. I must confess that I had to bend the rules a bit and continue to give them credit, otherwise they just couldn't afford to pay it because they were giving you the money they got in their wages to pay last week's groceries. I'd tell them to ease up a bit, just order a little 'till the Wednesday and then they could come in after we took stock on the Thursday and fill their larder again.

Working in the Co-op Shop

The Co-op were in these days reckoned to be the best employer in retailing. They had a pension scheme, which was something that most companies didn't have back fifty years ago, and their wages were higher than that of the competitors. The workers were all in the trade union. It was a closed shop in these days so if you worked in the Co-op, you were a member of USDAW. We had a national agreement with the Co-op and that meant that the employees thankfully had a better salary than they had elsewhere. The Co-op was reckoned to be more secure in these days, too – if you went into the Co-op, you'd a job for life, as some people used to say. In other places I suppose that was not the case.

Bank as you buy at the Co-op.

DIVIDEND left to your account in a Co-op. Society earns a good rate of interest and can be easily withdrawn at any time.

-and BANK on S·C·W·S goods for top quality and value

JOHN MILLER LTD., PRINTERS, GLASGOW

1950s Co-op ad

In the main, you had the branch manager, who was usually a male; you had the assistant manager who was a male, and the rest of the staff were female. There were very few women managers of shops – you now have women in charge of shops, and rightly so. The other thing was that you had your full-time staff, and you had a regular part-time staff who came in and worked Thursday, Friday and Saturday. That was regular. Nowadays, you have a store with about four hundred staff and about seventy per cent of those are part-timers or casual, some only working four hours a week. One of the big problems nowadays in managing a shop is matching the staff levels to the peaks and troughs of the business, but that can be done now by computerisation, so the whole job has changed dramatically.

Competition and the Co-op Movement

Fifty years ago, the Co-op paid a dividend and that dividend was valued, believe you me, by the customers who were the shareholders. They didn't have the same competition then as they have now. You had over two hundred Co-op societies in Scotland in these days and now you have seven independent societies. Just after the war, in the 1950s and the early '60s, there emerged the multiples, who competed and beat the Co-op in price. People were still expecting their dividend and also looking for the cut prices and it just couldn't be done. They then went for the cut price and the Co-op lost a lot of ground in that area.

The Co-op were the pioneers of many great innovations, but one of their problems was that they were overtaken by the competitors who did it even better. And of course Co-ops, because of their democratic set-up, didn't have the finance. Individual societies couldn't match the might of the multiple. They couldn't afford to spend, in these days maybe a quarter or half a million pounds on a new store. I'm talking about fifty years ago and that was quite a lot of money. So not only did the Co-op lose ground because of price, they lost ground because there were more modern and better equipped shops selling their products at a cut price, or a lesser price than the Co-op could sell it at. The Co-ops, because they were mainly small shops, couldn't compete.

Nowadays, the housewife shopping gets a better deal but there's a number of reasons for that. Shops are bigger and you now have large national companies such as the Tescos of this world with tremendous purchasing power. Of course, they can purchase huge volumes of products and sell them to the consumer at a reduced price and still make a handsome profit. It's better for the consumer, but I would say it's perhaps not better for the elderly and the people who are unemployed and the people who are on low wages and can't afford to have the convenience of a car to drive into the car park and fill up their trolley and put it in the car and drive home. People who are not in that fortunate position tend to shop at the convenience stores in the neighbourhood and the price for doing that is probably a higher price overall.

Margaret Macintosh
Teacher

Born 1936

I was born in Peebles in the Scottish Borders. My father was a shoemaker, a soutar, and for the first ten years of my life or so, he was a journeyman, he worked for someone else. In 1942, he and my mother bought a little shoe shop in Peebles and they had their own business but he still continued to repair shoes.

We always lived in our own house. My mother and father in that sense were quite unusual in those days. They had bought their own house when they were married, a small three-roomed, bottom flat of a block of four. Around about the time I went to university they bought a bigger, semi-detached house, still fairly modest, three-bedroomed house. There were five of us in the three-roomed house – I have an older brother and a younger brother. And my grandmother too, in the early days. My granny was in the wee room at the back. Three of us were in the bigger bedroom and my mother and father slept in the living room. Every night, right up through the time I sat Highers, they couldn't go to bed until we went to bed because they had to make down a bed settee. I remember my mother really getting quite cross with us, because we wouldn't go off to bed. We were young and fresh and frisky and still wanted to read and talk, but she couldn't get to her bed until we went out of the room. I now look back and I think, 'Oh, my poor mother,' because now I need to get to bed earlier.

My mother was fully involved in running the business. She did all the financial side of it and so she was often sitting doing the books, especially on a Saturday night while we would be reading or talking or whatever, all of us in one living room, which I think was quite big but memory plays tricks. She'd also have to do all the washing and the cleaning. I was helping in the house, but certainly without any of the modern conveniences. We had no fridge, no washing machine. We did have hot water but it was heated by a fire – there was no immersion heater – so first thing in the morning, the fire had to be lit. But there were certainly people that I knew who didn't have hot water so I think we felt quite privileged in a way. It was always very cosy too, with this roaring fire.

Modern Scots expect a bed, and a room, of their own – unless they choose otherwise. In 1901, the average density was 1.52 persons per room – and thus far higher for many. By 1991, the vast majority enjoyed densities of 0.5 persons or less per room. Homes have got bigger – and families smaller. At the start of the century, the fertility rate among women aged 15–44 was 120.6 per 1000; now, it is under 60 per 1000.

The War

I was three when war broke out and in Peebles, which is a little country town, we were pretty sheltered from any of the dangers of war. I remember rationing but it didn't affect us much, possibly because we'd a shop and had lots of farming customers. We sometimes had fresh salmon that had been caught in the river. Eggs were rationed, but we got eggs from country customers: there was a way of preserving eggs in a liquid called isinglass.

The eggs were carefully put in this isinglass and they seemed to be able to be kept for several months. We had this biggish container that held about four dozen eggs, and my mother carefully put the eggs into this liquid. The container sat on the top of a rather flimsy wardrobe in the little bedroom that my granny had been in – my granny had died by that time. In those days before Christmas and Easter the whole school went to a church service, at the end of term. We went by crocodile down to the local church. It was quite a big occasion for children and you wore your best coat. I must have been quite young, maybe about eight: we were going to go to church after lunch and I was desperate to get my coat because that was just so important. I went through to the bedroom to get it and the wardrobe door stuck and jammed. I jiggled it a bit and pulled the wardrobe over and pulled four dozen eggs in isinglass on top of me and on top of the bed. Of course, all the eggs broke. It was a terrible disaster, my mother's reaction was certainly that it was a terrible disaster. That's my chief memory of wartime, this business about the eggs and how important these fresh eggs were.

Growing Up in Peebles

We played in the garden and out in the street. We played peevers on the street very regularly, and played up and down the road and in other people's gardens. We had a swing in the garden. I'm not sure that there were any children's games that people don't play now. I don't remember the boys playing peevers – it must have been a girls' game. There was a local park that we always played in in the summer. My mother would come with us on a Saturday afternoon which was perhaps the only time that she were free to go, but from the age of about seven, we would go on our own.

There was very little traffic. I don't think any of my friends in primary school came from homes where there was a car. We certainly never had a car. There were bicycles certainly and horses – the baker's van was pulled by a horse. It was quite the done thing to go out and shovel up the manure for the garden from the street once the baker's van had passed.

MID-DAY, MID-TOWN
PEEBLES, *1953*

I think there was a strange age of innocence up to the end of the '50s. It certainly wasn't something you were aware of then. I often smile because some of the things my parents said seem to imply that it was anything other than an age of innocence and that times were changing terribly from the time that they'd grown up but looking back from this perspective, I think it was an age of innocence. For example, when I was going to secondary school, maybe about fifth year, there was a big scandal about someone called Lord Montagu of Beaulieu. This Lord Montagu was alleged to have been 'interfering with boy scouts', as the phrase goes. It was the talk of the place. Now I must have been sixteen, I had never heard of homosexuality, and I can picture myself yet going up and down with friends to Peebles High School, which was quite a long way to walk from my home, and we'd just talk about nothing else and, of course, we were greatly intrigued about what might have been going on. I think we were also greatly intrigued by the exotic nature of the pronunciation of his name – we were informed it was pronounced 'Bewly' so I don't know whether I was more absorbed by the intricate things this man had been doing or by his name.

My parents were quite strict and very keen for us to do as well as we could. I didn't go out Monday to Thursday evenings. We did our homework, we read and we stayed in. I felt at the time that I was under a lot of constraints, that my parents were too strict and it seemed to me that my friends had more freedom than I had. Friday nights we went to the Guides and then we strolled the streets looking for the talent, just as they always did. In Peebles in those days there were two cinemas – this was in a town of six thousand people – and Saturday night was the night for the pictures. There was always a queue at the cinema, right along the main street and then down the other street where the smaller cinema was. We didn't really choose the cinema for the film. We would walk along the queue and check out who was in the queue and decide on the cinema we'd go to depending on where the talent was going. It was very much a Saturday night practice. By the time I got to about sixteen, I felt I got a little bit more freedom. After the pictures you went to the cafe – we'd very limited pocket money, but there were two cafes as well where you gathered. Again you did a bit of glimpsing in the window to see who was there. I always had to be home at half past ten, on a Saturday night certainly until after I sat my Highers, and I resented it. That was a cause of big problems in my house because I think my friends got out later than that. But I remember thinking it was pretty good being a teenager. I think the word 'teenager' was around just about in the '50s. 'Bobby Soxer' was also a word we used. I was very conscious of it and enjoyed it really, being a teenager.

My parents were Presbyterian, and very religious. I came from a happy religious home, but we went to church every Sunday, Sunday School every Sunday. There were Roman Catholics in Peebles: with hindsight, I think there was quite a lot of discrimination and anti-Catholic feeling that never came out in any particular way. There was a Catholic primary school, all the children went to secondary school together, but there was an anti-Catholic feeling around in the circles in which I moved. Catholicism was associated with poverty, to some extent, but poverty brought on themselves, careless living and having too many children. There was really a lot of nasty stuff around and now I look back and think, goodness, but it just wasn't questioned then.

Radio Days

The radio was a very important part of your life. It was a big set that often crackled. You didn't get very good reception, but we always had the news on in our house and often light music – a particular feature was Saturday night. Saturday night was a really good night in our family. It was usually a very busy day at the shop and mum and dad would come home about six. The radio went on and we got the news and there was always football, sports results, and then you went into a programme of Scottish dance music. We knew all the bands, and Jimmy Shand was as popular then as he is now. We would dance around the room with the Scottish dance music. There was something called the Scottish Variety Orchestra which sometimes played Scottish dance music – we didn't like that at all. We didn't like them playing it.

Following the Scottish dance music, was a programme called *The MacFlannels*. It was a radio soap about the MacFlannels, who were a kind of working-class Glasgow family. Other families came into this soap and their names were all materials like the MacSatins and the MacTweeds and the MacCottons and so on, and their pecking order in the social status was indicated by the material. So MacFlannels were ordinary working folk but the MacCottons were a shade above that, they had kind of Kelvinside accents. We wouldn't miss it for anything and we got to know all the characters in the programme; we felt they were quite close friends. It was a kind of radio version of The Broons, actually: the goings-on between the neighbours and the kind of come-uppances and people trying to be better than the other. The daughter of the household was called Maisie MacFlannel, and she obviously wanted to be going up in the world. There was a grandfather in the family who lived with them who was a bit rough and coarse. He had an allotment and talked about spreading the dung on the allotment, and Maisie said, 'It wasn't dung, grandfather, it was manure,' and her mother said: 'Oh Maisie, if you only knew how long it took me to get him to say "dung".' That was considered very naughty, you know.

School and University

I went to the local primary school and high school, which was the comprehensive high school for the whole of Peeblesshire. 1948 was my first year in secondary school. Everybody went to secondary school, but you sat a qualifying test to be placed at a level, whichever class you went in. The classes in secondary school were A, B and C. A was certainly the double language, Latin and French, no choice. B was French only, and C was no languages. There was a very clear division so although it was a comprehensive school in the sense that all the children went there it certainly wasn't comprehensive in its structure within the school.

I think I was regarded as not the type to go to university, I was a bit of an harum scarum. I was always regarded as quite bright, but I'd an older brother who was bright and hard-working, a studious boy, and there was always an assumption that he would go to university. He did Latin and Greek in school and he always sat over his books. I had two close sets of cousins: each of my mother's sisters had a boy and a girl. The girls had not gone to university, it was sort of seen as a boys' thing. I thought in terms of my going into the civil service or the bank, something of that nature. In my fifth year, my first bash at the Highers, I got three Highers and two Lowers as they were called in those days, and I was slightly too young to enter the civil service. You have to be seventeen and a half and I was seventeen.

The rector pointed out to me that to go into the civil service I would have to wait and do a sixth year at school. Bright girls left at the end of fifth year and got a nice job, but I would have to stay on for a sixth year. I thought, what was I going to do in the sixth year? I might as well take another couple of Highers. Then I thought if I take another couple of Highers I might as well go to university. I thought, what temerity to think that I might go to university, so I went to see the Rector and he said, 'Yes, why don't you? There's nothing to stop you.' I then broached it with my parents and my father said, 'Certainly you can go, you're just as bright as your brother.' It was the first time I realised that I actually was university material. It had never occurred to me.

Going to university didn't present a financial problem. There were grants available by that time but my father was very reluctant to apply for a grant. It was something to do with pride. I think my mother persuaded him that there was nothing wrong with this and I remember – I think it was the beginning of my socialist ideas – being insistent that that was a perfectly acceptable thing to do. By that time, we had a shoe shop and it prospered during the war and after the war; it was actually quite a good time. I was never made to understand that it was to any cost, or sacrifice rather.

I went to Edinburgh University. I don't think I was shy but I felt terribly ill-informed. I didn't know what to do. I didn't know my way around. I'd an aunt in Edinburgh and you'd occasionally come in to see her and the odd time to a theatre sometimes, but I wasn't familiar with the city. My brother was there two years ahead of me but we weren't really close. We were on good terms with one another but we weren't like each other and I didn't seek out his advice. I felt very ill-prepared for the amount of study you had to do in your own time. I'd been so used to being spoon-fed at school. I remember thinking that the children who came from the Edinburgh schools seemed to have an advantage. At that stage, I wouldn't have been able to put into words what that advantage was but they seemed more sophisticated, more articulate and I felt a bit tongue-tied, particularly in tutorials.

A Career in Education

About halfway through my degree, I thought of going into teaching. There were two things I'd have liked to have done, journalism and social work. Again it's a symptom of my lack of sophistication but I had no idea how to get into journalism. Now I think, what an idiot, why on earth wasn't I a bit more forward. But that deterred me: I simply didn't know the route in. On social work, I was quite attracted to that and I began to take one or two steps to see if that was what I wanted to do. But I met a lad in university who I was very close to and we had a very serious relationship, a chaste but serious relationship, and I'd been thinking of getting married. In the '50s that was what girls did: it was the 'back to the fireside' movement that happened after the war. It was part of the programme – you got a job and you worked maybe three, four years, you got married and then you had your family and you stayed at home. I seem not to have had the vision to have seen beyond that; I now can't believe I was that innocent. Because I'd met someone and that was the beginning of the plan, teaching seemed like a good alternative, a good job for combining with a family, if one wanted to be working and being with a family. So that's what it came down to in the end.

I started off teaching back in my home town of Peebles. Then, when we got married, I went to Inverness and I taught in Inverness for a while. Then I taught in Portree for a while and then moved to Oban, all country towns. Then back to Edinburgh and I taught for quite a long time in Edinburgh. Once I started, I was very committed to the idea of teaching. In a sense, I think social work and teaching aren't that separate. Maybe now I regret that I didn't at any time consider moving because there's nothing wrong with perhaps being a teacher for ten years and then moving on. It's a funny thing about teaching – it kind of traps you in some sort of way. But I enjoyed my work. It was very hard work; I don't remember teaching ever not being hard. A lot of hours were spent at home, preparing your work.

I always saw education as a liberating thing for children. I was fairly radical in my views – I was of the view that education wasn't good enough if what it did for children was to make them conform. I've always believed that it shouldn't – that it should have done the very opposite, it should have made them rebel and give them freedom and liberation. That's always been a kind of motivating factor.

There was very little truancy, in my memory. Discipline was never particularly easy: it certainly is never easy in your first two years unless you have a very natural authority, and most young people haven't. Discipline was always an issue. But a huge change has taken place in society. When I was going to school and when I started to teach in 1958, there was still an assumption in society that the school, on the whole, was right, and parents very seldom contacted the school. It was still pretty traditional in what it was expected to do for children and in what was expected of children in terms of behaviour. The 1960s saw an enormous change, the '60s and '70s; there have been huge upheavals in society, it seems to me, and I don't think education has kept pace with those changes. I think they've done a lot in recent years to catch up but they've still not really caught up. Teaching's never been an easy job, but the kind of problems we faced in the '50s when I first went there, were very different from the problems that you face now – quite dramatically different. Now I think it is mostly social problems. The home and the school are not in the close alliance that I think they were in in the '50s.

PEEBLES: THE TRAINS
STOPPED RUNNING IN 1963

Part of that might be a loss of deference, but I don't think I would put it down to that largely. I think it really is the stresses that children and families are living in, in their home circumstances and the pressures on them from society. The expectations and the images that they pick up largely from television, that life beyond school and outside school is exciting and romantic. Children don't seem to be able to make the connection between what they do in school and what might happen to them later on. For many children, school is just something that they have to get through in order to get to that wonderful life out there. I've never myself been able to crack that, I don't know how you crack it.

Looking back, people are much better off now. There are still pockets of desperate poverty, we must not forget that, but more people are better off, more people have a much higher standard of living now. There's more freedom of expression – children are not frightened of teachers and that's a good thing. I think children's experiences of schools are much happier and they're able to be more creative than they were. But there's a loss of innocence. It's quite sad that children lose their innocence, at an early age. I'm not just talking about sexual innocence but all sorts of innocence; I think childhood has almost vanished. A lot of children just don't seem to have a childhood. They become teenagers at the age of eight and parents are largely at fault for that. I think it affects little girls more than little boys. I'm quite sorry when I see parents dressing little girls in adult clothing, putting wee girls of eight into bras and the whole doll thing, like Barbie dolls. It's very sad.

David Diduca
Jute-mill Worker

Born 1936

I was born and brought up in Dundee, in Charles Street, one of the streets off the Wellgate which is all gone now. The Wellgate Centre is actually standing in that area. I stayed there with my parents until I was married in 1960.

We were toffs. Most houses had outside toilets and their sink and bunker, if you like, was actually in the living room, or in a corner of the living room next to the window. We had one bedroom, a living room-cum-bedroom, an inside toilet, and what they'd normally term a scullery, which was a sink and a cooker and this type of thing. Mother, father, two boys and a girl lived there. By today's standards, it was overcrowded, but I didn't think that then. We just took it for granted because that's the way people were in these days.

My grandfather was Italian. The name's actually been changed. It's spelt now Diduca. In the early days it was Di Duca. My sister and I've been trying to find out when he came over. We know he originated from Itina in Italy; we're not very sure when he arrived but it was before the Second World War. My father was born in Dundee but we believe his older brother was born in Italy. My grandfather died before I was born, or could remember him although I can remember my grandmother, who spoke very broken English. My father was a Dundonian, if you like, who believed that he was a Scot rather than an Italian so I don't even speak Italian.

We were quite keen to go out and play. We didn't need to be thrown out in these days. The countryside wasn't that far away; it was probably forty minutes' walk because the outskirts of Dundee weren't so widespread in these days. Even if you jumped on a tram car, you just run to the terminus and then minutes from there, you were in the countryside, so it was much easier to get there than it is today, unless you have a car of course. But things weren't always as happy as these days because my mother died when I was twelve years old and I was the oldest. Then it wasn't the case of coming home from school and running out, it was the case of all muck in and clean up, get things ready for the tea and this sort of thing.

When we were older, you'd go to the dancing: the Palais de Dance which was in Tay Street and Kidd's Rooms and special evenings. You went to a little dance hall called Robey's which was up the Overgate type thing. It was interesting and enjoyable. We went to the dancing for the music as well to meet girls – I enjoyed both.

I went to school at Cowgate and then Stobswell. At school-leaving, it was a different outlook then from what it is now. In those days you were looking for an apprenticeship of some sort. In my own particular instance, it was joinery, but that never materialised. I became a mill mechanic and I worked with Jute Industries as it was called at that time. It later changed its name to Sidlaw Textiles. I started in 1952 as a ludge boy and in October of that same year, I became a first-year apprentice as a mill mechanic. I eventually worked my way up to become engineering foreman in Tay Works, in Lochy Road.

In 1924, the Dundee jute industry employed 41,220; in 1945, 20,000; in 1974, 9400; in 1991, 1806; in 1995, 400. And in late 1998, what was declared to be the last-ever shipment of raw jute docked there.

I started when I was fifteen years old and I thought there would be work in the mills for the rest of my life. During my final years at Sidlaw Industries, I was offered a job with the oilfields and decided I enjoyed the job I was doing and decided to stay. I was there for a further six years. Tay Works actually closed down in 1981, although I was made redundant in December of 1980 and I was three months looking for work. It's actually full-time employment looking for work. Eventually I found a job in Arbroath with Haliburtons Engineering, manufacturers of oil machinery.

I met my wife at Bow Bridge and we got married in 1960. She was a weaver and I was an apprentice weaving mechanic at that time. It was very noisy at the mill, but the apprentice would normally do a bit of work and a bit of dodging. You always managed to end up somewhere that you wanted to be, standing next to the loom, looking as if it had been broken, or as if you were interested in the loom and talking to the weaver. It wasn't so difficult when you were standing side-by-side, rather than two looms away like the other weavers were.

You accepted the noise, the dust. They didn't give you any hearing aids or hearing muffles for the noise or anything like that, but everybody done that. It was totally acceptable in these days. Totally wrong, probably, but totally acceptable. I am actually bothered with my hearing to a slight extent. I have difficulty in a large room where there is some background noise, and you don't hear people talking that maybe you should do. You don't catch all the words.

I was a shop steward for a small period: in Sidlaw or Jute Industries days, everybody was involved one way or another with the unions. I think it was probably a good thing, looking at the way today's bits and pieces are going in industry. It's probably time for them to come back, but not so left wingish, if you like.

An awful lot of people were thrown out of the mills over the period between 1950 and 1980. I was extremely lucky only to be idle for three months. I was again made redundant in '85, after five years with Haliburtons, because the oil industry started to go down. Then I got a job with the Scottish Crop Research Institute and I was there for five years and then went back to Haliburtons for a further three years. My current job in the Jute Museum came up and I was extremely interested in what they were doing. I also believed that Dundee people deserved something like a textile museum because it was part of their history and I wanted to be involved in that.

I probably disagree with the way the town has actually developed in as much as I believe they knocked too much down. If they applied themselves to doing buildings up rather than knocking them down to make way for new buildings, the older environment, such as the Overgate and the Wellgate, would have been a tremendous attraction to incoming visitors. As far as I'm concerned I think it's a shame and a mistake.

John & Peter Douglas
Cinema Projectionists

Born 1937

We were born in Glasgow, in Hyndland. Our father worked for a tobacco company in Glasgow and our mother was a housewife. She didn't work at all... once she got twins, she had no choice. Actually, it was a terrible shock for our parents when we arrived. The main reason was that in those days nobody knew if they were getting twins or not, and I gather they had to rush out and buy one of every other thing that they had already bought for one baby. We don't have any brothers or sisters – it was such a shock when we were born, the two of us, that they thought they were never going to do it again.

We lived on the top floor of a tenement and it was quite a lot of work for our mother if she wanted to take us out – getting the pram down the stairs first, a big twin pram, and then bringing one of us down and putting it in the pram and getting the other one. This meant going up and down the three flights of stairs every time – so a lot of hard work in those days.

The flat was a two room and kitchen – they were pretty good for that era actually, but still, looking at them today, it's a completely different way of living. They've all been modernised, but in those days it was the old range and the old kitchen, which also served as a bedroom, with a sort of bed recess for a double bed. And, of course, you had the other main bedroom and a sitting room and the hall and the bathroom. This is where we were lucky compared to a lot of people. A very long and narrow bathroom, with a huge bath. You don't see baths as large as that these days.

In the kitchen, you had a bunker – it was a wooden structure which looked as if it was made out of floorboards, and was painted. At least once a week or a fortnight, the coalman used to come with his horse and cart and lift the hundred-weight sacks onto his back and climb all those stairs, then come into the kitchen and dump this sack of coal into the bunker, which took two, three hundredweight. A housewife's job in those days really must have been terrible because whenever the coalman came the whole place was covered with dust. She had to clean the kitchen every time the coal was delivered. She also had to

NOT ALL GLASGOW TENEMENTS WERE SLUMS: A SCENE FROM THE CITY'S PROSPEROUS WEST END IN THE 1920S. NOTE THE MOTOR TRAFFIC, AND THE SEEMINGLY OBLIVIOUS PEDESTRIANS

Anniesland Mansions, Anniesland, Glasgow

clean the common stair. It worked on a rota basis. The stairwashing day was twice a week, and quite often the more affluent managed to get a lady to come in and do the stairs for them. Of course, the higher up you lived in the tenement, the less wear and tear there was on the stairs and therefore not quite so much dirt because not so many people travelled up to the very top.

War Days

We were two and a half when the war broke out. That brought big changes. Our father was called up – he was in the Royal Naval Volunteer Reserve – and was away quite a lot during the war. When he was based down near Portsmouth, at Lee on Solent, we moved down there. They expected an invasion at any time from the Channel Islands, which the Germans had occupied. When we were down there in about 1942 or 1943, there were tanks and live ammunition all along the front. That really was a war-ready community. We lived there quite happily as children; of course we didn't realise in those days the gravity of it all, but we survived the war.

Even though we were so young at the time I still have recollections of the enemy aircraft going overhead every night. We spent most nights down in an air-raid shelter in the back garden, an Anderson Shelter. It was sunk into the back garden. We always thought we were doing very well because my mum and dad, to give them a bit of false spirit during that time, would have a little whisky now and again. We at our age of about five would think that we were having a whisky as well, but all our father did was to pour out the whisky bottle into a glass with his finger over the top of it. Which meant of course we thought we were getting whisky when we were drinking lemonade. But we loved our whisky.

What persuaded us eventually to come up to Glasgow for good was when the flying bombs started. My mother felt that she couldn't cope with that, so that was the decision to come up north, while my father was still serving in the Navy. In Glasgow, we moved just up the road a little bit to 113 Novar Drive and that was another two room and kitchen, rather similar, but at least it was only one floor up this time.

When we first went to school it was in Lee on Solent, in a little wee country school for about the first six months of our schooling, before we came back up to Glasgow. Then we were lucky enough to go to Hyndland School – all our school life, really, from Hyndland Junior to the Hyndland Senior Secondary School in Clarence Drive – that was really our main basis and a very good educational grounding it was too; in those days, it was a very good school.

After the war, our father came back and rejoined W.D. & H.O. Wills, the cigarette firm. He worked with them when he left school in Bristol and he rejoined them after the war again and was based in Glasgow 'till he retired. We lived all our lives with our parents 'till they died. Round about 1965, when our dad was about due to retire, we decided to move from Glasgow to Dumbarton, and that is where we live now. Dumbarton was really only chosen because it had a good public transport system – this comes from not being able to drive. Of course, us working these very odd hours, we had to have an easy way to get into the centre of Glasgow and also back home at night from the centre – that's why we moved to Dumbarton.

Growing Up in Hyndland

In Hyndland, we played in the streets... no cars in those days, of course. If you go down the road where we lived now it's just a solid line of cars, residents there can't even find enough place to park their cars. But in those days, there were very few cars about and, in fact, the whole of the street actually was air-raid shelters, brick shelters all down on one side of Novar Drive. It was completely different and we used to play all round the streets and down the back greens, the back courts as they were called, Kick-The-Can and things like that. Cowboys and Indians was another great favourite, another taboo game these days, of course. There was a bit of Tommys and Germans as well.

Our parents were quite happy to let us go in our own direction. They didn't have any great plans for us, no preconceived notions as to what we should do. Both John and I have very bad eyesight. We've had that ever since childhood: we were semi-albino when we were born and we used to, when we were toddlers, even walk into lamp-posts and things outside. So we've always had bad eyesight and this gave us a slight problem as to what we should do.

We got teased a little bit at school – that's normal with kids, with anybody who's slightly different for any reason. We had the twins syndrome first, of course, which was in some ways an advantage because everyone knew us. We used to get fed up in the playground with kids coming up and saying, 'Switch around and let's try and tell which one's which,' and all this. We used to get really fed up and bored with all that. But yes, there was a little bit of bullying because some of them did spot we'd poorish eyesight. But that's just part of life, of growing up; you learn to accept it and get over all these things. Like the bad eyesight itself, it's never really stopped us from really doing most of the things we'd ever want to do. The only thing in life that really we've not been able to do because of the eyesight is drive. But there again, we don't really miss that because we've never had it to miss.

Our mother did dress us identically as children; it was the done thing in those days. That's where the difference is today. We've always been told that we seem to be just one personality instead of two personalities, that we've lost something through that. But we haven't really lost anything because we've never known any different. We usually wear the same type of thing but in slightly different colours, just to stop people from getting too confused.

The Beginning of an Obsession

We'd never been to the movies, but we listened to the radio. We used to listen to Auntie Kathleen and the *Children's Hour* and *Dick Barton, Special Agent*. We actually had tears in our eyes when Dick Barton finished after many years. Then, in 1949, when we were twelve, the little girl who stayed downstairs from us said one day out of the blue, 'Would your mum and dad let you go to the pictures?' This was to the Saturday morning children's show at the Ascot at Anniesland – the building is still there beside Anniesland Station in Great Western Road. We said, 'What actually is this all about?', and she said, 'Well, you see films and other things – I think you would like it.' So we asked our mum and dad and they said yes, so off we went with Janette on the Saturday morning. That was our first introduction really to the cinema.

We went in and the first thing they had was community singing. There was an 'Uncle' on the stage, who turned out to be the cinema manager, and an 'Aunt' who played the piano, and they used to put slides on the screen and you used to sing all these songs. They were songs that would be well known round about the wartime or just after the war. From that you went on and saw a cartoon film, and then after that the Uncle would come back on the stage and invite children up to do their party piece. Most children went up and sang the songs they learned at school, or recited the poems they learned at school – which was very boring to a lot of the other kids. A lot of the other kids didn't really like all this at all. We decided that we wanted a bit of this fame – it was the microphones actually that we fancied the idea of. We would corner the market by singing the pop songs of the day. That's what we did, we went up and became quite popular, and we found ourselves being on the stage nearly every Saturday morning.

After the little stage shows, they then ran a serial which was Cowboys and Indians or other types. We'd have an episode each week of some film or other and then that would then go onto the Feature show which would be something like Roy Rogers or Gene Autry. It was great days at the children's cinema club. There was the old song that you used to sing every Saturday morning, of course, which was the cinema club song – the ABC Minors went to the ABC, that would be the Grosvenor in Byres Road in those days. The one we had was the Gaumont-British Circuit and we used to have this one:

We come along on Saturday morning
Greeting everybody with a smile
We come along on Saturday morning
Knowing it's well worthwhile
As members of the GB Club we all intend to be
Good citizens when we grow up and champions of the free
We come along on Saturday morning
Greeting everybody with a smile – smile – smile

With going on stage on Saturday mornings, we got to know the cinema manager, and eventually started going to some of the shows after school. In those days, it was continuous performances – it seems very strange in these days of separate performances that you could walk into the middle of a feature film, sit all the way through and come out in the middle of that same film again. But we went after school to the four-thirty performance, watched the film, and by the time it came about seven-thirty or eight o'clock, the manager was standing in the foyer in his full evening dress, bow tie and everything. We stood and talked to him and thought, 'This is going to be the job for us' – standing there in this evening suit, that was what we wanted to do.

A Career Choice When we got to the age of sixteen, our father said, 'Right, I've got to know if you want to leave school now or you want to carry on in education' – probably through income tax or allowances or something. We said we'd like to get a job as a cinema manager. So we went along to the Head Office of the Gaumont Cinemas in Glasgow and talked to a regional engineer there. He told us that you could not go on to a managerial course until you were twenty-one. But he said, 'If you like to serve your apprenticeship as a cinema projectionist, by the time you've finished your apprenticeship you've got all of that behind you to go on to the managerial side.' So at sixteen we left school and started a five-year apprenticeship as a cinema projectionist – yes, it was a trade in Scotland. We became members of the National

Glaswegians were among the biggest film-fans in Britain. The first purpose-built cinema, the Electric, opened there in 1910, and by 1929, and the coming of the talkies, there were 127. In 1950, on the eve of the TV revolution, the average Glaswegian was going to the pictures 51 times a year (the English average was 28).

Association of Theatre and Kinematographic Employees – NATKE, the trade union; Tom O'Brien was General Secretary.

Having completed the apprenticeship, we stayed as projectionists. We discovered what a really bad job the managers had and what a reasonably good job the technical staff had and we preferred to stay in the technical side. In those days you weren't on your own in the projection booth. The cinema which I [John]went to work in first was the Capitol Cinema in Ibrox. That cinema had five of a projection staff – three were on one shift and two on other shift, so you always had somebody to talk to. It was a nice wee cushy sort of job, not too difficult. Unusual hours of course; we had to do unsocial hours but we were quite willing to do that. All our days working in the same business, we always worked unsocial hours – if we had had every night off in the week, we wouldn't really know what to have done with it. We weren't particularly interested in dancing or going to the theatre. We were part of the entertainment industry. When you look back to it, in the early '50s, that industry was a really wonderful thing. Every night of the week you would have a queue around the cinema waiting to get in for the nine o'clock show.

There were the films you liked and the films you certainly disliked – at the suburban cinemas such as in Ibrox, the show changed twice a week. You had Monday, Tuesday, Wednesday then Thursday, Friday, Saturday. No opening on Sunday in those days at all. So we had plenty of different films coming in and also of course, a Saturday morning matinee for the children.

When we first started they said, 'No way will we have you two in one cinema working together'. It wasn't company policy that relatives – especially close relatives such as twins – worked in the same building, if they had other places. And therefore when we first started, I was in the New Savoy in Hope Street and Peter was in the Gaumont, Ibrox – the Capitol, Ibrox, as it was in those days. We moved about though, when our apprenticeship finished, I eventually ended up in the Odeon in Renfield Street. About a year after that, Peter went to the Gaumont in Sauchiehall Street and so we were both promoted to what was called 'city-centre cinemas' – that was a sort of promotion you had at that time, to get into the centre of the city.

AT THE OUTSET OF A CAREER IN THE MOVIES: PETER (LEFT) AND JOHN AT THE PROJECTOR, 1953

The Cinema: a Glasgow Institution

In those days, the city-centre cinemas got the first release as it was called, and then, as the weeks went by, these pictures would begin to appear in the outskirts cinemas such as the Anniesland one, or Ibrox, or wherever, and that's the system they used to work on. It's only in recent years that they've started this mass-release business, where you can look at the newspapers and almost every cinema is showing the same film.

The taste of the public was different in different parts of the city. Something which would go well at the Ibrox cinema would not necessarily go down at all well at Anniesland, and it's just a completely different clientele. At Ibrox, they might like westerns, but hate musicals, whereas in the centre of the city it might be the opposite way round. It's very difficult to tell just what films would actually be good-running films. Quite often a film which has been a bit of a flop in the rest of Britain can turn out to be quite a good money-maker in Glasgow for some reason or other. I don't know why that should be, but it sometimes happens.

Comedy films such as *Genevieve* and some of the early *Carry On* ones, and the Ealing comedies – things like that were all very good products and well made, but there was an awful lot of rubbish from British film studios in those days, compared to the American films of the day. The not-so-good Ealing comedies like *The Titchfield Thunderbolt*, which were very sort of southern English, they didn't do very well at all. Audiences came to see them on the back of publicity from England because there wasn't much else to see but they came out bitterly complaining that they hadn't liked it. It's only in recent years again that the British industry has really begun to make a quality product.

There was somewhat of a captive market in those days, because there wasn't very much other entertainment – there were the music halls and radio, but that was basically it. That's why the cinema in those days was so popular. It was a habit too – people went along regularly, every Monday and every Thursday, or at a weekend if they wanted to winch in the back balcony. There was a lot of that and the projectionist had the best view of that.

Some cinemas had special seating for the lovers, of course, as well. The La Scala had the settees and Green's Playhouse had the couchettes. And who knows what was going on there... mind you, they were pretty open, you couldn't really get up to much. The back row was the best place, because that's the darkest bit usually. Of course, the usherettes were under instruction, if they thought something a little too advanced was going on, to shine their torch. You couldn't have any hanky panky or anything untoward happening – the customers might complain.

Showmanship was a very important thing in those days: the closing and opening of curtains at the appropriate points and the right kind of lighting, the colour of footlights, and the right type of music – everything was extremely important. Today, in a lot of places, it's on with the film and that's it. Even the front-of-house staff were all in uniforms with epaulettes, and we'd run out and open your car door for you if you were rich enough to come by car to the cinema.

Certainly, all that you see being eaten in cinemas nowadays would never have been eaten in those days. The range of stuff that was available at the old kiosk in the cinema consisted of bags of sweets and some Kia-Ora sort of drink in waxed-cardboard containers with a straw. Those who really were wanting to do it a bit posh might buy some chocolate mints from the kiosk. At the interval of the film, the

sales girl would go trooping down to the front and stand with this lit tray filled with little tubs of rather watery ice cream. The spotlight would hit her as a sales trailer went on, advertising the ice cream and the drinks. We had to operate the follow spot.

In the early days the projection room was filled with things like slide lanterns and the projectors of course, and the spotlight for the sales girl. All very important in those days. In theory, the projection room was supposed to be soundproof, but usually if you had any sort of breakdown the audience reaction would be whistling, and possibly stamping of feet as well, and no soundproof projection room would be away from that noise. We used to hear it as we were trying desperately to get the thing back on the screen again, which usually meant just actually re-lacing the film through the projector and starting the thing up again. Actually, a breakdown in those days was much, much easier to handle than a breakdown these days with all the new automation that they have in cinemas now. It's very rare these days but if there is a breakdown, it's much more difficult to sort out in a short time. In those days you could usually get the film running – if you were a decent projectionist at all – in about thirty to forty seconds. But that still seems like an eternity to somebody sitting in the audience.

If an audience didn't like a movie, they used to get up and go out. It still happens today. It was an odd occasion if somebody really felt riled about something or other – maybe they thought they weren't getting value for their money. In those days, knives used to be quite well known, but they used to rip things like the seats and things, or go into the toilets and do damage in there. But generally speaking, you wouldn't get people throwing things at the screen, not like the live entertainment shows in Glasgow. Particularly at the Empire, if they didn't like a show they'd throw pennies, or in one place supposedly they didn't like some nude show so they threw their ice creams.

If they did throw things at the screen, it's probably because they just wanted to get up to some mischief. Children in the front – and this is quite popular even now – they throw bits of popcorn at the screen and of course it sticks to the screen. In those days we used to paint the screen. The projectionists didn't do it, but they used to bring in firms who sprayed the screen and they could only spray it for so long because all of the little holes in the screen. Of course, the cinema screen was full of holes, partly to let the sound through from the speakers behind the screen. But these holes would get blocked up in the days when they used to spray screens, and then the cinema owners would have to pay out money to actually change the screen. A screen these days is very much more a high-tech piece of equipment and actually lasts much longer, but costs much much more.

The Advance of Television

The Americans knew long, long before we did that there were going to be problems with television – they tried all sorts of things like bringing out new screen ratios, Cinemascope and things that they would hope would manage to defeat the television. It never did, of course, and when television came to Britain, it had the same effect as it had in the United States. People began to find that entertainment in the front room much easier than having to go out to what might have not been the best and most comfortable cinema in the world. In fact, some of them were pretty poor in quality for seating, and even the sound and picture in some cinemas wasn't all that you might expect it to be – rather scratched and noisy. The cinema then had to look to its laurels because it did lose business.

The smaller cinemas on the outskirts of towns began to find that their business was going down so much that they had to do something about it. In a lot of cases, they jumped on the bandwagon of a thing that was beginning to become popular in the late '50s early '60s: bingo. In a lot of these places, it was so easy just to stop showing films and start playing bingo, and that's what happened.

One particular cinema in Glasgow that was affected in the pretty early days by the downturn was the Paragon in the Gorbals. It was owned by our company and the only experience that we ever had of it was going out on relief, because they were always short of staff. But the Paragon consisted of benches instead of seats, with gas lighting around the walls – and this was in the '50s and '60s. It had no set seating capacity, because it depended on how big the audience were, bodily. They used to put them on these benches and when one fell off the end, that was that row filled. So they hoped for a lot of thin people. It was an old converted wooden church – a terrible place, it was. But that was one that was affected very early by the downturn.

Life After the Silver Screen

We worked forty-four years in the cinema and we felt that after all of that time that we had had enough of it. We did enjoy our job but there were other things that we wanted to do. Our main interests are our local drama group, our local church, hospital radio. We wanted to go abroad and see people who we hadn't managed to go and see, because when we were both working. We both ended up in the same cinema. In fact we are the only people that were joint chief technicians in one cinema – it was the only place in Britain where they did that – because we were twins and they really wanted the cover in that particular cinema. It worked out, but that meant that we couldn't go on holiday together; one always had to be there on the job.

We've always been twins that have stayed together. Apparently, they did a study on twins many, many years ago and the conclusion they came to, that whenever identical twins are born, there's some predetermined cause that either makes their life go in a 'V' shape – in other words, they diverge from each other and each go their own separate ways – or there are identical twins who stay a parallel course, and it seems to be through fate rather than trying to change things. We seem to be the ones that have stayed on the parallel track all our lives with the same interests. Mind you, it has its advantages for hobbies: if we both have a hobby which might include buying a new CD player, for instance, it only costs us half price. The only difference between us, for some reason or other, that I can't eat eggs. I've never been able to eat an egg and that is the only difference between Peter and myself.

In the drama group, we want to be backroom people: we do the sound and effects and things, rather than tread on the boards – we're not so much keen on doing that. We like to be in the background, as with the cinema business where the projectionists are always in the background. They have to be there – if they weren't there the cinema would stop. They can do without managers and usherettes, but a cinema must have a projectionist, and so we've always been there in the background and felt an important part of the production. But always there in the background, never really to be seen.

Sandy McDonald
Church of Scotland Clergyman

Born 1937

I was born in Bishopbriggs in Lanarkshire. My wife always tells me I was brought up in a posh house: it was a three-apartment semi-detached house in Bishopbriggs with an inside bathroom, which was big-time! Compared to my wife's circumstances, it seemed very grand that we actually had a bath. That is, I had a bath if I shared the water with my brother. We had a Saphona fire, eventually – to get hot water in the morning was a treat beyond treats. When I started work my dad and I had our coats on when we shaved in the morning, the house was so cold, and you'd to boil the water. You boiled the water while you made the porridge but you had your coat on. That all sounds unbelievable but it was true and a feature of life that we just accepted.

My mother was a mother and housewife for all of my life. She didn't go out to work at all, but was very busy in the home and in the community. My dad was a joiner to trade. His father had a sawmill in Callander driven by a water wheel, one of the last ones in Scotland. That went bust with the collapse of the banks in 1929 and they moved to the Gallowgate in Glasgow. Then my dad and his father went to work in Lithgow's shipyards. They were both very good craftsmen. My dad continued at the tools for the early part of his life and then went on to train as an architect. But he couldn't qualify because his folks couldn't afford to send him to university. Eventually he became a director of a company called Laird's in the east end of Glasgow. When the war started old man Laird pulled out and my father and Laird's son were left to sort out the business. They managed to do that and finish off the jobs that they were doing, but it also went down. Then my dad went to work for Glasgow Corporation as it then was. He became the person in charge of the

REV. McDONALD AS MODERATOR OF THE CHURCH OF SCOTLAND

joinery work throughout the war and then the building of all the main Glasgow housing estates in Garthamlock, Easterhouse, Castlemilk and Drumchapel, and was responsible for all the joiners employed by the Corporation. He worked there until he retired.

My family was religious – churchgoing, and very faithful churchgoing. I was baptised in Kenmuir Church in Bishopbriggs within the first six weeks of my life, and I was taken there probably every Sunday from then on, in the Young Worshipper's League at the front of the church. We sat and listened to sermons that made me make mice with my hanky: I was making the kids laugh beside me – it was far more interesting than the sermon. On two or three occasions, the sermon stopped while Sandy McDonald got told off. Then I usually got a telling-off, if not a belt on the backside, when I got home for causing such trouble and embarrassment for my folks. But I went on to Sunday School and then the Youth Fellowship. I was in the Boys Brigade from the minute I could get in, and I'm still in the Boys Brigade – it played a very big part in my life. My Boys Brigade Captain influenced me deeply, as did my Sunday School teacher, who's now a famous Glasgow architect. I'm sure he still looks back on the days he had me in Sunday School as some of the nightmares of his experience. But they were all influential in what happened in terms of my own spirituality, I think.

School Days

I went to Bishopbriggs Higher Grade School – now that's a joke. Although I loved being there, to call it Higher Grade was really a laugh because of the war, among other things. Most of my teachers were retired but had been brought back into service because so many had gone off to serve their country in one way or another. So we had an amazing mix of teachers. Our school was bombed as well during the war. Towards the end of the war the building that was bombed got re-roofed and that became the first what we called 'dinner school' – the first school dinners that were ever provided I enjoyed in that school at four old pennies a ticket. It was nearly always soup poured out of a big jug – nearly always looked the same and more or less tasted the same – and was often followed by things that many people to this day remember, like semolina with a blob of red jam in the middle: not very determinate jam, but red. Or sago, or tapioca. The great favourite was the day we had caramel tart, which was boiled condensed milk spread across thick pastry, and that was the day you went for extras!

But that was my schooling – I stayed there and did, in the A class, French and Latin up until the third year and then I went to Whitehill Senior Secondary in Glasgow.

Holidays

We mostly went to live in other peoples' houses in places like North Berwick, Largo in Fife, Brodick in Arran, and Millport. I think my earliest holidays were in Millport. But North Berwick sticks in my mind. It took me longer with my family, during and after the war, to get to North Berwick than it takes me now to go to New York. We started out from Bishopbriggs in a tramcar, then you would get to Queen Street Station where the queue would be right outside and away along past the Copthorne Hotel, maybe nearly as far as the City Chambers, because you couldn't book trains. You sat in the queue on your cases and moved slowly forward as they brought more trains in. You had your sandwiches with you and flasks, and you would have your first lot of sandwiches and the first flask before you got on the train! Then you would get to Edinburgh and you wouldn't be sure when the next train would come that would eventually take you to Drem. And then you stood on Drem platform until a North Berwick train came and you eventually arrived to go to live in the house.

If you were posh – and I suppose if I lived in a semi-detached house in Bishopbriggs I was posh – you got not just a house, but one with attendance. That meant that my mother bought the food but the woman who owned the house, or lived in it – it was often a council house – cooked it for us. They lived in the hut in the back garden so that we could have their house. I remember once in Largo in Fife we had a house, and everything tasted of paraffin. From the breakfast through the mince and potatoes at lunch-time to the cold meat salad at teatime – all tasted of paraffin. It took us a while to work out that the woman doing the cooking cooked on a paraffin stove and she had to pump it up like a Primus stove, so everywhere and everything tasted of paraffin.

The holidays were very basic. The great thing was that you went in large crowds 'cos lots of families took their kids to the same place. Sometimes the dads only got there for a week, they didn't always have two weeks' holiday. Sometimes we went for a month, big-time, we got the house for a month. The mothers and the kids went and Dad would arrive whenever he got holidays from his workplace.

We didn't have a car; in fact the tram was our lifeline to the rest of the world, and then it was the trolley buses. They were the thing for the dances. I would sometimes get a bus to Netherlee Scout Hall to dances and the trolleybus was the feature of that. But we could go from Bishopbriggs for a penny when I was younger, from the terminus at Bishopbriggs right over to Pollokshaws or Rouken Glen and there to the baths. We did go to Springburn Baths but it was a real treat to go to Pollokshaws Baths, and that was a penny in the tramcar. But we took it for granted because the vast majority of folk didn't have cars. We once had a North Berwick holiday in a car during the war – somebody always could get things and one guy could get cans of what was called Red Petrol. That was petrol that only farmers or fishermen got but this guy got a five-gallon drum of Red Petrol and someone else had a Rover. So Dad bought the petrol, we put it in this guy's Rover and he drove us to North Berwick and that was a treat to get going in a car. Also a crime. Oh yes, but it was a great treat.

*The War Years:
Shelters, Spitfires
and Snowballs*

My memories of the war vary tremendously. I remember the building of the shelters, and the Italian prisoners. The man that ran our ice cream shop was interned and among others was used to build the shelters in our street. All the folk in the street knew him well, they'd known him for years, so he got well looked after along with his colleagues.

The rationing comes to mind. Nearly everybody in that street – Kenmuir Gardens – knew somebody that knew somebody that worked somewhere. Somebody that worked at Lees Factory, old Mrs Jones' son, I think, got a box of Snowballs once a month. When the Snowballs arrived all the kids in the street queued at Mrs Jones' door and you got one Snowball. Parcels came from Canada that had lollipops in them; the other thing in those parcels was Kraft Dinner, which was macaroni and cheese in a packet. That's my first memory of anything that resembled Italian food,

NATIONAL
REGISTRATION

IDENTITY
CARD

but it came from Canada. When the Canadian parcels came, again all the kids came to our door for a share of ours.

On one occasion, a German fighter plane flew over, being chased by Spitfires. Our next-door neighbour was out waving her brush at it. That's a childhood picture in my head – of her shouting and swearing at this pilot and sort of urging on the Spitfires that were chasing it; it crashed eventually in the Campsie Hills.

The man next door to us was in the Home Guard and he had a rifle. I don't think it could ever have fired anything but he always carried it, and during the night when the sirens went we would get paraded out into the shelter and he would stand at the door on guard, saying, 'Who goes there?' It would be someone like the old woman up the road with her shawl wrapped around her, but he always challenged her and anybody else who came. But inside the shelter everyone brought either flasks or bowls of soup and sandwiches and all kinds of things, and we lived inside this place until the all-clear went and off we went back to our homes.

We started off going under the living-room table: that was supposed to help us in case the roof came down. But we eventually went to the shelters right through to VE Day and VJ Day, and having bonfires in the street. My dad, as a joiner, had collected all the ends of wood to burn in our fire 'cos coal wasn't easy to get. He gave me a right old doing because I went in with all my pals and nicked all these bundles of wood to build this huge fire out in the street, but it was a great time of celebration.

A Student at the
University of Life

At the end of the war, during my last years at school, I didn't really have an idea of what I wanted to do, other than leave school. I had always been interested in sales and things related to selling, and it seemed to me the folk that had it made were what I called commercial travellers in those days, because they got moving around. I did once try and persuade my dad to buy a chip shop 'cos it did seem to me in those early days that folk had it made who had chip shops. My father persuaded me and the rest of the family that this was not a good idea. But eventually, many years later, I worked in a chip shop for a few nights as a minister, just to get the feel of it and sometimes I regret he didn't buy one.

When I left school, I did walk out of Whitehill and got myself a job in Arthur & Company in Queen Street in Glasgow, a wholesale textile warehouse. I was 'the boy', who did everything from wrapping parcels in the basement to running about at everybody's behest to find and do everything. The only good bit was that I could buy cheap shirts. But I only stayed for six, eight weeks and then was interviewed for a job with the then city sawmills, for management training. That really was the beginning of what I thought was going to be my life's work. I got a great training. The very thing I'd wanted out of school to avoid, I began to do in a much more demanding way from October to March every year: five nights a week at what was then the Scottish College of Commerce, now part of Strathclyde University, and Stow College, which is still, of course, in Glasgow.

We were going to the cinema or to dances, but that was kind of slightly dodgy at times – in certain Christian circles pictures were a bit doubtful, kind of evil. And dance halls where you actually touched – in the most appropriate way, of course – your girlfriend, were even more dodgy. And yet I remember that you could go to parties and have necking sessions that you could hardly breathe after and that was alright, but pictures and dance halls were a bit iffy. However, I went to all of them. That's maybe a confession that I shouldn't allow, but I did.

We went to the college dances in the Scottish College of Commerce in Pitt Street, which is now Police Headquarters. The relative formality comes to mind: everybody went around with blazers, you got your blazer with a fancy badge on it, and a pair of flannels. That was also the first time that I was aware of black people. That sounds really surprising perhaps to many, but there were not a lot of black or ethnic minority people in Glasgow at that particular time, except in colleges and in university.

But the dances were great occasions. It was a regular Saturday night, and folk went there to make friends with people of their own age. They were highly organised in many ways, some would say very rigid: the men were at one side, the women at the other and we moved towards each other in order to get the right girl for the dance. There were just sort of traditional patterns related to that sort of thing: you always would check on the girl's name – I mean, she might have been a Catholic. It was quite important. In the same way that when I went to the sawmill for an interview, they wanted to know what school I went to; that was to find out whether or not I was a Catholic. I mean, these are just terrible things, but that went on. If you went home and said to your father, 'I was with Mary McGonagle tonight ... ,' he'd say, 'Right, that's the last time you're seeing her and I never want you to go near her again.' You were never totally sure other than that you realised her name must have sounded a bit Roman Catholic. Desperately bad things, but they went on, judgements like that made in firms and in society.

At the sawmill, despite being paid under thirty shillings a week – £1.50 – I had to turn out with a starched, white, stiff collar, not a plastic one. I had to carry a spare one in my pocket because if I'd been in the yard most of the morning and the collar got wet and started to bend, I had to have a fresh one to put on at lunch-time. I had to always have a tie on, and although I never wore one at any other time I always had to wear a hat – foremen in those days were hatted because you'd to distinguish between the workers and the staff.

But we had amazing characters. The things that happened in terms of employment in those days I still find nearly unbelievable. We started men at half-seven in the morning, they worked till half-four or five, depending on the time of year. They got no tea-break in the morning; if they were caught smoking they were paid off instantly, and we paid them just over three pounds a week. If they worked all day on a Sunday when we were stocktaking, they would get sometimes one pound something, and as a staff member I got two and six, to buy my so-called lunch. We had one foreman I remember quite vividly: if a man gave him trouble he would lay him out, punch him and flatten him and then say, 'Right, ya *******,' (I'll not repeat what he said), '... get up and get on with your job or you're fired,' and the guy would get up and get on with his job.

We also had a person that we called 'The Shithouse Clerk': he was the guy that was instated really by the time-and-motion study people, who insisted that men were taking too long in the toilet. Too bad if you had the runs or something ... you didn't have curries in those days, it would just have been a Glasgow pie that had got to you ... but they would go and clock in to the toilet. After so long, the Shithouse Clerk told them to get out, irrespective of condition. In those days, you couldn't put money on horses legally, so it was in the toilets that that was done. That did take a bit of time – the foreman Carter was the bookie's runner and he collected the lines, and the place to put your line on was in the toilet. So maybe the time-and-motion study men – who were a bit of a joke in some ways – had something in that guys were pushed out the toilet if they took too long.

We delivered all our timber in Glasgow by horse and cart, and they timed how long it took to put a horse into the shafts and take it back out again. They sat, wearing their caps and carrying their stopwatches, in front of a load of timber with a carter dressed in a very scruffy old bunnet. These images will stick with me till the day I die, but just another world ... hard to believe that this was all happening and I'm actually still young enough to be at work.

Eventually I became a certificate member of the Institute of Wood Science and took various diplomas in Business Management, interrupted of course by two years in the Royal Air Force as a National Serviceman.

I went off to the RAF, kitted out at Cardington, went to train on ground wireless. The one thing that I didn't think I could do was the thing that they decided I should do. I was offered a commission if I stayed for an extra year, but no chance –

I went on, in fact, to a bomber station at Binbrook and took charge of the transmitting station there. It was really during that time that I started to feel a call to the ministry, but knew that really, I'd signed up to be a business manager in the timber trade. In fact, after the RAF, I went back there for a few years before I started studying to go to Glasgow University.

But National Service changed my life. I had a great childhood, I had great parents, who looked after us tremendously well, but I had a sheltered childhood. For example, I went into the RAF not knowing what a homosexual was. I learned very quickly, but I went in not knowing. I'd heard about 'poofs', but I just thought they were men that wore lipstick. That was a measure of that time, of course. I was actually out of the RAF the first time I heard about lesbians: I was in a hotel lounge and this television programme came on and I thought it was something to do with the theatre. I don't think it was just innocence, it was a feature of the time: things like that weren't talked about. But the RAF certainly opened my eyes – in any billet I heard the so-called dirty stories, the like of which I had never heard in my life. I laughed, or sort of took part, because I often didn't understand what they were about. You learn very quickly in that kind of environment, however. I learned how to look after myself, I learned to look after my affairs, such as they were – the practicalities of living your life away from home, which I had never done. I learned about human relationships, about people's backgrounds that were very different from mine, and a mix of people from the whole UK. Although I did often go to the camp church, I was often the only one in the billet that went. And for so doing I got bringing back everybody's newspapers and maybe helping clearing up after the ones that had been drunk on the Saturday night and had been sick all over the place – that was the option if you got up early and went to church. But Sandy McDonald was a very different person, I hope a more mature, a more responsible and certainly a better educated – in the broadest sense – person, because I spent my two years in the Royal Air Force and I never, ever regret it.

Mary Strathie
Mill Worker & Housewife

Born 1938

I was born in Galashiels, in our house. My mother was a waitress and my father worked in the tweed mills as a warper. It was a terraced house – one room, one bedroom and an attic. My brothers slept in the attic and had to go up a ladder to go to bed and my parents slept in the living room. There was a kitchen but no bathroom. Hardly anyone had bathrooms in Galashiels – it was all outside toilets. I didn't have an inside toilet until I was married at nineteen. That was usual in Galashiels. Very few houses, only big houses, had inside toilets. I don't know if the mill bosses, when they built the houses, thought that we poor people needed inside facilities and of course, it wasn't considered hygienic to have toilets in the house. I think it was more prevalent in Galashiels than in other towns. People from outside Galashiels called Galashiels people 'pail merks' because they said that they kept pails in the house to go in and they got the marks round their behinds. So they were called 'pail merks'.

I started school just near the house – the school isn't there any more – and then went to the burgh school. We moved when I was about seven to a much bigger house with three bedrooms. It still had an outside toilet but it was nearer, just down the stairs. I can remember the electricity being put in when we moved in, because I remember the electrician saying, 'How high can you reach?', so that I could reach the switches. I would be about seven when we got electricity after the war.

I can remember my mother doing the washing in an outside wash-house in one of these big tubs. I remember seeing my mother stoking up that fire under the boiler and doing a whole wash – that was in the winter too. Because I'd two brothers and my sister and my father, it was a big washing to do. I can remember being bathed in the tub after the washing was done and I used to be scared because I was sure it was bottomless.

My mother shopped every day because we didn't have a fridge. Monday it was mince, Tuesday it was stew, if it was fish and chips, you knew it was Friday, that sort of thing. There was no lasagnas, no pizzas, anything like that; my father had a really bad ulcer and I can remember he ate boiled fish or tripe every day, for about seventeen years, I remember. He had fish . I'd be about thirteen, I think, when he went into Peel Hospital. They had just started doing the operation where they take about two-thirds of the stomach away and he was the first person at Peel Hospital to get that operation. The transformation on him afterwards, it was unbelievable. He could take a drink and he could eat things. He was thrilled – you would be, too, after eating fish for seventeen years!

I hated school. I went through all my school days being told I was stupid and it dawned on me, when I started to read about people with dyslexia, that's what had been wrong with me. You always felt that the teachers thought, 'Oh, it's the stupid lot, we don't have to bother', except for two teachers: Mr Mackenzie who was an English teacher – he seemed to see a spark in me which nobody else did – and Mr Foggie, my art teacher. I can remember in my first year at high school, Mr Mackenzie used to get us to read stories like *The Wind in the Willows* and things like that and be the characters in them. I wasn't a brilliant reader because of the dyslexia but he must have seen that I had some acting ability. He said, 'You know we're doing *A Midsummer Night's Dream* and there's a part of a fairy in it called Puck and you know you'd be really good at that, Mary,' and I said, 'Nah, I don't think so,' but he gave me the book. I knew I couldn't read some of the words, I didn't know what they were but, oh, I'd loved to have been in it. I remember standing at the hall door where they were doing the auditions and I heard them all speaking. I knew it would be all the fourth, fifth and sixth years doing this play and I really wanted to go in but I couldn't pluck up the courage. Next day, Mr Mackenzie said, 'You didn't come to the readings, Mary,' and I said 'Nah, I didn't want to be in it.' I always regretted not having the courage to go into it.

After I'd written *The Derners*, my play about the mill workers, two of the ladies that were in the play were school teachers and we were standing after rehearsal; one of the ladies said to me, 'Mary, you are clever, writing a play' – I've waited until I was fifty-three to hear a teacher tell me I was clever.

I always went to all the local live shows, the local opera society things; I loved theatre. I spent four nights a week at least in the picture house. I loved the films. We lived about five hundred yards away from the picture house in Galashiels and it changed its programme twice a week; then there was the Playhouse, which was down the road a bit and it changed as well, so I went about four times a week. I saw everything. There's hardly any of the old black and white films that come on [television] that I haven't seen. Musicals were my particular favourites. The only one I remember not liking was *The Three Stooges* – I've never liked them. I can remember going to the cinema on my own when I was seven. You wouldn't let a child go now to the pictures on their own.

I loved swimming. I was in the swimming team and swam for Scotland at school level. I always had dancing lessons as a child. That was one thing my mother always did scrape enough money together to give me and I loved them. I was very healthy, although my mother didn't always think so because I used to pull stunts not to go to school. I would have aches and pains, and cry with it, 'Oh, I don't want to go, I've got this sore stomach.' I remember them thinking for quite a while that I might have had polio because of all these pains in my legs but it wasn't, fortunately.

Even when I was pretending, I remember worrying that they would have to get the doctor and that would cost money. My mother did have to think about that. We didn't realise at the time that we were poor because everybody was in the same boat. It was not so bad when I came along because my brothers were a good bit older than me and they had started to work. My oldest brother's fifteen years older than me, the next one's ten years, my sister's nine years. I was a 'mistake' so things really were a bit better off when I can remember it. But I remember my mother saying, when the boys got pennies: 'Come on, put them in your bank!' and it was the gas meter.

The games I remember playing were in the street mostly and it was brilliant because, you know, there wasn't a lot of cars going up and down and nobody used to shout at us for running across the roads, I think people expected children to play in the streets – Kick-the-Can, skipping, beds – all the usual games. One person stood in the middle of the road and the rest of the crowd were on the pavement and you said some film star's initials and if you got it right, you got to move one step – there'd be six or seven of us all standing in the middle of the road. I still remember playing in the street at games when I was fourteen or fifteen. I don't think we developed quite as fast as they do now. You still wore your ankle socks and dressed as a child, very much so, until you left school. I can remember wearing ankle socks to my first job.

MARY'S FATHER, ADAM RENTON, AT WORK, 1955

My father'd been in the First World War and was injured; he'd lost a finger and his hand was curled round, so he couldn't go to the Second World War. He was a warden. I remember him always going out on duty and I remember being taken out my bed one night when the siren went off. I think it would be the night that Clydebank was bombed and I was taken down to a neighbour's who lived downstairs. I don't know if they thought we'd be safer there but I remember it being the middle of the night, being wrapped in a blanket and taken down. And I remember rationing. I remember taking jelly, solid jellies to the pictures instead of a sweet, and you sat and sucked that in the pictures for ages. We must have had really good nails, I think. [Jelly was said to make fingernails strong.] I can also remember taking rhubarb in a screw of paper with sugar in it and dipping the rhubarb in.

Working Life

I left school at fifteen and very few of my contemporaries at that time went on to college. It was only really rich children that went to university. My art teacher, Mr Foggie, saw I had some talent in art but I wasn't good enough to go on academically to college or anything; the only place he could think of me using my art was in a photographic studio. He knew the man in the studio and got me a job there, learning to retouch negatives and touch up photographs and things, and working in the shop. I can remember my first wage was seventeen shillings and sixpence and that was working the six days, with a half-day on a Wednesday. That only lasted about ten months. My friends were making about five pounds a week in the mills which was a big employer then and I thought I'd give the mills a try. There were about forty tweed mills then.

I went as a weaver. I can remember, we didn't get tea breaks or any official stopping time. We all smoked and we used to go down to a smoke room next to the toilets, a dismal place. There was no door on it, so even in the winter it was freezing.

In 1901, more than 200,000 Scots women were employed in the textile industry; by 1991, it was less than 25,000 – and has fallen since.

There were two benches down the side of a long table and a big round metal bin in the middle of the table, full of ash for putting the cigarettes out in. If you were in there too long, the foreman came and shouted you out. That's where all the gossiping went on.

MARY AT WORK AT THE MILL, CHECKING FOR BROKEN THREADS, 1955

It was very noisy – there could be thirty or forty looms in a weaving shed – but we still managed to have conversations. You learned to lip-read. I'm a bit deaf now because of working in the mill, I think. You always know weavers when you see them speaking out in the street, the older women, they talk right into each other's ears or they'll watch people's mouths when they speak.

Weavers were all women then. Darning, too, was always a woman's job. Tuners who mended the loom, they were the men. I can remember doing my training down at Netherdale – it was the technical college then – where you went to learn the weaving. There was a lot of students from Stornoway. They all came down to learn the business down here and we used to socialise quite a lot with them. They used to have parties and we used to get invited to those sometimes. I can remember one student, Ken Harris Mackenzie from Stornoway, he cornered me in the stairs one day and said, 'What does a virgin have for breakfast?' I was still quite shy, I'd just left school and I said, 'Well, I have a roll and jam.' After I thought about it, oh, I was so embarrassed. They were nice chaps, though.

The mills have slid into decline, which is a shame, but people don't want lovely tweeds now. There's so many fabrics that are much easier to look after. Of course, the electronics industry sort of took over when the mills went because there was a good workforce possibly. I went into the electronics when there wasn't much work in the mills.

Marriage and Motherhood

I stayed in the mills till I married at nineteen, my first marriage, and then I went back periodically. When the children were small I'd go in and do an evening shift – my husband would finish his work at five and I'd go in on an evening shift.

I met my first husband at the Edinburgh Palais. There was a lot of the big band stuff there. Bill Haley, of course was very popular, and I remember going up to the Empire in Edinburgh and seeing Johnny Ray. We used to go up in a busload and see the stars, Frankie Laine and all those. I was on holiday with a friend and we were

THE DARNING FLAT,
GARDINERS MILL, SELKIRK,
c. 1948

at the Palais. He came from Portobello and he was a merchant seaman. Seventeen years we were married and then divorced in the late '70s. It was still a bit frowned on, but it was necessary.

Before the war, it was very unusual for anyone to get divorced in Galashiels, just as having a child before you were married was frowned upon a lot then too. I was a virgin when I was married at nineteen; I thought everybody was but I found out since that was quite unusual. When I got engaged to my first husband, the first thing my mother said to him was, 'Now remember that's an engagement ring, not a wedding ring,' and that was it. And it was really because I was scared, I wouldn't have hurt my mother for anything. I find now that some of my friends are saying, 'Oh, I wasn't' and 'I wasn't.' I think there's quite a big change in women over the generations. I can remember I did a late shift, and I can remember my husband bringing my son, who was about one year old at the time, along for me to come out the mill to change his nappy because it was a dirty one. He wouldn't change that although he'd have changed a wet one. I came out the mill, changed the nappy and went back to work and he took the baby home. I mean, I put up with things then, in my first marriage, that I wouldn't now; I just wouldn't.

Betty Smart
Bus Conductress & Publican

Born 1937

I was born in Kirkintilloch, an only daughter: nine sons and and I was the only girl. We were a big happy family and we had quite a happy childhood. We stayed, first of all, in a four-in-a-block and then when they built the semis – which were fantastic – we moved to a semi-detached, and then to what you called a steel bungalow, then back to a semi-detached.

I was coming up for seven when the war finished so I can remember parts of the war. I can remember my siren suit; me and my brothers had wee siren suits. We used to get put under the table when there were any planes coming over. I remember during the Clydebank Blitz, we were put under the big thick kitchen table with our siren suits on. Six of us were put under the table when the sirens went; my mum got us all under it.

CLYDEBANK AFTER THE BLITZ

With the rationing, I remember, we got tins of dried egg. We'd a big family so we got more tins than maybe somebody else and it was a treat if my mum used to make lemon curd with the dried egg. Thursday was banana day, a fantastic day. There would be queues outside the Co-operative to get your bananas and the broken biscuits. I used to get sent for tuppence worth of broken biscuits for the family. These were good days. My mother's Co-op number was 4015 and I've still got it. I still use it; it's 4015 Kirkintilloch Co-operative

I went to St Ninian's School in Kirkintilloch. I started in the old school in the Parochial Hall, Union Street, and then we moved up to St Ninian's High when we were eleven. I was up there till I was fifteen and then I left and started work in a foundry, making cores. My aunt worked there and she got me in but it wasn't what my mum and dad wanted. It didn't seem a suitable job for a girl but I wanted to try it and I thoroughly enjoyed it. I left there and went to a grocer's shop and then I went to the nursing.

In the old days in the Co-operative, there was also private shops. I went on a bicycle to all the toffs' houses and took their orders. Mrs MacLean who owned MacLean's Garage in Kirkintilloch, she was very very fond of me and I used to go for her order on a Tuesday and she'd take me in and give me a wee cup of tea and scrambled egg and I used to tell her all the gossip in Kirkintilloch. She loved me for that. I found out that her daughter was the secretary of Woodilee Hospital. Well, you were really no supposed to start in Woodilee Hospital until you were seventeen and I was only sixteen and a half but I spoke to her and told her that I was dying to be a nurse and she got me in. So I started to study to be a psychiatric nurse and I loved doing it. I was at the nursing until I was eighteen.

When you left school at fifteen, well, you were still classed as young. A fifteen-year-old now is an adult but I was never an adult until I reached about eighteen; then I was kind of looked on as starting to be adult age. When I was fifteen I used to go to the pictures, me and my pal Sadie; we used to go down to the fruit shop and get two oranges and two apples and go to the pictures. If we had the money, we'd get a couple o' they penny caramels, those big caramels. Till I was about seventeen, we went to the pictures and we used to go into the Empire as well. I went to see Max Bygraves and Des O'Connor at the Empire and to me, this was a great night out.

Sadie went to Australia and I stared palling about with Anne when I went to the nursing. I heard about the Locarno Ballroom in Sauchiehall Street from the other nurses and there we went when we finished our shift. Our shifts were very hard, you started at half six in the morning and that was you till eight o'clock at night. If you were good and got all your work done, the sister would let you run down at five to eight, five minutes early to get the eight o'clock Woodilee bus into the Locarno. It was brilliant, it was great. I loved it, I loved it.

It was rock-and-roll then. It was ballroom dancing as well but it was mainly rock-and-roll. Those were the days when the fellas chased the girls but nowadays, the girls chase the fellas. We used to stand in a row with our handbags between our legs and they walked round about you as though you were a herd of cattle looking to see what one they were going to ask to dance. They'd say, 'Are you dancin' hen?', and if we didnae like them we'd say, 'Naw, it's the way we're staunin'. They didnae like that and so they left us alone. I liked the Locarno and many a friend I met there.

On the Buses

Two or three of my friends went to the buses and they said the money was good so I put my notice in quietly at the Woodilee – never told my parents – and then started on the buses. My father blew a fuse; he said his only daughter wasn't going on the buses but I went anyway and I thoroughly enjoyed them. I went as a clippie – there was no such thing as a woman bus driver then. No, they were all men drivers. You'd never have dreamt that a woman could've drove a bus in they days but that's all changed now too. The driver was at the front of the bus and you were at the back. If it was a double decker, there was no doors, and in all kinds of weather, you'd to stand there. Whether you could hold on or no, you'd just stand there. It was quite a tough job.

The drivers treated the clippies with the greatest respect. There was a lot of old- time drivers there, there were some great old drivers, the like of Frank Brannan, he was like a father figure to the conductresses. If you were on with him for your first shift, Frank guided you. Jimmy Woods, an Irish guy who'd come over, he was

A CLIPPIE IN UNIFORM

one of my first drivers and he was absolutely hilarious but they made you at ease. And they looked after the conductresses; if there were any thugs that came on the bus or that, the driver was out the cab in two minutes time, you know. They had great respect for their clippies in they days.

The clippies were smart in they days and so was the drivers. You'd to wear a white shirt with a stiff collar, we'd to buy the paper collars. You got twelve for half-a-crown out of Knox's the Tailors and where I worked, Lawson's Buses, we were very, very smart clippies and drivers. You were given a coat and trousers for the winter time, a costume for the summertime but at all times you had to wear a white shirt and a black tie. Collar and tie and the driver wore the leather gloves through his lapel here and that was the way they were dressed then. They were very very smart. To me, the buses were different from what they are now. You were proud to be a clippie, you were like a soldier, you were immaculate. You got to know all your passengers and they got to know you. The pit buses were the best, getting the miners in the morning. I loved the pit buses, there was a lot of talent then. Big, rugged men. I loved it. You'd get young men standing up and giving their seat to a woman or an older person; if any pregnant lady came on the bus, you'd see somebody get up and gie them a seat. You were allowed eight standing on your bus. If you had a double decker it was eight downstairs, if it was a single decker it was eight on the bus and if you had, say, six ladies standing, you'd guarantee there's six men would get up or six boys would get up and give the ladies a seat without hesitation.

You could crack a joke but you never had the abuse you get now. Even when your bus went into the depot, the bus was a lot cleaner than they go in now. People throw things on the floor but in those days oor buses were spotless going back. I'm no' saying nobody put a sweetie paper in the seats, a kid or that, but that'd be all you'd get; you never got the abuse. I wouldnae be a clippie now.

You were either day shift, back shift or spreadover. The routine was you started at six in the morning or five-thirty, that was you till four, or you took up your shift at four and that was you till midnight. That's the way it worked. Spreadover meant you could start at half past five in the morning and finish at ten or eleven, then you were back out again the back of three and that was you till seven; that was called a spreadover shift. It was mostly to accommodate getting the workers to their work, and getting the schoolchildren in the afternoon.

I had a lot of fun on the four to midnight shift. I seen all walks o' life on that. We used to sit in Glasgow Dundas Street – that was the terminus – and every Saturday I was on the last bus, at twelve o'clock leaving Glasgow. I used to see all the courting couples saying goodnight to their boyfriends or their girlfriends. You saw all the elite, that you thought were gentlemen, kissing their fancy women goodnight. I used to get a kick out of that and then they'd come on the bus and give you a wee wink, as much to say, 'You didn't see me'. You never, ever told. In those days you never, ever told.

Once I got trouble on the late night bus; I got hit over the head by a machine but I hit back and we got the police that night. But that was just one boy who was drunk and it was really verbal abuse: he was actually fighting with his pal and I asked him to stop but other than that naw, we had no trouble whatsoever. Only that one sticks out, that I can ever recall, in all my years on the buses.

It was fun and you were treated with respect. When you go on a bus today, the driver hardly talks to you whereas in oor day we knew everybody that came on that bus: 'Good morning Joe', 'Good morning Jeannie, how's your granny. How's your mammy? Has your mammy had her wean yet?' 'Has the hoose been decorated yet?' That was the kind of things we said. Now if you go onto a bus, if you don't have the right money you've got to get back off that bus, the clippie had the change.

In my day, by the end of a shift, we never had any kind of fear that we were carrying quite a lot of money. And we had a lot of money. On a Monday morning and a Tuesday, those were your weekly ticket days when anybody that was travelling from, say, Campsie Glen to Glasgow all week, they'd pay quite a few pounds for their ticket. So we were carrying quite a few hundred pounds by the end of Monday night or Tuesday and a Saturday was your busy, busy day. But nobody was frightened, no. I walked when I worked as a nurse, I walked from Hillhead to Woodilee through an old bing at quarter to six in the morning in pelting rain and dark, and I wisnae frightened. Nobody bothered me. I did that for years. I'd walk from my house to the bus garage at quarter past five in the morning in mist and fog. None of us were frightened. We were quite safe in those days, in the '50s and '60s.

After I got married I went back on the buses and it was still safe. You had a lot of fun. You were proud, very proud to go to your work and to have a job. To give your mother a wage packet you were very proud. Everybody loved giving their mammy a wage packet. I couldnae get enough overtime so's I could give my mum extra money – to the youngsters in those days it was pride, and pride with your parents. Nowadays they'll hardly gie you dig money.

I stayed at home into my twenties, bringing home wages. It didn't occur to me to move out. My father was a great believer in his family. I remember once my brother, Jack, who was a year older than me, was working with these boys and they told him they were giving their mums dig money, lodging money (you didn't say dig money then it was lodging money). My father came home from the night shift one morning and there were four pounds on the mantelpiece. He said to my mother, 'Helen, what's the four pound on the mantelpiece for?' She said, 'That's your son Jack's. He wants lodgings, he wants to pay lodging money.' So my dad walked in, packed a bag, hauled Jack out the bed, gave him his four pound and said, 'If you're wanting lodgings, laddie, you go and be a lodger somewhere.' That was my parents' philosophy. My mother's philosophy was that you paid your wage and then when you got married you got a good send-off. She gave you everything you needed – clothes, money – to start you off. Right up to the day we got married, we paid full pay to our parents. You thought nothing of it. I don't mind anybody ever having lodging money then.

I met my husband on the buses. He was a great outdoor man, he liked fishing and all that. I happened to be on the Blanefield run and he had had a wee drink this day. I asked him for his fare and he handed me a ferret – I nearly died and I squealed and the driver stopped the bus. It was all in good fun but I never forgot it to that day: 'Four to Kirkintilloch please' and he went into this bag and handed me this ferret, you know. Oh, my God. In those days when I was on the Blanefield bus, we used to travel up and you'd stop at a farm and a lady would come on; I'd say 'Fares please!' and she'd hand me a half dozen eggs. But that was accepted.

I got married in 1961, and I stopped work. I had a girl and then I went back on the buses. I went back to a different depot, the Milngavie depot. When I fell pregnant with my other daughter I worked in an off-license stacking shelves. And when my second daughter was born, I went back on the buses again, you know. That's the kind of things we did. I was three year on the buses and then I left and went back on them for two years after I got married. So I did a five-year stint on the buses.

New Directions
After the buses, I started working in a pub, then I bought my own pub. I've always got on great with the public and to me, going back years ago, the public house is where you get all the laughter and the banter. You met a lot of stars that come into your pub. Billy Connolly used to come into my sister-in-law's pub and I had Danny McGrain and Jock Stein; these people came into my pub and we became friends and they helped me with my charity work. To me that was a great life, the pub work. Great for meeting people from all walks of life.

I left and went to London for eighteen months. I lost my mum, my husband was a bit brutal and my marriage was breaking up. So I took the kids to get away; I just packed their bags one day and off I went. I worked and I made a lot of money and I came back here. I couldn't get a house in Kirkintilloch at first so I got a house in Possilpark. I stayed there for three years then I moved back to Kirkintilloch. But when I was in Possilpark, it was a terrific place. I was born and bred in Kirkintilloch but I've worked a lot of my life in Glasgow, and without any prejudice, I'd say there's nobody to compare with Glasgow people. Castlemilk, Drumchapel, the Garngad. I've met them all, they've come into my pub, I've done a lot of charity work with them and they're the salt of the earth. I don't give a damn what anybody says, if you need something, Glasgow people are the best people in the world.

I got a job as I said in the pub, met my second husband and I've been very very happy since – I wish I'd met him forty-odd year ago. We've had a great life, you know. We'd another daughter so I've got three girls and two boys, and eleven grandkids. I know all about life; I think I'm a modern mammy and granny, but some people say these were the bad old days – I'm afraid they were the good old days. Yes, there was a lot of things happened that we maybe didnae see that's coming out the closet now but when we were young you could play in the streets. I walked two and a half miles to school, I never once was stopped, I never once was interfered with. To me the youngsters had more then. Take, for example, Christmas Eve, Christmas Day. Do you ever see a kiddie oot with a pram and doll or a cowboy set? Christmas morning you used to open your curtains and there were wee boys in the street with their cowboys and wee girls – they've taken it all away. I've never seen my granddaughter playing peever, I've never seen her playing ropes. To me the government, the people, society have taken the youth and took the childhood out of our kids. A kid at nine now is not a kid – they're classed as a teenager and I think that's all wrong. Mothers have got to educate their children now a lot earlier than we did because of the bad things in life. My God, I was seventeen before I knew what the birds and the bees was and it did me no harm. It did me no harm. It was the same with my kids. I let them enjoy their childhood and then I sat them down when they left school and told them about the birds and the bees; it did them no harm and they did me proud. I don't believe in the Tories, but as John Major says, 'Back to basics': I quite agree with him there. We should go back to some of the things in the old days. I think we'd have a better world.

Sheila Mackay
Community Activist

Born 1939

Early Memories

I was born in Inverness and I've always lived just here, just beside where I was born. My earliest memory must have been when I was about three and a half and my mother had gone into the nursing home to have my sister. Myself and two or three of the other local youngsters were playing in a field. The father of one of them came along – he'd come home on leave from active service – and he had a banana; he broke it into little bits and gave us each a piece. None of us had ever seen or tasted banana before. I remember thoroughly enjoying it but one or two went 'yeuch'.

I had a happy childhood – it was the country and we could wander about the fields and the moors and nobody ever bothered us. I'm sure we did some very dangerous things. I know I fell in the burn many times and hung my vest on the pear tree beside it to dry before we went home, but yes, it was wonderful. We had lots of freedom.

As soon as the frost melted, we played marbles – girls and boys, it didn't really matter who played – and everybody had what we called in Inverness, the 'steelack'. The Invernessians have a great habit of sticking 'ack' onto the end of their words; I think it comes directly from our Gaelic ancestors. The steelack, the steel marble, was the prized one. The glass marbles, they were difficult to get so if you got marbles it didn't matter how chipped and cracked they were, they had to last. We dug a hole in the ground – that's why you'd to wait till the frost melted – and his was called a 'punky'. You had to try and get the marbles into this punky with the steel marble and there was great competition. As the weather got better, it was skipping for the girls; the boys of course wouldn't take part in that except to annoy us. And then 'skeechie': we played that everywhere, there wasn't a road anywhere that hadn't got the skeechie mark. We played that right through the summer, all the usual games like hide-and-seek and so on. Every burn, and there's a lot of burns around, we used to put on welly boots and wander through, although maybe not even welly boots, as not everybody had them.

When the winter came that was quite magic because there was very little traffic, so everything was crisp and absolutely virginal white because there was nothing to dirty the snow and turn it into slush. Looking back, it must've caused hardships for our parents, because they had to get fires lit and it's difficult to get into town for shopping. I remember particularly the winter of 1947, just at the end of the war. My father had taken back a pair of wooden clogs after he was demobbed – I don't know where he got them from. Our school was about a mile or so away. There was obviously no school buses or anything in those days, so you just had to walk. I can recall very clearly walking home with these clogs on in this very bad winter night. The snow was deep and there was barely any street lighting – you wouldn't let children walk like that now. The snow had packed up in the wood in the clogs and it was two or three inches thick. I couldn't get any further and I was standing howling at a wall when round the corner came a small platoon of soldiers. One of the young lads at the back of it must've seen this poor little girl crying beside the wall and he broke ranks, ran over and showed me how to bang the shoes against a wall to knock all the snow off. Then he just ran off. It must've taken a good hour to get home and no doubt my mother was wondering frantically where I was. I think this is one of the changes: you wouldn't allow a young child to go out and walk on the roads now but then they had no alternative.

During the war, we got a big outing in a car, about once a month. There was an elderly couple and they had an old Austin Seven. They were the most funny-looking old pair. He was a retired stationmaster and always wore his hat and she was a little dumpy lady who looked like something out of the *Woodentops*; she wore a full-length, black dress always, her white hair in a bun and she was the spitting image of Churchill. Once a month they went to town in a stately procession. They got into this old Austin Seven and there was about four or five neighbours, including us kids, all got into this car with them and proceeded to town, probably not exceeding fifteen miles an hour. We were so excited about actually going in a car because nobody had a car and there was just an occasional bus.

War Memories   During the war there was very little in the way of treats, neither was there money and even if you had money there was very little available. I can remember the jam-making. All the sugar we got was saved up right through the year and then we all used to walk miles to pick brambles – three or four miles up the road. We spent all day gathering brambles and came home just purple – purple mouths, purple hands, purple feet. Then the jam was made and it was strained through a sort of straining bag that my mother hung between two chairs overnight, and it was the most delicious bramble jam and that lasted.

The food during the war was really pretty disgusting. Powdered eggs, which was all you could get unless you were lucky enough to live on a farm, had a very

HIGHLAND SHOPPING IN
THE INTER-WAR YEARS

peculiar taste that I don't think is ever forgotten. Butter was practically non-existent but there used to be a ration of margarine and then every so often we would be allocated a little bit of butter. My mother used to mix the butter with the margarine to make it go further. There was one particular allocation of butter she got which must have been rancid, and of course it spoiled the whole lot so we went for about three or four weeks with neither butter nor margarine. Meat was non-existent, many a time our meal at night was either potatoes and onions or potatoes and milk. One thing I do remember was an elderly aunt who lived on an estate up in Ross-shire. Just before Christmas, she would send the Christmas Chicken down. It used to arrive at the door off the bus – there was only one bus a week – and it would come off the bus to the door with a label round its neck. It was dead, but it was fully feathered and the kitchen would be full of feathers because we all wanted to pluck it. Occasionally we got a rabbit, but again it landed on the doorstep, completely intact and fully clothed.

We were reasonably fortunate in that there was a little croft next to us when I was a child and they had a few cows and pigs and hens. When the hens were laying the eggs, a lot of the eggs were preserved in what they called 'water glass' and sealed in big stone crocks, like big flower pots almost. This water glass preserved the eggs but they never tasted quite the same. The crofter's wife kept them in the little scullery under a sink; one year there was a very bad flood and the burn beside their house came over and it was flooded. When everybody went down to help, the eggs were floating about in the kitchen, they were just bobbing about on top of the water.

I suppose, again, this is something that wouldn't happen nowadays but I really worked quite a lot before I even went to secondary school. At night when I came home from school there was always work to be done on the croft, like cleaning out the byre, cleaning out the hen-house. My job was taking the cows home from the fields, which was just a little bit along the road, and I would get on the back of the big red cow who seemed to be the leader of the pack. The cows knew their own route, and would just walk along the road down the brae into their own particular place at the byre and then they were milked. All the milk was put into the little milkhouse and then the byre had to be cleaned and everybody in the area had a little churn, maybe two little churns or so, depending on the size of their family. Once the milk was put in the churn I would take it out and deliver it door-to-door, walking, and the empty churns would come back and then after that it was probably well into the evening and we'd go home. There was a little shop along the road, where everybody got their messages – there was no supermarkets or anything, people didn't go to the town for their shopping – and once I was a bit older I used to work there after school and during the summer holidays, just serving and delivering messages and so on.

Keeping Healthy   Our old cottage, which had been a shepherd's bothy, was bitterly cold, and every winter my sister and I were usually in bed with bronchitis and asthma. There used to be a steam kettle that sat on the old grate and steamed to help our lungs to breathe. As soon as we went back to school, or as soon as the cold weather started, my mother would soak sheets of brown paper with camphorated oil and that was stuck down between your vest and your liberty bodice. The embarrassment and humiliation of crackling all the way to school and in the class crackling and reeking of camphorated oil, and everybody saying, 'What's that smell?' and 'What's that noise?'! She insisted that we wear this because this was an old wives' tale; she read the Doc's page in *The Sunday Post* every week and that was your current problem for the week, and if the Doc said it, you did it. Whether it helped or not, I don't know, but she firmly believed it.

And if it wasn't Syrup of Figs, it was Castor Oil, Cascara, Sennapods, Epsom Salts, Andrews' Liver Salts, Bile Beans, Ex-Lax or any of a dozen other proprietary jollops. So many laxatives, and so few unshared indoor lavatories.

Every Friday night we got lined up and we had to take Syrup of Figs. There was absolutely nothing wrong with our bowels, but you had to take your Syrup of Figs, a big spoonful, and I swore when I was about nine if I ever had children I would never give them Syrup of Figs. You ended up the whole of Saturday night holding on to your stomach until eventually the inevitable happened. That was until I got to about eleven or twelve and totally rebelled. My mother was only four foot eight so I topped her by about an inch by then! I can still remember the pains in my stomach, my sister was the same. She was obsessed with bowels, my mother – it was typical of the time. There was an old medical book in the house, probably written about 1850, and if anything was wrong, she went to this book. 'Eye of Newt and Leg of Toad' – if it was in the book, she would've boiled up and made us take it! But oh, dear, how we survived!

School Days

I went to the Crown School, a very old school in Inverness that's still on the go. It had originally been a secondary school, but then in the early '30s, it became a primary school and it was wonderful. I remember the first day I went there. It was wartime and we didn't have many toys and I can recall quite clearly going up to the headmistress to ask her when we could get to play with plasticine. I'd heard about it and the name intrigued me, I'd no idea what it was but I knew that you got it in school. I remember thinking that the hall we were sitting in was this huge chamber, it just seemed so enormous, and yet years later when I took my own children back there it was just a tiny little hall.

Most of the teachers were very strict but very fair. It's very different now when there's only twenty-seven in a class: we had about fifty children in our class, all the way through, children of mixed abilities and backgrounds, and it must've been quite difficult for the teachers to try and get them all learning at some standard. But they were very fair. There was one or two I recall who were extremely strict to the point of being quite brutal. One springs to mind – she would take up the old wooden duster for the blackboard and throw it at whoever wasn't managing to answer their mental arithmetic questions. That was one of the things that we all dreaded: every morning you had to do this mental arithmetic and if you didn't get your answer right, by golly! But it did teach us – I don't think there's anybody of that generation now couldn't immediately tell you what six eights were. Now you would never be allowed to assault children as some of them did then. But most of them were very good teachers and very patient. You learnt to read – there was none of the phonetic spelling and all the fancy ideas that they tried out in the '60s and '70s which quite clearly have never worked.

When I went to secondary school, it was quite a change – the primary school of the Inverness Royal Academy had been a fee-paying school at that time and it wasn't all that long since they had started taking in children from everywhere, not just those who could pay. It was an excellent school, very academic – Latin and all the classics. In fact, I think that they won the old BBC *Top of the Form* [a schools quiz] programme on more than one occasion and they did turn out some very well-known people.

In those days, you had the choice of going to the technical school – the boys got woodwork and all that sort of thing and the girls got domestic science, which was terribly sexist in modern-day terms. Or you went to the Academy and took the academic course, probably with a view to carrying on to university. I did the qualy [the Academy entrance exam]; it was the bursary you called it then. It was all written and included everything really – a little bit of things like biology, and general nature subjects but it was really your maths, your English and your history and geography that you rose or fell on.

One memory sticks out very clearly, the day that the bursary exam results were read out. We had a super teacher, Miss Smith; she worked very very hard with all her class and everybody was on pins. There was quite a few whose parents were reasonably well-to-do and obviously had aspirations, who didn't pass and one or two of them were quite hysterical. The headmaster came and handed the papers over and the results were read out. There was nothing sent to the house, it was read out there in front of all your peer group and the humiliation for those who had hoped and had been encouraged, not to say bludgeoned, by their parents into doing well and didn't, it was very very hard going, it was terribly tense. Were you going to pass or were you not?

There was a tremendous amount of pressure on eleven-, twelve-year-olds, who had no clear idea of what they wanted to do. Who does? And it may not be necessarily that they went to the best school – there may have been some that went to the academy that would've benefited from going to the technical school and vice versa. It was a tremendously traumatic experience for twelve-year-olds. I remember making myself quite ill about it, wondering if I would cope with going to this school. Coming from a very poor background – my father was a guard in the railway and my mother did some cleaning in the school along the road – and then going in with all the solicitors' and the doctors' children, it was a shock. I didn't particularly let it get me down and most of them were okay but there was a few snobby teachers who definitely favoured the better-off children. But most of them were pretty good.

A lot of friendships split up as well. The schools were about two miles apart, and each of these took in a catchment area from the whole of the town so, for a lot of old friendships with people you'd been in primary school with who didn't make it to one school or the other, that was it. You started moving in different circles.

At fifteen, I probably could've had a university career ahead of me, but my father became ill and he had to give up work and there was no money coming into the house. I decided that I was going to leave school. My parents said 'No, no, no' and I said 'Oh yes, I've got to make some money.' At that time you could get any sort of job you wanted. The rector, who was a tremendous character who died several years ago, tried to persuade me otherwise but the main problem was that I had outgrown the blazer that I'd had for three years. At that time, the blazers for the academy were very expensive and you had to wear one. I knew my mother and father couldn't afford to buy me a new blazer; I didn't tell them that but that was the reason that I decided to go, because I couldn't go without a blazer and my blazer was done.

Off to the Town

I got a job in the office in a butcher's shop. It wasn't much of a job but it was good fun and it taught me a lot of things. Having been brought up in the country and so naive, it was a whole learning curve to start going to work in the town. All these men and butchers, they were, well, a bit rough sometimes. We started work at eight o'clock in the morning till six o'clock at night. An hour off for lunch, half day on Wednesday, worked all day Saturday and at that time everybody for some reason bought their meat on a Saturday and there was queues out the shop and away along the street.

My wage was one pound, eight shillings and ninepence (£1.44 in modern-day terms). I had one shilling and thruppence off for my tax and gave one pound my mother. When you think that a pair of nylons cost you nine shillings and elevenpence! You would have to save for weeks, and if you got a run in your nylons there was an invisible mender and they used to repair them for thruppence a run, because you couldn't afford to throw them out. If you were really desperate you could put this brown stuff on your legs and then draw a black line up the back for your seam.

Dancing the Nights Away

I did that for three years and then I'd met my future husband by that time; he had just come out of the RAF having done his National Service. When we got married, I was just eighteen. I met him in the Islands, which is a very pretty place in Inverness, down by the riverside. There was always a band and open-air dancing there in the summer, and the trees with fairy lights. Everybody went on a Wednesday night to the dancing. That really was do-it-yourself entertainment in many ways because all the local lads would get up a band, or what have you. All the country areas around had dances on a Friday night and busloads of youngsters would go out to them: to Strathpeffer, to Drumnadrochit and on a Wednesday in what you called the 'Cally Hotel' – a wonderful hotel, a beautiful design, I don't know why they ever knocked it down. They had their own resident orchestra. The Northern Meeting Rooms – which have sadly also been demolished – would have all the big bands and singers of the 1950s: Ted Heath's Band, Ronnie Aldred from the Squadronaires, Dr Crock and his Crackpots. We could be at a dance Wednesday night, Thursday night, Friday night, Saturday night and still be able to get up and go to work. Very few drank, maybe some of the wilder lads, but nobody else. You had orange juice or what have you at half time, but there wasn't a bar as such. I mean everybody went there to dance and enjoy the music and did all the rock-and-roll and what have you, jiving.

There were places where the younger ones could go to as well. We had what was called The 50-50 Club where there was dances on, and it was tea and buns at half time. You met boys, obviously, or girls and it was very much the social centre of life, it was terrific. But you had to be home by a certain time: there was no wandering about till two, three and four in the morning, and you had to come home with somebody, if you didn't have a boy to walk you home. We used to come up the road, gangs of us altogether, probably making a bit of a noise but nobody was drunk and there was very seldom fighting. The only fights used to be the soldiers that were stationed at Cameron Barracks; they would pick fights with the local lads and everybody would sort of gather round and cheer them on in the middle of the dance floor.

There was very seldom crime until recent years – maybe a bit of drunk and disorderly, but no vicious crime. There was little bit probably when the Teddy Boys were on the go – there's no doubt that some of the local ones who'd got into the Teddy Boy movement used to have the big lapels on their jacket and they did have razors sewn on them. With some of them, I think, it was just purely showing off, but mostly there was very little crime in those days. This was probably about forty years ago. Since then there has certainly been a big difference and there have been some quite nasty and vicious crimes, murders and so on over recent years. Although one of our most infamous murders was done by a local man – a double murder quite a few years ago. A child was murdered and then somebody who found out about it.

Inverness in Transition

It wasn't until the late '60s and into the '70s as Inverness started expanding with the oil-related industries, that a huge influx of population moved into this area and it changed Inverness completely. From being a fairly isolated place – I mean the A9 [the main road from the Central Belt through to the north of Scotland] as we know it now hadn't been built – there were air flights to all over the place. When they started opening up the Highlands, basically, it was like the second version of what happened after the '45 [the failed 1745 Jacobite Rebellion], when they started putting in roads and the canal and so on, so that you didn't have to walk over the mountains to get into the Lowlands.

Some changes are good, some are bad. Inverness, and probably all the Highlands, for centuries were very parochial. I think to a great degree we sort of resented incomers and there is still a little bit of that resentment, that these people seem to be coming and taking over our lives, a perception that it's all these incomers that are getting the best jobs, especially in all the quangos that have been set up. I'm not sure that's true – there is an element of it without the sensitivity to know, or the sense to find out, what the local people actually want. And I think that's something that saddens me quite a lot.

A lot is probably just a historical effect of being isolated from the rest of Britain for so many thousands of years. We were parochial, there's no doubt about that. We had very much our own lifestyle with mostly Highland people, even two hundred years before probably a lot of people moved in then, but they became adopted and merged into the sort of Highland society. Then it all started changing again. I think the speed of change frightened quite a lot of people – it went from nowhere to the fastest-growing town in Britain. It's widened our horizons and I think it's given our young people a much greater opportunity to go out into the world and see other things.

On the down side I think that we're in danger of losing a tremendous amount of the essential character of the Highlands. We've lost a tremendous amount of our culture in many ways. The old Highland culture of translating our music and song down through the generations and handing it on – that's gone. People aren't taking the time to sit back and think about their own culture and heritage. And if you think about the culture and the heritage of the Highlands, that's something which has been all over the world. Indeed the descendants of the Highlanders who live in America and Canada and Australia and New Zealand, I think they're much prouder and more conscious of their own heritage than we, the descendants of these people who'd a dreadful life of poverty and oppression for so many years – and I think that's something we should remember.

I think that we are probably trying to run too fast in many ways. Certainly the pace of change for the indigenous population is something that they're not entirely happy about. They were remembering, as I suppose everybody of that generation does, the tremendous community spirit where everybody helped everybody else. Just thinking back on an example not long after the war: the old cottage where I had been born and brought up in, it had originally been a shepherd's bothy with a bit added on. The bit added on, which had happened to be my sister and I's bedroom, had just been built on the ground which is why it was so cold. In the winter, the frost would be glittering on the inside walls of the house, not the outside. One day my bed fell through the floor; all the neighbours turned up and everybody mucked in and we got it sorted out. I'm not sure these things would happen nowadays.

As far as changes in women's lives go, women have gone from being the kitchen slave, basically. Looking back on my own mother, she practically put the spoon in my father's mouth. He was a lovely man, he was a very gentle, kind man, but he accepted that that was her role. You can still see mothers to this day bringing up their sons like that. There has been tremendous changes, and I think the revolution possibly was the pill, which gave women the freedom to decide whether they were going to be mothers at certain stages in their lives, and to control the number of children they had. That is probably the main revolution because it gave them then the ability to decide did they want to go out to work when their children were in school, or did they simply want to stay at home and have a family or be part-time in both, which is probably the most sensible option. Over the last forty years, most women's perceptions of their role in life have changed dramatically, and I think that's accepted now. But having said that, the Scotsman is still not somebody I think who deep down really believes that a woman shouldn't be at home warming the slippers, making the meal, looking after the kids. I think it's sheer financial necessity that has forced them to accept it, but there's not very many of them that really job-share, shall we say, in the domestic situation.

Looking Towards the Millennium

My hopes have in the last few months especially, turned into concerns. I joined the Liberal Party thirty-four years ago because I really believed Scotland should have its own parliament. Since the campaign started a year ago I've become more and more concerned about what is actually going to happen. I don't like the way that the two main political parties in Scotland are handling the whole thing. I have very strong reservations about what might happen were an independent Scotland to emerge out of devolution because, frankly, I don't believe the figures that have been put forward are adding up. Also, I think we are in danger of retreating into ourselves. Scotland still has very much the ethos of, 'Where you get ten Free Kirkers, you'll get ten Free Kirk churches.' It's an old Highland saying. Now, however much they may argue that Scotland is a unit, if you like, it's not. The Borderers, the Central Belt folk and the Highlanders are different. They always have been because they are descended from completely different cultures and they have their own aims and aspirations. I think I have a very great fear that the Highlands are going to lose out. That'll be sad because we've lost a tremendous amount in the Highlands, balanced by some gains. But I think we could be in danger of losing a lot more than we gain and that really does concern me. It concerns many people up here now.

Max Cruickshank
Youth Worker

Born 1941

Home Life

I was born in Edinburgh, just around the time of the war. I had a great childhood. My parents were good but older. My mother was in her forties when she had me, so we were very loved children. Although my parents were very much working class, for some strange reason my mother managed to persuade my father to buy a house, a bungalow with a garden, in quite a nice suburb of Edinburgh. We were the kind of keelies in the street, as it were. Now that I look at it, the house seems quite small. It was all bare boards and lino covers and no wall-to-wall carpeting, no central heating. We didn't even have hot water easily available, you had to boil the kettle on a gas stove in order to wash the dishes. It had a tiny wee kitchen, a wee bathroom, a living room, two bedrooms and what was called the parlour – it only got opened up for visitors and high days and holidays. But we had quite a big garden, so that was nice.

I used to be embarrassed because, although we lived in a good house, we couldn't really afford it, so we had to make ends meet. My father used to make rag rugs – you took one of the old sugar sacks and tore up rags and made these rugs that fitted all round the house. I was embarrassed because other people had proper carpets in their house. I always used to hate to bring my friends in. Years later, when I was about twenty, I went touring with a friend in an MG sports car around Scotland to the hostels. You were supposed to walk or cycle but we would get within two miles and walk in. We went to an old keep in Stornoway, in the Highlands and we walked in on a Sunday morning to have coffee and this beautiful hotel had rag rugs on the floor and I thought 'Wow, I've made it at last. The fashion's gone round and come back and they're now in fashion.'

Now with all the central heating we have things like asthma problems and so on. We never had a heated bedroom. It was always freezing cold. So you either went to bed with someone else – you often shared a bed with one of your brothers or sisters. You'd be into a freezing cold bed, maybe with a hot water bottle, maybe not. We didn't have showers. You had to have a bath. My mother certainly had the big tin bath. I never experienced that but the tin baths were still around at that time. A tin bath in the middle of the living room: a bit embarrassing, I think. We were one of the last to have a television and, much later, to have a telephone. Fridges were almost unheard of, as were microwaves, gas cookers, fancy cookers, videos. We used to have tape recorders and the old 78 records, then it moved on to the 45s and the LPs. Now we've got the CDs and the CD-ROMS and that kind of thing. It's amazing the electronics development in that period of time.

My mother had been what you used to call 'in service'. My mum and dad were both from rural communities up in Aberdeenshire – he'd come down to be a train driver which then was a very prestigious job, and my mum was in service. She was a servant, and there was different levels of servant. She ended up being a cook for doctors mainly, which then was quite a high-class servant's job. She was a very good cook, and although we had very little money, she could always cook very good things. We would have things like fish soup which nowadays is very much in vogue, and soups of all kinds. But mince and tatties I suppose was the big one. Things like jelly and custard were definitely on the go, and we had a little bit of garden where we could grow vegetables so we always had cabbage and kale and sprouts and leeks and onions and potatoes. That was very common in those days – people grew a lot of vegetables so they were very fresh. And we did have pies. My mother used to make mince and bean pies, a big big treat. Meat loaves and things like liver and kidney that nowadays people balk at but were very popular then. We had very little meat in any particular meal but it would always be bulked out with bread or potato and vegetables.

Entertainment

We played a lot in the street because in these days there was no traffic around. The main thing you had to avoid was the milk horse coming round, leaving its manure on the streets. You could play long and hard on the streets then. We used to play things like Kick-the-Can which kids won't know about these days. You kicked the can and then you all went and hid by the time someone found the can who had to go and find all the people. We played football, of course. We used to roller skate, and played things like rounders and the cleek, the old-fashioned cleek up and down the street. I used to walk on stilts quite a lot. We had what we called 'guiders', little kind of trolleys. We built them ourselves with a wee kind of trolley thing with wheels on it and we used to race down the streets on that. There was no traffic to run into in these days. You could come wheeching round the corner and you could almost guarantee there would be nobody there. It was brilliant.

As a family we used to play board games and things like that. The whole family would all join in great massive jigsaws that seemed to take weeks – it would be moved off the dining room table and put back on. Monopoly I can remember: certainly the adults and maybe my older brothers and sisters would play Monopoly for hours on a Sunday and we'd be allowed to sit and watch. They played card games and I think they gambled but I didn't quite understand that bit of it but they certainly played cards and got awful ratty about it. Things like pontoon and brag, were quite popular. Scrabble came in later and Ludo, and we played Snakes and Ladders. All these games were very much part of family life.

It was a very alcohol-free time. My parents only had alcohol at New Year. My dad used to buy a bottle of stout on a Friday when he got his pension and he would boil it up for some reason and put sugar in it because it wasn't sweet enough and that would be him, one half pint of stout a week. Mother only had a drink at New Year, a glass of sherry and she'd be absolutely out the box. Advocaat and lemonade, that was the other one – a sherry or an advocaat and lemonade. You'd be a prostitute or something if you drank anything else. Amazing.

My family were very much a singing family. My mother used to play the harmonium, a kind of organ and you had to pump it with your feet to get the air through it and we would all stand around and sing, all the old Sankey hymns which meant you had to harmonise so everybody joined in. That was great fun. My father played the button melodeon. He was very much like me now. I tend to do the same thing. He went off, he hid in the kitchen, shut the door, played his entire repertoire about three times a year. You were allowed to listen and even go in but you couldn't interrupt him. He had to play it from beginning to end and work through all these very old folk songs and well-known Scottish songs. Our family loved that, and the whole singing traditions carried on right into adulthood. Two of my sisters have become well-known folk singers and I sing; we sang in the church choir and different choirs like the school choir. We loved it. It's sad: kids nowadays don't have that kind of experience. It's much more piped kind of stuff and instant stuff that you buy. Although, I'm a youth worker and often I get out the guitar and play songs that the kids don't know and they love to join in, especially if you can hand out the hymn sheets as it were, hand out the music and then they can all join in; funny songs and sad songs, it doesn't really matter to them. I think we should do a lot more effort to get people singing again.

My parents hardly ever went to church, just the high days and holidays, but they insisted the children had to go, certainly until you went to work and we didn't really object to it. The Youth Fellowship was there, the Scouts, the Guides, the Brownies, the parties and the trips of one kind or another. The church then was almost like your community centre. Turning up to the actual church services wasn't a big problem to me or my sisters because we were in the choir and we didn't have to listen too much to what was going on, we just enjoyed the singing. It was certainly a big part of our life and virtually all of our friends went to church one way or the other, Bible Class, Youth Fellowship and so on. It's very much dwindling now, except perhaps in the Catholic community. It amazes me how the Catholic community does still manage to attract young people and very ordinary working-class people. I think the Protestant community has much much more deteriorated in terms of the numbers in the tenements and so on.

Holidays

My dad was a steam train driver for forty-six years and when I was about ten years old, he legally took me on the platform, up on the train and we went all the way to Fauldhouse and back one afternoon, which was brilliant. All the railway staff used to get free passes. That was the only way our family ever got a holiday, or a weekend away – we would go somewhere with our free pass. We went to Liverpool once and to Aberdeen and Buckie. We used to go to Loch Lomond and the train company also owned the boats in Loch Lomond so we went for a trip on Loch Lomond, an afternoon tea and had chip supper on the way back. That was brilliant. Holidays are another big innovation because then we were pretty lucky. Lots of our friends had never been on holiday anywhere.

As teenagers we went cycling a lot and camping – youth hostelling was a big thing then. My sisters were really bold and brazen and they used to go hitchhiking. Can you imagine? It was thought of as being really, really way out for girls to do that in these days. They would leave on a Friday afternoon and they would be all the way to Inverness by teatime. They used to go to the berry picking at Blairgowrie for their holidays and things like that. You'd live in huts and spend all day berry picking and all night singing and drinking and stuff.

School Days

Primary school at that time was Craiglockhart Primary in Edinburgh. One of my main teachers was Norman McCaig, the very famous poet. He seemed to have some kind of liaison with a Miss Smith, to be spending too much time with this woman teacher, so we were all scandalised about that, but I remember him very well.

Primary school I really loved. It was a very old-fashioned kind of school. We did have a play at one point and I ended up being the dormouse in *Alice in Wonderland*, but that was quite a traumatic experience for me, and I've never been able to act ever since – it did me in for life. We used to have a slate and a slate pencil instead of paper and pen. Then we had the inkwells and we had to write very properly with the ink.

Corporal & Capital Punishments

When we went to our secondary school, I was absolutely horrified because they had the belt; they had it in the primary school as well but I don't remember it very often being used. But certainly in the secondary. I went to Tynecastle Secondary in Edinburgh and we had one wee granny of a teacher who taught maths, whose name has gone out of my head, probably because it was so traumatic. She took the view that the only way to control classes, and especially classes with boys, was to belt us all at the start of every class. We all got two or three of the belt, just automatically when we arrived, which absolutely horrified me. I had terrible problems dealing with maths after that because you spent half the lesson recovering from this violent experience. So I'm glad that's gone by. I think at that time, teachers really believed that belting was the only way to maintain discipline. And yet the teachers that you really respected were the ones that didn't belt. We had a geography teacher who also did all the Bible kind of stuff and he completely enthralled us by filling the entire blackboard with fantastic pictures. As he spoke, he illustrated, and by the time of the end of each lesson the whole board would be covered with pictures. He was brilliant. We didn't get a massive amount of religion at school – we certainly had assemblies and choirs and went to church things occasionally, but it wasn't rammed down your throat.

One thing that I remember from my childhood is being horrified at the idea that we would hang people. During my childhood, the last hangings happened in prisons in Scotland. I think Peter Manuel was probably one of them, I can't remember the detail but I can remember we sat by the radio and listened to the news and I was absolutely appalled. I couldn't make the relationship between what the person had done and the idea of actually taking somebody out and hanging them. I'm a lifelong anti-capital punishment supporter; it still horrifies me that they had that. And they also used to have birchings as well, which have long since gone. About two years ago someone asked me about birching and I phoned up the inspector in the Isle of Man who, in theory, is still responsible for birching. Although it's been banned by the European Community, it is possible that they could birch people if they wished. I had a long conversation and a correspondence with him about it. He was saying that he would be the first person to have it banned because it was his responsibility to deliver it and administer it and he said it just did not work. If anything, it encouraged the real thugs to come back for more because that became a status symbol. One of the big changes in our life is moving from that very violent way of dealing with people which we've now realised doesn't work. But this view is very unpopular, because if you arranged for hangings on a Saturday afternoon on Glasgow Green, I'm sure the crowds would turn out to watch people being hung or birched. You've always got to hope that politicians and lawmakers are ahead of the trend in their thinking so that we don't bring back things that are totally outrageous and quite immoral really.

Off to Work

I left school at fifteen and went straight into an apprenticeship. In these days it was quite easy. I actually wanted to be a joiner and my mother insisted I should be an engineer instead and I thought well, why not? Ferranti used to recruit apprentices every year and there was a massive kind of Saturday selection day where three hundred boys – there would be no girls, I suspect – had to turn up at the McEwan Hall in Edinburgh and do some kind of IQ tests and exams, to select twenty apprentices. I got one of the places, to my amazement. So I became a highly skilled instrument maker, an engineer.

The apprenticeship was five years and that was a great time. We had an apprentice school for a couple of years and then we went to the factory. When I was an apprentice still in the factory, we used to work two nights a week overtime and Saturday and part of Sunday – it really was a very, very busy working life, very tiring. I ended up teaching in the apprentice school. I broke my leg at one point and they hired me back to teach technical drawing. The factory was a bit more difficult. That was my first experience of factory life and people who were a bit different from me. One of my main memories was how crude the women could be. I mean, to adolescent boys, who looked like ten-year-olds and probably were sixteen, they were pretty horrendous. I used to get sent up a lot and embarrassed a lot, so that was quite difficult, especially since I had quite a churchy background. Even into my late teens, I tended to go to church and Youth Fellowship and those kind of organisations.

Starting Youth Work

People now think that life is quite violent, but around 1961, life in Edinburgh was quite violent. The kind of violence that people remember in Glasgow was also in Edinburgh, in Leith in particular. You went to the dancing and there was massive fights and battles and a lot of drunkenness. There were street gangs all over the city. We had all the Teddy Boys and the Mods and Rockers. They were just guys trying as always to be macho and use up their massive energies. Fired by alcohol, they became incredibly aggressive and found an opportunity to express that. This was before the drug scene hit Britain. The motivation was totally alcohol driven. We didn't see drugs around at that time at all. You heard about it. I remember I overheard about this incredible Chinese restaurant, the first Chinese restaurant in Edinburgh, I think, up the top of Chambers Street, where they've now built the new bit of the Scottish museum. There was shops there, and shops above the shops, and in there was an opium den – Chinese people went there to consume this illicit drug, opium. Now I had no idea what that was at the time but it just seemed really way out and wild. It's quite ironic because now a large part of my work is in drugs education and counselling.

Particularly on the Friday and Saturday nights, people would go and get very drunk and then turn up at the dance halls. You're talking about maybe two thousand people turning up at the Palais de Dance in Fountainbridge in Edinburgh. Two thousand young people is quite a handful at the best of times but as the night progressed, different gangs would appear and, inevitably, there would be battles. What horrified me the most wasn't so much the violence of the young people, but the violence of the adults, the bouncers and the people who were supposed to be controlling it. They seemed to love to be utterly violent to people, throwing people through doors and smashing them with tables and kicking them downstairs. That partly motivated me to think that there must be a better way to work with young people than being violent to them.

Everyone was talking about trying to do something about this. A guy called Ron Beasley who was an amazing character, a youth worker at that time for the Church of Scotland, had this idea of opening up a Beat Club, a nightclub that young people could go to. They would work with these street gangs – I suppose their main intention was to try and give them some kind of religion. It was also very much a social thing, about trying to work with them, and I got involved because it seemed like an interesting idea and I was a very practical person. I could make things and they needed doors hung and floors laid and painting done and furniture built, so I got involved purely with the intention of helping to build it and then I would leave. But I got totally enthralled by the idea and got involved. I'm surprised I did because most of the people involved were students and very intellectual kind of people, very religious kind of people who weren't my scene at all by that time. They were incredible characters and once we started working with the young people, it opened up all kinds of interests that have kept me going for the last thirty-five years.

Youth Work in the New Towns

I left engineering and trained as a professional youth worker. I went then to New York for a short time and worked with a street gang and in the drug scene because I wanted to understand more about that. I had a sixth sense that this was going to be a big thing here and I was right. Also, because I had been working with street gangs here, I also wanted to see how the Americans did it. Then I came back and my first job was working with an ecumenical team ministry, which was a big experiment in Livingston New Town. I was the detached youth worker there – my job initially was wandering round the streets, meeting young people and trying to work with them, and eventually setting up all the youth work around the new town. New Towns were basically about trying to rehouse the people from the slums of Glasgow. Livingston was about the fifth New Town, I think. They were seen as a massively successful experiment in moving people out of slums into greenfield sites where all these new innovations could happen: new houses, really decent houses with central heating, hot water and proper facilities, decent schools, lovely environment.

It didn't quite work out as simple as that because it's not that easy to change communities. In general, it was a fantastic experience trying to innovate things, particularly on the youth-work front. I was naive enough then, at twenty-six, to think I could change the world. So I had this wonderful idea that would do away with all the traditional youth clubs and youth work, Scouts, Guides, the BBs and Girls Guilds as they used to be called, and do something different. But within three years people were clamouring for the old. Their parents and their grandparents remembered the BB and the Bible Class, and they wanted their kids to have that, so it was quite difficult. But we did do a lot of innovative stuff and it was a very exciting place to be. It was like the Wild West: you came to a greenfield, drove in the trucks and set up camp and started. That was great fun.

The biggest problem in introducing new things was changing adults' perceptions more than changing young people. Young people would have gone with the flow, but adults hankered for what they thought was best about their childhood or about their upbringing; they wanted this inculcated into the life of the community for their children. But New Towns, all of them, tended to attract very young workers and young parents so you had a cycle to go through. The first phase was very much about babies, toddlers. My wife was one of the people that pioneered the whole idea of pre-school playgroups in Scotland, which was very much more a mum-run than a dad-run, organisation for pre-school children before we had nursery provision. That was a big thing. There was a desperate need for mums to meet during the day in particular. All the men were off at work, most of them had work at that point, good well-paid work and long hours. And we then had to create opportunities later on for younger kids and then for teenagers as time went on. Then it would be young parents and then middle-agers. Now it's very much about pensioners. You've had a whole kind of cycle over the whole thirty years.

One of the most important things I was involved in was when we created the first charitable company in Scotland, called the Craigshill Community Development Project, which was about trying to create an innovative community facility, not a community centre. The idea was it would be like a chameleon – as the chameleon changed its colour according to its background, we would change our approach according to the needs of the community, so we would start with babies and work on to pensioners. I'm absolutely delighted to see that that facility, the Craigsfarm Centre, has done all of that. It has simply evolved as thirty years has gone on and changed its needs according to the community. So I'm very proud of that.

The Burgeoning Drug Scene

I was a teenager in the 1960s when the whole drug scene happened but I completely, totally missed it as a young person. People often say, 'Well, you must have known about it, you must have heard the tunes,' and so on, but we were totally naive. The nearest I heard was the Chinese opium den.

But once I saw the situation in New York I was absolutely gobstruck and horrified. I remember coming back from America and thinking two things in particular: the first thing was, would we be so stupid as to copy all of that because they used to say that most things that happened in America, we did twenty years later. The second thing that bugged me was the people I was working with, the drug addicts and it just got right up my nose. I didn't have a lot of sympathy for them and I eventually twigged that the problem was that they were like big weans, like two-year-olds, at the 'terrible twos' stage of life where we try to assert ourselves and it's 'me, me, me', 'I, I, I', 'I want, I want, I want'. That's what horrified me: that basically the main problem with drugs wasn't the deaths, it was that it stunted people's maturity, it stopped the process of growing up. It stopped the process of working through the normal activities of life and the normal dealing with problems to become a mature adult.

So, I was very clear in 1965, when I came back from New York, that I wanted to do something to combat that. I naively imagined it would be possible, just by telling people and working at it, that we could avoid all the problems they had in the States. The horrendous thing is that we've copied absolutely everything. Everything that has happened in the States – the whole drug scene – we've copied, including all the approaches that don't work. I'm utterly frustrated that after thirty-eight years of working at it, basically we've made almost no progress. We're just about to make some breakthroughs now, I think. It's taken all of that time and I think we have a horrendous problem on our hands. We live in a very hypocritical society that is drug-driven, by the medical profession, by the pharmaceutical companies, by the alcohol industry, by the smoking industry, by the belief that you can solve anything by popping a pill. We simply haven't learnt enough about that yet to be able to combat it.

I'm a very positive person in terms of my belief that we can change things. I honestly believe that if we listen to young people, and work with young people to solve these problems, then we will get there. A difficulty has been that in the past, adults, particularly adults in authority, think they know best. They've been totally clueless, they've been working in the dark. They haven't listened to what young people are telling them. Once we get to the situation where we start to listen to young people we will then be able to create alternatives. The drug situation is a multi-billion pound international business that has been developed over thirty years, and these guys are not going to go away easily. The only thing that will hurt them in any way at all is if fashion changes and young people or adults say: 'I'm no' having it. I don't want it. I've got a better alternative.' We've got to work to create that better alternative.

I have a company at the moment called 'A Right Pair of Chancers' and they're creating a second company called 'Gie's A Break' – and Gie's A Break would be going out and gie'en folk a break, you know. Let's have some fun. Like the old days where we used to sit around as a family and have fun and do all kinds of stuff. Let's teach folk again to have fun. That way, folk might find that there are other alternatives that are not drug-induced. and that would be really helpful to them. So I live in hope that we will create that. Young people aren't daft but they're easily exploited and it's adults that exploit them. It's big business, whether it's international Mafia, international pharmaceutical companies, international sugar companies, international salt companies. It doesn't matter. In the end of the day our society is driven by the need to create wealth, and almost anything goes as long as that kind of goal can be achieved. We then think we can buy off later the problems we create and I think what I've learnt in my lifetime is that you can't buy it off.

Looking to the Future

I think the new Parliament offers tremendous opportunities. We've got to lay that against the utter cynicism of the population towards politicians – a lot of my generation have fought long and hard to have a Scottish Parliament and we hope and dream that that will give us the controls and the powers that we need to make things better. But if we continue with the kind of politics that we have at the moment, which seems to be all about soundbites and sleaze and politicians manipulating things for their own ends rather than the community, then we have no hope at all. My hope is that we can involve ourselves in a much better situation, but I think we need to educate the population to believe again that you can effect change. I don't think at the moment that most adults let alone young people believe that in any way we can effect change.

One of the things that stuns me is that childhood now is a much more isolated, lonely thing – this has partly come about because of the safety thing, but also because of transportation. I mean parents drive; I think eighty per cent of children are driven to and from school. They don't walk any longer so they are no longer fit. They don't socialise on the way to school and the way back. Many kids come home and then go into their own bedroom – we never had our own bedroom. They have their own space, very much more privacy than we had. They can then hide away there watching television and videos, playing computer games and can easily become social isolates. For me, that's one of the things in the future that we really have to work at. I honestly believe that many children will reach their adulthood having been in a very isolated social situation, a less healthy way than it should be. I think it's absolutely urgent that we convince young people, at least, that we can effect change and get them as heavily involved as possible in their local communities, in their local youth-participation programmes and their own organisations. Then, at the end of the day, as we prove to them that it is possible to effect change in their patch so therefore it must be possible to effect it on a national and an international and a world basis. There's a massive programme to be done there and I'd love to be part of that.

Tommy Fleming
Hairdresser

Born 1942

An East End Boy

I was born in 20 Glenlyon Street which is deep in the East End of Glasgow between Gallowgate and Duke Street. As a very young man, the one thing that got me really clean and healthy was swimming. I got picked up at about seven years of age, became a competitive swimmer right up till I was about fourteen. I swam for Glasgow, swam for West of Scotland, captained the school swimming team, all these sort of things – they kept me well away from a direction which I don't think I'd have liked to have gone in. I could've ended up possibly in that sort of gang syndrome that was going about the East End of Glasgow in those days. There could've been pressure to do that, only I excelled in swimming. They thought I was a young lad doing well, so they more or less stayed buddies with me and didn't expect me to go about in gangs, causing problems and trouble for other people.

This was in the very early 1950s. There was no fear – even of the gangs that ran about the streets in those days. Strangers, kids, old age pensioners – they were sacrosanct. These sort of gangs would never, ever touch them. It was almost the tribal thing: if some other gang came into your area, that's when trouble could start. I don't think anybody's sacrosanct now. Possibly the drug element changed all that. I'm not saying all these gangsters of yesteryear were all noble people – they were violent, horrible people. But they never touched strangers and never touched old people or kids, that I do remember.

We stayed in a room and kitchen, and even had an outside toilet. But it was lovely, I just loved it. I've very happy memories of the whole scenario. I remember as a child I suffered from migraine, and used to have attacks regularly; whatever caused that I'll never know. Both my parents worked but they could leave me, key in the door, and neighbours came in constantly to make sure I was okay. Could anyone imagine leaving a key in a door anywhere in Glasgow these days? We played football, non-stop. I'd two brothers who were exceptionally talented at football. I was very ordinary, but I was a football fanatic. I was born a stone's throw from Parkhead [Celtic Park] which tells you where I went every Saturday afternoon. I went with my brothers. My father enjoyed football but he didn't go very often. I used to go as a four-year-old, waiting for the gates to open at half time to get in free. That's my earliest memories. I

THE HERO GETS MARRIED: CHARLIE TULLY IN 1947

remember Charlie Tully but I was very young. It was really primary school stuff but I do remember being absolutely mesmerised by the man's talent. I thought he was the most wonderful thing I'd ever seen.

I remember the anthems the supporters used to sing at Parkhead – they were actually more hymns than anthems. They were taken out of the church realm and that was the songs that were sung until the famous one by Glen Daly [*Sure, It's A Grand Old Team to Play For*] and that's changed lots of things. Now all I seem to hear is people writing songs for Celtic supporters. In the old days, it was specific songs, always stuff like *Hail, Glorious St Patrick* and *Faith of our Fathers* that always let you know that Catholicism was involved, but as the years rolled on that seemed to fade a lot and it's just Celtic songs now.

As a child, I wasn't really aware of the religious divide in the West of Scotland. I've got very strong views on how it's actually got worse. When Jock Stein joined Celtic, it was exactly the same period that the troubles in Northern Ireland got worse. I felt the pressures on both sides of supporters got really embittered and I think that's what caused what goes on today. I remember going to what was referred to as the 'Jungle' [the North Stand] at Celtic Park; people find this very difficult to believe, but I used to go with pals who were Rangers supporters. The Jungle at one stage was close to being neutral. Scarves actually criss-crossed there, and the same at Ibrox opposite the main stand, you occasionally saw the scarves crossing over and this is where the sort of peace-loving supporters used to go and support their team. But when the police in their wisdom started segregation then the Celtic supporters headed for the Jungle so they could be close to their arch-rivals Rangers and this is where the Jungle started building this reputation up of fanaticism. But in my youth it wasn't like that – the fanaticism was behind each goal.

School Days

A BOY AND HIS BIKE

I went to the school closest to Parkhead, St Anne's Primary School, and had a wonderful education there. In my day, qualifying exams were part and parcel of school. Luckily enough, I sailed through them with flying colours. I had to – I had two brothers who'd done it before me and the qualifying teacher made sure I never forgot about them. I ended up at St Mungo's Academy, which was one of the best schools in Glasgow at the time. The Marist Brothers [a teaching religious order] there were pretty strong on discipline. Towards the end of my schooling the indiscipline started creeping in slightly, but this was the start of all the 'blackboard jungle' and the teenage rebellious attitudes coming out of the States. But the Marist Brothers were up for it.

I used to go to the cinema, all the local fleapits, every one. I was an ABC minor, I used to go on Saturday mornings, singing my little heart away – couldn't sing a note, but I used to sing away. Watching Flash Gordon, Batman and Robin, Rex of the Mounties, Rocket Man – oh dear, I can remember all these series that were on – I used to love them. Tarzan was my hero, I think it's because I could swim, and Johnny Weismuller was my hero, except I could never understand what 'Umgalla' meant – this was Johnny Weismuller's favourite word. Elephants came, lions ran away, thousands of African natives dispersed rapidly when the word 'Umgalla' was used, and still to this day I don't know what it means.

I was hooked on Ayton Biscuits, a sort of diamond-shaped biscuit, with chocolate on top and just plain dark biscuit underneath. I was hooked on them and used to eat them all the time. I also remember when lots of 'gingers' – to use a Glasgow expression – came out. The only pop drink was just very simple lemonade, then all of a sudden Irn Bru was reintroduced after the war, and you got pineapple juice, you got lots of variety all of a sudden; all the variations now on the shelves. We used to get lots of ice lollies when I was a kid – chocolate-flavoured ice lollies and that sort of thing.

Career Choices

Prior to leaving school at fifteen, I had a second cousin who was a lot older than me, and I used to visit her and her husband. She used to 'Hilltone' her hair, which was basically a bleach from the chemist. She used to ask me to apply this at the back because she couldn't see it. So every time I went up, I used to put the stuff on for her and her words were, 'Thomas, you're going to be a natural hairdresser.' From that point forth, I thought hairdressing was slapping this stuff on people's hair, I didn't realise there was a lot more to it. But she implanted the thought in my head. When I left school I went for jobs – furrier, dental mechanic even. Then my brother, who was living in London, informed me that one of the top London salons had just opened in Glasgow, or was in the process of opening. We phoned up and I got an interview; I went along and sex raised its ugly head. I was sitting there – a wee boy from the Gallowgate waiting for an interview – and I saw these glamorous girls round the reception area. I'd never seen anything like that in my life before – it was really straight out of Hollywood. I thought, 'I've got to get a job here,' and I did.

At first I told my pals I was working in a barber shop, I didn't tell them it was ladies' hairdressing. I was worried. I was genuinely worried, I thought, 'this is going to immediately make me gay'. Then one day, we were sort of hanging about a street corner and one of the real neds (I shouldn't say that, he was a pal of mine) said to me 'You are a lucky so-and-so, you go to work clean and you come home clean. We go to work, we come back filthy, got to go and get scrubbed down – I really envy you.' And that sort of settled things – then I realised things weren't too bad. Only on one occasion I remember getting funny looks. In those days you used to apply treatments to ladies' hair and you had Chanel No 5 or Arpège. Sometimes I used to come home with my hands reekin' of the stuff and that's when I got the funny looks. But everybody knew I was boringly straight.

When I first finished my apprenticeship, an unknown London hairdresser came up to – of all places, Partick Burgh Halls. Somebody says, 'I've heard this guy's really good, let's go along and see him.' I went along and I was totally mesmerised. The man is now internationally famous: it was Vidal Sassoon. He and Maurice and Rosemary, who I met later in London, did a show, but only for hairdressers. The public would have been aghast: in those days everything was back-combed, everything was high, full, wide, couldn't get it high enough or full enough. These three hairdressers produced hair that could move. When people moved, the hair moved, and I thought, 'That's for me.' London was it, and eventually I went down looking for work and got a job.

Swinging London

I was a Scot in London, in the 1960s, the Swinging '60s. Oh, I went down with the chip on the shoulder, didn't I? To prove that I could be better than them, given half a chance. I worked in three salons, and in two of them I became top stylist. I loved it. I first got a job in Harvey Nichols and it was wonderful then. It was just awe-inspiring, the whole place.

I did loads of celebrities. I did quite a lot in Glasgow before I went down, pop stars like Connie Francis coming in. She was a strange girl – she was very reclusive and underlined quotes from the Bible while I was doing her hair, and I just found it strange. This was when I worked in Steiners, where I trained. Lots of the theatrical people lived in the Central Hotel in those days so we got them in as clients. I was nervous about them coming in: the thought of it got me going. But I was quite a confident young lad about my hairdressing ability so I wasn't nervous once I started.

The loveliest person I ever dealt with was a girl called Miriam Karlin, a Jewish actress, and she was the nicest human being I'd ever met. She was well known, being on a very hot series called *The Rag Trade*. These kids were piling on top of her and she sat them on her knee and told them stories the whole time I was dealing with her hair. To me, anybody who's good to kids like that in that situation was wonderful.

The biggest disappointment was Margaret Rutherford. I thought 'Now this is somebody that I think must be so funny and humourous' and I got really excited about it. In she came, I asked her how she wanted her hair: not a word. She'd a handmaiden with her and this lady told me everything that Miss Rutherford wanted. Not a word was passed – it was the biggest disappointment of my life.

The most glamorous person was Vivien Leigh. She was appearing in the King's Theatre; she was beautiful, but she was tiny. I was really amazed how small she was – I'd envisaged somebody about five foot eight – but she was lucky if she was about five foot.

Jiving in Glasgow

I missed the soul of Glasgow. I missed the humour, and every time I came home for a weekend I thought, 'No, the crack's really still great up here. I will come back'. Lots of friends I worked with in London started moving off to places like South Africa and Australia, but these sort of places didn't appeal to me in those days. I was even offered jobs in America and I was a bit frightened of that, a bit frightened of the States. Then two lads that I'd worked with in Glasgow were on an expansion programme and they were looking for a salon manager and talked me into coming back. Quite honestly I haven't regretted it, I've had a wonderful time since I came back.

People in the United Kingdom may find this strange: everybody jived in those days but Glasgow had something that other cities didn't have and I think it was a direct connection with New York almost. It was something peculiar to Glasgow, it was a cult. Maybe Liverpool did it but I was never aware of this. But it was straight out of Harlem. A few years back, I went a Caribbean cruise with my wife and there was a big band playing and I was doing a bit of jiving, jitterbug stuff. This couple came over, Americans, and said 'Where did you learn to do that?' I said 'Glasgow.' He said, 'You've never been to New York?' I said I'd never been to New York in my life. I got up with his wife, he got up with my wife and it worked, it really did. Also, I've a lifelong ambition to go to Harlem. I don't think it'd be as easy now, but I'd love to go and dance in a place called Mama Rosa's (I think) jive club with locals. It still goes on to this day: it's kids that are still taking it up.

Possibly the real appeal was because it was American. I'd gone to see *Rock Around The Clock* when I was still at school, and thought that's what I want to do: I want to dance like these kids. I thought they were out of this world, I'd never seen anything like that before. My parents still go to the dancing, my older brothers were going to the dancing – none of them jived. And I said, 'That's for me.' A new jazz club opened up in Glasgow and in those days clubs didn't get a licence to drink, they only got permission to drink on opening nights. My mate's uncle was a publican and he supplied drink for the opening night. The following Sunday my mate and I went up to get the empty crates. It was about eight flights up in Union Street and as I walked in, *The Girl Can't Help It* by Little Richard was being played. There was this lad dancing and I says, 'Little Richard's here.' It was a guy who I'm still friendly with, called George Leslie who's Afro-Cuban and a wonderful human being. He was doing the dancing that I'd seen in the film *Blackboard Jungle* and I says, 'That's for me.' So I was still at school when I started it, at fourteen years of age. I've loved it ever since.

I used to work in a famous club called the Londella, I was in the Logan Show for three years running, jiving, and it was just incredible. I even signed autographs! The first professional gig I ever got involved with was with Alex Harvey who was Scotland's Tommy Steele. No harm to Tommy Steele, but Alex Harvey was miles better than Tommy Steele. He was a wonderful character and that whole part of my youth was very educational, let's put it that way.

Glasgow Style The fashions were very much American. London hadn't peaked as a fashion centre then. Paris had but Paris catered for, dare I say, early-middle-aged people in those days. The American college student was what everybody wanted to look like. That was it, what you saw in cinemas, was what you wanted to get. I used to go up to Bob Fletcher's, a shop in Cambridge Street, to get all my shirts and trousers. Very American, these shirts were all named: Mr B which was Billy Eckstein shirts, Tony Curtis shirts, Dean Martin shirts. And Ivy League shirts: the trendy guys in Glasgow used to get Ivy League shirts 'cos they were all stripes, various dull colours, autumn colours. In those days, you had to be immaculately dressed: everything had to be snow white, almost stiff collared, silk ties, three-button suits. If you didn't have that, you then went the American college route and that was the sort of styles that was going about in those days.

These three-buttoned suit guys, they were referred to as Moonies – nothing to do with a religious sect, but with a dance called the Moon Dance. The mods came from them, that's for sure, mods came from Glasgow Moonies. The Beatles suit of '63 came

*THE HEIGHT OF FASHION;
c. 1959/60*

from Glasgow Moonies. When I was in London I met Manfred Mann and I was talking to him about it. He said he used to send up to Glasgow to Esquires to get shirts and suits made and he said the Beatles used to do it as well. They used to send up and order these special shirts. The little guy who worked in the shop was called Arthur Black. Arthur opened up his own little workshop in St Enoch Square and I'm sure he supplied most of the pop people both north and south of the border.

We went to see Jerry Lee Lewis. I've seen the biopic film of him, of how when he came to Britain and nobody went to his concerts, they booed him. That never happened in Glasgow. I don't think the fact about him marrying his thirteen-year-old cousin had broken when he was in Glasgow; I think that came to press later. St Andrews Halls was packed. We saw Bill Haley when I was a schoolboy. My mate and I took turns staying up all night to get a ticket, front-row seats. We queued about four hours each. Went home, had a quick sleep and came back. That was not done in those days. He played in the Odeon Cinema. It was one big cinema then, it wasn't a group of cinemas as is now.

After we'd gone dancing or whatever, we'd have a poke of chips. Chips would've been the only thing because nothing else was opened in those days. You came out of jiving about half past ten, quarter to eleven and that's when Glasgow died, unless you belonged to a private club, like the Piccadilly Club; they stayed open late. Teenagers would never be members of a private club and generally speaking, people were in their bed for half past eleven, twelve o'clock – that's when they're getting ready to go out now.

Changing Morality

Morals have changed in Glasgow. The worst thing I ever touched was alcohol and I was never heavily involved with it. The very first time I was in a pub, I was the youngest of four of us. Three were eighteen-year-olds and I was about fifteen. They all got knocked back when they went up to order and they asked me to go up and try as a last resort and I got served. I don't understand to this day how the guy looked at me and served me, 'cos the other guys were two or three years older than me. I didn't even drink. I can remember many a time being stopped from trying to get into pubs.

Drugs! The only thing I knew about drugs when I was a kid was what I read in cheap novels from America. Hairdressing was a trade where drugs filtered in quickly but it never got to me at all, never interested me. Now the drug culture is actually accepted, even by people who don't like it, who want to fight against it. They still accept it – it's just part of 'Oh, you cannae do anything about it'. I find that a hard thing for anybody to say if people are dying with drugs, thugs are becoming millionaires with drugs, yeah we all sit back and say 'Oh you cannae do anything about it, it's got too big a grip now,' – surely somebody somewhere must have an idea how to stop it. My idea is taking kids out of school, taking them round hospitals where you see amputees lying – drugs have caused that, dirty needles. I've got kids and I know it's horrible to think of them going into hospital to see people in severe pain, but it might just be the catalyst that could stop them from going in that direction. Because as a parent I worry, really worry. Everybody tells me 'You're old fashioned – drugs are the thing.' I suppose I am.

The Future for Scotland

I think Scotland's got to go a stage further than it is now – we have to have more control of the economy that has been ruined by Mrs Thatcher, may I say. I'm not her biggest fan. Why can't we get the oil? Nobody can tell me why – people say nobody'll invest – it's the oil companies that invest. You're not looking for Scottish individuals to invest. BP invest, Esso invest, Texaco invest, as they invest now. Are they going to stop investing if Scotland all of a sudden owns the oil or owns the revenue from the whisky? I'd like us to see more share of what we ourselves produce, and I'm a firm believer we produce the oil; it is geographically there for all to see. I think a stage further: I would love to see this place becoming a tax haven. I think it's a possibility if we could get to grasps with everything that economically is sound in our country, if we ourselves get the benefits of it. I don't think I'll live to see that though. Maybe, just maybe.

Bruce Findlay
Rock Manager & Impresario
Born 1944

I was born in Edinburgh at the Simpson Memorial Hospital. We lived in a place called Chesser, near the abattoir. As kids we used to go up there and herd the cattle and the sheep up with the farmers, the shepherds; we were doing it thinking they were being auctioned. I never really contemplated that they got slaughtered. I didn't equate the meat on my plate with these animals up in the fields there. There were huge fields which we played football in, huge fields around there that are now houses. We sledged, there was a nice slope on one of the hills. The animals were brought there in cattle trucks and we used to go to the auctions, which were great fun as a kid.

My mother and father divorced when I was quite young. When I was born my father was a policeman in Edinburgh but after they divorced my father moved to York and worked in Rowntree's chocolate factory for the next twenty or thirty years. My mother obviously had to make ends meet and she went out and did books for a radio and gramophone shop in Falkirk. She encouraged the boss to buy up a little record shop that had gone bankrupt in about 1952 or '53 and she opened this shop in Falkirk. My mother's passion for the records is the reason I got into the music business. The shop was called 'Angus MacDougall's'– great name – and through the '50s it became legendary. My mother reverted to her maiden name, Miss Shearer, and she became very well known to the music industry and the record company.

School Days
I went to Stenhouse Primary School and then got a bursary to the Royal High School, in Regent Terrace. You had to do an 11-Plus and an entry exam and that got me into the Royal High but I hated it. I was reasonably bright up until that age, about twelve. Academically, I did all right; I was always near the top of the class but I just failed at the High School. I was miserable. I didn't like it, it was a boys-only school, I found it very snobbish. I didn't come from the right background because I'd divorced parents. I left as soon as I could, in 1959, when I was fifteen years of age.

I think the parents of all kids, then as now, wanted them do respectable things – get good exam results, go on to college or university, become a doctor or something like that. I don't think my mother was any different and it was frustrating for her because the school would say that I was not as bright but I played truant all the time. I rebelled – I don't feel good about that necessarily but I certainly don't feel bad about it either. The notion of going to college only appealed to me because I thought students were really hip. I'd have loved to have gone to art college or drama college, but I didn't have the qualifications so I used to hang out at the Art College, pretending that I was a student. In the late '50s, students were hip, the way they looked, the way they talked, they were slightly rebellious. We didn't really have a British rock-and-roll scene in the late 1950s, not until the Beatles and the Stones came along. I identified more with students or American Beats – Jack Kerouac, and all that.

Juliette Greco, France: all things French I thought were incredibly cool. Fashion, music obviously turned me on, rock-and-roll, pop music, American music. There was very little in Britain. Karl Denver I liked, he was a Scots guy. He had a South African song called *Wimoweh – The lion sleeps tonight*, a great song. He did an original version, he just wailed, *Wimoweh*, in this falsetto voice. But the music scene in Britain itself wasn't really very good.

A Cool Cat in Falkirk

Up until I left school, we were still in Chesser. My older brother Brian had to work, to help sustain me and my mother, so he went off to work in the same company as my mother: hi-fi, radio, television. He drove my mother back and forward between the shop in Falkirk and Edinburgh. It's only twenty-five miles, but it was the wee windy road, quite an exhausting day for my mother. The car was a little Morris Minor-type van, which Brian used to go round on his calls to repair televisions. Television now was up and running, and the shop was doing so well in Falkirk, that Mr MacDougall built a new shop with a flat above for my mother, and we moved there in late 1959. I hated the idea of moving to Falkirk. I was from Edinburgh, for goodness sake, but Falkirk from 1959 until I left was fabulous. It was a great town, great people and there was a great sense of humour.

I started to work in the record shops as soon as I left school but it was seen as a temporary job. In those days it was traditionally a job for girls, between the ages of eighteen and getting married, so it was never seen as a career, record retail, not then, even although my mother was doing extremely well. I did several jobs over a period of a year: labouring, working in a sawmill, in a brewery, as an office boy. Finally I got a job with the bank. I nearly joined the RAF: passed all the tests and then went off to a place called Holton, said goodbye to my mum, family, friends, because I wanted to become a pilot. I was sixteen. I only learned before I finally signed the documents that I would have to sign up for fourteen years. I thought 'No, to hell with it, I'm sixteen, I can't make up my mind,' so I didn't do that.

I came back in disgrace, and was persuaded to try to get into the bank. I worked for the Clydesdale Bank and I was brilliant at telling, counting, dealing with the customers. It was an old-fashioned bank, pen and ink and script, and pounds, shillings and pence – no calculators, no adding machines. That was a great training for me but again it involved having home studies, exams and documents. I wouldn't study, and after eighteen months of this they said: 'Look, Bruce you've got to get some exams, you can't stay on,' so I said, 'Fine, I'll leave.'

This was the rebellious side of me, the need to be cool, and to try and grow up and become a person in my own right, as all kids do. I was going through a horrible period: your hormones are working overtime and you're fancying girls. I was going to a lot of dances by this time. Next door to the record shop in Falkirk was the Manor Cafe which had a juke box and a big heavy Coca-Cola machine; you put thruppence in and got a Coca Cola out. That was where me and my two best friends, George and Gordon, used to hang out, trying to look cool.

It was mostly the Teddy Boy thing in those days, but I didn't like it, it was just too macho. The bike thing, on the other hand – remember, the coolest actor in the world was Marlon Brando and the coolest image in the world was Marlon Brando in a leather jacket on a motorbike in *The Wild Ones*. In the bank, though, my hair was never too long. Everyone still had these sort of army haircuts, or else there were

Teddy Boys and that greasy stuff – horrible. Mine wasn't, I never used grease or anything and I'd curly hair so it was always fairly neat. Put a suit on and anyone looks smart. I wore a suit to work. The first suit I ever got was a Daks suit. It was about £15, at least three weeks wages, a really expensive suit at the time. Anyway, I only wore it to work, I couldn't wait to get out my suit. I'd come home immediately from work, fold my suit neatly, and into the jeans and the big baggy jersey and then down to the cafe to hang out. My two pals, George and Gordon were very cool bikers – they wore the gear, sure, leather trousers, leather jacket, but they were also into jazz. We used to go to Edinburgh on the bikes and hang out in Bungee's, Studio 3, La Boheme – all the cool cafes that were beginning to open up in Edinburgh. Rock-and-roll was so bad then that the coolest thing to like was traditional jazz, and the whole beatnik thing which was in fashion. We wanted to believe that it was much more than that, that it was a possible way of life, but you're sixteen, seventeen, growing up now, beginning to earn some money, but completely unsure of what the world's really all about, struggling to find out and having great fun challenging it. Then one day – the 17th of September 1961 – a Sunday, my aunt got married, which was a very unusual thing in Scotland, getting married on a Sunday. The reception was in Grangemouth and George and Gordon decided to pay a trip to see me at this wedding reception. On their way down, they were in a head-on car crash which killed them both. I attempted suicide that night and they locked me up for the next two weeks in hospital. They said I was going to have a nervous breakdown, I was just an emotional teenager really upset. I wanted to die, it was all terrible self-pity, horribly cruel to my mum, my brothers.

On the Road

All this changed my life: when I came round, I left the bank. I had very itchy feet, so I thought I'm going to hitchhike round the world. Me and another pal called Des set off hitchhiking. We had no money at all. We got as far as Brighton and I managed to get a job in a hotel as a barman. I was seventeen so I lied about my age. I was there for about six months and saved about £60 which was quite a lot of money in 1962. With that money, we went off to France. It ran out very quickly, but I got work in the South of France in Baneuils-sur-mer in a vineyard for a month or two. The winter of 1962, '63 was the worst winter on record I think at that time – snow, they'd never seen snow like it down this far south. Then I moved into Spain, sold encyclopaedias to American servicemen in Seville for about a week, until I realised it was an absolute con. I went on to

On the hippie trail: Bruce in the 1960s

216

Morocco, and I thought, 'Great, I'm on to my second continent.' This was now four or five months in to my hitching, surviving on next to no money. It was a great experience though; when I got to Morocco, it completely ran out.

You weren't allowed into Gibraltar without money, but Gibraltar was British, so I managed to con my way in, slept rough, and telexed home from a post office. I got twenty quid sent out and started to hitch home. From Portugal, penniless now, I got a lift all the way to the north of France, got dropped off, and was trying to make Dunkirk when this young farmer picked me up. He tried to speak English and I tried to speak French: 'What are you doing?', 'I tried to hitchhike around the world and I only got as far as Morocco.' He said, 'Do you want to go home?' and I said 'Nope, people are going to take the Mickey out of me when I go home 'cos I didn't make it.' And he said 'We've just moved out of our old farmhouse, back into the chateau which the Germans occupied during the war. I'm redeveloping the farmhouse, the farm; it's a small farm, would you like to come and work for the summer?'

So off I went, drove a tractor, learned to ride horses bareback, rounding up cattle on this guy's farm, it was brilliant. I was there for three or four months. During that time, 1963, the Beatles were happening in Britain. My mum's sending me out records and the *New Musical Express*, and I thought, 'I've got to get home', I wanted to be part of the something that was happening in Britain. I really felt like a young man now, I've travelled the world, well, France. You're young and naive and it was a long way for people like me – going to bloody Edinburgh and Glasgow was a long distance from Falkirk, never mind going to Morocco, and Tangiers, and smoking that funny tobacco stuff.

Interesting Times, Interesting Substances

Me and my pal had shared a little apartment in Baneuils when we were in the south of France – three bedrooms, well, three rooms. We befriended a couple of hitchhikers who came through the village, a German boy and girl, very cool. We put them up for the night and the guy said, 'Look, do you fancy a little bit of this, the weed?' and I said, 'What is it?' We'd heard about reefers and things, I wasn't that naive, but I'd never tried it, that was the first time. When we got to Morocco, it was just everywhere – it was the beginning of what became known as the Hippie Trail. There were beatnicky Americans living in Tangiers, all talking about their world travels, what they were doing, where they were going.

It was just about the time that the Indian route was beginning to open up, and I intended to hitchhike all the way. I didn't quite make it, but I met lots of kindred spirits. You would identify with someone with a certain hairstyle or a look in their eye; it was a bonding between certain types of people, when you went into a certain café or into a certain shop. You'd just recognise kindred spirits and these two Germans were like that – we must have talked to them in the street or in a café in Baneuils. I never saw them again. Funnily enough, I've got photographs of them.

I kept a diary, every single day – it was so pretentious but I'm quite spiritual and I like to try and think of what life's all about. Once I was absolutely penniless on a road south of Barcelona somewhere. I didn't know where I was, on my own, and I hadn't seen a car for about six hours. I thought, 'Nobody knows where I am, if I curled up and died here nobody would know.' I don't know why, but that amazed me. It was a turning point, really. It's quite meaningless: my life in the whole grand scheme of things and stop worrying so much about what the meaning of life is and just get on with it.

To be absolutely honest, I thought grass was wonderful because it calmed somebody like me down. I sort of chilled out, relaxed. The most important thing when you're young is finding an identity for yourself. Older people look at us when you're young and laugh and tease you: 'What're you wearing that for?' I do it with my own children, I can't believe the words that come out of my mouth: 'Get that horrible noise off,' 'What are you wearing those clothes for?', 'Why are you going out with that guy, he's horrible' – all the things that my mum used to say to me.

Back in Swinging Scotland

1963 was fantastic. Bungee's was a hip club, really cool, very beatnicky, hessian walls, dark, perfect. Another place opened up called the Tempo Club behind John Knox's House. When I came back in 1963, my mum got me a job in Patrick Thomson's. Patrick Thomson's was on the Bridges – it's now the Carlton Highland Hotel – but it was Edinburgh's biggest department store, bigger than Jenner's. I was in the record department and a lovely middle-aged lady worked there who knew nothing about the Rolling Stones and the Beatles. The Beatles were just happening, the Stones were about to happen, the whole thing was bursting – I got the job there and I very quickly became the buyer, and I was good.

In Scotland, rock-and-roll was only just beginning to happen. There was an Edinburgh band called The Athenians who were terrific; Arthur Orr was the singer, and Ally Black, who's got Shapes the furniture shop, was the guitarist and a real show-

The sensational Alex Harvey

off he was. He's not now; he's terribly modest now. They were a great band, as good as you could get in Scotland in a way though we never saw them as necessarily challenging the Beatles or the Stones. At that point, The Place opened which was mostly jazz – it was much cooler to go to The Place. The Gamp opened opposite and that's where the Athenians played. But I only went to the Gamp once or twice. I went to The Place – to bring in rock and roll they had Alex Harvey, the big soul band from Glasgow, and that was one of the most exciting things I've ever seen – he was fabulous. Another band called The Blues Council, also from Glasgow, were so sophisticated, very sort of Georgie Fame, Ray Charles-y – they were the crossing over from jazz into rock-and-roll. It was becoming hip to like rock-and-roll, and all this rhythm 'n' blues stuff, the Stones in particular.

Today everyone remembers the Beatles and the Stones and all the great bands; they forget all the crappy bands we had as well. The top twenty was as it is today: we sold lots of the other stuff: Herman's Hermits, Freddy and the Dreamers, Peter and Gordon, Billy J. Kramer and the American equivalents, Frankie Avalon and things like that. But we were selling a hell of a lot of the Stones – the great thing is that the most popular records were in fact the best records as well. The Beatles and the Stones were the biggest selling records and they were fabulous, and the Small Faces later on came through. The charts actually had a lot of good records in them, but they'll always have the lightweight throwaway-type records.

By this time, I was quite mature for a nineteen-year-old, having done all this travelling and doing different kinds of jobs. I had a new kind of confidence that I didn't have before. I felt as good as anyone else. So I didn't pass my exams, I didn't go to university, but I was hanging out with people who were and I was working and they weren't, they were still at university at nineteen. I became very well known as the record buyer in Patrick Thomson's. My mum then said, 'Why don't you come back to Falkirk and I'll put you in charge of the pop side of the record shop? You're great at it.' I said 'Great, but I'll need a flat. I'm not staying with you, we'd just fall out.' So they got me a little two-room flat, with an outside toilet but it was a flat. I was a nineteen-year-old kid and I had a flat of my own in Falkirk, you beauty.

Rock-and-Roll's Time at Last

The shop was really beginning to explode, the record sales were phenomenal, thousands of these kind of records. Other shops began to catch up but we were ahead of the game. I was good at buying and selling records. I was the manager of the shop and realised there was a career in record retail.

A club called La Bamba opened in Falkirk, and it was better than any club in Edinburgh or Glasgow – it was the Place in its own way and really good bands played there. People used to hang out in my place, including the bands, and I began to hang out with the bands that played at La Bamba. I knew Jethro Tull before they became famous, Dean Ford and the Gaylords. The Vikings were almost resident at La Bamba. They were from Perth and the leader of the group, Alan Gordy, went on to form the Average White Band. Hamish Stewart, who was the lead singer with Dream Police, also joined Alan and the Average White Band a couple of years later when they moved to London, as bands used to do in those days. There were lots of good local bands, lots of English touring bands. It was a small club that would hold maybe three hundred or four hundred people maximum so they didn't want big names. You got names before they were big and that's what makes these clubs great. It's the same today. If you go to the Attic in Edinburgh or King Tut's in Glasgow, you see lots of new bands before they've made it. You can say 'Oasis played here', not the Oasis we know from Loch Lomond, but better than that because you love to discover things. La Bamba became a place to discover new bands, new bands wanted to play it. It was a very good audience there and there was a scene in Falkirk, a lot of young hip people. As Pete Irvine would say in *Scotland the Best*: 'Falkirk's a cool place.'

Coinciding in 1963 with the whole rock-and-roll thing, hipper than all of it was Bob Dylan. The Falkirk Cycle Hut ran a folk club, so our folk section in MacDougall's record shop was really big. It had gone from being a bit Teuchter and finger-in-the-ear to these hip young singer songwriters – Caroline Hester, a young

Joan Baez at that time and Bob Dylan. Dylan was just perfect, the perfect image and so Falkirk had not only a very cool rock club, pop, beat club, it also had the coolest folk club. Roy Guest opened up The Howf in Edinburgh opposite St Giles, and another in Dunfermline and young folk artists like Robin Williamson and Mike Heron and Owen Hand and Bert Jansch played in these clubs and in the Falkirk club. It was a very hip scene, the folk scene and the rock scene, and they were appealing to similar kinds of people. There was a crossing-over. It's separated again recently and folk's coming back to being grumpy and old-fashioned. They don't seem to encourage anything new and revolutionary; it's not folk.

Success has its Ups and Downs

In the next few years after '63, I had jobs here and there, then my girlfriend moved to King's Lynn with her family. It wasn't too difficult to fall out with my mum's boss, Angus MacDougall, and I just ran off to King's Lynn: 'Right, stick your job, I'm off, I'll get a job in London, I'm great.' I went up to London one day and just walked into a record shop and said, 'Do you have any jobs?' They said, 'What have you done before?' I told them that I had a bit of experience and after a few other questions, they gave me the job, in a shop called Discy. This is now the mid-60s, I worked in London for the next year. We got married, my wife got pregnant, and we moved back to Scotland in 1967, with the family, still happy and hippie and enjoying it.

London in 1967, flower power, was a great year, a great experience but I couldn't wait to get back. Priorities began to change – my desire to be hip, cool and in the middle of it all remained, but as a secondary thing to being happy and having a home and thinking about the child and where it was going to be born. So coming back to Scotland was a joy and I came back with all the London experience. London's great, but it's no greater than here. And we can be as good. When I first came back I got a job in Graeme & Morton in Stirling, and it was the year the university opened in Stirling, so all these young people arrive in Stirling from nowhere and Graeme & Morton didn't know what to do with it.

The turnover in the record department went up ten times in six months. During that time, my brother also fell out with Angus MacDougall and said to me, 'Bruce, I want to start a record shop. Could you help?' I said, 'Sure, I'll help you', and I did. His shop was called Brian Findlay's Record Emporium, and it opened in Falkirk in late 1967. He also built mobile discotheques so I was DJing and helping him with the record sales and running this record department at Graeme & Morton. I was keen. The shop did so well that my brother said, 'You're going to have to join me.' So I resigned at Graeme & Morton and I joined my brother Brian.

We opened the shop and very sadly, my mother died a week later. But we'd got the shop opened and it was a great moment because it was our own, we weren't working for other people, we were doing it in our own right. A guy called Simon Stable, who wrote for the underground magazine *International Times*, wrote about our record shop. They wrote about very hip, weird records, The Fuggs, Captain Beefheart and Frank Zappa and said things like, 'You probably won't be able to find these records in your local family neighbourhood record store and those of you north of the border you might find it even more difficult unless you go to the Brian Findlay Record Emporium in Falkirk.' I'll tell you, the power of the press, the cool, influential press: we just got flooded with people from Glasgow and Edinburgh coming to our shop in Falkirk.

Falkirk, with the best music shop in Scotland! It was great: I'd built up great contacts with America and we had all these American imports. Britain was so slow at releasing these new underground artists like Joni Mitchell and Neil Young and the Grateful Dead. They were just seen as artists who would never sell. They waited to see how it was doing in America before they would release records in Britain. That could sometimes be six months so we had a six-month run on these American imports and became very famous for this. The day that students got their grants in Edinburgh, my shop in Falkirk would do such incredible business, at weekends, with all these kids. Stewart Cruickshank, from the BBC, would come through to Falkirk from Edinburgh to buy. He was one of my first customers. He was great, he was like a fifteen-year-old schoolkid, exactly the same as he is today. Talk about enthusiasm in guys that are hitting their fifties: there's Stewart, still as enthusiastic. Pop music does get you, believe it or not, and you can stay with it. Most people give it up after three or four years, it's just a little phase in their life, like puberty, but not for me. So Bruce's Record Shop came out of all that. We had to move to Edinburgh then for the next shop and that was really the beginning of our claim to fame.

After a few years of that, I was actually beginning to make some money, did the bourgeois bit: bought a nice cottage in Culross, nice wife, two kids, two cars, divorce. We just drifted. I think I was too preoccupied with the business, ignoring my wife, being tired, coming home and only talking about records, records, records. It was easy to satisfy material needs because I had money, but that's not enough. I wasn't taking care of the family. I realised then that the whole twee living in the country, where you don't come from, in a twee little restored house, with lots of twee people was not my cup of twee after all. So it was back to Edinburgh again. It was too late to try and save the marriage, but we moved back to Edinburgh.

The sign of success

Avoiding the time warp trap

I'm certainly as enthusiastic now about music as I was thirty years ago, but then people who are into football are still into football after thirty years, people who write about politics are still writing about politics after thirty years. I'm still an enthusiast, I like youth culture, I like the rebelliousness of young people trying to struggle to find themselves and the music that comes out of it. I was at La Belle Angele last night, which is the coolest club in Edinburgh to see new bands, live bands. I don't mean club in the sense of dance clubs, old men's clubs or drinking clubs, I'm talking about rock-and-roll venues. Finlay Quaye played his first couple of gigs in La Belle Angele, Geoff Buckley, Radiohead, Annie Christian, the band I'm just starting to manage.

With young people, there's an element of tolerance of me because I won't go away but I think a lot of young people do like me because I'm genuinely enthusiastic about them. I'm not cynical; I don't say, 'I've seen it all before.' Well, I do sometimes because I have seen a lot, and when people are being totally retro, I'm not impressed, they're not pushing it. The first Oasis album was not a complete Beatles rip-off, there were elements of originality in there and excitement but their last album was a complete disaster because, as far as I'm concerned, musically it was saying nothing. Radiohead have made an album arguably as good as any of the classic albums of the

'60s or '70s, the Sergeant Peppers of this world. I think Radiohead really are up there with that kind of an act. And it's harder because we are now more sophisticated, we've had rock-and-roll for nearly fifty years.

It's funny, it's never seriously entered my mind that I ought to be in New York or California or Detroit, because I love Scotland, pure and simple. Absolutely. East, West, Hame's Best. I love Scotland, I like the smell of Scotland, the air, the sky, the trees, the sea, the lochs, the mountains, the people. I love it to death and I particularly love my home town of Edinburgh. It's a great place to live, great people, very cosmopolitan. You know those posters 'Join the Navy and see the world' – no, join a rock-and-roll band and see the world.

A QUIET SMOKE IN THE '70S

I've been everywhere: Japan, South America, America, Canada, all over Europe, everywhere. I've talked at conferences in the Eastern Europe before it all came down and in America and in the south of France. I helped to organise the Nelson Mandela concert at Wembley, I was very heavily involved in Live Aid, the American end of it in Philadelphia with Bill Graham. So I've had great thrilling moments, truly thrilling and all from my Edinburgh base. You don't have to stay in these places. The best thing is to get to them, check them out, and just realise how wonderful Glasgow is, or Edinburgh, or Aberdeen, or the whole of Scotland. We've a great country and anyone who talks it down gets a big smack in the face from me. It's a great place to live.

Ronnie McDonald
Off-shore Oil Trade Unionist

Born 1946

❧

Early Life

I was born in Airdrie. My father had just come back from the war and I was a classic post-war baby boomer. I went to school in Coatbridge – Old Monkland Primary School and then Kildonan, which eventually became Clifton High School. I absolutely loathed school, I must say. The day I left was the happiest day of my life. I don't know why I hated it so much. I think I had a few bad experiences at primary school – like one particular teacher who was liberal with the belt and corporal punishment. I suppose that alienated me. To that extent I lost interest and just marked time until it was the day to leave. I went through the motions and managed to survive it. I managed to stay in the top class but essentially not through any effort, I have to confess. It's quite appalling looking back – nothing to be proud of.

I was prone to going away for whole days, and two or three days at times, just wandering. I enjoyed roaming – simple as that. It caused a great deal of worry in the family but that's what my main propensity was as a child – not being where I was expected to be, and not doing what I was supposed to be doing.

I hadn't a clue of what I wanted to do when I left school. I knew what I did not want to do and that was work on one of the local steel mills which provided about ninety per cent of the employment in Coatbridge. That did not appeal, so essentially I just went where I was guided on leaving school. I became an office junior in an old, established accountancy firm in West Regent Street in Glasgow: John S. Gavin & Son, long defunct. I started there in early 1962. In fact, the boss, John S. Gavin, was the son of the original founder and he was well past sixty, so it was a firm that had been active in Glasgow from about the 1860s. All the original furniture was there – everything except the quill pens. They made one concession to modernity and they did have a phone.

Certainly I met a lot of interesting people. It was a busy firm but unfortunately I didn't last long – I was sacked before the first anniversary of my employment there. I had been in trouble a number of times, and the final straw came when Mr Gavin discovered me mentioned in the front page of the *Evening Citizen*. I'd become fairly deeply involved in the Campaign for Nuclear Disarmament, and on my third arrest for civil disobedience, that was the final straw. Mr Gavin said, 'This is not in keeping with the image this firm wishes to project,' and that was it.

My father was very angry. At that time, the issue of nuclear disarmament had the country in some turmoil. The Labour Party had been split asunder and we'd just gone through the Cuban missile crisis and that sort of thing. It was very much the live issue of the day and I felt passionately about it, hence my total involvement in it. Unfortunately, I got into severe trouble as a consequence.

Out Into the World

So, I went away to sea. I joined the merchant navy and spent the next nine years just slapping about the world on old cargo boats. These were perhaps the best nine years of my life so far. I was a seaman, just a deckhand. It was a magnificent life for a young, single man. In those days Britain still had a merchant navy, of course, and it was possible to go down to the Broomielaw in Glasgow to the merchant navy pool and look up at the board and choose a ship, if you wanted to go to Japan, or spend half a year in the Pacific, or wherever. It was a tremendous opportunity. Those days are gone and I look back on it with fondness.

In my mid-twenties – around twenty-six, twenty-seven – I began to get the impression that life was passing me by. One by one, all my friends had gradually become married and were starting families. That was one aspect. I just felt like a change essentially. In the early 1970s I became a construction worker, mostly on steel and tower crane erection. That was very interesting. It met the basic requirement that I have in life – constant travel – and so I worked all around the United Kingdom, on some of the biggest projects of the decade. I thoroughly enjoyed it.

Apart from that, I think one thing I did despair of was the decline of the town I was born and brought up in. Coatbridge had always been a busy, industrious town. When I left school in '61, '62 there was no such thing as unemployment. Every school leaver literally had a choice of three, four, five jobs. Or university if the inclination was there. But by the early '70s all that had gone, and this was not as a consequence of industrial decline generally in the nation, although things were changing. It was the direct consequence of the centralisation of the iron and steel industry, the centralism pursued by both Conservative and Labour governments. So the steel mills and strip mills gradually shut down in Coatbridge. By the mid-'70s it was in a deplorable state. Unemployment was high and really it was a town where the young were leaving school without opportunities. Perhaps I noticed that more than those who did not leave the town, and I find that sad and disappointing. I find it also quite extraordinary that the Labour government, whose policies brought this about and caused this to happen in the town, continued to enjoy unreserved, virtually ninety-five per cent electoral support in the town. I find that quite extraordinary.

Britain's Black Gold Rush

So I went into steel erecting just about the time the oil industry was starting up. I had been living in London and doing reasonably well from a personal point of view. On a number of occasions I came up to the oil-rig yards on short-term contracts for my employer and on one occasion I was asked to remain and take permanent employment there. I became permanently employed at Kishorn in 1977, building the Ninian Central. It was an exciting project, the biggest object ever built in history. All the superlatives you could use to describe that project – you'd just exhaust them. Although we had only a glimmer of a perception of the importance of the project for the nation at the time, the fact of the matter was that that installation had to be out and on-stream by 1979. Upon this installation, more than any other, Britain's drive for self-sufficiency in oil and to get the IMF off our back depended. So nothing was allowed to impede maximum production on that site. It was quite an extraordinary experience, one which I think a lot of people were damaged by and a lot of those who worked there are still angry about.

It was a very, very dangerous job. The injury and death rate was quite extraordinary but mere trivia like safety standards and men's lives and limbs were not particularly highly rated. There was a blatant and horrifying disregard for safety and an acceptance, virtually on a daily basis, that there would be an attrition rate. So much so that the site had established its own hospital with its own staff – partially because of the site's remoteness, of course – but nevertheless the three or four beds in the hospital were continually occupied. It was that bad.

Having said that, there were positive things too. Thousands of construction workers were brought together from all over the country. The Kishorn camps and the other camps up at Sullom Voe in the Shetlands and over at Nigg Bay: it was like the Wild West. It really was. The money was good by any standards, and that's what attracted the men and may have encouraged the men to tolerate the bad conditions. I think some of the local construction workers reminisced about the mid-war years when the big Hydro projects were underway, and compared Kishorn camp particularly to some of the camps that existed in the Highlands in those days. The Highlands had already seen one such influx of construction workers. It was short-lived. By the early '80s most of the camps had been dismantled and the workforces dispersed.

The camps were reasonably comfortable. I remember at Kishorn, ocean-going ships were brought in because such was the demand for labour; one time two ocean-going ships were moored alongside, absolutely chock full of construction workers. Some workers were living rough on the site. You'd look up a big pipe and there would be two guys sleeping in sleeping bags. It was quite an extraordinary place.

Drink. That's all there was to do at Kishorn. We had two bars. One in particular, the legendary Wellie Bar, where people knocking off after a twelve-hour shift just went in with their oilskins on, and they drunk until closing time and went to their beds and grabbed a few hours sleep, and were back up in the morning and back at work. The money that passed across that bar must have made it the richest licensed premises in the history of Scotland. It wasn't very good for safety standards though, but it's a free country and the guys were earning the money and it's up to them how they wish to spend it.

We all thought this was just a flash in the pan, that we should get the money while the going was good – it was as simple as that. The general perception was that within a decade it would be over – indeed that seemed to be confirmed by about 1980, '81, when the orders for off-shore platforms started to dry up and the pressure really was off by about 1979. The government had achieved, essentially, its initial goal of self-sufficiency and had, through the savings in balance of payments in oil income, paid the IMF off and really got the country back on an even keel. Production started to peak around that time so, as I say, the oil companies pulled back, reduced their level of exploration and production, and that seemed to confirm the perception that we had had all through the 1970s, that it was a one-off bonanza.

I went on to the next construction project: from on-shore construction sites to off-shore work. A couple of big projects started off-shore in the early '80s. In fact, it is a bit of a paradox that the general activity did decline at that time. Nevertheless, the biggest single project ever embarked upon off-shore commenced around '81, '82, when Marathon built the Brae platform which was the biggest hook-up (the hook-up is the construction and commissioning phase) so far at that date. In fact, one time they had the record of 1800 men off-shore in one location in one day, sometime towards the end of 1982. It was a phenomenal project.

The Need for Activism

Essentially, off-shore's the same work. So much of the work is done on-shore in the rig yards and then it's taken off-shore and it's the same: the same construction workers, the same skills, the same practices, the same end results, and the same safety standards. I was quite horrified by some of the practices I saw and some of the risks taken on that particular project. It was around this time that those of us who were active in the trade union, became more acutely aware of the absence of the key aspects of health and safety regulations, and this was a contributory factor to the situation off-shore and the further realisation that this had not happened inadvertently. In actual fact, the light regulatory touch was something the government, both the Labour Government in the '70s and subsequently the Conservative Government, were happy to see continued. So we saw (a) our safety jeopardised, our lives at risk, and (b) a virtual conspiracy on the part of the regulators to not fully regulate and control the industry. By about '80, '81, '82, around those years, that had become something that we were getting very, very concerned about indeed.

It was cold-blooded calculation that it wasn't worth spending the extra money to offer the extra safety. The oil companies had to be presented with a line of least resistance – the minimum impediment was placed in their way in the '70s to facilitate the rapid development of the oil fields. In actual fact, I've discussed this with some of the major players subsequently who were around at that time, including Tony Benn. Tony Benn, as you know, was the Minister for Energy responsible for these achievements. I find it, just as an aside, quite extraordinary that Tony Benn is regarded with some derision in some areas of the media. In actual fact, if you look at the record of ministers in all governments since the Second World War, he's one of the few ministers who can actually say, 'Here is a project I'm going to complete,' and actually he did it. He's the man responsible for ensuring that Britain became self-sufficient in oil by the planned date. So he oversaw that project and, yes, he acknowledges that the business of extending proper regulatory controls off-shore was something that was not given priority. He and others have also admitted that it was the intention to rectify that eventually, but unfortunately in 1979, the binmen of Wandsworth intervened and Mrs Thatcher came to power and that was the end of that.

I'd always been active in the trade unions in every industry I've worked in: when I was at sea, and when I was in construction on-shore. I never had any ambition at any time to actually become a part of the union, an office bearer, as it were, but the concerns that really started to come into sharp focus by about '82 compelled myself and others of like mind to really try and get to grips with the situation.

Time to Organise

One particular night really it made me so angry and so concerned, that my activism in off-shore oil really stems from the events of this one particular night. The platform we were building, the Brae Alpha, was still unoccupied. We were living alongside in a large crane barge and we moved to and from work across a bridge from the barge to the platform. In heavy weather, which in the North Sea is more the rule in winter time, it was very difficult and dangerous at times, and I do recollect this particular night there were four hundred men waiting to cross the bridge to change shift and the weather becoming pretty severe. It was clear to anyone looking that there was bound to be an accident, that this bridge was not going to remain in place much longer. But the construction superintendent, desperate to get his men across and get on with the work, was insisting that the men cross. The master of the barge, on the other hand, he was becoming more and more worried that the weather was sweeping his barge closer to the platform. He wanted to let his anchors go and get away as rapidly as possible. And in front of four hundred men, this master mariner and construction superintendent argued quite viciously about who was in charge and who was to order the men across the bridge and who could order the men not to cross the bridge. We stood there without a leader, without the protection and essence of the Health & Safety at Work Act, at the mercy and vagaries of these conflicting imperatives. The weather intervened and settled the argument because the bridge crashed into the sea. Had it done so when we were crossing the bridge dozens of men would have died. And this was literally only weeks after the Alexander Keelan rig disaster in which over two hundred men had just died.

That really was the starting point of the campaign of a group of off-shore workers to really take matters in hand and try and get things sorted out. We no longer had a Labour government who may have been sympathetic to our plight. In fact we had a government embarked at that time upon a war of attrition against trade unions and organised labour in general, just around the time when we realised, as working people, that we really had our own destinies in our own hands here, that the only changes that were going to come about were those that we could force. 1982 was not the most propitious time to develop such a strategy. We had no choice.

Through the mid-80s, '85, '86, a group of about thirty or forty off-shore workers worked quite hard, within their respective trade unions and off-shore, to convince our fellow workers that organising was the only option we had here. But it was the rule of fear: people were frightened to join unions and those who were in unions were frightened to admit that they were members. Quite literally, the industry was run by fear. Victimisation was blatant and rife. So we really didn't make a great deal of headway, I have to say that. It wasn't really until the inevitable big disaster happened that the off-shore worker and public opinion swung behind the campaign. That was Piper Alpha. But, you know, three hundred and fifty, three hundred and eighty other men – depending on how you calculate the statistics – have died. Piper Alpha is not the only disaster to have occurred, it's merely the biggest.

Throughout the history of this industry, as there was in the past with coal mining, there was a permanent disaster going on, day by day and week by week. It had become almost regarded as normal, and an inevitable consequence of being off-shore, working with these products in that environment – frankly, that's absolute nonsense. There is no reason why the environment out there and the working practices out there can not be as safe as they can be made. We have the technology.

The regulations existed on-shore that, had they been applied off-shore, would have assisted in the process. It was just a question of not spending the money.

In many respects it has gotten better since Piper Alpha. I think the potential for a major multiple death disaster on the scale of Piper Alpha has receded a great deal. But I have to say that the industry is still kidding itself on. Where the industry is kidding itself on and trying to kid the public on, is that the ordinary toll of injury – the so-called trips, slips and falls – have somehow been contained and the trend reversed. That has not been the case at all, unfortunately.

A great deal of positive has happened and in some respects we are on the right road. But a great deal has still to be done. The one missing element is the one that we have experienced since the mid-'70s – the basic human right of workers at their place of work to organise collectively on their own terms, join in a union of their choice, and where a majority of them are active and members of that union, that they should have rights of representation. That's taken as a normal basic human right in the whole western world. If you still say it in Britain's off-shore oil and gas industry you're still regarded as a dangerous subversive. But it's the one missing element. We have the right to representation, we have the right to representation collectively, and as long as the industrial relations system is set up to resist that, put that aspiration down, then the safety regime as a consequence will be forever incomplete.

Looking to the Future

I'm still very active with the trade union. I've produced a magazine for them called *Blow Out* and I still assist with tribunals and that sort of thing, but I'm no longer an office-holder in the union. I'm really between jobs. I'm really unsure of what I want out of life; but what's new? I'm completely unambitious, that's my problem. If I do have one ambition at the moment it's to recede back into the anonymity from whence I came. If I've ever worked at an ambition, hopefully that's the one I will achieve.

I have to say, I have thought about being a member of the Scottish Parliament – there is no doubt that those who work in the oil and gas industry, particularly in the off-shore section of that industry, require and deserve input into that political process that's about to develop in Scotland. In that context I have given it some consideration. I haven't totally excluded it but what really tempts me to say that the Scottish Parliament, in that regard, will be a complete irrelevance, is that, first of all, the fiscal and regulatory regime under which the off-shore oil and gas industry work will continue to be administered from Westminster – it's as simple as that. In terms of basic human rights, trade union rights, individual workers' rights and collective rights, those matters too will remain firmly within the ambit of Westminster. So in the two areas in which I have a passionate involvement, the Scottish Parliament's remit will simply not run, and that's a ridiculous situation and something that perhaps could only be remedied by independence. Who is to say? Let's just say I'm watching developments at this moment in time.

I think I'm settled here in Aberdeen. I do like the city – the quality of life is excellent. It's got everything really that I could ever require in life and so I think I'm stuck here, frankly. One of the pleasurable aspects of living in Aberdeen is the complete absence of any notion of religious prejudice or religious bigotry. In

Aberdeen they do not care a jot and don't even know, by and large, what religion you are. So that dimension that you are constantly aware of, in one form or another in the West of Scotland, is completely absent here. And I find that one of the most refreshing aspects of living and working in this part of Scotland.

Ingirid Jolly
Musician & Housewife

Born 1946

My dad worked in the cathedral – he worked there for thirty-two years and my mum was just at home – she looked eftir the family. To begin with, our house was very much just wan room with everything in it, and two small bedrooms upstairs, an outside toilet; no hot water, one sink and one tap, and a black stove for cooking on. When I was aboot eight we moved to some hooses that had been used for keeping the Wrens during the wartime; there were two lots of houses like that in Kirkwall. One was the Buckwhy hooses which in a way were maybe slightly better hooses, and another lot at Hatston. And they were just used to house fowk for a year or two until they got proper cooncil hooses.

I went to Kirkwall Grammar School. In fact I havnae been oot o' Kirkwall or Orkney for more than three weeks at a time, ever. In a way I enjoyed school, in that I did really tak' an interest in me homework. But you would've been discouraged fae speakin' Orcadian in the school. You know, as pert of your lessons anyway. And in fact I think at that time bairns weren't encouraged to talk very much. Even noo I find it's maybe less easy to talk in that kind of way than maybe young folk noo, who are used to talkin' in class a lot.

You were allowed to go outside in the evenings. There was very little traffic. In fact just the odd horse and cairt still at that time. Lots of fowk still didn't have cars or vehicles. That's the early '50s, it was nothing like what there is today.

A lot of folk had relations oot of Kirkwall. I know that we had a few relations in Sanday and one or two in the outer isles. We were very pleased to go there and certainly some of their habits were a bit further in the past, you might say: folk getting up at midday and working till midnight at nigh,t instead of up at eight and stop at six.

All the bairns played things like catching games, and lots of skipping games and some other things, you know, hide and seek. I suppose in a way Christmas was one of the main things for bairns. Although there were things like the county shows on, I only remember going to it once when me uncle took me when I was eight. And I think we often looked forward to fowk coming home in the holiday time, like relations and so on, because they would tak you a run somewhere. Sometimes they had a car, although I got very car sick. I always liked to get oot. Plus the fact we had family picnics, and me father's side of the family would often hire a bus in the summertime and as many of the family as could – that'd be maybe forty or fifty folk wi' bairns – would go oot to somewhere like the links in Birsay, and tak' a picnic and food and kettles for heating water, and have games on the links. That was a good day.

Our family didn't really go out to eat very much at all. We might do it occasionally in the summer when relations were home, but other than that we just ate at home. But some families certainly did that on a regular basis, they'd have High Tea or something. High Tea was quite a treat for folk at that time; it wasn't so much

going oot at night for dinner. The first time that a Chinese or Indian restaurant opened here, maybe twenty years or so ago, I think folk thought it was quite an exotic idea. Lots of folk patronised it and thought it was a good idea and enjoyed it very much.

THE ANNUAL FAMILY PICNIC

I think me first trip oot o' Orkney was when I went to Shetland with the inter-county netball team, and I'd have been about twelve or thirteen. The next time I left was when I was about fourteen, and me father had been asked to go on a tour of some of the cathedrals and abbeys in Scotland connected with his work. He took me doon as far as Aberdeenshire and left me at a ferm there, which I enjoyed very much 'cos I liked to work on the ferm.

Choosing a Career

When I was younger I'd always been interested in ootdoor activities and I was very keen to get oot o' the toon as often as I could. And whenever we went to the country I was very pleased to do any work in the ferming community, if I could do that. So I thought I might try that. But just before I left school I applied for some work for a year's experience in aboot twelve different farms in the north of Scotland and one in Orkney, and met with a very mixed response. Some of them said, 'Oh, we don't need anybody to help us at the moment,' or, 'We don't want a student.' Some people didn't answer at all, and a few said, 'Oh, we really don't want a girl.'

I think what I had hoped to do was have the year's practical experience first – that was what Craibstone [Agricultural College] seemed to require before you went off there. Another thing was, I think I was so happy to be here, I didn't especially want to leave Orkney to do something else. And so I did the fifth year at school after I just left and took a job in a shop here – a general store really with lots of different things in it. I was 18. I think at that time I maybe wasn't quite motivated enough into anything else, apart fae what I had thought aboot originally, and I felt it wasn't getting anywhere, but I wasn't motivated enough to leave here and try it.

After I worked for a short time in the shop, I went to a dental-receptionist job which I enjoyed very much. And then I went to work in a bank for aboot three years before I had me family. I haven't really had a job since then, apart from home and family.

Teenage Pursuits

When we were seventeen and eighteen, there wasn't quite so much drinking and pub-going as we find nowadays. Certainly folk did tak pairt in that, right enough, but I wasn't really a very typical teenager – I didn't go to dances very much.

I got married quite young – I was aboot twenty-one. He's been a fish merchant since he left school – he's a few years older than I am. We met really partly through music and partly through an interest in the local ba' game [a type of football game played in Kirkwall at New Year].

Getting into Music

It was mainly traditional singing at that time. You find I think that at most of the concerts here at that time there was quite a lot of singing going on, and a few musical turns as weel. And maybe noo it's almost the opposite way aboot, that there's more music and less singing. But at that time there was a very small folk club that was going on for a short time in the Ayre Hotel here. A friend of mine and I used to go along to that a few times.

But then I became more and more involved in local music. I think it really stemmed from the fact that I met up wi' a man here called Hugh Inkster who played the fiddle. I was playing the guitar along with the local Strathspey & Reel Society. I was playing very modestly, just a few chords. Hugh asked if I'd play along with him for something in the St Magnus Festival. So I was a bit nervous of that and said I wasn't really up to it, and he said, 'Don't be silly, come along and have a shot at the hoose,' so I went along and had a good few tunes and I realised then that I was very keen to play along with instruments. When we were younger there was quite a thriving orchestra, and opera as well, and that's kept going you know, throughout the years. And drama as well has been quite an important thing. But noo that we have the St Magnus Festival and Folk Festival that gives a boost to the interest of that particular part of music, you know.

Traditional music's been reviving now all over the country. and in many respects all over the world, but while we were small it was very much looked doon on as something that was very old fashioned and just for the auld folk. Whereas noo you find young folk are often appreciating it. If you go and play in a pub, for

INGI IN A TYPICAL PUB SESSION IN THE OLA HOTEL BAR, 1993

instance, lots of young folk who you would not imagine would enjoy it, come and say that they really do like it.

I think here lots of folk tend to quite enjoy Irish music as much as Scottish music. And a touch of Shetland music thrown in occasionally, and there's quite a few Orkney tunes too, of course, and a few Orkney songs. But we're pretty cosmopolitan I think in what we like to play. And when we have a session we don't mind if somebody wants to come in and do a bit of bluegrass, which doesn't happen very often, but one night we were having a tune in the Ayre Hotel here and one of the ex-drummers oot o' the group Nazareth turned up and had a shot on the table. So that's what we like – just folk to come and join in.

My favourite song is, funnily enough, an Orkney song called *Orkney Anthem*. I really do like that. It really tells the story of what Orkney means to the person who wrote it, and was written by an architect about a hundred years ago. But the music was written fairly recently by a local man called Ivan Drever who you might have heard o' – he plays in Wolfstone.

Our elder daughter is quite a good fiddle player too, although she hasn't done so much recently since she had her family, but she's just beginning to get back into it again. And my youngest daughter – she enjoys it very much.

Even if they said 'Oh mum, don't be silly, you're too old to go and do that,' I don't think I'd pay any attention. I think people have to do what they feel is right for them. Music's really the sort of main interest and enthusiasm of my life now. I also would have to say that I really do very much appreciate the friendship o' a lot of folk that I know here. They and my music really are the things that are most important to me. And Orkney as well.

Reflections on Orkney

Orcadians definitely feel different from Scotland. You feel that you're apart or separate from the mainland of Scotland, there's no question aboot that. It's no' that you feel an aggression towards Scots of any sort – it's no' that serious.

I suppose really if you've been born and brought up here, where a lot of the names of the places are Norse, and maybe the feelings have come down through the centuries of how things have always been – that maybe that's why we feel more on the Norse side of things. But maybe in a way too much is made of that as well, because it's a very mixed-up community here and there's been folk coming into this place for thousands of years or more. Thousands of years.

I feel Orkney's changed quite dramatically since I was young, and although it's probably inevitable because of all the influence o' media and folk comin' here, I still feel it's a bit of a shame really.

In some ways the incomers who've settled here have made it quite invigorating, because they've come with lots of good ideas and I think a place could possibly stagnate unless there's some fresh blood put into it occasionally. But there has been quite a number of folk come, and you begin to wonder if it might be swampin' the general Orcadianness of the place.

I sometimes think too that bits of Orkney have been altered to the benefit of tourism, and it's altering it to the extent that it doesn't look natural any more. An example is the Broch o' Birsay, and the point there at Buckwheat just across from the Broch, where it's become a place that can be comfortable for tourists; I think they should just go and see it as it is.

The most striking change here might be the fact that people in general have more money to do whatever they like. I think that might've altered how folk do things to quite an extent. And I feel sometimes noo people are more interested in acquiring things rather than, well, you know ... and people going oot to work to do things, to get things – it's more important to them than finding out how the people roond them are doin'. I'm talking about in general, obviously you get the usual differences between the really well off and the folk who aren't well off at all. But in general most folk have a vehicle of one sort or another.

A lot of folk here travel quite a lot. Quite a lot, really, to the Mediterranean or Florida. I like to travel. I would love to travel all sorts of different places but I don't just quite get roond to it somehow. But not the Mediterranean, I don't think. I'd quite like to go to Iceland – some of the Northern latitudes.

Jim Watt

Boxer

Born 1948

Early Life and
Memories

I was born in Bridgeton in Glasgow. My father was a baker. At that time, my mother was a housewife, and my father died when I was five so I was brought up just by my mother. By that time we had moved to Possilpark and my mother went back to work full-time in the Ruchill Hospital in the laundry section. We lived in tenement flats. Both were room-and-kitchen and both had the luxury of an inside toilet. I don't remember the first one, but the one in Possilpark had an inside toilet which at that time was a luxury.

I went to Saracen Primary School in Possilpark. I enjoyed primary school and had good fun there. Obviously I liked sport best but I was fairly bright, I was usually in the top two or three in the class at primary school but when I went to Possil Senior Secondary, I found the competition a bit tougher. I also lost a little bit of interest, just like everybody else growing up and thinking about other things. I didn't achieve any great education. I was all right obviously, I wasn't a dummy but by that time I had reckoned sport was probably where my attention should lie.

At that time you could actually play football in the street. There weren't so many cars and I remember the only criminal record I had growing up was a ten-bob fine for playing football in the street. Actually, most of my friends had that on their criminal records; playing football on the street was very popular. It was a crime but usually the police turned the other way. Now and again a car would come along and disrupt the game but very seldom. But now you wouldn't have a chance.

Nobody really worried that you could get into worse trouble if you were out playing football on the street in the evening. I had a different upbringing than most. Being in a one-parent family back then, when my mother was a widow and working, I had the key of the door round my neck at five years old, on a string which I never took off. I was home first from school into the house – I had a sister who was four years older than me – and when I opened the door I just took the key out, into the lock and then put it back down my shirt again. So I had a little bit of responsibility that a lot of kids probably didn't have. I think the only way our family could exist would be with a little bit of trust and a little bit of responsibility.

I was probably about twelve years old before we actually got a television. We didn't watch an awful lot of television. Back then, your parents thought it was unhealthy for you to hang around the house, so you were really thrown out every night and that's the way you grew up. You expected to be outside; you didn't think about sitting inside doing things at home. Even when it was raining you would find somewhere to go outside the house.

I had a little go at golf, and round about July when Wimbledon was on, you'd get hold of an old tennis racquet, put an old clothes-line up and knock the ball over the line and so forth. You played the tennis round the back courts where the washing lines were. We tried everything. The boxing was one of the things that I tried, just

235

for a laugh really, but I found that I was quite good at it and stuck in, even though I was far keener on football.

Boxing and football were the two major sports for the working classes. When I say I tried some golf, that was going up with two clubs and nicking on at the second hole at Ruchill club because you didn't have the money to pay to get on. And the tennis was just a joke as well, round the back. So really the sports you had a chance of getting involved in were boxing and football and at that time, both flourished. But now today they're both suffering badly because the kids have got so many other choices, computer games and everything else which you didn't have back then.

I loved football and played for the school. In 1963 we had a very bad winter – it was still snowing right through to April. We ended up where we had too many games to play and not enough weeks to play them so the teacher had to withdraw the team from the league and I had nothing to do. I saw a sign on the wall advertising the Cardowan Amateur Boxing Club, so a friend and I went along to a boxing club, again just for something to do. We'd no intention of taking it up seriously. We had tried everything else, karate clubs, judo clubs, the tennis, the golf. I was in my last year at school. I was fourteen years old.

I didn't enjoy it. The first couple of times I got punched on the nose I didn't like it – nobody likes getting punched on the nose and I actually quit the club a couple of times. But the coach, James Murray, obviously spotted something in me and he came up to the house a couple of times and encouraged me back down again. But even then my heart wasn't in it. I didn't take to boxing like a duck to water. I thought it was a hard sport and not an awful lot of pleasure but my career got off to a flying start. I think my first four fights I won in the first or second round and I thought, 'Hey, this is a good game, this. This is fairly easy.' You get a little mention in the local newspapers, and it's amazing how that made you feel. By the time I found how hard a sport it was, I had been bitten by the bug, I'm afraid. I think the thing that appealed to me about boxing was that it was one-on-one sport. All the glory came to *me*, not a team. Well, when I played football I obviously enjoyed it and you enjoyed your own performance but boxing, all the credit and all the pain as well, unfortunately, was on me.

I was never conscious of a tradition of the lighter weights or wee guys from the west of Scotland being good at it. Several times I've been asked why Scotland's heaviest world champions are myself and Ken Buchanan and we both boxed at nine stone nine pounds. It's amazing but we don't know why this is. I wasn't really conscious of the tradition there because I hadn't been steeped in boxing. I didn't have a boxing history.

James Murray, as well as having an amateur club, had a professional manager's licence. That's frowned upon down in England but in Scotland, the pros and the amateurs worked fairly closely. Amateurs sparred with professionals and it was fine. So, within about six months of me starting as an amateur, an almost fifteen-year-old boy, my coach saw the potential and already we were speaking about professional boxing. My aim then was to turn pro. It was strange how it affected me. My main ambition was to win the ABA Championship. I won that in 1968 and got picked for the Mexico Olympic Games but I didn't go. I turned professional instead – I don't really regret that. People still say to me 'I don't understand, how could you refuse the chance to go to the Olympic Games?' But all my ambitions were in the professional ranks and I say: 'Well I've always wanted to be a pro.'

Hazards of the Ring

I never thought, 'I could get my brain scrambled.' Never once did that thought come into my mind. It's like driving a car. Every morning when you come to work you don't think, 'I'm going into this car. I could have a crash today. I could be killed.' You don't think like that – if you thought like that you'd get the bus and then someone else would kill you. If that thought ever comes into a boxer's mind he wouldn't be a boxer. You never think about the dangers. Any dangerous sport, mountain climbers, people who drive motorcycles and so forth, if they've got that thought anywhere in their mind, then forget it, get out of it. But it never, never entered my mind at all.

My mother was a very strong lady and she loved me to bits, as you can imagine. She thought I was the best in the world at everything. I remember I had one particularly hard fight against a man called Sean O'Grady in a world title fight. There was blood all over the place – I was cut, he was cut – today the fight would be stopped straight away; it was horrendous. My mother, when I asked her about it afterwards, she hadn't been the least bit worried because she always felt I was in control. I don't think that was normal for a mother but she had total confidence in everything I set my mind to do, so she never worried about boxing. She never looked upon the dangers of it. She always said, 'Well, Jimmy knows how to look after himself. He'll be all right.' It was just the way she coped with everything.

The World Championship: Scotland and Boxing

Boxing's an individual sport. You think about yourself and nothing else – it's the only way you can survive. So I would never have thought that I was carrying the hopes and fears of a nation. My fight at the Kelvin Hall in 1979 was the first world championship match in Glasgow for about thirty years. It was just after Scotland's dismal showing in the World Cup over in Argentina, so I think Scotland as a whole were demanding success at the top level and it fell to me. The press jumped on the fight and as you can imagine, six weeks before it, you couldn't pick up a newspaper in Glasgow but there was something about the fight, maybe a full page, and they made me very aware of the fact that they demanded success. Scotland's a wonderful nation, they get behind their heroes but they are very

WINNING THE CHAMPIONSHIP, 1979: JIM AND HIS MOTHER IN THE RING AFTER THE FIGHT

demanding and they let you know what they expect of you. So I was made well aware that defeat was unthinkable.

Ten thousand people were at Kelvin Hall and the atmosphere was incredible. I remember coming from the dressing room, behind the pipe band and the hairs were standing on the back of my neck, it was a wonderful feeling. The strange thing is, it didn't help me – it probably tightened me up in the earlier rounds because I think I was so terrified of blowing this. I was thirty-one years of age so it was the only chance I was going to get to become World Champion. But once I got through the early rounds, into the middle rounds and then in the later rounds when the fight really became hard, that's when I felt the crowd really lifting me. When I needed them, they really lifted me and I think I needed them that night. Things came through all right.

Scotland will win again. Scotland has never been a major force in boxing. Back in the '50s we had a lot of good fighters but we've never been a major world force. But every now and again, every ten years or so, someone comes along just to remind the world that Scotland's still about the place. First, there was Benny Lynch and then little Jackie Paterson; in the next decade, Walter McGowan, in the next decade, Ken Buchanan and in the next decade, Jim Watt. So it'll happen again. We used to have a lot of good championship class boxers, like Evan Armstrong and Tommy Glen Cross, people like that who didn't win world titles but could give any world champion a fair run for their money. We've lost that at the moment but that'll come back within the next couple of years. Boxing in Scotland is thriving at the lower level, so those boys will come through. We'll never be a major force but we'll definitely produce more world champions in the future.

I think Glasgow people, and Scottish people as well, are aggressive little people when it all comes down to it. We're gritty and maybe we just don't gel too well as a team. Maybe we're a race of individuals. Boxing's an individual sport and then there's people like Alan Wells, for example; a wonderful athlete, but again, an individual, so maybe the personalities we have, maybe we just can't wrap together. There are men and women runners, squash players, snooker players, boxers ... all wonderful athletes but all in individual sports. Maybe we're all just little glory seekers at the bottom line.

Sectarianism in Boxing

We have boxers from Protestant areas and Catholic areas, and sometimes you see that the supporters are wearing colours, but I've never heard any abuse hurled at a boxer for religious reasons. I don't ever remember seeing that, thankfully. We've had some troubles in boxing – thuggery, again not too often, thank heavens, but not religious bigotry. One of my earliest memories, when I was just a young kid, was when I boxed over in Ireland. I boxed a fellow called Sammy Lockhart at the Ulster Hall in Belfast. I went into the ring and Sammy came into the ring and they introduced Sammy first and he got a decent applause, and I thought: 'I wonder what I'll get.' When they announced my name the roof lifted, everybody screamed, it was like I was boxing at home – I found out later that Sammy was a Protestant and they didn't care what I was but they knew Sammy was a Protestant, so I got the biggest cheer in the place. I couldn't believe it. That was the Ulster Hall in Belfast. But Irish people are wonderful. If that was how they felt, it was good enough for me.

*Boxing Today: a
More Complicated
World*

We have loads of religions around the world because one couldn't get on with the other and pretty much the same has happened in boxing. Boxing has four ruling bodies. It's obviously financially motivated as well. The ruling bodies are making money out of it. Boxing has survived having four world champions – if you have four world champions it means you don't have any, that's fairly logical, but the fact that boxing has survived the confusion once again shows you its popularity. As long as there are good fights, as long as the top guys in each division meet each other eventually and we have great boxing matches, it will survive. I probably couldn't name half of the world champions today. When I was boxing we had twenty world champions – two ruling bodies with ten weight divisions. Now we have four ruling bodies with seventeen weight divisions, so sixty-eight world champions. It's obviously far easier now to win a world championship – it's not the same achievement, but on the credit side, many more boxers are making money now, so that in itself is good.

There's a lot of opposition to boxing now obviously from the British Medical Association, but boxing is thriving. Little Nas [Prince Naseem], who's the hero of the moment, boxed in Manchester recently in front of about 12,000 people. and it was surprising the amount of young people in the audience. Probably the greatest thing Nas is doing for boxing at the moment is bringing young people into the

*Jim Watt, fashion guru,
1980*

arena, buying tickets, not sitting at home watching it on the telly. Boxing is still by far the highest paid sport in the world, at the top level. Mike Tyson, Evander Holyfield, made about $20 million each for one night's work. I know basketball players can get $20 million contracts but that's for a season or three years, not for one night's work. All the television companies want to see Mike Tyson and Evander Holyfield fight for the third time. That money's generated not by a fellow with a magic wand bringing it out of mid-air but because it's still one of the most popular sports in the world.

I know heavyweights will get this kind of money and there are flyweights who won't, no matter how good they may be, but I don't resent it, for a couple of reasons. First of all, my dream came true: I was champion of the whole wide world and I've got a lovely lifestyle now, thanks to that. I was more fortunate than most. I had six world title fights and three of them were against top Americans. American television came into the equation in my fights and so I made a lot of money. But it's not all about money. If I was sitting here skint and I had blown all the money I had made, I would still have been champion of the whole wide world. That's the bottom line – when all the money's spent and it's all behind you, you've been champion of the whole wide world and it's wonderful. So I have no complaints about it whatsoever.

If I was a miner working down the pit I wouldn't want my son to go down the pit because I would know how hard it was. Boxing's the same. If a son of mine wanted to box, I would support him and make sure he did it properly but I wouldn't want him to do it. I never encouraged either of my two sons to take up boxing and it's not really just because of the sport: it's following a famous and a successful father. It's a tough enough game when you're anonymous but when you're a target, it must be impossibly tough. So I would rather my sons didn't take up boxing. But I would definitely do it all again.

Scotland Today: Change and Equality

You can see how Scotland's changed in the way the country has come on. We take things for granted now. I sit at home and think back twenty-five or thirty years: How many people had a telephone back then? How many people had a motor car? How many people had two workers in the family? I think men and women working now is probably the biggest change. People keep talking about the problem of unemployment but they forget that if you go back thirty years, the man worked and the woman stayed at home. Now that all the women are working you've got to expect unemployment. I don't say that it's right or wrong; quite right, equality, we're equal now. But go back thirty years, the man was the man and the woman walked a couple of steps behind. That's the biggest change I see – women have caught up with us. They even want to box now. One got a licence recently. I wish they wouldn't do that, I really do. I don't mind them being equal, but, please, keep the boxing gloves off.

Margaret Sinclair
Former PA/Secretary

Born 1951

❀

A Crofting Life

My grandmither lived in the country. Although we stayed in the toon, we spent most of the time in the country with me grandfolk. Every holiday, weekends, Christmas, the whole summer, we spent in the country. It was really just a crofting life: it was just working in the tattie rig, working wi' neeps, working wi' kell, working wi' animals, working in the pit-hou – just a crofting life.

RAKING THE HAY BY HAND, EARLY 1970S

Sheep

They were breeding their own sheep and were killing their own sheep at that time. It was a humane killing. The animal was just killed in a oot-hoose but I didnae want to see that – I wouldn't have been allowed even if I had wanted to. It was just at the tail end of the year when they were killing animals. The whole animal was used; my grandmither salted and cured the sheepskins and the animal was cut up and cooked in various different ways, boiled or roasted or whatever. The stomach was used to make a currant puddin'. The ither intestines was used for mealie puddin' and when the animal was killed, the puddins was putten in a basin in a salt pickle and that sat mixed up wi' watter until a tattie floated and it was left there until it was used.

I can mind going wi' granny to the well, because this was before running watter was in the hoose. She had two wells; there was one well for human use – I'm no too sure just how hygienic it would have been because there was a troot in the well – and the other well was used for animals. I can mind going wi' her wi' the puddins and they were roughly washed oot first. Then she took the lang wans in particular and stripped them between her fingers to mak sure that she removed a' the fat. They were turned ootside in and stripped again and watter was poured through them. I can mind holding the top of the puddin' wide while she poured the basin of watter through to make sure they were clean. They were used ootside in and they were cut into about foot lengths and the wan end was stitched and then they were filled wi' the puddin' mixture and stitched up again. I can mind just a darning needle and thick thread and her just over-stitching. They were good, the big puddins, the wans with the currants in them. They were boiled for a couple of hours and then left to cool and then sliced up and fried. Puddins are still made. Folk in the country districts, if they still have their ain animals, will still be making puddins but they have a smell, as you can imagine, and for anybody who has been brought up and used tae it, it's just a delicacy and you think: 'Oh, great, I'm going to have puddins again.' For anybody that's not been used to it or brought up wi' it, the smell is nauseating.

We had an awful lot of soup because a small bit of mutton could mak quite a big pot of soup, tattie soup, vegetable soup, rice soup. That could be made on a bit of beef or mutton or in olden days a sweed sheep's head which was a different taste. Granny taught me about how you sweed a sheep's head. My mother could mind it just when she was small and I think they probably did it up until aboot the beginning of the war, probably because the head was sweed in an open fire but just after the war folk were getting Rayburns so they couldn't do it. I think that's probably when it died oot. When they were killing sheep, they took the sheep's head and split aff the lower jaw and then they held the sheep's head in tongs in the fire until it singed – you can imagine the smell that would be wi' that. They held it in the fire and scraped off the wool, and scraped and sweed until it was just completely bare, and they did the same with the lower jaw. Then it was put in a pickle for two days, the same pickle with salt and water until a tattie could float, and then the head was used. The head was split open and the brain was discarded – they didna eat the brain – but they were careful about the tongue. The tongue and the eyes, they were sweed as well, with the head. The eyes were removed and they were eaten. The ball was removed but the eye was boiled. It was a bit of a delicacy. Then they made soup on it and it had a different taste. It was really good and they looked forward to their sweed sheep's head. Apparently the meat at the side of the eyes was the best tasting bit. The tongue was boiled alang wi' the head in the soup, it was a great delicacy but they gave it to the bairns generally. The eyes was boiled in a mutton brew and maybe wi' a bit of onion and kidneys as well. But they very seldom ate the liver because liver fluke was prominent at that time. You dinna see it now because animals are treated but at that time if there was any marks on the liver whatsoever it was discarded.

They had home cures for sheep and animals. There was a burn that ran through the valley no far from my grandmither's hoose and there was grass growing in the burn that was called ga'garse. It was gathered and boiled up in a pot and the brew was fed tae animals if they had gall bladder trouble. I suppose that's where the ga' came frae. It had a strong, strong smell; when you cam in the hoose, you could smell it but it fairly cured the animals.

Pigs

My grandmother didna keep pigs but her folk kept pigs. My great-grandmother lived about seven miles from Lerwick. She used to walk into Lerwick every year and get her young pig. It was put in a hessian bag and she carried it home on her back. This peerie [small] young pig was kept in aboot the stove and they looked after it in the house for a few days. It did get ootside but they had it on a tether because if it got off, it would be her job to catch it again. On one occasion it did tak off and it gi'ed through the whole place and it took everybody the best part of a day to catch it again. After this few days, it was put in the pig sty and it never saw daylight again till the day that it was slaughtered. Granny said that they really had no affection for it: it was there, it was fed, it was looked after, but it was there to be fattened up to be slaughtered at the tail end of the year and they never thought that it was cruel or anything wrang wi' it, just being in the dark in the sty.

I thought it was terrible that this poor pig was just locked in a sty for months on end and never saw daylight. But she said that the pig was awful clean. It had its eating place and its sleeping place and the place it made a mess but it was very, very clean and well looked after. They werena allowed to see the pig being slaughtered. There was a man in the district that did the deed, as Granny called it, and he went aroond all the crofts and bled the pig. It was a great excitement because they were going to get ham again; they had mutton, and the rest of the time it was really fish, so it was fine to get this ham again. They cooked fresh ham for a day or two but it was really all just saltit doon and cured for winter use, but the home-cured ham was good. Same as the reestit mutton. My granny was reestin mutton when I was young. It was put in a pickle and left there for aboot three weeks; it was then dried and hung up on a rip above the stove, above the fire so the peat reek and the heat dried it oot.

Tattie Hooses

I don't know if there are any tattie hooses left noo at all, but my grandmither was using one right up until the 1960s and into the early 1970s. It kept the tatties a' year and they were just stored in there covered wi' hessian bags

The tattie hoose, early 1950s

tae avoid them gettin' windit. The name was windit but it really meant wind or frost, damp or onything gettin' tae the tatties. Otherwise they rottit.

The tattie hoose was made by my great-great grandfather – that would be the mid-1800s. It was in the backyard at the back o' the hoose. He dug oot a deep pit, aboot three or four feet wide and maybe eight feet lang, and you could stand up in it. It was probably comin' on for aboot six feet high and it was half and half, aboot three feet under the ground and three feet above the ground. Above the ground it was dry-stane wall; it was a good dry-stane wall, it wasna open. It had a tackit roof, a thatched roof and a door in the gable end. When you went in this peerie door, you had to bend doon to get in and then put your feet in first and sit on the edge. There was a box that you stepped doon intae and of course, there was no light in it at all. There was a passage right alang one side and wooden bits to hold the tatties.

There was just a earthy smell when you come into the tattie hoose.

The tackit roof gave through time and it was replaced wi' a wooden roof wi' turf. As my grandmother got older, she wasna having the quantity o' tatties and she stopped wi' tatties altogether when she was on her own. Eventually, the roof fell in so my aunt cleared it oot and she took doon the wa' at one side and she now has it for a sunken garden. She keeps roses in the tattie hoose.

Fish

My other granny cam frae a fishing community so in her hoose it was mainly fish whereas in the other hoose, it was mainly mutton. She wis my father's mother and she lived wi' us. When fishermen, like relations, cam into Lerwick wi' fish, they would cam alang the hoose wi' fish for her, a free fry fish and she just thought this was great. She would just be in the sink right away gutting this fish because wi' being in the fishing community, she'd worked at the gutting when she was very young. It was the only sort of employment that young lasses had at that time. So gutting fish was no problem to her and she'd have the fish in the pan and on the stove in nae time at all. She died when I was young so I just have the memories of a' this going on. I spent much more time wi' my ither grandmither and then when I got interested in it I gi'ed to her wi' my notebook and got everything written doon. So I dinna have the same memories.

Changes in the Shetland Diet

When I was young, we seemed to eat tatties every day, tatties wi' something at dinner time: it was tatties and mince or tatties and fried fish, tatties and boiled fish, tatties and mutton. Everybody had home-grown vegetables: tatties and neeps and carrots. We didn't have to buy them because of going to my grandmother's every weekend. A lot of times, dinner was a two-course meal. It was homemade soup made on a piece of meat. Then the meat was ta'en oot frae the soup – you didn't eat the meat in the soup – cut up and you had it wi' the tatties for your second course. And a bit of mutton would be boiled in a pot wi' vegetables and then the brew was used as a sort of gravy.

My gran cooked wi' peat just in the Rayburn. It certainly had a smell in the house. I'm no

FEEDING THE HENS

sure if there was a difference in cooking wi' peat or not. In my great-grandmither's hoose, they cooked on an open fire and of course they couldna roast anything. Everything was just boiled at that time and to have a bit of roast was something different. Their next-door neighbours had a Dutch oven – it was a big iron pot wi' a handle and legs and they borrowed this oven maybe two or three times in a year. You got a good peat fire going and the Dutch oven was placed in the fire and then the peats was built up aroond it. When the pot took heat the meat was putten in and the hot peats were put on the top as well – that was how they roasted in the Dutch oven.

I seem to think we didn't eat very much at teatime, maybe a boiled egg and bread or maybe sausages. We had dinner [the main meal] at dinner time [midday]. That began to change when folk were working. When women were at home then dinner was at dinner time but once women got out to work then it changed. I still prefer to have me dinner at dinner time but we usually have it at night.

For puddings, jelly seemed to be a great thing that was on the go, and custard. And then later on tins o' creamed rice. Everybody seemed to have a fondness for rice because away back, we made soup wi' rice; rice, vegetables and a bit of mutton, beef or sweed sheep's head in rice soup was good.

I canna really mind much about fruit when I was young, even. Oranges and aiples and bananas is really jist whit I can mind. There probably wis ither fruit aroond but it probably was quite expensive. Later on, I can mind plums, probably, but no' the variety o' fruit you get nowadays. But me grandmother had a gooseberry tree and berry trees and sometimes they grew strawberries.

Eating out was just a rare occurrence. Folk had nae money, really. I can mind going on car runs on a Sunday and we'd maybe go to a hotel and have high tea, but that was once a year and we went to the Hillsuite Hotel for high tea. That was the only times I can ever mind eating out when I was peerie. Maybe in the '60s into the '70s, folk had a bit more money, and eating out was mair common. It was just once, twice, a few times in a year, whereas noo some folk are eating out every weekend wi' all the restaurants that are here.

A Shetland Christmas

I always spent Christmas wi' my grandmither, my grandfolk, in the country, and Christmas in the country was always different frae Christmas in the toon. As bairns, on Christmas Eve we went guising, that was the first thing that we did; we all dressed up and we went guising aroon all the hooses. We had a sock, just a haun-knittit sock wi' a knot tied in the end so we werena goin to lose the pennies that folk gave us – we'd mak quite a lot o' money. We usually got ginger cordial or strawberry cordial, and a piece of cake or a biscuit in every hoose. We preferred the strawberry cordial because the ginger cordial was a bit too hot for us.

Then on Christmas morning of course, Santy Claus has always been. I remember wan morning – I would have been aboot seven – opening my eyes and seeing this big dolls' hoose at the foot o' the bed. I thought it was great. I discovered later on it had been in the loft for a while and was actually one that my great-uncle had made for me mother in the 1920s and my folk had done it up and given it to me. I still have it. You'd never believe what we had for breakfast on Christmas morning – boiled mutton. We didn't have it any other morning in the year but on Christmas morning, and for dinner we had roast mutton, vegetables and then we always had a trifle. Later on, we always listened to the Queen on the radio, because there was nae TV at that time. That cam to Shetland in 1964, I think, so we listened to the Queen on the radio. Me grandfather died when I was ten, so after he died we always went to the cemetery on Christmas afternoon.

There always seemed to be folk coming and going the whole day lang. It tended to be women and relations and bairns that visited through the day and then at night maybe, men cam aroond wi' drams. Women didna drink at that time, so the men just offered the men in the hoose a dram, they didna offer women but they didna sit and drink like they do nooadays. They had just one glass, and when they cam in the hoose then one man would ask for the glass and it would be quite a peerie glass, maybe aboot an inch and a half, just a dram glass. It would be topped up and then it would be offered to everybody in the hoose and they just each took a sip and handed the glass back and then when the glass had done its roonds, then the next person got the glass and the same thing was done again so it was just sips. Women generally didn't tak a sip, or if somebody was drunk and insistit, you just held the glass to your lips but you didna drink. It's still done in Whalsay – I believe it's the only place in Shetland where they still work with this one glass. That died oot I would think in the '70s.

In me grandmither's day they had a super custom at Christmas. This would have been from the turn of the century up until the First World War. They got up in the morning and they lit candles in every window in the hoose. Their hooses had astragals, that was the four panes, so they had four candles in every window. When they got up in the morning they lit the candles and a' the hooses on the opposite side of the valley were all lit up as well. When daylight came up the candles were blown oot and then, in late afternoon when it was beginning to get dark, the candles were lit again. They were on until they just went oot – they werena blown oot.

A Shetland New Year

At the New Year, we went guising on New Year's Night. We never did anything at Hogmanay. It was just New Year and that was it. We generally stayed up until midnight on Hogmanay when I was quite young – it was the novelty of staying up and taking down the old calendar and hinging up the new one and then we just gi'ed to bed. That was it. But New Year's Day, after New Year's Dinner, we'd get all our guising clathes and wir masks, and we'd all get ready. We'd all gather at the wan hoose and then everybody gied aroond a' the hooses. When I was peerie, before I was allowed to go out, we stood in the windows because folk had torches, had blinkies, and you could see them go from hoose tae hoose, waiting wi' great excitement for the guisers to arrive. They

GUISING AT NEW YEAR, 1973

usually had accordions and guitars and there'd be dancin'. You'd clear the tables and chairs – of course there were nae carpets at that time – and maybe have an eightsome reel.

Up-Helly-Aa

I was always in the toon for Up-Helly-Aa. It was great excitement on Up-Helly-Aa morning. You wanted to see the galley before you went to school. Frae oot our side window we could actually see the galley shed. We were sitting in the window waiting to see the galley come oot o' the shed withoot its head because the head could only get putten on once it got ootside. It was just an exciting day. It's the same noo. It is a great excitement wi' the bairns. When we was in school, the junior galley was just in the playground and we got oot to see it; the bairns noo are actually taken to see the big galley as it comes in. The bairns dress up and they make their paper Viking helmets.

When I was young, you could just feel something in the air, that it was Up-Helly-Aa day. Even yet you can feel it but I would say you have to have been born and brought up in Lerwick to actually feel Up-Helly-Aa. Onybody from the country coming in and seeing it – they dinna have it. It's no the same as actually having been born and brought up wi' it, when your very first memory is seeing the galley and feeling the excitement – it lives wi' you.

Jessie Watt
Teacher

Born 1951

My father was the skipper of a seanet boat in Lerwick and my grandfather had been coxswain of the first Lerwick lifeboat in the 1930s. When I was born, my parents lived in a little caravan down at Freefield, and I think I was about two years old, when my brother was born, that we got a council house for the first time. It was nothing special, just a typical council house.

We ate fish six days a week and meat on Sunday because fish was free, in effect, because my father was a fisherman. So I was brought up really on fish. We had traditional Shetland dishes like stappincrappin. It's a very unusual word, but it's good stuff to eat. It's made with oatmeal and livers and a lot of different fish just cooked very simply, on the grill mostly, or pan-fried.

My mother was a gutter, and I can actually remember the tail end of the herring fishing in Lerwick. I can remember my mother packing herring, bent over a barrel till she was sick and then going back and doing more packing. It was a very hard life and I can remember them with their clootie fingers, you know, they used to wrap their fingers to stop the knives and the salt attacking them. They got flour bags from the local baker, washed them and stripped them into bandages and then bandaged their fingers. I can remember being quite sick about it all when I was a child because my mother came home with the cloots on. Often she'd wash her hands and you'd go to the sink and there would be this pile of clootie bandages and scales on the soap. So I thought fish were terrible things when I was a kid. It's only when you get older that you realise what folk had to put in to that kind of work. It was backbreaking stuff, a very hard life.

GUTTING AND PACKING THE FISH, 1903

From when I was a child there would have been about forty herring stations in Lerwick, on either side of the harbour, some on the island of Bressay and some on the Lerwick side. You'd hear some of them pick up a tune and then all the stations would pick it up right along the whole water. It could be very dramatic with all these outdoor voices and all nationalities as well. I mean, you'd a lot of Irish people here, people from Great Yarmouth, the North of England and then you had a lot of foreigners in. It's always been a very cosmopolitan place, Shetland. You had a big influence from Dutch fishermen and from Germans and all sorts really. The population of Lerwick really doubled in the summer. You got 20,000 incomers. The fishing really was tailing off between the wars and then after the end of the Second World War, there was not nearly so much herring fishing or such big herring fleets coming in but I can remember the last two working stations.

Growing Up

I don't have many recollections of primary-school size but in secondary school there was about five hundred pupils when I was there. It's now about a thousand but that's the increase with the oil and I think it's stabilised just in the last couple of years. There was a terrible depression in Shetland when the population went way down before the oil era. But then it started to pick up again once Sullom Voe [oil terminal] got into full swing. I mean, there was a whole generation of young folk almost lost from the island but the advent of the oil gave the young men, in particular, the chance of staying home or getting a degree and coming back and working from Sullom Voe. So the population gradually increased again.

When I was a teenager, there was a single dance hall in Lerwick called The Planets, up Mounthooly Street and it was just a typical dive, you know, with one of these glittery balls on the ceiling. (It's now Puffins, a fancy furniture type shop.) You didn't have much chance to keep up with fashion when a teenager, you were working six months behind London and the mainland and if you went to a local shop and bought anything and you went to a dance then half a dozen other lassies had exactly the same frock on, so you tended to work a lot with Kay's catalogue and different mail order catalogues.

We did a lot of outdoor things. I taught swimming in the sea while I was at school and through the first years of university. This was the pre-swimming pool era and there was maybe about two hundred pupils at one stage swimming in the sea. But I would be scared to go in the sea now – it's blooming cold! You kind of get weaker as you get older. Everybody's central-heated now. You don't have an old coal fire and when you went to the bathroom you'd freeze before you got back into the warmth again.

Climate Changes

There's been tremendous changes in the weather. In summer, I remember running barefoot and the tar melting on the road, although that was just the odd day. The winter is a definite thing. When I was a child we had fairly deep snows regularly in the winter time and we went sledging. There was a lot less traffic around, so in Lerwick, we went sledging on the main streets. I can remember several times opening the door in the winter and the snow being right up to the top and having to dig your way out of the house. I can also remember boys at school, particularly from the rural areas, getting a week off school to dig out sheep. Now we hardly have any snow and if the snow does come, it doesn't lie longer than a few days. The Clickiman Loch in Lerwick used to freeze over, where the broch of Clickiman is and when the herring season was in its peak in the early days, they used to cut blocks of ice out, smash it up and keep the fish fresh with it. That was before we had freezers and that kind of thing. You would never get hardly any kind of layer of ice on that loch now. So it's a huge change in weather, from the ozone effect or whatever. There's been a definite shift. We're wetter and windier now with much higher winds but not nearly such deep and prolonged snows.

The Urge to Leave When I was at school, I wanted off the island. It's a very sheltered existence being brought up in Shetland. There was no TV in our house and I didn't see television until I was fourteen. But once this TV came in, I wanted to see the world. I mean, it sounded very exciting, the big city life, the colours and the clothes. I'd never seen a double-decker bus or a train before I went to university. So it was quite an excitement and a want to get off the island. I was left to make my own mind up. I think my parents realised that unless I wanted the same lifestyle as them, which was very much a labourer's lifestyle, I needed education and I needed to get off the island, at least for a while.

You learn about things through education and you know there's no way you can pursue that particular thing in Shetland. I wanted to be a geneticist from a fairly early age. I thought genetics was just a wonderful science. I knew so little about it and they'd hardly begun to teach it, certainly not at high-school level, so I just wanted to go some place where they were teaching this wonderful new subject.

When I got to Aberdeen I was scared of the railway station. It all seemed to be noise and bustle, and there was these flapping little signs that went round telling you where all the trains were going and their times but it was all too much. I could never find my way, but once I got used to that it was okay. There were still trams running in Aberdeen when I first went there.

I stayed in halls of residence my first year because you got to meet more people. They gave priority to islanders because if they were in among several other island folk, it helped them find their feet better. So it was a bit of a home-from-home for me: I think there might have been about eight Shetlanders in the hall of residence, that were of the same age, and from the same year at school.

Shetland Changing I'd come back on holidays at every possible opportunity but I never lived here, so I notice differences in the Shetland that I'd left. I think the big changes are the infrastructure: the roads, the standard of the houses, the leisure centres, I mean we really are terribly well-off for fancy leisure centres. The other changes are probably that there are bridges to a lot of the islands that had no bridges before. There's excellent ferry services to the North Isles which are subsidised by the council so it's easy for folk that would have been isolated on the islands to get into the centre of activity. I think what you're finding is a lot is a depopulation in the rural areas because the facilities for travel are so good and a lot more folk are moving into the town.

I think probably there are more English voices around. It's always been cosmopolitan in terms of foreigners, like the Dutch, but now there's more English voices around, many of them having come in for jobs in Sullom Voe or council jobs because they maybe had the right qualifications at the right time. But you've also got a couple of Chinese restaurants and an Indian restaurant and the children are speaking with a Shetland accent, so I think that's really quite cute.

There was a while when there was a lot more shops in Lerwick but I think mail order's taking over again. They can put a whole load of stuff up to Shetland and I think they charge £5 or something for delivery to the pier here so it's very difficult for local traders to keep abreast with prices. A lot of folk go to Marks and Spencers regularly because they're off the island quite a lot. More people go off for jobs or holidays or whatever, and they take full advantage of a shopping trip while they're at it.

Coming Home

Being off Shetland for twenty years, I was desperate to get back again because your values change as you get older. Part of my reason for wanting to come home was my own kids. I was based last in Birmingham in the West Midlands and I had a big salary and a big house but I wasn't happy with the education the boys were getting there. I realised that I was either going to have to come out of the public school system and put them to private schools or come back to Shetland. So it was part of my decision to come home and I'm pleased I did that. I think it's a very good education you get in Shetland and the boys have now both got a very excellent education. I think it's one of the top schools in Scotland, on these charts of comparability [national exam performance tables].

My sons were both in late primary, before they went into secondary school, when we came back. It was a big change from Birmingham. They enjoy it now and never want to go but maybe eventually they will. My oldest one is at Glasgow University now and he's fishing daft. He's away at the moment collecting whelks on the shore because the price of whelks just now is £1.15 a kilo, so he reckons he can earn £15 an hour collecting whelks.

As far as further education on Shetland is concerned, there's the FE college which does quite a range of different courses like weaving, knitwear courses and I think, a bit of engineering. There's also the North Atlantic Fisheries College in Scalloway, the ancient capital of Shetland. I actually had a lot to do with its setting up. I was the Co-ordinator and Acting Principal for a year when I came back to Shetland. It's designed to take the Shetland fishing industry into the 21st century and it really is a Rolls Royce solution to Shetland's training needs. It teaches all subjects in the catching side, navigation, all the Department of Transport courses, all the fish processing courses, engineering and also aquaculture, fish farming and all of that side of things. And it'll do things like first aid courses, hygiene courses for factory workers so it covers quite a range of education in the fishing industry. There are some postgraduate students based there now and also quite a lot of foreign students coming in for particular courses so it's again a cosmopolitan type place.

Bashir Maan
Businessman & Councillor
Born 1926

Coming to Scotland I was born in Pakistan and it was the damp, dank night of 28th of February 1953 that I came to Glasgow Central Station. The only connection I had in this country was in Glasgow, a Pakistani businessman who was living here. I had never met him but I had corresponded with him. There was no particular connection with Glasgow from my home town or my family. During the Raj, students always came to Glasgow and Edinburgh. The Scots who were in the Sub-Continent in the 18th and 19th centuries initiated our educational organisation; it was, I would say, ninety per cent Scots who did that. Because they were educated at Edinburgh, Glasgow, St Andrew's or Aberdeen, naturally they sent all the students from there to Scotland. You'll see in the university records that until 1920, before Gandhi started the campaign for boycotting British schools and universities and everything, about thirty to thirty-three per cent of the total number of students came to Scotland and only two-thirds went to the huge country of England and all the universities there.

I wanted to come out and study. In the Sub-Continent in those days, and even today, education is very costly. Parents have got to pay for it and my parents had paid enough for me to be sent to the university and I decided to come out to study further, not depending upon them. So that's how I came to Glasgow. The idea was to better myself, to have a degree here, and go back and get a good job. That was the idea. But I didn't go back. The reason was when I came here there were five hundred to six hundred Indo-Pakistanis living in Scotland and the great majority of them, I would say about ninety-five per cent of them, were concentrated in Glasgow. They had no organisation to help them: there were very few people who could read and write English that were sufficiently word-proficient in the language to be able to help them in their problems – and their problems were many. It was the time just after the Raj, and prejudice and discrimination were prevalent, far and wide. They had no statutory rights as we have now under the Race Relations legislation. Anyone was at freedom to discriminate against you, to put you out of his place, not to let you in any pub, hotel or club, or not to rent you a house. There were a lot of problems and I got involved right away because I had knowledge of the English language. I could speak and understand and therefore I started helping my compatriots, both Indians and Pakistanis. That made me get involved too much and that then affected my studies. After two years, I gave up my studies – I realised that perhaps I can do better here instead of continuing my studies and neglecting the work that I'm doing with the community, so I gave up the study and joined them. I also became a traveller.

First Impressions Two things happened to me in the first two days that I was here. The first day – I asked my friends if they could guide me towards any historical monuments in the city of Glasgow and they said, go up to Cathedral Square because there was the Provand's Lordship and the Cathedral. So I went there but I forgot my way coming back home. I was really lost so I asked one or two people. They tried to point out to me but, being just raw and not being able to understand Scotch, I just couldn't make any head or tail. Eventually I stopped an old man and tried to explain to him I was staying in Hospital Street, next to the Gorbals, and that I wanted to go there. He tried to explain to me for about five or six minutes and realised he wasn't getting anywhere. So he held my arm and walked off, signalling me to follow him. He brought me to Hospital Street, showed me the nameplate and then he says 'What number?' '135,' I said and he took me there to the close. 'Okay?' he says, 'Cheerio.' That was one thing which really brought home to me the friendliness of Scottish people.

The second night I was going upstairs, I saw a couple winching in the close. To me it was a shock, the greatest shock of my life because I had never thought that young people, or anybody, could be showing their emotions, private feelings, in open view, in public. So my heart started to beat very quickly and I ran upstairs. I opened the door and I started shouting at my friends, 'You should see outside. There's a boy and a girl, a boy and a girl…' and I couldn't make any sense out of what I was wanting to say to them so they said, 'Come in, come in and quiet down. What is it?' So I explained and they said, 'Is that all? Well, you haven't seen anything yet.'

The Early Asian Community in Glasgow

After the First World War, most of the Asian community were seamen and in the Armed Forces. Unfortunately for them, as soon as demobilisation started, all the coloured seamen – the term at that particular time in vogue was 'coloured' whether they were black or brown, from the Sub-Continent or from Africa or West Indies – were paid off to make room for the white soldiers who were coming back home from the Armed Forces. They were left on the scrapheap with nothing to do. Most of them somehow made their way back home, wherever they had come from. Some of them persevered here, doing odd jobs or selling trinkets in the streets, but they did not succeed in making a good living.

One day, one of them went to a Jewish warehouse man in Crown Street, asking him for a job. The man was being honest and he said, 'Listen, don't go round looking for a job because you won't find one. No one will employ you in these days, particularly the white people. But I'll tell you how to make a good living.' He said, 'I can give you drapery goods, on credit. Take a suitcase, fill it up, go out and sell them. Persevere; it will be hard but you could make a good living.' So this man did it. Within a few weeks he started to earn quite a considerable amount of money and when his compatriots saw him doing that, they also joined him. That's how they entered the peddling or travelling trade. The Jews and Irish were, until then or just before then, the pedlars. Now they were getting out of that trade because they had done well. Indians and Pakistanis filled up the vacancy in that field and they did well. That was in the early '20s. Then they started calling over their relatives and their friends from India and Pakistan.

Till the end of the '20s, the community was only about sixty to seventy people but every decade, it increased two- or three-fold. By the time the Second World War started in 1939, their number had grown to five hundred or six hundred, peddling and making a good living. They were living by then in Edinburgh, Dundee, Aberdeen, Elgin and Inverness, and some had even penetrated to the Outer Hebrides. But once the war started, and rationing introduced, all the factories were closed to make room for the production of armaments. They couldn't get the wares which they sold, so they were forced to come back to Glasgow. During the war years, they couldn't go back home because the sea wasn't safe and there were no passages available, so they concentrated in Glasgow and that's actually when the community started to organise itself, to get roots in this country.

In Nicolson Street in Glasgow, there was a shop opened by a Pakistani who used to import some things from Pakistan and India and some from a big warehouse in London – London had always a sizeable community from India. So this shop supplied us with cooking ingredients, garam marsala and all these things. But there were no shops for our meat; there were no Muslim butchers, and the Muslims could only eat halal meat. There was a butcher in Stockwell Street who used to keep live chickens. We would go there, buy one and kill it ourselves according to our rites round there in the back of his shop. He cleaned it for us and we brought it home. It was always chicken that we ate in place of lamb or beef, because we couldn't get halal meat. In early 1950s Glasgow the neighbours would have had a fit if they had caught us cutting the throat of a sheep but we could get away with the chickens. Soon after that, the environmental laws and regulations stopped anybody keeping chickens in a settlement where people were living.

The Community establishes itself

The community remained static till after the war, and then the process of Partition [of the Indian subcontinent into India and Pakistan] started. There was no traffic between Scotland or England and the Sub-Continent for the two or three years of the Partition and the Independence. It was only again in the early '50s that the new arrivals began to come to Scotland and the community started to grow because everything had settled down in the Sub-Continent. People got in touch with their relatives and their friends over here, asking them if they could come over.

Up to the late '50s , the economy of this country was going very well; there were a lot of places, particularly in England, where there were a lot of jobs – factories, particularly in textiles, had jobs that were lying empty and they were very pleased to have anybody who could come along. But in Scotland, the only thing Indians and Pakistanis could do was peddling and because people were getting a little more affluent, there was far more room also for others to come in and enter the market. In the mid-'50s , the City of Glasgow Corporation Transport Department, and those in Edinburgh and Dundee, started recruiting Indians and Pakistanis. Before then they had always refused to entertain any Indians and Pakistanis. I remember myself, in 1953 and '54, one or two people who were told in no uncertain terms 'No, there's no room for you.' But when they couldn't find the people to run their buses then they opened the door.

In 1957, the recession had started in Yorkshire and many of the mills were closing down, so there was a lot of unemployment. Many of the Indians and Pakistanis who could speak and understand English well were hired here. They had to pass a test before the Corporation took them on. They wanted to make sure that they would be able to understand what the passenger is saying, where the passenger wants to go, how much he has to be charged, therefore they had to pass the test. All those who were capable enough to pass came to Scotland and joined the buses and from then on their way of living and working here started to change. Before that time, ninety-nine per cent of them were pedlars, but from then on, the numbers of those who were employed started to grow. They started also to join certain factories, particularly those which had dirty and dull work which the Scots shunned. But very few West Indians ventured up to Scotland, I don't know why. By the early 1970s, there were only one or two West Indian families here. The majority were Indian and Pakistanis and that's still true today.

A Muslim in Scottish Politics

I started to get involved in the domestic politics of Scotland, not just the Muslim community representation. In 1968, I was the first ever Pakistani – and Muslim as a matter of fact – in the UK to be appointed a Justice of the Peace. I got a lot of publicity. Nowadays there are so many Justices of the Peace that nobody knows when one is appointed, or who is appointed, but in my case it was a unique thing. A lot of people got to know me and in the same year, David Marshall, who's now the MP for Shettleston, got in touch with me. He was not only the organiser of the Labour Party for Glasgow but he had been a trade union official and was in touch with a lot of Pakistanis who were in the buses. Through them he got to know me and coaxed me to become active in politics. I had joined the Labour Party early in 1965 on the persuasion of the then MP Tommy MacMillan. He was my MP when I lived in Townhead and he persuaded me to join the party. I had been just an ordinary member who just pays the sub, but when David Marshall approached me, he said, 'Well, you've got so many people now and so many problems that if one of you was in politics, it will be easier for you to solve their problems. It would be good for the community.' So he talked me into it.

In 1969 I was put on the panel of candidates [for a local council seat] and was selected to stand for Kingston. Before me they had tried to win that seat from the Tories with [the late] Geoff Shaw, and Pat Lally but both of them failed. Geoff Shaw failed because there was a huge number of Catholics in that area and they won't vote for him, and Pat Lally failed because equally there was a forceful number of

ELECTORAL SUCCESS: GLASGOW'S FIRST MUSLIM COUNCILLOR 1970

Protestants and they wouldn't vote for him. The chairman of that constituency party was Harry Selby who also became an MP later on. When I got selected he told me, 'Bashir, you know why you've been selected, it's because you're neither a Catholic nor a Protestant. We think you're a neutral person and you might be able to win the seat for us.' So that was why I was selected and I did win the seat. It was a great upset for the Tories and there were headlines in the press. I had won against the expectations of everybody. All the media pundits had been saying: 'It's very good of the Labour Party to give a chance to a coloured person but the time hasn't come when the Scots will vote for a coloured person.' This was the type of attitude that they adopted in the media, and when I got elected, everybody was very, kind of, amused; one of the papers had the headline: 'Bashir Bashes the Tories'.

My business had also helped me a lot in introducing me into the community. I think that was another factor which helped me because when I went out to knock doors to do some canvassing, door, people would say, 'Oh, we know you' – they had seen me on the television or heard me on the radio or had seen my picture because of my business activities and I think that was another reason for my success.

The Modern Muslim Community

The total ethnic minority population in Scotland is between 60,000 and 70,000 now and out of that, the Muslims are about 35,000. The Pakistanis would be about 25,000 or 26,000. The rest of the Muslims are from all over the world – from North Africa, from Middle East Arab countries, Iran and, of course, Malaysia.

The first purpose-built mosque in Scotland was the big one in the Gorbals. We started building it in 1977 and it took us about seven years to complete it. The first phase was completed in two years, then we had to wait for more funds. The funds came, and we opened it in 1984. The community raised most of the money itself. We did get about half a million pounds from abroad, from the Middle East, but £2 million was raised from the community itself. There were certain people who really sacrificed a lot to see that project completed.

Now there are quite a lot of people in the Islamic community who are third generation, children and grandchildren. Most of us are worried because we feel that Western society has put its religion aside; people do not believe any more in religion or morality as dictated by Christianity and we feel it's affecting our children also. The mothers and fathers try to teach as much to their children as they possibly can, but there is a worry, naturally, a very great concern. We would like children living according to the ordinances of the religion, to be moral, be honest, be upright and be unselfish, whereas the Western society has gone totally opposite. That does worry us and that's why we try to do as much as humanly possible to keep our children within the fold. We have arrangements for their religious teachings, their religious up-bringing in the Mosques, in the Sunday schools, in the evening classes, also in the homely atmosphere of the house.

We have centres for the older people where they meet but otherwise we have no clubs as yet. One thing that the Muslims cannot have are clubs where drink or dance or something like that is practised. Muslims may not consume or serve drink, nor can they sell it – it's against their religion. Islamic law is very strict where drink is concerned. I've sold it, but I was committing a sin and that's why I stopped, when my conscience really pricked me. Where drink is concerned, Islamic law says the manufacturer, the purveyor, the storer, the seller and the drinker are all the same.

Secondly, it has never been our culture to have clubs of that sort. It has always been our culture to meet at religious places. Hindus meet in their mindirs, Sikhs meet in their gurdwaras and Muslims meet in their mosques. But we do meet on certain occasions like weddings, which we have in hotels. There the whole community gets together – the weddings are very big things where five hundred or six hundred people will get together to celebrate.

Community Relations

When I first came here, I was helping a very small community from the Sub-Continent. Now there are much much bigger communities, both Pakistani and Indian, and also Hindu and Sikh communities. Generally the relationship is very cordial. Most of us know each other from back home, the first generation particularly, and those connections are being passed down to the children also. Most of the people in Scotland have come from one particular area which is now in India, the Punjab. There is a part of Punjab which is on two banks of the River Sutlej, the north and the south banks, one is called Nikudar and one is called Gigroun. That is where most of them, ninety-five per cent have come from. Of course, since then many people have come that do not belong to that area but the original people, the people who came here between the wars and up to 1960, were mostly from that particular area. Secondly, we have lived together for 1000 years, the Muslims and Hindus in India before the Partition, so there are a lot of things we have in common. We have a common culture and language, most of us speak Punjabi – Hindus and Muslims – so all these connections make us, I think, quite close to each other. They unite us instead of dividing us. Of course, it's the politics that divides us, and whenever there is a struggle between India and Pakistan, naturally the feelings do become a wee bit affected but otherwise we're all right. We have never been to the stage that you might expect between Orange and Green; we have never attacked anybody here or been aggressive or somebody been hurt. The only thing is that you probably mentally just keep away from each other in case you say something or you hear something which kind of affects your feelings and makes it worse.

When I first came here in 1953, there was still prejudice – very much so. I remember the neighbours always kind of harassing you on any excuse, and one that there used to be was the smell of cooking. We would come home in the evening, most of us, and start cooking and if it was summer the windows were open. Soon they would be banging on your door, and shouting, 'Close the bloody window! The smell of your cooking is annoying us!' Now, that smell has become so popular.

In terms of prejudice, I think the legislation has made a difference because people now cannot say to you or dare to do things to you because they know they'll be breaking the law and be penalised for that. But the legislation can only deter people, not change their attitudes. Unless we change attitudes, prejudice and discrimination will remain, because it is in people's minds, it is the myths and misconceptions which generate discrimination and prejudice.

Home

I used to go to Pakistan every year till last year. Last year my father died and I don't know if I'll continue that ceremony of going every year or not. My mother died about twenty years ago. That was the link. My brothers and my sisters in Pakistan are all well settled. I have even some property coming to me from my father but whenever I go back to Pakistan, I always feel like running back to Scotland. I always start talking like, 'I've got to go back home now.' I have lived now far more years here than where I was born and brought up so though I think for the first generation, at the bottom of your heart, at the bottom of your thoughts, you still long for where you were born, in practical terms you will never leave. I won't go back to Pakistan to spend the rest of my days there. It's too hot and I have no friends there. All my friends, all my contacts, all my interests are here. What would I do if I go there? It would be all right for a few weeks. People would come and visit me and I would go and visit all my relatives but what after that?

Raymond Ross
Teacher & Writer

Born 1953

I was born in West Lothian and brought up in a shale-mining village. The shale pits didn't die out until the mid '60s. My grandfather had come over from Ireland to work in the pits and my father was a Polish RAF serviceman who met my mother at a dance in the mining village of Whitburn. When they first met, they conversed in Latin, he having very little English and she having no Polish. My mother was brought up a Catholic and it was simply after a dance she said to my father, '*Deo Gratias*,' ('Thanks be to God') and my father replied, '*Et cum spiritum tuo*,' ('And may the spirit be with you also') which was the correct response from the Mass; so my mother said, 'I knew he was a Catholic, so I can have another dance.'

THE HAPPY END TO A LATIN COURTSHIP: RAYMOND'S PARENTS

A lot of Polish servicemen stayed on in Scotland because they couldn't really go back to Poland. My father would never set foot in the country while the Stalinists were still in control. They were declared the biggest private army in the world after the war but they weren't really welcomed, even by a lot of the Liberals and the Labour Party. They were denounced, nobody wanted them and I think if the Government could have shipped them back to Poland they would have, but after Katyn [the site of a wartime massacre of Polish troops by the Russians] and all that they couldn't. So a lot of Poles like my father changed their name, they naturalised and had to become British citizens. Most of them were great admirers of Churchill but they were denied pension rights and things like that if they didn't naturalise. They didn't have to change their name but they chose to because there was always that kind of threat hanging over them.

There was often a divide in the Polish community in my experience, because there were those who really tried to retain their Polishness and there were those who wanted to become more British than the British, if you like. I think my dad fell into the latter category so I was never brought up speaking Polish but I think if my mother had been Polish, it would have been completely different. I think I would have learnt Polish but my father really wanted us to be British. I turned out to be a Scottish nationalist and I'm sure was a great disappointment to him.

After the war, my father worked as a waiter and after that he started his own business, which was a wee shop in the village and the post office. We were rather a small village but there was a German family, there were several Ukrainian families, quite a lot of Polish families, obviously a lot of Irish or Irish-Scots, and a French family: quite a big mixture for a wee mining village really. There was quite a lot of poverty. My father never went down the pit but that was the kind of thing you were threatened with when you were a child: 'Get to university or you go down the mines.'

Fledgling Nationalism

I think I became a Scottish nationalist when I was at school. I can remember in Primary Three at school, when you were doing Bannockburn and Robert the Bruce and the Wars of Independence and all that, it just really fired up the class. I can remember going outside, nobody wanted to be the English and get slaughtered, so we all charged around in the one army as it were. It's quite funny because, if you'd gone back two or three generations, the whole school would have been Irish, Polish, or whatever. I think that's quite funny. I don't know, I just think that if you're Scottish, you're Scottish. I think it's only in recent years that I've thought the fact that you get passionate about these things could be more to do with your Polish blood or your Irish blood – I mean I have got Scottish blood in my grandmother's side, but it's dormant.

Sectarianism

Geographically, West Lothian's nearer Edinburgh but culturally, it belongs to the West. There were regular Orange marches on the Saturday nearest the Twelfth of July. They would stop outside the church – it was always timed for when Mass was on – and they would stop for twenty minutes and bang the drum and shout or whatever. We had this old Irish priest and he just used to stand and hold the altar and just stare at the wall for half an hour until they'd gone and then continue. They broke into the church and smashed it up and stuff like that. It was definitely there: so you were a left footer and you knew that, and you were a Tim. You were a 'sausage roll' to boot, that was a Pole, in the local rhyming slang. They knew I was a Pole because my eyes were too close together. I mean, you're talking about small villages where everybody knew everybody else and you went to a Catholic school so, you know, people knew your background.

Where I was brought up in West Lothian, it was Billy Wolfe [SNP] running against Tam Dalyell [Labour]. As kids, I can remember being told that if the SNP came into power then all the Catholics would be kicked out of Scotland. There was all these myths about Billy Wolfe's grandfather's shovel works, and the way the Irish labourers were treated, and the whole tie-up between the Labour Party and Catholic education. It's quite laughable when you go back to it but it was certainly passed on to you as a genuine belief at the time. Now we've seen the disappearance of the working-class Orange Tory vote – people voting Tory because it was Orange – and there's been a breakthrough in the old perception that working-class Catholics would never vote Nationalist because they perceived the SNP as being an Orange organisation.

I think sectarianism comes and goes. A lot depends on what happens in Ireland as to how real it is or how bitter it is, but it's definitely still there. There's two ways of looking at it, I suppose. One is that it's a cancer on the body politic and the other is that it lets off steam between different sections, and you can look at separate schooling and all sorts of things that lie behind it. I always think that it lies in the past; as Scotland matures, it's something that should be solved. I think if the Irish war or situation is genuinely solved, which it may or may not be, that's obviously going to have a knock-on effect. You can go back to John Maclean's words: 'Scotland will not get a Republic until Ireland gets hers.' Sectarianism in Ireland and in the west of Scotland are related but I think partly it belongs to a British identity. As that weakens, and I think it is weakening, then it should be less relevant. If you do have an independent Scotland, what does Orangeism or Loyalism mean? It should wither.

A Literary Renaissance in Scotland

You come over a bit of Scottish literature at school, but it was at university, where I went as a mature student, that I read Hugh MacDiarmid – in particular, *A Drunk Man Looks At The Thistle*. It was a modern, intelligent voice, a very satirical voice and it expressed quite a lot of sentiments about Scotland that I think psychologically drew me in immediately. This was at Edinburgh University in the mid-'70s: there were a few academics who were interested in Scottish literature, but this was a Scottish literature course – there was no degree. The course was quite small and if you were interested in Scottish literature, you were regarded by the establishment of the English department as a wee bit quirky, backward even, or sometimes even a bit dangerous, if you were politically nationalist as well. I think they half expected you to be carrying Semtex around in your pockets. Of course, this was the time of the devolution thrust. The universities were trying to get out from the Scotland Bill so they could stay with the University Grants Committee. Of course, what happened was that Thatcher turned round and used the UGC to slash their grants and their funding and it kind of served them right, I suppose. But there were a lot of English academics and there was that panic, that comic panic, that they were all going to run over the border, and so wandering around George Square with an SNP badge on studying Scottish literature made them look at you a little askance at times.

That's definitely changed over the last twenty years, definitely in universities. You can do Scottish literature/ethnology degrees now and they are much more accessible. If you say now that you're doing a degree in Scottish literature, people go, 'That's very good,' whereas twenty years ago they'd have said, 'Oh, but will you get a job?' Well, you weren't going to get a job anyway, I don't suppose, but it's more mainstream now, because there's more confidence, and it seems more natural to people to start looking at the world from where they are.

Not only are there more people studying Scottish literature but it's much more acceptable to write in Scotland – in Scots even – and about Scotland, particularly in prose now. I think the renaissance was poetry at the beginning. There was always something self-conscious to a degree about writing poetry in Scots but I think now people just write in whatever register they want, prose or poetry or theatre, and that's just accepted as natural. More people are writing and there's more attention paid to it in the press and the media. When we launched *Cencrastus* magazine in 1979, just after

Cencrastus

AUTUMN 1994 • £1.95

CENCRASTUS

THE CURLY SNAKE No.49

MACDIARMID VERSUS THE FOLKIES
RLS TROCCHI MORGAN
SOCIALISM AND SCOTTISH IDENTITY
IAN MCCULLOCH PICTISH ART
IAIN CRICHTON SMITH
POETRY • MUSIC • FICTION • REVIEWS

THE MAGAZINE FOR SCOTTISH AND INTERNATIONAL
LITERATURE, ARTS AND AFFAIRS

the referendum [on devolution], in its own wee way it was a kind of declaration of faith in Scottish culture. We had to carry a lot of reviews, for example, of Scottish books, because the main press didn't cover them. That's not the case now: a Scottish book is leapt upon and if it's got enough sex or violence or whatever appeals to the supplements at the time then it'll get punted. There's maybe a danger there, because it's fashionable now. But it would have been inconceivable as recently as the early 1980s that a Kelman or a Gray or a Welsh could be a major literary figure in London and be on the Booker Prize short leet. Fashions may come and go but it is no longer possible to go back to marginalising Scottish literature. It might be that people will talk about Scottish writers, Kelman or Gray, just as who they are, as we would talk about a big American writer without appending the national adjective 'Scottish' to it. I think that's quite important; it would be a real sign of maturity, that we'd made it. Why do you always have to say 'Glasgow poet' or 'Scottish poet'? Seamus Heaney now is just Seamus Heaney, people don't say 'the Irish poet, Seamus Heaney'.

It's partly our own fault, because we continue often to behave in a rather parochial way: we claim Candia McWilliam or William Boyd despite the fact that they are not resident in Scotland nor do they write in Scots or about particularly Scottish topics. You can play for the Scottish football team if you have a Scottish granny. But the other side of that is that the cringe is still there. People still put themselves down a bit. I teach with the Open University which is quite interesting because you meet a lot of adults of different ages and backgrounds and they ask you what else you do and so on. When you start talking about Scottish literature, you get really complex and strange responses, like, 'There is nothing beyond Rabbie Burns,' or 'What is Scottish literature?', so you know there's still a long way to go. The media or the chattering classes know a lot or they're in touch with a lot, but there's a lot of people who still are not. The big thing there is the education system, which is still constantly under threat of being eroded, of being anglicised further.

The Future for Scotland

I don't think that there's any doubt that we have made substantial progress in recent years, but I still don't think that we can sit back and relax on it. I think Thatcherism really damaged Scotland quite badly. Edinburgh's good at hiding its poverty, until recently certainly, decamping people out to big schemes which basically become ghettos. England always had these inner-city problems, as they were called in Thatcher's time, but in Scotland it's the schemes outside the city centres that are

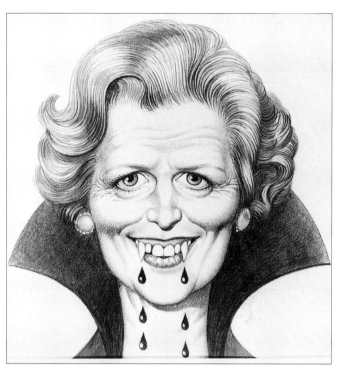

NOT SCOTLAND'S FAVOURITE LADY

the main cause of concern or should be cause for action. I think Edinburgh's a poorer place than it was through the '80s – all the beggars in the streets that you see nowadays. There was always dossers and guys you knew from the Grassmarket, you sometimes knew their names and chatted away to them and gave them money, but now there's just so much homelessness. I think something has to be done, something positive. Going back to visit my dad in the '80s, going into Bathgate, I noticed there was a smell that I hadn't smelt since I was a child. You'd sit in a cafe and you'd think, 'What's that smell?' – it was the smell of poverty. That's come back and I think it's something that has to be sorted.

I think Scotland should look on itself as an emerging nation, as they would say in the United Nations. Politically we're still inept, corrupt even, but there's a promise of a parliament, which could be the glorified county council that Tony Blair wants or it could mature into a fully fledged sovereign parliament. As somebody pointed out, you can't sing or write or poeticise your way to independence, you have to have the political edge, the political maturity, the social maturity to do it. But culture is obviously part of that, or it's part of culture.

Jim Wallace
Member of Parliament

Born 1954

Childhood

I was born in Annan, Dumfriesshire. My father was an accountant and my mother had worked in the Annan telephone exchange up until the time she married, and then went back just as it was going over from a manual exchange to STD – it must have been in 1962 or '63. Up until then there were people wearing headsets and saying 'What number do you want?' Mum had to do a duty rota on a Sunday; I went in with her at ten o'clock on a Sunday morning. She had to ring the fire siren for the practice and just seeing her flick that switch when the siren went up round the town for the voluntary fire brigade to go and practice, that's a memory I do have.

The house I first lived in had been my grandparents' house and my parents moved in there when they got married. Then we moved into a council house where my grandfather lived with us. When I was five, we moved into the three-bedded bungalow my parents still stay in. I went to Newington Primary School which was a very short walk away from the bungalow, and then I went to Annan Academy. I walked to primary school and at secondary school I cycled. February 18th 1970 – I was walking to school because it was very snowy and very icy and my mother told me it was safer to walk to school than go on my bike. Two hundred yards down the road, I fell and broke my left wrist. After that, my father drove me while I was injured and that then became a habit, although I walked home in the evening. But nobody worried about my walking, or cycling.

THE OPERATORS AT ANNAN TELEPHONE EXCHANGE, EARLY 1950S. JIM'S MOTHER, GRACE, IS STANDING AT THE BACK BY THE WINDOW

CROWNING OF THE QUEEN OF THE BORDER AT ANNAN RIDING OF THE MARCHES, 1961. JIM WALLACE IS CLOSEST TO THE FRONT STEPS

We played in the streets, we were quite fortunate. When we moved to our parents' present home we were absolutely on the edge of the town; we used to play in the wood right across the street, played football in the street. You put your jackets down to make goals and you picked sides. In the summer sometimes we managed to find three stumps up against a wall and had a cricket bat. Certainly if you could get outside you went outside – we didn't all rush home to watch television. I certainly remember pre-school, all the familiars of *Watch With Mother*. Monday was *Picture Book*, Tuesday was *Andy Pandy*, Wednesday was *Bill and Ben* and Thursday was *Rag Tag and Bobtail* and Friday was *The Woodentops*. There was the usual diet of *Blue Peter* and the quiz programmes and things like that in the evening. It was fairly balanced.

I think, like every boy, I certainly had a spell where I wanted to be a train driver but I had just turned nine when Harold MacMillan resigned and Home became Prime Minister. I was fascinated by it. Then, following Alec Home becoming Prime Minister, our then MP, Neil MacPherson, was elevated to the House of Lords. During the subsequent by-election, I remember meeting the Labour candidate and some of his supporting MPs, including one Tam Dalyell. I got a political bug then, and if someone had said then in 1963, 'What do you want to do?', I'd probably have said 'be a Member of Parliament'. By the time I got to school, I think I'd certainly formed an interest in being a lawyer or being a civil servant.

University Days

I was possibly the first from Annan Academy to go to Cambridge. There certainly have been some since. I'd always assumed I would go to Glasgow or Edinburgh or Aberdeen University. I got pretty good Higher results and someone said to me 'Have you ever thought about trying to get into Oxbridge?' People complain about some universities and the way they treat Scottish qualifications but I had no problem. I had to sit an entrance exam like most of my other contemporaries at Cambridge but they accepted my Scottish Highers in terms of the other qualifications that had to be met.

Going from Annan to Cambridge was a shock, although I'm not quite sure whether it was the cultural shock or the sheer homesickness. It was the first time really that I'd been away from home for any length of time. In many respects I don't think it was as big a cultural shock as I had expected – it was not full of English public school, stuck-up students. Basically, I found a lot of people who were of very similar backgrounds to my own, and in fact, the friends whom I made in my first twenty-four hours there are probably to this day some of my closest friends.

I went to Downing College. I had no connection with any college, but I had always indicated I had certain political ideas and Downing seemed the obvious place, given the name, linked to Downing Street. My choice of college was honestly as basic as that. As things turned out, it was a college that had a very good reputation for law and I was very well taught there. Downing also had a reputation for English, but the year before I went, there had been college riots which were all related to the English faculty, and in my year no-one was taken in to study English. I think there was a sort of moratorium to allow things to quieten down – Leavis had not only gone but his portrait had been removed from the dining hall.

I was a member of the Union and took part in Union Society debates. In my first term at Cambridge, Chris Smith, now in the Cabinet, was President of the Union. I was involved in what then was called Pressure Group for Economic and Social Toryism (PEST) which would now be called the Tory Reform Group; I actually was a member of the Liberal Party at the time, but for some reason the local Liberal Club put me off during my first term there although by the third term, I'd joined them. The National Chairman then of PEST, Keith Raffen, is now a member of the Scottish Liberal Democrats, and indeed, one or two others of these days I have subsequently met up with at Liberal Democrat events. I campaigned for the Liberal candidate in Cambridge and eventually left PEST because it was becoming slightly difficult to campaign. By then, Mrs Thatcher was elected Leader of the Conservative Party and I think many people on that wing of the Conservative Party were seriously disappointed. We had the two 1974 General Elections whilst I was there and I took an active part in the local Liberal campaigns and ultimately became treasurer of the University Presbyterian and Congregational Society.

A Career in the Law I did economics in my first year, then decided I would do a second part of my degree in law. At the same time as all that, because it was actually an English law degree, I decided I wanted to come back to Scotland, do a Scots law degree and qualify as a Scottish lawyer. I came back and did a two-year degree at Edinburgh University and got my LLB. I think I probably always wanted to be an advocate, and indeed before I'd even left Cambridge, I'd had preliminary discussions with the Faculty of Advocates to find out what the entrance qualifications were so I knew which subjects to take when I went to Edinburgh. It's probably all part of the psychological make-up that makes you want to stand on your hind legs and argue.

I qualified academically, was called to the Bar in '79. The Faculty was then still very much Edinburgh Academy and the New Town, but these were possibly the days when Glasgow-based criminal practice was beginning to take off, when Glasgow

Chambers were set up and recognised. It was still relatively small – I go back occasionally now and don't really recognise most of the people there and certainly find that a lot of my contemporaries say the same. That's a very good thing: the Faculty has increased in size, it's probably a reflection too of the volume of work, not least in the criminal courts that's to be done. But then it was still a relatively small place.

This was a noticeable period of change; certainly the girls were starting to come in but they were still fairly thin on the ground. There had been a number of women Sheriffs but there still weren't that many girls around. I was called to the Bar on a day when I think there was thirteen of us in all called but there were no girls among us. In fact, they held two callings, and that was thought at that time to be quite an event. In some respects this was maybe the start of the growth in the number of people becoming advocates.

Law & Politics

As a student, I stayed in a flat, renting a room, and stayed on there until I bought my first flat in Edinburgh, probably about 1981. I'd been the Liberal candidate for Dumfriesshire in 1979, my home area, and then shortly thereafter, the South of Scotland Euro-candidate. I have the claim, which no one will ever be able to take from me, that I was the first person ever in a European election to lose their deposit because the South of Scotland was the first result declared – it was a makeshift campaign.

In 1979, I was also engaged in the referendum of course, before the Euro elections. I had a correspondence with the Returning Officer in Lothian because I was registered both in Lothian and in Dumfries and I wanted to come off the Lothian register so that my non-vote would not be counted as a 'no' vote. The Returning Officer refused to take me off the register. I don't think anyone outside those who were campaigning for a 'Yes' vote in Scotland every fully realises the depth of anger caused by the arbitrary forty per cent rule [the Government-imposed rule for the referendum that forty per cent of the Scottish population had to vote in favour of devolution for it to be implemented]. This has of course overshadowed the fact that the 'Yes' vote actually won, which people sometimes tend to forget. So I spent quite a lot of time in Dumfriesshire in that referendum campaign: as these things turned out, both the prospective SNP and Labour candidates had resigned, very shortly before, so when the referendum was called I was the only prospective 'Yes' vote candidate. Hector Munro was the sitting Member and, of course, was taking the 'No' vote. In some respects, it actually helped me in the ensuing election campaign because I'd had two or three weeks really of being the advocate for the 'Yes' campaign.

Two weeks after I was called to the Bar, I had a very acute dilemma: I got a phone call from Archie Kirkwood, now one of my Parliamentary colleagues, to say that David Steel [the then Liberal leader] was looking for a new Parliamentary bag carrier, to head up his office and was I interested in the appointment. Possibly if I'd actually been asked two weeks before I was called, I might have actually gone but I declined. I wanted to practice law and I was doing reasonably well. It's always difficult to evaluate your own performance, and clearly I was marked as a person who was very politically committed, but then a lot of people in the Faculty of Advocates are very politically committed – you go back through old election results and you find some interesting battles between QCs in various Scottish constituencies. So it wasn't a disqualification and then, of course, I was fighting the Liberal cause so probably no-one ever thought I was going to be elected.

I did mainly civil work, I had the odd foray into the criminal courts but it was mostly civil. I could think of one or two very interesting experiences in the criminal courts, but my own predilection and talents lent themselves more to civil work than criminal. One of the frustrations was there was nothing better to get your teeth into than a good complex problem, but usually these were the ones you were under tremendous pressure to have your opinion back the following day. But, as a junior, I did enjoy tackling the civil problems.

I devilled to Brian Gill, who's now Chairman of the Scottish Law Commission – I think that the sun rises and sets on Brian Gill. He was a first-class devil master. He would give me a lot of responsibility to get on and do things and then took the time and the patience to go over it with me. Certainly, I couldn't have asked for more from a devil master, and then, after my calling, he was always around to give advice. I have got the greatest time and affection for Brian.

About two months after being called, I was instructed to act for the Scottish Conservation Society in the public inquiry as to the Atomic Energy Authority's proposals to drill boreholes in the Galloway Hills for the disposal of nuclear waste. It was an inquiry that lasted for about five weeks, so that was a steady income for that time. There were some senior QCs there – Malcolm Morrison, Bruce Weir – and it was a very good learning experience, not just about the law, but about the issue. It was the thing I perhaps enjoyed more than anything else about being at the Bar is that you've got to turn your hand to so many things. Don't get me wrong – I was not an expert on nuclear power, but I knew a lot more about nuclear power and how nuclear reactors worked and nuclear waste and vitrification processes and geology and and the hydrology of different geological structures, by the end of that.

Likewise, I remember being involved in civil litigation over the Ballachulish Bridge, where I remember actually going out and buying the Penguin or the Pelican guide to engineering terms and you actually had to get some knowledge of basic engineering. I actually enjoyed that. It's not unrelated to what you've ultimately got to do as a politician because one day you can have to deal with the current crisis in agriculture and the next day it might be fisheries, the next day it might be some complex social security problem. I think the training I had as a lawyer has, I hope, helped me in good stead.

Leisure Pursuits

The only sport I'd every really taken up was golf and I think the lowest handicap I ever managed to get down to was about sixteen, and I regret now that I very rarely have time to golf. In the last two years I've started taking horse-riding lessons but I'm still very amateurish and unaccomplished at that. My problem was that my main pastime was politics, not least when I was trying to nurse a seat some eighty-five miles from Edinburgh. That did actually take up quite a substantial amount of time. I was on the Scottish Liberal Party executive and by 1982, had become the Vice Chairman so that actually was taking up a lot of time. The problem, of course, was that when I was elected, my hobby became my job and I don't think I've ever quite got round that. One other thing I used to do, when I was in Edinburgh as a student and then in my early days at the Bar or my devilling period, I used to sing with the Edinburgh Royal Choral Union, I did enjoy choral singing.

In Edinburgh, there were some good plays on and you watched them but not on any systematic basis. Frankly, I used to hate Edinburgh during the Festival. There was always people there enjoying themselves with so much to do and I would be walking up to Parliament House to go and draft my next divorce summons and I used to think how nice it would be to escape from all those people having a holiday and go and have a holiday yourself.

From Dumfries to the Islands

I actually thought Dumfries was a winnable seat. The percentage share of the vote which I got in 1979 was the roughly the same as Menzies Campbell got in North East Fife and Ray Michie got in Argyll and Bute, both of whom won in 1987. Remember we're talking about '81 when the heady days of the Liberal/SDP Alliance – when Shirley Williams was winning Crosby, Roy Jenkins hadn't quite won Hillhead but he had a resounding result in Warrington, and Dumfries I certainly thought was winnable. At that point we then had to negotiate with the SDP over the share-out of seats. David Steel came to the meeting in the South of Scotland as a representative of the Roxburgh, Selkirk and Peebles Liberal Association, and basically thought that it would be a good idea if Dumfriesshire was given to the SDP. He took me aside and said, 'You'll do this for the good of the party, won't you?' I suspect he was right because Roxburgh, Selkirk and Peebles under boundary changes was about to become two seats, and the Liberal Party was getting them both – and indeed, subsequently won them both. Having nursed the seat for five or six years, I'd gone from fourth to third in 1979, been the first Liberal to save my deposit since 1945 and clearly thought that there was more progress that we could make, so it was a pretty brutal part of my life. I was very upset, but ultimately I had to bow to the inevitable. My local party was certainly happy to go for another fifteen years before they invited David Steel back to a constituency function although he was the next-door Member of Parliament. I hated it, but I knew he was right.

Therefore as the 1983 General Election approached, I didn't have a seat to fight. I had temporarily been a PPC for Kinross and West Perthshire but that seat was being completely carved up under boundary changes, so they couldn't guarantee me the nomination. I subsequently applied for Orkney and Shetland when Jo Grimond announced his retirement. I had never set foot in either Orkney or Shetland. I went up during the first weekend in January 1983, to Orkney on a Friday and then to Shetland the following day. It must've been one of the wildest weekends of that winter and I was just absolutely captivated by the place: the power of the sea crashing in at the Bay of Skaill in Orkney. Shetland in really foul weather, it either grabs you or completely turns you off – it grabbed me. I'd always said I would not put my name forward for a seat that I could not identify with and live in, and I had no doubt after visiting here that I could actually live in it. One of the interesting insights into that is that Orkney and Shetland are not Highland. We talk about Highlands and Islands – they are certainly not Highlands. A place like Kirkwall is about the same size as Annan and it's a market town too, the centre of an agricultural area. I don't want to draw the parallels too far but I found it was a place I could readily identify with, and likewise Lerwick. So I felt that yes, I could feel at home here.

I was engaged to be married. When my then fiancée, now my wife, got engaged to me she thought, 'It's all very well getting engaged to him, he has politics as a hobby but he's a Liberal, he won't be elected!' My wife came from Milngavie – her cousins were in the flat next door to me in Edinburgh and we met at a party in the flat. It never occurred to her that we would do anything other than set up home in Edinburgh; in fact we'd bought a flat in Edinburgh for when we got married. I'd flown back from Shetland on a Sunday to Aberdeen and got a train from Aberdeen to Edinburgh. She recalls meeting me at Waverley Station and the first words I said to her were, 'Oh, you'll just love it, you just see the sea crashing in!' She decided she would make up her own mind whether she loved it or not and came up with me for the selection meeting some two months later. She said she felt it was right, and certainly we have never regretted it one bit. Indeed every election now, my children in particular, both of whom were born in Orkney, they get paranoid that I might lose my seat. There's no way they ever want to leave Orkney and I've been given that ultimatum. 'We'll buy a farm,' said my daughter before the last election, 'if you lose.' Where the money was coming from to buy the farm, I don't know, or how I was ever going to farm it without any detailed farming experience, I don't know, but yes, we've been very happy.

The 1983 General Election was held up by the media as a classic four-cornered fight. Jo Grimond had been the Member of Parliament for thirty-three years and people said, 'Well it was all a personal vote, it wasn't a Liberal vote at all. It was Jo's personal vote.' The Labour candidate, being a Goodlad, was the only local candidate, she was a Shetland lass. The Conservative candidate – and the Conservatives had traditionally been the runners-up – was David Miles who had been the Member of Parliament for Banff, and the SNP candidate was the sitting MEP, Winifred Ewing. Every candidate had something going for them. The difficulty is that you do not canvass in the traditional way in which you would do in the cities. There's a wonderful passage in Jo Grimond's memoirs describing where he tried a different tack and asked someone, 'How do you think the people will vote in this Parish?' only to be told, 'Mr Grimond, they'll vote as they see fit.' You just don't ask outright, 'How are you going to vote?' No-one really had much idea, but what I knew for a fact was that if I was the Liberal who lost Orkney and Shetland after thirty-three years that there probably wasn't really much future in the party for me. I mistrust personal votes; now, of course, I'm told that my majority is all a personal vote and I say 'Look, I got here with a majority of four and a half thousand when I had only ever been in the place for six weeks – don't tell me that was a personal vote.'

The Orcadians and Shetlanders didn't question the fact that I was a 'sooth-moother' or a 'ferry-louper', the two expressions that are used. Many of course remember that my predecessor, Jo Grimond, had been a Fifer. It's a place that's got a very strong community identity and which actually does not take well to those who come in and tell people how it all should be done. But it's a very welcoming place if you are prepared to come and work with the grain, and become part of the community. It's also got to be remembered that there's a great sea-going tradition in both Orkney and Shetland. They are islands but the people are not insular. They have a wide world perspective, I mean I only need to look at my postbag. Going round, people ask questions on not just local issues which of course are important, but there is an interest in what's going on in Scotland, in Britain and in the wider world.

Home Rule

This is a constituency whose MPs have had a long identification, with varying degrees of commitment, to Scottish home rule, and yet it's an area of Scotland where people will say that they identify more with Scandinavia than with Scotland and that they'd rather be run by London than by Edinburgh. But I think these things go in phases. If you read Jo Grimond's memoirs, he says that when he first won Orkney and Shetland in 1950 from the Tories, the biggest cheer he got at his eve of poll election in Kirkwall was when he gave his commitment to a Scottish parliament and Scottish home rule. He reflects how unusual and strange that was given the experience in 1979 when both Orkney and Shetland rejected a Scottish parliament by considerably greater margin than any other parts of Scotland. So it's not something that's always been the case. From the 1950s, the time of the National Covenant, there clearly was a mood, but I accept that that view had obviously changed. The 1979 referendum result was the same.

I've never hidden my commitment to Scottish home rule, it's been on every election address I've had, and I was identified with the Constitutional Convention. None of my constituents were in any doubt as to where I stood on this. I think, if anything, the concern has possibly been over-centralisation, and particularly what we've seen as a Central Belt domination. That's why I made it clear that I would not have supported a Scottish Parliament that did not have proportional representation. That was essential because every party should have a stake in all parts of Scotland. You won't get the domination by one party which has a disproportionate share of the vote in Central Scotland. I think that was an important factor in producing a 'Yes' vote at least in the principle of the Scottish Parliament in both Orkney and Shetland in September 1997.

I think too, that the eighteen years of a Conservative Government also had an effect on people's perceptions. I was never slow to remind them that it was a London parliament that imposed the Poll Tax against the wish of the majority of Scots. The Central Belt Scots didn't want the Poll Tax any more than Orcadians or Shetlanders wanted the Poll Tax. And I think the centralisation, particularly of local government services, which the Tory government embarked upon between 1979 and 1997, also helped change perceptions again, so that we did actually manage to get a majority.

That's why I also attach considerable importance to the Scottish Parliament when it is up and running, that it must take proper account of the islands areas and have means by which legislation can, if necessary, be tailored to meet islands areas. It's not usually the major issues; it's often detailed practical things. I can think of one or two practical issues where the fact that you were trying to apply legislation, however well-intended, to an islands area just simply didn't work in practical terms. For example, some environmental waste control which means that the sand that you dig up to set building foundations on one of the North Isles will have to be disposed of in Kirkwall, that's complete nonsense. The Scottish Parliament I hope will operate on a scale where it should be able to either identify it beforehand and amend the legislation accordingly, or when anomalies do arise – because with the best will in the world you're not going to predict everything – there should be a mechanism for resolving that quickly. I think that will be a test of the Scottish parliament, as to how sensitive it is to all parts of Scotland.

Orkney and Shetland: Today and the Future

When I think about my time here in the Islands, I think about just how much things have remained the same. Communications are still a problem. The airline services fluctuate almost every six months – it depends on the new timetable as to whether they get better or get worse. I'm afraid at the moment we seem to be going through a period where they've got worse. The shipping service is constantly a source of concern because of the cost and the different services which are on offer. I've always maintained that the most important issue to the islands is transport, because it affects so many other issues. Agriculture depends on transport. If you're fishing, you've got to get to a market: that depends on transport. I don't believe that any government – and to be fair, from time to time, some have tried – has cracked it yet and I hope again that the Scottish Parliament can devote more time to looking at issues of transport in the islands.

I arrived in Orkney and Shetland after the oil industry was well established. I think probably the biggest change people would notice are those who have got the experience of pre-oil and post-oil. These are major industries: I have the biggest oil terminal in Western Europe in my constituency. They have had an impact, you can't get away from that, but I value the way in which it has not actually affected the community. I still find here a very deep sense of belonging and community. You can't generalise, but it is probably still safer here. I've got a twelve-year-old daughter and I know that she'll go into town on a Saturday and I don't worry about it – no more than normal parental worry, but about the same as when I was a twelve-year-old walking the streets in Annan about 1966 or '67. You can't say that of every Scottish town. The fact that people actually do leave their cars unlocked – oh, it's an island, you cannae take a car very far. But it's things like that: in spite of a major industrial development within our isles, that sort of quality of life is still here.

We've got very good education and it's a place where the traditional Scottish importance of education still rings true. Where we are really going to see I hope, some positive and exciting developments is what actually can be achieved here through new technology, particularly communications. In the past, Orkney and Shetland must have been some of the last places to be touched by the industrial revolution. Some of the islands were only connected to the grid within the last twenty years, but here we are with a new information revolution, a telecommunications revolution where distance needn't matter, and the fact that the sea is there needn't matter.

In sixteen or seventeen years of being in Parliament perhaps the most important question I asked was in a Scottish Grand Committee debate that the Liberal Democrats initiated on the economy of the Highlands and Islands. I asked Michael Forsyth, the Secretary of State replying, if he'd make a commitment to the University of the Highlands and Islands and he said, 'Yes'. If you'd seen the shocked look on his official's face, when he gave that unequivocal reply in open debate! Potentially, the University of the Highlands and Islands is going to be a very exciting development: a campus that's not just going to be focused on Inverness, but spread out throughout the Highlands and Islands, making use of new technology, linking in with traditional industries and with arts and archaeology – there's a lot of potential for that. Taking a longer timescale, going into the future and looking back, I would like to think that the revolution in telecommunications and developments like the University of the Highlands and Islands will have a lasting effect for the good in communities such as Orkney and Shetland.

Neil McCallum
Reformed Bank Robber

Born 1955

I was born in Parkhead, Glasgow. My mother was a cleaner and my father was a labourer and we lived in a council house. I went to St Michael's Primary School in Parkhead until the age of nine. I just played truant for the last two years, until I was eleven and then I was taken into care. I enjoyed the schoolwork, but I didnae really enjoy school. It's a strange difference but I was kinda bored at school. I think that's what led to my truancy, and then onto petty thievin'. When you're a child and you're walkin' aboot the streets durin' the day, you're liable to get up to mischief, and that's basically how I started off the way that I'd went later in life. Just started off with stealin' little things out of shops, for the thrill of it, or to get sweets, and that was it!

THE FIRST COMMUNICANT, 1962

I have an older brother, an older sister and a younger brother. My older brother got into trouble a little when he was about thirteen. Just petty thievin' but he learnt his lesson: he was never involved in trouble again. My older sister became an unsuccessful shoplifter and has spent several prison and remand sentences in Cornton Vale. My young brother is a drug addict who has quite a lot of problems and has just finished a prison sentence himself.

Thinking back about everybody who was in my class at primary, I was the only one that actually went down the wrong path. I was a loner to a certain extent. I liked my own company and everything to me was an adventure. Up until I was nine, I have so many happy memories as a child. I loved waking up in the morning because it was a new day, and if the sun was shining and my heart was beating, I just wanted outside and to discover things. In school you cannae really do that, because you're confined to classrooms and teachers threatening you with the belt if you try to get oot.

I remember getting six o' the belt quite regular from one teacher, a science class which I'd no interest in whatsoever. But rather than just sitting there and saying nothing, I became disruptive. The guy was, by this time, at the end of his tether and sometimes I'd get a slap across the legs. It's not politically correct now, looking back. But when I went home and told my mum, these sort of things were accepted because I was becoming a wee bit disruptive even in the home.

When I was bunking off school, I just used to go walks. I can get dropped off anywhere in Parkhead and take you anywhere you want to go. Trying to give you the name of a street is almost impossible for me, but I knew the whole physical layout of Parkhead, which stood me in good stead in later years when we had all the gang fights in the late '60s. I knew escape routes that most people didn't even think existed.

It wasn't really common for boys and girls in Parkhead to get into trouble, not really. I mean, the neighbours were brilliant. If you can imagine back to the 1960s, to what Glasgow was like with the tenements: everybody in the close was like an aunt or an uncle. If your own parents weren't in, you were always taken into somebody's hoose and given a piece and jam or a cup of tea, made safe. I cannae recall any others who'd actually went down the road that I eventually went.

Going Downhill

By 1967, I had a few previous convictions, breaking into shops and into my grandda's pub – he was the manager. I'd taken the keys out his pocket on the Sunday morning and went down, took the money out the safe, locked the pub up and put the keys back in his pocket. It was a lot of money, £600, away back in 1967. I'd went to school the next day and took all the kids oot and bought them sweeties galore; I can assure you I was the flavour of the month!

I don't think my grandda ever forgave me for that really, because it caused so much trouble in the house. The suspicion actually fell on my uncle William, my dad's younger brother. He was only eighteen and he'd been getting into a bit of trouble himself. The police were going to charge my uncle and I didn't want him getting the blame for something I'd done, so that's how I eventually admitted it. This was my first custodial sentence; I got sent to an approved school – St John Bosco's in Fife – for that.

The approved school was a big shock. I'd never been separated from my family, other than for maybe two weeks in a remand home. It's a total culture shock. For the first year, I kept to myself, well away from everybody. I wisnae opening up to anybody. Approved school then was run by the Salesian Brothers and it was kind of strict. There was no formal education whatsoever: you got some English and arithmetic and that was it. I ran away twice and that meant I was having to stay there longer, so it took me two and a half years to get home. But when I look back, I think I grew up with a bit of resentment for my family because I'd felt that my mother had rejected me. I still loved my mother and my family but I felt a wee bit detached from them. I don't know whether that was the experience of the approved school, or whether this was something else that was developing, but I felt it wisnae really my family, that I was different. Something had happened to me, and I couldn't really explain what. That maybe decided how things were going to play out later on in life for me.

I was a child with some sort of talent; later in life I showed that I had the educational ability by achieving O-Levels and Highers and going on to college. That ability was obviously there but I don't think the service was geared up to try and work with individuals. Even then, in the '60s, they were having problems with the probation service. There always has been a backlog of cases throughout the social work services and that means sometimes kids like myself go through the system and nobody picks up on it. Bad for me that it was twenty-odd years down the line that I eventually managed to turn things round. I'm hoping that things are a wee bit better now for kids, and more emphasis is placed on trying to reach them, finding out what it is that really makes them tick, rather than just making them trying to fit into wee square holes.

I received several thrashings from my mother and they were thrashings – it wasn't what you would call a normal punishment for a child. By this stage, my mother was absolutely losing the place, because I was driving her demented. My younger brother had just come on the scene, and was causing her so many problems, so a couple of times she cracked and I copped really hard punishments. People use the argument 'we'll punish them' and 'that'll just stop them' – believe me, my experience is that's not the road at all. All that taught me was that violence was acceptable, and that played a major part in my life from the ages of thirteen on up to maybe thirty years of age.

Gang Life

I got involved with the gangs but not until I was about thirteen and a half. I got introduced to them almost by accident. One day – I'd just been released from the approved school – my mother had sent me to the shop with a £5 note, to get fags and some messages for tea. When I was getting the change handed to me, I seen four members of the local gang standing out the door and I just knew instantly they were gonnae try and take the money aff me. But I was more frightened of my mother than of them; there's no way they're getting the money off me 'cos my parents couldnae really afford a fiver going missing. I'd always been a scrapper at school – wee schoolboy punch-ups – I was never afraid to have a fight. But I'd developed a technique where I could really handle myself against people my own age. So when I came out the door, the four of them had surrounded me and says 'Gie's the money.' I just bust right through them, I don't know how fast I ran but they couldnae catch me. I ran up the hill, and the next-door neighbour Ella Boyle came out. I pushed the money into her hands and turned round and squared up to them. At the end of the day I'd been offered what they called a 'square go'. The leader of the gang offered to fight me himself and I battered him, and I was invited into the gang. That was my introduction to the gang.

I'd come out of the approved school feeling alienated a bit from my own family, and all of a sudden the gang was on the scene, and they became my family. The gang was an extended family: all of a sudden I had all these sort of pals and brothers, the big boys. They actually became my role models – unfortunately – but that was the way things were in Parkhead. It was easier for me to fit in with the gang than to stand myself against quite a substantial number of young boys.

The gang culture was that you got pissed oot yer heid and then you went fightin'. So I was introduced to bevvying and I took to it like a duck to water. I wanted to out-perform everybody: I had to drink more than them; I had to be braver than them; I had to go fightin' more people than them. It was almost like an extension from the childhood days where all the 'square goes' were fought 'roon Murphy's back. All the kids would gather 'roon there and it was like an arena set up, watching all these people having their wee fights, seeing who was winnin' and who wisnae. Fitting into this culture was something that wasn't alien to me. I felt this could replace what I was missing from my own family.

Serious Trouble

I didnae reach the adult court until I was fifteen years of age. After my first approved school, I was then put into another one for breaking into a shop. I was transferred to St Mary's in Springboig and then, after three months, up to Oakbank Approved School. I was absconding all the time to go back to the gang. On my last leave from Oakbank, I was drunk and I got into a fight with a policeman so I was sent to a further approved school, St John's in Springboig.

I ran away from there just before Christmas in 1970 and obviously, being on the run, I'd nowhere to stay, so I was staying with pals. One day we got into a gang fight; there was about seven or eight on each side. Later that night, I'd occasion to see three of them going into a cafe, and I just went right in behind them and stabbed the three of them, managed to get the better of them. I used a broken bottle and a bit of a knife; I was only fifteen, but this was me getting my own back on the gang for earlier on. The cafe owner got assaulted 'cos he tried to stop me as I was going out the door. But this is how stupid I was: this happened just round the corner from my house! The cafe owner knew me! Everybody in the cafe knew me! I'd been so caught up in seeing the three of them going in, I never even thought of the consequences. I was going in to show them that I was better than them. And this sort of culture comes back to haunt me later in life. I wish that I thought things through a wee bit better.

The gloves were off now – this was me getting the treatment. I was sent to Longriggend Remand Unit, which is basically for untried sixteen to twenty-one-year-olds. I was sent there originally at thirteen years of age when I'd escaped from one of my approved schools because I'd been certified unruly. So any time I was getting remanded it was to Longriggend. I went there for a full three and a half months, and I was held in the schoolboy section. Two young boys had committed suicide 'roon aboot me, and I found one body myself hanging from the wall. It was kind of frightening for me – I'd realised I'd went beyond what had been childish behaviour, but I was now within a system that was going to treat me as an adult. I went to the High Court and I pled guilty to the charges but I couldnae begin to give any explanation about why I'd done what I'd done, other than to say they were members of a different gang, and that's what went on. I got sentenced to three years.

The problem for the Secretary of State was I was under sixteen years of age. They had no, what they called then, real secure units. They didn't want to send me back to an approved school again for me just to walk away and be back on the street and obviously causing more mayhem. It was decided that I would go to the Young Offenders, even though I was only fifteen. Young Offenders is primarily for people sixteen to twenty-one; sometimes, if somebody's twenty-one and a bit, they keep them in there rather than transfer them to the adult prison. But this was my introduction to what you would call the penal system now, the punitive side of it.

I was only about four foot eleven when I was fifteen, when I went into the Young Offenders. The lesson I learnt straightaway was what I'd learnt out on the street – you have to look after yourself. A couple of people approached me and tried to bully me and take my tobacco and my money, my wages. I went and got an iron bar, just woke up one morning, went right in and set about the biggest one oot of the two of them, and I never had any problem from anybody again in the three years I was there.

I was still unruly, even within the Young Offenders: I'd done my full three years, I wisnae released early. I went in at fifteen and a bit and came out eighteen and a bit. No attempt at rehabilitation; nothing to address my violent behaviour; I was beginning to develop a drinking problem – there was nothing done about that. I was literally held in custody for three years and then thrown out the door. Basically I went back oot still a fifteen-year-old – I hadn't grown up mentally. I was looking for the gangs and the gang fights again; I was almost hooked on the violence now.

I'd never tried anything other than booze at that stage. That was not really on our scene. We'd heard some of the older boys talking about uppers and downers and pills but I'd grown up in a male culture where drink was socially acceptable, so drink was the sort of natural extension for me; sort of, 'this is what I consider to be manly.' So I kept to drinking, quite a lot of us did. When I was in the Young Offenders I was introduced to cannabis, but I didnae enjoy it then. I actually made myself quite sick the first time: I was given a bit and wisnae told that it was enough for two or three. I just put it in one and I was absolutely ill and that put me off any types of drugs whatsoever. I wish it would have put me off bevvy.

We used to make the home brews, and occasionally the staff would find them. Sometimes they didn't. But the one thing I did learn – and it made me stop taking the drink in the prison – was that when I got drunk, I got violent. I wouldnae take normal banter from people; I would take it personal then turn it 'roon against the person and that would give me my opportunity to fight with them. I'm glad that's all over now, anyway.

A Glimmer of Light

In the Young Offenders, you were locked up every Friday night because you all had to clean your cells oot. Other nights you were allowed oot on association. I'd came up with this brilliant idea: I'd go to the Governor, who was Andrew Gallagher at the time, and say to him I wanted to form a discussion group, on a Friday night. This was an excuse to get out the cells and a few of us were into it. I went to him and says, 'Look Sir, I want to start a discussion group.' And he says, 'Well, what sort of topics are you going to be talking about?' 'Cos I've always been a nationalist, I says, 'Well – ways to get Scotland's independence.' He says, 'I know just the man for you – go and see a guy called Skip Watson in the cobbler's shop.' So I went round and walked in. This guy's sitting in the cobbler's shop, and I says, 'Skip Watson?' He says, 'Aye.' I says, 'I'm Mac, and the Governor sent me 'roon about this discussion group.' He started to talk to me and he was an Englishman. I says, 'Ya bugger, Gallagher, you've sent me to an Englishman to talk about Scottish independence'.

This is where I would say the beginning of my education began as an individual, as a person, and the beginning of a very good relationship. That man gave his own time up on a Friday night to come in and start this discussion group with eight young people who had long-term sentences. He introduced us to writers like Steinbeck; plays and things that I'd never done before, and he started to challenge us, he educated us in a way that we actually started to challenge ourselves. One of the most important things that I think he'd ever brought in was a student magazine from Edinburgh University. Inside it was just four wee cartoons and a storyline but it made such an impact on me, although it wasn't really until later years in life that I was really able to do anything about it. The first cartoon was the boss shouting at the worker. The next shows the worker shouting at the wife. The next cartoon shows the wife shouting at the wee boy, and then the wee boy going out and kicking the dog. It was all about misplaced aggression and that was when I started to understand myself. I didnae know how to deal with it, but it gave me an insight into myself and how I was reacting to things. I would have an argument with a prison officer and then a prisoner would bump into me and I'd take the violence out on him. I wisnae following it back to what was originally setting the anger or frustration, that eventually caused the anger to come out against somebody else. Later in life, that came back to me and it played a major part in my own rehabilitation after that and being able to control myself to a certain extent. But the rehabilitation was still some way off then.

The idea of parole and all that had just come into the prison system in the late '60s and was kinda new. There was a spirit of liberalism within the Scottish Office at that time, and they were trying some new things, but it was on a sort of ad hoc basis. It was just by pure chance whether you were involved or not, rather than on any systematic approach like saying, 'Well, let's try this on a small scale at first and if it works, let's introduce it to the mainstream.' Nothing like that was ever done. Anything that was learned by the prison service seemed to be just put on a shelf and forgotten about. I find that distressing to a certain extent, because if you've got information that's available to actually alter or influence people, surely the onus is on you to do that. Because the public need to be protected from people like me when I was younger. I was just going out and creating more victims and they had me for x amount of years by this time inside. Surely something should have been done. I'm not blaming the system, but I believe there should have been safeguards within it to actually pick up on that.

Two Steps Forward, Three Steps Back

When I came out, employment was practically out the window. People were asking me what sort of education I had. I had to tell them I'd been in approved schools, that I'd just finished three years. I had no secondary education. So I just took to the bevvy again. I just tried to blot everything out with drink. All my old pals had grown up: some of them had married, some of them had kids. They weren't interested in gangs. Basically, I started hanging about with fifteen- and sixteen-year-olds because it was the gangs, the violence I was seeking, the craving for the fighting and all that.

I knew how to break into shops quite easily. My favourite target had become pubs. I could eye up a building and work out a way into it without setting any alarms off, and empty the stock. I wasn't selling the stock – I was drinking it with my pals. I remember at one point my father saying to me later on in life, 'I'm glad you got prison, because you'd have been dead within another three months.' Things had become so bad with the drinking with me, but there was nobody I felt close enough to, to try and talk to.

When I was discharged, I went back to live with my parents. They'd moved from Parkhead now to Tollcross, and Tollcross had always been a bad area for me because of the gangs. A lot of people there had bad memories because I had managed to chib a few of them, as they said in Glasgow: slash a few of them during the gang fights. I was a wee bit wary going back into what I considered enemy territory. Although I was sleeping there at night, I was in Parkhead during the day, and that's where all my thieving was happening. I was actually what you would call a one-man social menace in Parkhead at that time. Nothing was really safe from me, apart from old ladies and things like that. I got brought up that you didnae steal aff yer ain and you didnae take liberties – these things were beyond the pale. But any shops or cars or vans was fair game for me, and I was doing it on a regular basis – twenty, maybe thirty, offences. By now, I was a well-kent face to the police. When I was caught, sometimes I would plead to some of them and other times I would just keep my mouth shut. I'd imagine they're still on some record somewhere as unsolved.

I remember coming into Parkhead one day and being picked up by the police and driven back to Tollcross. I was told that the next time they seen me in Parkhead, I was getting done for breach of the peace. Now that lasted for about ten weeks: an unofficial curfew on me. But anytime I was seen down there I had to run away and my mother had to lie for me to say that I hadn't been in Parkhead that day, or I'd have got put away. They just had enough of me – I would imagine the police would have been happy if I'd have got a substantial sentence and just taken out the way. I admit, I was quite out of order.

In the Young Offenders, it's a college of crime; that's exactly what it is, learning from each other because you've nobody else to talk to. They're the people you associate and spend your time with, so the one thing you always ask each other is, 'Well, what are you in for? How did you get caught? How did you do that?' I learnt how to do fraud, not a thing that I ever done, but somebody had showed me how to do fraud from the big stores. There was other people who'd been in for armed robbery. It leads on and, before you know it ,you've got almost a complete education of criminal activities if you want to turn your hand to them.

So I was always just sticking to the pubs and the shops, for the money to finance my drinking problem. I hadn't even begun to think about earning things in a profitable sense and putting money aside, maybe for a rainy day or to better my own situation. Everything I was getting was just going down my gullet – I was just drinking myself to death at that point.

Peterhead and Prison Politics

In 1977 I was sentenced to five years at the High Court for breaking into a person's house. The person was supposed to be away and we were actually ransacking downstairs when he came down and in the mêlée, the guy got stabbed. That was the only time ever I'd sat down when I'd been convicted and thought about what I'd actually done. I'd always remembered my dad saying to me, 'Never take a liberty.' OK, we were drunk. I could make all sorts of excuses about it – I did for long enough to myself – but we could easily have got away from that guy without using a knife on him. He was only stabbed once, but that's beside the point. He didn't know what was happening to him, he was only protecting his property. That was the first time ever I'd sat down and felt absolutely ashamed. Twenty years later, that shame is still with me. I'd always justify it by saying 'Well, he was holding my mate down,' and if somebody was holding your mate down, you sort them out and you get your mate away, that was it. It was later on that I started to think about it. I actually deserved more than five years to be quite honest; it was out of order. My co-accused was to get six years because he was done for the stabbing.

But I then went to Peterhead for that five years in 1978 and this, believe it or not, was the start of something entirely wonderful for me to a certain extent. People sometimes say to me, 'How is it that you can go through prison for so long and come out the person that you've came out, and not be affected to a large extent by what's happened to you?' When I went to Peterhead Prison, conditions there were really archaic, absolutely terrible. It was basically a dumping ground for everybody who was considered a problem within the prison system. I went there when I was twenty-one years of age but I'd never been in an adult prison: up until that point, it had only been Young Offenders. But I find myself in Peterhead Prison and lo and behold, there's four or five young pals that I'd been in the approved schools with, in the Young Offenders with, in borstal with – and now I was in Peterhead with. They'd come through the same system that I'd come through. And when we got there we looked about and says, 'Aw, Christ, this is no' right whatsoever – what can we do about it?' I got involved in prison politics at that point.

This was to cost me later on, physically, and in extra years in prison. I got involved in one major riot, and one rooftop protest with two of us, which cost me a further three years, nearly, in prison. It cost me about eight teeth. It cost me serious injury to my liver, injuries to my kidneys, internal injuries which were explained by saying I fell off a roof seventy feet onto concrete. They wouldn't take me to hospital for three weeks – I found that strange. If somebody falls seventy feet onto concrete, surely you phone an ambulance straightaway – you don't wait three weeks. But that's

how they explained my injuries away and I got out after completing my full five years. So I'd done my full three years in Young Offenders, I'd now done my next one which was the full five years. I got out in 1982 after being locked up in 1977.

Meeting Violence with Violence

Being brought up in a culture of violence, I never objected to what the prison staff were doing to me, when the violence went down. I'd been brought up in a way that if you're prepared to fight with somebody and you come out second best, that's just the luck of the draw. During one of the riots, one of the staff had actually got a slate stuck right in his face. He was in intensive care. There was other staff being slashed and stabbed – it was really physical violence for four days, hand-to-hand stuff. After the four days they were going to get us back when they got the opportunity, so when the violence went down against me, I just sort of accepted it.

Looking back on it, from a societal point of view, it should never have happened because the punishment was in staying extra years in prison, but I never questioned that. I just accepted it and thought, well that's how I would have done it; if somebody gave me a hard time for four days, I would have responded the same way. It shows you my way of thinking was still connected to 'violence is OK'.

One of the periods of isolation or solitary confinement I was on was for a year. This was after the riot in '79. So I had a year in my own company. I'd always said that I was quite happy with my own company, but they played a lot of psychological games against us, just to play our heads about. I started getting books on psychology to play them back. One of the things I discovered was one of the control methods for controlling a group of people who have a shared experience. To break that bond you keep them in isolation close together and eventually they turn on each other. Well after a year, we had never turned on each other, and that bond had existed for all that time. That for me was a reinforcement again of the gang culture because these were people who had went through a shared experience again as well, and there was a common enemy. The prison officer was a common enemy. So I'd got strength.

After the riot in '79, I'd got the beating up – well, that would probably be disputed from the prison staff – when I was seen to after coming off the roof. The next day, when they were bringing us out, we were all stripped naked and we were taken out one at a time. When I came out the cell, I'd looked and seen two lines of prison officers all just standing with baseball bats, pickshafts and riot sticks, just hitting the ground and waiting for me. I thought, 'God, they're going to kill me.' Then I realised as I started to walk between them I fully expected to be hit on the back of the head or the back of the legs to bring me down. And I got a strength, I don't know where from, but I had an insight. I said, 'No, they're not going to hurt me – they're wanting to humiliate me, they're wanting me to crawl.' And that's where I got my strength from. From that point onwards I lost all fear from the prison staff. The only thing they could do to me was kill me. That was all they could do. Anything else I was quite happy for, and I would fight back all the way. Once I realised what the big picture was – it was about breaking me as an individual, humiliating me – I got the strength to resist.

That cost me later again when I was in prison because I was doing extra amount of time because I felt the system was unjust: it didn't ask questions about people, it just kept people locked up for x amount of years. Prison officers were

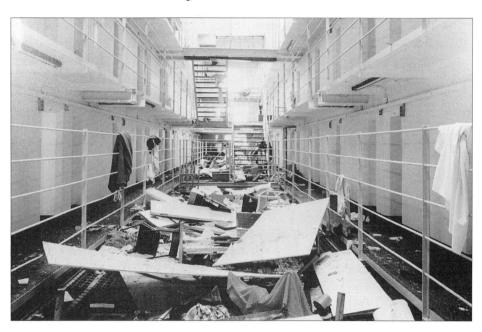

PETERHEAD RIOTS, 1988

getting fat salaries for doing nothing but locking doors. Why shouldn't they be social workers? Why shouldn't they be doing group work? All these things now that we know are sadly lacking in prison, because prison is still being used basically as a dumping ground. People are there for ten years or whatever, come back out and society expects them to be normal. How can you be normal after ten years of that treatment? It's not normal at all – it's an abnormal society we're putting people into, so people come out after x amount of years and have quite a lot of problems readjusting. That usually means trouble for other victims.

Escaping Prison's Revolving Door

When I got out in 1982, I was out three months, because by this time I'd said to myself, 'Never again am I going to allow drink to get that hold on me.' I'd been attending Alcoholics Anonymous for two-and-a-half years of that five years at Peterhead. I knew I'd a serious drinking problem, that if I drank I'd get violent, and I didn't want to be violent to anybody again without just cause or what *I* consider to be just cause. But I'd met a friend in there who told me where I could get guns, and all of a sudden I was saying, 'Here, I don't mind being a bank robber, I don't mind being an armed robber, 'cos if I'm going to be coming in and out of prison for the rest of my life, I'm going to get money for it. I'm not just going to come in for beating people up or anything like that.' So I got out in June 1982 and was back in by November for an armed robbery charge. Not very successful, my life of crime. You should know by now crime doesn't pay ... long term.

I got done for twelve years for an armed robbery. When I'd got out in '82, I set a wee team up, eyed up a place, went in, done it. As we were driving away, one of the other two people behind me let the shotgun off and shot our driver in the hand, he had to go to hospital. It was like Keystone Cops stuff, I'm having to kick out the windscreen of the van as we're driving away because it was all shattered, and I'm saying to myself, 'This is a bloody nightmare, this is not the way it's supposed to go.' The robbery itself was sweet, that went without trouble or incident to anybody. But it was Keystone Cops stuff and I was eventually caught.

I remember Tony Tunilla and Mike Fairley – they were in Peterhead Prison when I was there in the '70s. This was the Army of the Provisional Government. They went and robbed a bank which had shut the previous week. There was quite a bit of humour about that. In fact I've actually used that story in some of the work I've been doing with some of the young offenders now. 'Cos it's about the best-laid plans of mice and men: they'd been eyeing this place up for three months and didn't even realise it had been shut. I found that quite humourous – just as I did when I look back at my robbery when the shotgun went off. I went, 'Oh, Christ man, I've been caught. Oh no, not more years in jail – how long am I going to be in for this time?' I look back on it and say that could easily have been my head rather than the taxi driver's hand because the guy was sitting directly behind me and I felt the shot going by me. I could've been dead there. I was beginning to look at my life and question it. I thought, 'I could be facing another twelve full years here in Peterhead' 'cos that's where I was sent back to when I was convicted.

The only time I pled not guilty, was for the armed robbery – I was working as a security guard for Lafferty's, which was a building firm. They were the only people who would employ me. He was taking on quite a lot of people out of prison and giving them basically a night-watchman's job. It was paying good money – it was a lot of hours but it was keeping me out of trouble. It was £200 a week I was clearing, but that was for a hundred and twenty-three-hour week; they were really horrendous hours.

I just went back to prison ... I mean that was what life seemed to have decided for me. I'd never thought of anything at any time to say, is there anything I can do to alter this? I'd got my twelve years and I'd settled in, and I went, 'Christ, back to Peterhead Prison'. All my old pals were saying, 'Right, let's get back into the politics, back up onto the roof.' I went, 'No, no, no,' I says, 'I want to do this sentence and get out eight years later,' with the two-thirds remission. The pressure was really on me to actually be involved again but I'd made up my own mind: 'No I'm going to try and give this a go. I've made a right mess of my life up till now. This is the first time I'm going to try something about it.'

The education unit at Peterhead was very limited. It was like a Portacabin and the classes that were available were very limited. I had had no formal education whatsoever from the nine years of age onwards but I'd said to myself, 'Well bugger it, I'm going to give a crack at these O-Levels.' I sat three O-Levels and I got them. And I went, 'I can do these things'. So the following year, I sat three Highers, in Peterhead, and I was absolutely amazed because this was something that I'd never tried before. To prove to myself that I could do something, I knew that education would have to play a major part. I knew I had to be educated to understand myself, so that I could control myself and the environment round about me, whereby I wouldn't be doing things on the spur of the moment. I could avoid drink, I could avoid violence – it wouldn't be the attraction to me that it was. I was just replacing something that I'd valued with something that I felt was of equal value.

I was at Peterhead for a further five-and-a-half years and then transferred to Greenock Prison; Greenock had then opened up as a short-term thing for long-termers because there was quite a lot of overcrowding within the prison service at that time. Greenock was absolutely incredible as a prison, in the way it was laid out. It was a small prison. You could get to know everybody, and it was OK amongst the prisoners, there wasn't the hassle in Greenock as there was in Peterhead. I remember my first experience at Peterhead, walking down the corridor and somebody leaning over me and stabbing the guy right in front of me. I literally just had to step over the guy's body and keep walking, I couldn't stop because everybody would think it was me then.

Looking to the Future

I've been in Peterhead, Barlinnie, Greenock, Shotts, Dungavel, Edinburgh, and Longriggend. Prison is now changing to a certain extent. I've noticed the changes over the years; there was some attempt at rehabilitation in the late '60s, and early '70s. From the early '70s, it went down to a more punitive regime and things were getting clamped down a wee bit. All throughout the '80s, it was basically a lockdown because of the amount of riots that they were having throughout the prison system. There was very little work getting done.

But recently I've been detecting that there's a new shift – I'm believing there is and I'm hoping there is – within the Scottish Office. There is a recognition that when people are in prison, something should be done with them when they're there to rehabilitate them. This is a thing I've been arguing publicly to be done for seven years now. Recently, believe it or not, I've been invited in by the Scottish Prison Service, to Polmont Young Offenders, to a new initiative they've launched there in November 1997, although I've only been working in it for the last month myself. This new initiative is actually taking young people who are coming in for their first custodial sentences and isolating them from the mainstream young offenders, thereby avoiding the 'colleges of crime' theme. It involves outside agencies like SACRO, like APEX, like the Cat A Theatre Company – people who are not normally seen as figures of authority, who come in and work with these young kids to try and get them to see the error of their ways.

One of the good things that I can bring to this is that I'm a reality that they've got to face when I sit down and say, 'Well look, son, I was you and this is where I went. I didn't want to go there, but I still ended up there. Unless you think about it now, that's where you could possibly be.' I'm quite skilled, I've done quite a bit of group work, I've been to college and I've been a youth worker for seven years. So I know what I'm doing. There's quite a bit more to it than that, but basically that is my message now and that seems to be the message coming from the system: 'We have to do something to stop you coming back.' That had never been present when I was there.

I've not drank for five years now. I think the last time I was ever really tempted for violence was when I was living in a flat in Gullins Close in Edinburgh. I could hear a young girl getting beaten up in the flat down below me and I just wasn't having it at all. I just don't like anybody that uses violence against women – I went down and intervened and I threw the guy out the flat. But if he hadn't have went, I knew I was putting him out. It was one of those things that it was in my mind. I just couldn't listen to the lassie crying for help and nobody answering. There was still that twist in my own mind that I couldn't phone the polis, 'cos then I'd be a grass. So the way for me to answer that was just go down and sort it out, and if it needed violence, it would have been just fist violence; it wouldn't have been any weapons or anything like that. The last thing the guy expected was me coming through the door and grabbing a hold of him 'cos he thought, 'Well, I'm on my own here beating her up'. I think I frightened the life out of him just with the fact I walked into the house. But I don't get any other urges for crime or anything like that. I was asked the other day when I went into the Young Offenders, 'Do you still find it strange coming in?' I said, 'No, because I know what I'm coming in for, and I know I can come out' – that's the good thing about it.

Once you educate yourself to a certain extent it's a natural process that follows on. I don't think there's any way going back. I'm saying just now that I don't think I'd ever go back, but who am I to say? Next week I might walk round and catch somebody else beating up a woman and hit them too hard and something serious could happen. I could end up in trouble with the law then. I mean, I could still see myself responding physically to somebody else's plight, but I don't see myself going out and using violence against anybody. That's beyond me now because I've understood what was driving me. It was basically my own anger and frustration that I'd blown it at an early age. Rather than face the consequences or do something about blowing my life, I just continued to blow it because it was far easier to get drunk and just blame everybody else, than blame myself.

Life on the Outside   It was really very hard for me when I came out, I came out and I'd set myself a limit of six months. I says if things don't start to happen for me after six months, I'm seriously going to have to think about what I'm going to do with my life. I was talking about educational opportunities at this time. I'd got these Highers and O-Levels but it had been a few years since I'd got them, I didn't know if that was going to get me into college or not. I wanted to try further education and the hardest thing for me was filling in my time during the day. The danger areas that I'd recognised were during the day and early evening. I don't mind late at night being in the house because you can watch the telly, listen to music and then go to bed.

So when I came out I did voluntary work in a cafe, a drop-in centre with SACRO in Edinburgh, and I did that for three years nearly. That took up most of my time during the day. At that time, I attended college at night to give me an access course into community education – a three-year degree course, and I was accepted. Hopefully I'm graduating in June this year. I had a couple of years' serious illness because my liver trouble came back to haunt me. But the last seven months I've been back to myself and this is me picking up all my voluntary work and other work now and hopefully making a difference to young people's lives.

Ian McIver

Freelance Journalist

Born 1956

Early Life and Education

My parents were originally from the Western Isles and both had been working in Glasgow and met down there. I was born in Glasgow but just a few years after I was born, they decided to come back to the islands to look after the family home. So I came back, lost all my English, was plunged into a Gaelic community and became a monoglot wee Gael.

The house was a standard crofthouse at Bernera on the west side of Lewis, supported completely by the standard crofting activities like sheep, cattle and whatever could be grown, which was corn, hay, potatoes, vegetables. The main activity was sheep. We had about one hundred and fifty sheep, which was the usual thing. In those days – this was in the '60s – it was a lot of work without much reward for it. From a very early age you were expected to help out with the rounding up of the sheep, the planting and lifting of the potatoes. Even more work involved in cutting and drying and taking home the peats. It was all very much self-supporting.

I went to school two miles from home at Bernera School. There was thirty of us in those days, the school roll has slipped back considerably, about half that, since. The first couple of years were taught through the medium of Gaelic because all the kids then spoke Gaelic. Within a couple of years things changed. I think the curriculum was going to change into English anyway, but quite a few people from the Glasgow area moved to Bernera and the playground medium changed pretty much overnight; it hasn't gone back to Gaelic since. There was the influx of these youngsters from the Central Belt and Gaelic died that year when they came. They were like me – their parents had returned after having worked for twenty years in the Central Belt as policemen, dockers and they were coming back home, that was the pattern.

My secondary education was at the Nicolson Institute in Stornoway. Staying during the week at a hostel, looked after by a warden and a few teachers was quite a traumatic change from being at home every night. There was up to a hundred of us from the outlying areas. It was very much a melting pot, in as much as we quickly had to learn how to get on with each other, many different types, many different personalities. I recall the trauma of leaving home, that's crystal clear to me still but I look back on it more fondly because of the friends that I made and the general improvement in my character. I think I became more aware of others by having to live so closely with others in a similar situation away from home. And lifelong friendships were forged in our joint university because we had some interesting characters who were in charge of us, and I think some of the light relief centred on poking the most terrible fun at some of these people who were trying very hard to keep us right. Some of them are now very good friends of mine. In a community like this when you leave school, you keep bumping into your teachers. You realise that they're very much human beings and you become good friends with them, but at the

In 1901, 0.63 per cent of Scots spoke only Gaelic and 4.53 per cent (202,700) spoke both Gaelic and English. By 1991, only 1.4 per cent of us had any Gaelic, and none were mono-lingual. Oddly, at the point when Gaelic died out in the playground, officialdom not only repented of forcing it out of the classroom, but began using it in official literature, and subsidising it on TV and radio, the two media which had perhaps done most to kill the language in the home.

time they were very much – not figures of fun like the day-to-day teachers were in the school, the ones that you also saw after school – they weren't as much figures of authority as people that you gently provoked.

There were still weekly boarders until about ten years ago – more from the Uists, the southern isles, they took over our places because the transport situation to the outlying areas of Lewis and Harris became better. Of course, in Uist they now have their own school so some from the most southern isles stay in Benbecula during the week. Certainly, up here, there isn't a hostel as such any more – I'm not sure if anyone is staying in lodgings, so I think something along the way has been lost there. I'm sure there's many benefits to be had from being at home but I think if I had been at home, I would have missed out. Some people had the choice of not staying in the hostel and travelled, and I think it's true to this day that I look back on those people as somewhat losing out on the opportunities that we had to make such friendships. I think that's very much part of a small community, and I think those friendships are possibly one of the reasons why I gave up my job in London a few years ago and came back. I just missed the camaraderie of being part of this community.

Off to the Great Wide World

After school, I worked in a shop here for a while, desperate to become a journalist. *The Stornoway Gazette* knocked me back and told me to go away and get some experience and come back. And I realised very quickly I would have to leave the island – I don't think the *Daily Express* or the *Daily Record* even replied to my letters, so it was a case of getting away somewhere. I joined the RAF just to leave the island and see the world, or let the world see Ian McIver.

I didn't get to see a great deal in fact. My first posting was the nearest RAF base to Stornoway, RAF Kinloss, which I was much miffed about. But I got detachments to places like Gibraltar and Naples which were the furthest afield I went, although I did fly from Kinloss on various sorties and I worked in West London.

I'd signed on for six years but left after a year early. Although I quite liked the way of life in the RAF, all working together, I was a single man so stayed on the camp – not dissimilar to the way of life I had staying in the hostel, living with the people I was with during the day. I decided that I didn't want to be a career airman, I still wanted to be a journalist, so I left. I came back for a few months to work in the Arnish Fabrication Yard here, near Stornoway. The nearest I got to being an investigative journalist, which was what I really wanted to do I suppose, was to become an insurance investigator. I worked for a company whose main work, initially in Manchester and then in London, was investigating people's insurance claims. An interesting time that was too, because usually the ones who were considered dodgy came to us, so it was a case of gathering evidence and writing it up in report for big insurance companies. Fascinating work, I loved it but I still wanted to be a journalist.

I then decided that London had to be the only place where I was going to get the break. So I was working for an organisation called the Institute of Metals, doing admin work for them, and establishing contacts with journalists and people in the London area, helping with tip-offs and basically helping them out for very little, if any money, in my own time. I was there for a year when I saw an advert in – I think it was the local paper here, which I was getting in London – saying that the BBC were looking for someone to present a late-night Gaelic programme for young people. I applied for the job and got it and I came back to Stornoway once again.

I was pleased to be back. I was pleased to have a job that was more interesting, more challenging. And because it didn't take up all my time, because I was broadcasting at night, it gave me the opportunity to work during the day in the newsroom and help out on the news side. When I left four years later because I decided there was nothing for me in Scotland, that experience stood me in good stead. I went down to London and within a week got a job on a weekly paper in south London. I left two years later as the Chief Reporter on that paper. Back here again.

Back to a Changed Island

I'm now a freelance journalist – have been for six years, and it's amazing the way I keep coming back, or shuttling between London and Stornoway. But I think now, having met and married my wife and having a family, I think she has finally tethered me down, and I suspect that the end of my shuttling back and fore has finally come.

There are – and I hear it when talking to young people all the time – things that they want, as we wanted, and we've got some way to go. However, we do have a lot of things to be grateful for: wonderful sports centre, wonderful groups, you know there's not many interests that you can have that you won't find some group doing here. An amazing amount for such a comparatively small community. But I think it's that age, between sixteen and twenty-five, that will probably feel the lack of the facilities like the ice rinks and the bowling alleys.

When I grew up in Bernera, one didn't stray out much on the Sabbath but to go to church. One didn't play around with a ball, even at the back of the house where the neighbours couldn't see 'cos it just wasn't done. You stayed pretty much indoors. If it was a really good day there was nothing wrong with going for a walk, but you didn't walk past other people's houses to make it obvious that you were out on a Sunday. That has changed. Even in the remoter, far-flung parts of the islands, people are not observing the Sabbath as we did. Even the people who are very much adherents, they do not object so strongly to people being out and about, to youngsters even kicking a ball about and to cars flocking to beaches, which they did not only disapprove of, but vocally disapprove of, when I was very young. People in the village would ask people not to congregate at the beach if they did and that was of some puzzlement to visitors, being asked not to congregate on the beach. That sort of thing doesn't happen.

There is still a large body of opinion that the Sabbath is special, something to be cherished, something that we should not allow to change too much. And to outsiders that must seem a bit strange because it's a day for leisure elsewhere. But there is still a strong body here, much stronger I think than anywhere else, although there are always those who in their own private ways observe the Sabbath. Here it is such a significant minority, 'cos I think it's still a minority rather than a majority who are strenuously for the keeping of the Sabbath. But the majority I would say are happy to go along with that because they appreciate that it's something that makes us different. It is something peaceful, something which can be enjoyed and even though it can be a dashed inconvenience not having shops open, not having ferries and planes running, people are still happy to go along with that. I am surprised after all this time that that hasn't changed, but I'm pleased at the same time.

Sex is something which is more talked about, without a doubt. I think that is probably the pervasive nature of the media, rather than anything that is happening in this community that is different to any other. Not just dramas on television, the news brings us our daily dose, particularly these days. So the old inhibitions – and there were inhibitions in this community, so many substitute phrases for particularly bodily functions, particularly in Gaelic – if they're not gone, they are going, and as elsewhere, people are more relaxed about their reproductive systems and everything that goes with it.

I think generally people, even here, are more relaxed about homosexuality. The churches are maintaining – I think without exception in the established churches here – a strong standpoint. They're maintaining a hard line on homosexuality and it's sinfulness as they see it. And because there is such a significant body in this community – I'm not saying a majority but a significant minority – who accept the teachings of the churches, then it is going to be a live issue where perhaps the attitude is perceived as relaxing elsewhere. I think it could only be in small communities that it becomes quite such a strong issue, like Sabbath observance. Gay sex is seen as something that's pretty much not up for discussion as far as watering down attitudes, so people will not disagree with that openly very often.

I look back at the various stages in my life and what the community was like. It has changed tremendously as far as I'm concerned, although I sometimes think maybe it's me that's changed. Certainly, it seemed to me that it was a place where very little was happening twenty years ago, because I remember my own desperation to get away, and I felt that to live properly one had to leave. I think most of my contemporaries thought in a similar vein. Twenty-odd years down the line so much is happening here, and I think probably information technology and everything else is such that you can now be anywhere and be in touch with what's happening. And this community, although it has its problems in many ways and lack of opportunities – as was the case for me and my contemporaries then – it is certainly a place where there's very exciting things happening, and there are opportunities in certain spheres and fields. And the way of life is so much improved, everything from the quality of life that people have working here to education and leisure facilities. It's not a place that I'm desperate to get away from; even if I wasn't married and settled, I don't think I would be so desperate to get away. It's still got that wonderful community feeling which I just didn't experience anywhere else. Probably because I was raised in this community, but I think it's just the general quality of life. I mean, I spent years battling through the traffic in south London. I cannot now but look back at the fields and the shores and the general atmosphere of this island and say 'Thank goodness I'm back here.'

June Lake
Promotion Person

Born 1963

I was born in Paisley by accident. My mother went into labour as my father drove down a cobbled street and she was rushed to Ross Hospital and I was delivered there. My parents stayed in Shawlands, Pollokshields. They were both antiques dealers. My father died five years ago and mother died in January 1998, leaving me with an antique shop to sort out on top of everything else.

Children's Games

As a youngster, it was just so different from the way it is now. We had a television but we didn't really watch it very much. You tended to play outside all day until you got bawled at to come in. We went to each other's houses for tea and played with dolls, the things wee girls like doing, playing with my friends, knitting, sewing. I played board games like Monopoly and checkers and things like that. I don't know if kids still play these things. There was no computer games.

Because of their business, I spent a lot of time with my parents and my grandparents. My grandmother was a great influence in my life. I spent a lot of time in the shop. I used to go there at lunchtime and at four o'clock after school. I would have my meals and then go out and play. Round the corner from the shop in Shawlands, there was a huge bit of waste area where there was stones you could climb over and hide and I remember just squads of kids just playing there. We played in the street. Nobody really bothered, nobody worried. My mum would come and look for me at six o'clock when it was time to go home.

There was no sense of danger whatsoever. I remember playing behind the school as well where there was derelict houses. I don't know if any parents actually knew, you know, but we used to play there for hours, taking our toys down there to play. We used to play something called Chinese ropes where you knotted elastic bands together and you played different games, like how high you could jump. We would also play our peever with our stones. There was a big factory behind my house, a stonemason's, and we would get the odd stones and sometimes one of the guys would smooth it for us and we would play peever. You could play that anywhere. I don't see any children playing in the street now, maybe just small children but always with parents supervising, which is kind of sad.

Schooldays

I went to school at Shawlands Primary and then at Shawlands Academy. I think it was a different school from what it is now, there was sort of a cross-section of children. There was children of every religion and every race and everybody got on really well, there was no racial tension. There was Jewish children, Protestant children, Chinese, a few Catholic children, children from mixed marriages – this was the late '60s, early '70s. I think the school that I went to now has quite a lot of problems.

I liked languages, although I don't really speak any now. I also liked English, and writing stories. My father was English, he came from Sussex; he loved the

English language and I think that was maybe where I got it from. He wanted me to learn big words and I had big words that I had to learn every day. When I was about two years old, he had me saying things like 'disinfectant'.

When I went on to the Academy, I started thinking about what I might want to do in life, but it's nothing to do with what I'm doing now. I wanted to be an author. I wanted to write, for the first two or three years, then I wanted to be a lawyer at one time. I think I was obsessed with *Petrocelli* on the TV – a hit programme of the '70s or the early '80s. I remember watching it and thinking 'I want to be like him.' And I loved *Ironside* and *Perry Mason* and all these programmes.

The Facts of Life

I discovered boys from about five, I think, at the first school dance. That was when I discovered that boys were much different than wee girls because they were violent. We'd had a school dance and I'd been eating the usual crisps and ice cream and lemonade and one of the wee boys said, 'Did I want to dance?' and he picked me up and turned me upside down and I was sick. I remember thinking 'Wee boys aren't as nice as wee girls.' So I learnt quite early on that they're not like us.

My mum told me the facts of life when I was about eight or nine – basic things about menstruation and whatever because I think all the women in our family had actually turned quite early and she thought she'd better warn me. When I was eight and my mum was thirty-nine, she had my sister. She was told it was the change of life so she thought, 'I'd better explain to Juney what all these things are' and then the next thing was she discovered that she was pregnant. She just thought, 'I'd better just go through all the details with her.' So I had a sort of grounding before they told us in school; well, they didn't tell us very much at school. There was a thing called 'Section Six', which everybody knew was the facts of life. But it was always greatly exaggerated by people in the years above you, so you thought it was going to be like a blue movie, like *Emanuelle* or something and it ended up being birds and bees or pictures of donkeys doing it. You got to cut up a frog and that was it.

I was a bit of a late developer really. My mum wanted me to concentrate on my studies so I was about sixteen or seventeen before I started going out with boys. I always had boys that were friends and I went to youth groups and different things. I was the PR officer for a youth group and I was quite tied up with that, so I was always with crowds rather than with having specific boyfriends. I was always interested in dancing. I had my dance classes, tap, ballet, majorettes – that kind of thing. It's like children who are into sports a lot tend to not have boyfriends but they have such a wide social life that perhaps they aren't that bothered about having a specific boyfriend.

A Change in Direction

In 1979, when I was sixteen, I left school. I went on an exchange course in Israel for a year, studying archaeology and the language and history. When I came back from Israel, aerobics had taken off, Jane Fonda was at her height and my dance teacher had actually started doing aerobics classes as well. I put on a bit of weight when I was eighteen or nineteen, and I thought I'd better do something about it if I wanted to dance professionally so I joined a health club, doing running and weight training and low- and high-impact aerobics.

I went to Cardonald College for a year to do more Highers and O-Grades. That was when, as my mother puts it, I fell among thieves because my dance teacher had formed a group called Hot Feet. She asked me if I wanted to dance with her and I thought that would earn me a bit of extra money, so I started dancing. We used to do things like the Can-Can and different sort of theme dances, things from *Cats* or from musicals. We used to dance in clubs and different venues, up and down the country. I liked it – well, I liked earning the money to be honest – and then I didn't get quite as many Highers and O-Grades as I needed to do law. I thought, 'Oh, well, I'm earning money now anyway, I'll just stick with it.' Then I started doing beauty competitions and modelling and it just went from there. My mother until her death would say to people: 'Well, June's only doing this just now. She will go back and study.' But my poor mother never got to see that, never got her wish.

Into the Boxing Ring One of my friends had been a promotion girl for the St Andrews Club; she got married and had a baby and asked me if I would take over. Earlier, in my own career, I had done amateur fights which I didn't like as much so I'd thought I'd not bother with that. In 1992, she asked me to take over for her, and I've done it ever since.

In the ring, I inform the timekeepers and the officials of what round they're at and what's coming up. I think it's really just a novelty as well. It incites a few riots but it breaks up the tension of the fights. We're there for entertainment, to put a bit of glamour into the show. Years ago, it was little boys who used to do it. You'd maybe find that some of the actual match makers now started out as little boys going round with the numbers. Maybe it was an American idea that it became girls; then I think they decided that they liked that better. It's funny because in the St Andrews Club, no women are allowed in; it's men only and sometimes, apart from the odd waitress, I'm the only woman there.

For a special event, if it's a big televised event, I have some sort of special outfit – for a Chris Eubank fight, I think we

June Lake

Height 5'5"	Bust 36C
Waist 23"	Hips 35"
Dress 10/12	Shoes 5 ½
Hair: Dark Brown	Eyes Brown

PHOTOGRAPHIC, HANDS, SWIMWEAR

Hair and Photography by TAYLOR FERGUSON

JUNE'S PROMOTION CARD

had top hats and tails – but normally we're wearing the sponsor's T-shirt. As with the American influence, everything's sponsored, but it's more a leisure, sports- orientated look. It's not the way it was ten or fifteen years ago when the girls wore a swimsuit or a bikini; it's come quite a long way from that. It's a bit more respectable.

I like boxing. Actually, I think from years of sitting watching it, I do enjoy it. Sometimes, you watch a really good fight between two men who are at the pinnacle of their careers and are very strict professionals, and you can't help admiring them, people who put that dedication into their sport. But it can be quite alarming; sometimes when you're sitting quite close to it, you maybe get splashed with blood which can be quite daunting.

The crowds are all right. I mean, you get a few cheeky remarks and a few wolf whistles but I'd probably worry if I didn't get them, to be honest. But I've never had any hassle whatsoever. Certainly, at the fights that I do, they're all members of the St Andrews Club so they know that if they got out of line they wouldn't be allowed back in.

Changed Behaviours

I'd say that women have a lot more respect now than they used to have. I think you find women in higher powered jobs and there's more women bosses. I think women have a respect that they maybe didn't have before and it's filtered down to my job as well. In the job that I do, years ago, I would maybe be expected to be a professional ornament. They hired girls like myself to hang about and make something, like a car or a supermarket, look good. But now, at the motor show, for instance, they take the girls and train them about the cars so you've got to be able to talk about the car and have a basic knowledge. I would say that people accept now that women have brains and that when women are in a profession where they have to be attractive, that's not all there is to them. You still get guys who just like to have a bimbo hanging about to make them look good and I suppose you get the casting-couch syndrome in every walk of life, in every business and office but you just learn to handle it. With years of experience, you just learn to say, 'You're joking, pal, aren't you?' Basically I'd say now men tend to expect women to think and be able to handle different situations.

The Future

I recognise that it is not a career for life. I'm actually surprised that I've got away with it for as long as I have. It's a lot of hard work. I think that, for some girls, it maybe comes naturally. I'm aware of how much I drink or eat and if I've got a big job coming up, I know I've got to get a lot of sleep, a lot more sleep than I needed ten years ago. I'm just happy as long as the phone's ringing. I find now I'm organising more events. People that I've worked for for years will maybe phone me and say, 'Oh, June, we've got a big dinner coming up. Could you get me ten girls?' or, 'We've got a big sporting event, we need hospitality, could you organise it?' So maybe that's an avenue that I'll go down. I quite enjoy corporate hospitality and working at that.

Maybe I'll have a family, in the fullness of time. Women don't panic about that as much now, I don't think. Obviously, the biological clock is ticking – I hate that – and you do have a time where it's going to run out but I don't think women sort of panic in their late twenties the way they used to do. My mum said she had me at thirty-one and she was the oldest person in the maternity ward. I've friends who've had their first baby at thirty-seven and thirty-eight, and I think that's another thing in women's favour. But it's still a struggle for women because you still have to take that time off. In any other job except mine, you could probably work up until you were nine months pregnant but nobody really wants a nine-months-pregnant woman doing the ring.

Nowadays, I think we're maybe more health-orientated. Figures have always shown that we've got the worst heart disease and heart attacks but I think we're becoming more aware of our diet and certainly I can see from promotions people's reactions to things. There's more vegetarians, a lot of people eating less red meat, and people are more into exercise. I think Scottish people for some reason were the slowest on the uptake for that but we're definitely now starting to look at our bodies and our health and think, 'Oh, wait a minute, maybe we should be doing something', but I'd say it's more the younger generations.

People are more aware of current issues, political issues as well. Scottish independence, I think that's got people thinking about the future. We tended to be a very much a fatalistic race: 'Oh well, what will happen will happen.' I think people are now generally thinking more about their lives and about their children's lives and the world that we're leaving them.

'Karen'
Shoplifter
Born 1966

I was born in Edinburgh in 1966 in the Simpson Memorial Hospital. My parents stayed in Niddrie, where I was born and bred, and which I was proud of. It was a notorious scheme and I'm quite glad that I did get brought up in Niddrie because it made me streetwise, it made me *really* wise. When I was born, my mum worked in Pollock Halls for students, for residents who stayed there and she cleaned their flats. I've got three sisters: one older and two younger. I left Niddrie when I was twenty-one and I now live in the city centre, beside Arthur's Seat, beside where the Parliament's getting made.

I went to a Catholic primary school, St Francis', then I went to secondary – Holyrood High School. I enjoyed primary but secondary I disliked. I was good at school. I was shy, but good. I'm still shy, to an extent. I did work at the lessons but my mum had died when I was twelve, just as I was going into secondary and I just think that I lost all my confidence. When I was doing my work, it was like, no' a waste of time, but I never had enough confidence when I was sitting there doing my work. When I was younger I used to always say that I was wanting to be a hairdresser. Now that I've got to this age, I would like to be a lawyer. But there's no chance of that now.

I liked hockey, netball, basketball. I was a right sporty person when I was younger. We'd play things like peevers, Chinese ropes, and Kick-the-Can. We would get wood and old prams and things like that, nail them together and make a guider. Just using our imaginations. I've never seen anybody for years play any of those games. I think they're all stuck in front of the television, playing PlayStations and Nintendo 64s. I've got a daughter of eleven now myself and I never see anybody playing any street games, peevers or nothing.

Rich Pickings, Easy Money

When I was sixteen, I left school and I went to live with my auntie. Then I worked on a YOP, a Youth Opportunities Project. I worked there for a year and I got £25 a week – that was in a printing department. After that, my uncle had a pub so I worked as a barmaid for a few years. Then I turned to crime. I was at the age where I think I was quite vulnerable and naive, and all my friends, like, they were shoplifters and they'd go away shoplifting. They'd come back and they'd have lots of clothes for theirselves and this and that. So I just tried it and it was that easy: we'd go to Princes Street and we got away with it all the time, so we just kept on doing it.

You just go into the shops, look around, make sure nobody's watching. Once I got away with it the first time I thought, 'Oh, that's great. I'll try it again.' Got away with it the second time, and it went on from there until you do get caught. After we got caught, you got remanded and then we'd go back up to court and I'd probably get a three-month sentence.

They did have the security tags and you could still beat them – you can still beat them now. If there's a will, there's a way. First of all, you need to remove a security tag. But there's ink bugs – when you go out the door, the alarm doesn't go off but you burn them when you get back home. You know how to get them off without damaging the garment, the ink bugs. The other bugs you just maybe go in the changing rooms, get them off or what have you, so it's harder, but you can still do it. Jenners is quite a hard shop to steal out of. I've stole out of it but it's very, very hard.

When you first start you really just go for anything. When you've been at it a wee while, you go for the dearest things, and then you start getting orders, orders for this, orders for that. It makes it easier when you do go into shops, and what have you because you know you've got an order for it, you're getting it sold as soon as you go back home and that money's lying there waiting for you. I've took television out of hotels, I've had a microwave before. You have to be brass-necked about it. If you're brass-necked about it, you get away with it. If you're in the shop and you're acting quite suspicious then that's when you get caught. You've got to go in there with a positive head that you're going to get what you're wanting. But I never shoplifted because I had a drug habit or anything like that. I just loved the money – it was easy money.

My wee cousin, he's in Glenochil at the moment, for shoplifting, which I think he took after me. I think when I used to come in with all the clothes, when I was getting money handed to me, when he was younger, I think he must have thought it's easy this and that. He just grew up and went ahead for it himself.

Getting Caught

The first time I ever got caught I was twelve years old and I got taken home. My granny watched after us at this time because my mum had died, and my uncle was there. I was just taken along to the police station with my older sister – she was sort of our next of kin. She took me along to the police station and a policeman just gave me a caution that if you do it again, blah, blah, blah, you'll get in serious trouble – trying to put the frighteners on you. I don't think it worked. When you get caught again, you just wait till you go up to court and see what happens. If you got away wi' it, you'd go away shoplifting again, probably straight from court.

I met my ex-boyfriend when I was eighteen and we've just split up after a fourteen-year relationship. I met him in Niddrie. When I was with him, when we first met each other, he was like in homes and things like that and he was always getting in trouble with the police. If he was getting lifted by the police, he would start fighting with them and we'd get charged with police assault, breach of the peace and drugs, using cannabis. I've smoked it for seventeen years.

Life on the Inside

When I first got remanded in custody, I did get a shock. I thought Cornton Vale would be like a man's jail, it would be quite frightening. When I first got there, it was like a Wendy House; you were locked up with another girl and it was so easy – this is going back maybe eleven, or twelve years ago. You got locked up and you got let out. Television was there for you, videos, and you got your visits every day except a Sunday. So it never gave me a shock the first time I ever got remanded. After that remand, I would have got three months convicted, which means you go to a different part of the jail. It's the same jail, in the same part but a different, convicted part where it's a totally different ball game. In remand, you're not allowed to do any work or anything like that but when you're in convicted, you get up at seven o'clock in the morning, you've got to start working at eight through to four o'clock during the day, making mail bags. The last time that I was in, it was making shrouds, which was quite morbid.

In my younger days, I had maybe done about ten remands and I've done three three-month sentences. The last time, four years ago, I was in for seven days and in January of this year, I was in for seven days, for possession of CS gas and hash. The jail has totally changed now. Before, if the prison officers had lain back any further you'd be taking the keys off them and walking over them. It's so changed because of all the suicides. [Cornton Vale has an unenviable public profile because of a spate of suicides amongst young women on remand during the late 1990s.] It's like they're scared to shout at you, it's just totally, totally changed, really changed. It was harder when I was first there and now it has totally changed. I think all the prison officers and the Scottish Prison Service are scared in case Cornton Vale gets closed down.

There were some lifers, in for killing people. Most were shoplifters, house breakers, prostitutes that cannae pay their fines. I've never really heard of anyone being in for bank robbery. I would say that most girls that are in prison at the moment, it's probably for petty shoplifting or petty this or that.

Most in Cornton Vale are Glaswegian girls and I would say they'd be shoplifting to buy drugs, because of their track marks on their arms and what have you. I've seen young girls in prison that take drugs and I've looked at their arms and I've thought, 'My goodness, that's terrible.' I cannae look down on them because I've done it myself but when I think back to myself, I never, ever got my arms in that state. I'm talking about maybe seventeen-, eighteen-year-old girls.

You do get medication in prison. You get methadone in Cornton Vale but I've never took it, but most girls get methadone which I think was a good thing for the girls that did use heroin outside. Myself, I take valium, diazepam. You got your diazepam, so it sort of helps you out a little bit. They never give you what you needed every day, but they do help you out.

Stuff comes in through the visits. I've never had any kind of parcel, like drugs, handed over to me in Cornton Vale but it does get brought through. When I'm in prison I sort of keep myself to myself ,and just get on with all the girls; whatever they've got, you just turn a blind eye and let them get on with it.

I don't think prison reforms anybody. I mean, if they do their remand or if they get a sentence, they'll do it and they'll go back out and they'll do whatever they have to do to get their drugs again. If it's money that they're wanting or whatever, you'll always go back out and do the same thing, so it doesnae help.

Life on the Outside   My daughter's quite a deep, deep lassie but I do sit down with her and speak with her. I say to her, 'Are you happy? Are you ...?' We speak about this, speak about that and she seems to be a happy-go-lucky lassie. But she's a very, very deep girl. She really likes school. She'll be going into Primary Seven this year. It's a mixed school – there's so many different minorities that go to that school. It's a really good school.

I worry that she might take to shoplifting or get involved with drugs. I say to myself, 'Well, if she's going to learn, she's going to learn from me' and I really think that she's no' going to turn to drugs and she's no' going to turn to shoplifting. I can't say that for sure but I think she's got to learn through me and her dad. Because her dad's on methadone, when she's seen him every night he was sort of sleeping so he was never a father-figure to her. He's been out of prison for eight years. I would say that he's probably seen more of Young Offenders than he has convictions for over twenty-one.

My ex-boyfriend was on heroin, and so was myself, but I would say that I wasn't addicted to heroin – I'd say I was maybe needle-happy. All my friends done it and it was 'go with the flow'. If you never done it, you were a sort of daftie or sensible, and if you did do it, then you were one of the gang. Then it just all stopped because all of a sudden HIV came out. I got a test in 1986 which was negative and I would never, ever go back for another test in my life because it's so frightening. No' that I'm feared, because I've never ever jagged since. I've never used a needle since 1983.

One Day at a Time   I worry about going back up to Cornton Vale because of the charge that me and my ex-boyfriend are going up for. We're charged with firearms for the CS gas and a half ounce of cannabis. Half an ounce isn't much but I've got previous convictions for drugs. It's a saying that the husband always takes the blame for his wife or what have you. But my man is no' taking the blame for me, so that's why I'm split up with him – he's no' a man if he's no taking the blame.

I got the CS gas in America in 1996. Even if you've got previous drugs convictions, you can still go on holiday to America, but you can't emigrate there. When we got to America I was getting all paranoid – what if they stop me when I get to America and say you can't come in here because you've got convictions – but we got through fine. When we were in our complex, in our hotel, a woman got robbed at gunpoint. I've got bad anxiety so I started panicking and took panic attacks and my daughter was screaming, she was wanting to go home. The policeman told us to go and buy CS gas. We've never ever used it but we stupidly brought it back with us.

Now I'm on High Court bail so I can't really afford to get into trouble. I support myself just with my Income Support, my book, and just try and get on with that, which is hard. When I look back at my life and I made money this way or I made money that way, it's quite hard. I can't really afford to go down town and start shoplifting because if I get caught then I've broken my bail and then I would go to prison. I've got to think of my daughter here. I'm no scared of prison but the only thing I'm worried about is my daughter. I can do the time, but it's my daughter. Because she's at that age and she's well looked after when I'm away but I just worry and I miss her.

Now I take every day as it comes. I never ever plan anything. I take every day as it comes. I wake up and say, 'What am I going to do today? What kind of day is it the day?' That's how I find my life.

Since this year has come I'd like to go to college or get a job. I think I would prefer to go to college, and do something that's going to suit me. Maybe I'd get a bursary, some kind of grant or something like that. If I was at college and it was something that I really really wanted to do, I could swear on my mother's ashes – and I'd never go back on my mother's ashes – and I could put my hand on my heart, that I would never turn to crime again.

A Woman's Perspective

Carol, Betty
Sheila, Noreen & Nicola

Introduction

Carol My dad was an engine driver. I live in Strathblane now, I've got two boys aged sixteen and eleven, and I work for myself, I do freelance stuff. I come into the BBC quite a lot because I used to work here and still do a lot of training with people on assertiveness and that kind of stuff.

Sheila I was born and brought up in Inverness, I got married at eighteen, had our first daughter at twenty-one and the next one at twenty-four. One's thirty-eight and does quite a lot of work for the BBC, the other one's thirty-five; both are married. I've got a granddaughter and grandson in Dunblane and two little grandsons along the road, so since I retired two years ago from Inverness District Council, I combine my time as Chairman of the Highland Senior Citizens' Network, Chairman of the Inverness Local History Forum and Secretary of the Community Council, with picking up grandsons from school, taking them home and occasionally getting to my bed and going to sleep!

Noreen I got married at twenty-three and it was twelve years before we had my son, David. Unfortunately when he was just six, his father died and so I've been a single parent since. I've lots of hobbies – gardening, amateur drama, writing, etc. – and a very full life.

Nicola I'm twenty-one and I was born and brought up in Rutherglen in the south side of Glasgow. I've just moved in with my boyfriend, about three months ago, which was a big step. My family were all behind me and my gran was especially behind me. She thought it was fantastic, which my mum was really shocked to hear, because when my mum was moving out when she was getting married, she was totally against the idea of my mum and my dad even being together when they were decorating the house for one thing.

Betty I'm married with five children – three girls, two boys. My oldest daughter's thirty-seven, my youngest is twenty-six. I have eleven grandchildren, aged from nineteen to two. I think I've done every job – nursing, owned a pub. I've done charity work all my life, I believe in equality, I believe that every man and every woman has their rights and everybody's equal in the eyes of everybody. I hate snobbishness – people who are born with a bool in their mouth, fine, but I hate the ones that put the bool there that never was, because we're a' Jock Tamson's Bairns. When you go at the end of the day, nobody asks you 'Did you stay in Milngavie or Kirkintilloch?', 'Did you stay in Lenzie or did you stay in Battlefield?', because no matter where you are, it's not where you live, it's how you live.

Teenagers

Noreen When I was fourteen or fifteen, the war was on and that made everything quite different. There was no clothes: you wore a pink jersey with a purple anything, because of clothes rationing. You weren't so keen as they are now on dressing and hair – you just felt yourself that you were lucky. But we had great times, it was a much simpler life. You didn't go far because you couldn't travel, so you got to know the people round about you much more closely. There was a freedom, strangely enough, that the teenagers don't have now. That's what I feel.

Sheila It was probably a wee bit different in the Highlands because there was quite a lot of dance halls in Inverness. There was a hotel with a huge ballroom – it was beautiful but unfortunately no longer there – and another big building, the Northern Meeting Rooms, which was used to entertain the gentry and such. It attracted all the big bands because there was always a good dance-following in Inverness. All the villages for twenty, thirty miles around, all had a Saturday or a Friday night 'hop'; buses used to be packed to the point of being dangerous going to them. The girls never drank, I mean, you really were a fallen woman at that time if you drank. The boys, especially the country lads, they always used to have a half-bottle stuffed up their Fair Isle pullover which was hidden behind the wall around the dance hall, church hall or whatever. There was a regular tramping back and forth from the dance to outside, and each time they came back they were a little more refreshed and the dancing got even more violent, to the point of hurling the poor little size tens across the floor. It was good, but there was never any drunkenness. There was a little bit of fighting occasionally, but it was good fun. Everybody thoroughly enjoyed it and we went back and forth in groups, but absolutely free.

Nicola I'd my first drink when I was thirteen, as did many of the people I know at my school. Many people actually took their first drug at thirteen, which was a bit shocking: they had their first drug before they had their first drink. There was a group of girls and we used to go into the city centre of Glasgow to the dancin', the 'under-eighteens', we called it. I used to get the train in at six o'clock and it would finish by nine o'clock and we'd go home – I had to be home for half past ten. The guys that always went there were all about sixteen or seventeen because you know they say guys grow up later than girls. We'd always go to the train station and drink a neck out of a bottle of Strongbow, and I would be really drunk by that time. I'd go and I'd be all giggly. I think I did it too quickly actually – I was drinking in pubs when I was sixteen. I never drank a lot at the time but every weekend you'd have, you know, a few drinks.

But it was just the norm. It's the norm now for people to take drugs at thirteen, which is a shame, really. A lot of people don't take it that far, it's just more experimental but thirteen was the age I remember, and a lot of people I know tried drugs.

Noreen In my day cigarettes was the equivalent of drugs and at thirteen that was when you tried to smoke. I tried and hated it. Luckily.

Sheila I tried it and hated the taste – I threw up.

Betty I was twenty-seven before I smoked. Actually. I didnae like it at all, but it was at a bereavement; it was my gran. We were sitting at a wake and the cigarettes were getting passed round and quite automatically, I took one. I just felt it calmed me, and after that it was a wee Woodbine, five or ten Woodbine. I've continued smoking ever since.

Nicola Now it's cannabis joints that are the norm. Cigarettes is becoming sort of a wee bit unsociable, and people say, 'I'm going to stop smoking but I'm still going to smoke joints,' as if to say that it's more socially acceptable to smoke a joint.

Betty When I was thirteen I played at French ropes, I was brilliant at French ropes. You played ball. Boys never entered our mind at that age – we played with them but there was nothing sexual.

Sheila There was a bit of disgust at boys at that age, really.

Betty Aye, if a boy said anything to you at that age, you were dumbfounded, but I find that my grandchildren today are missing out on a lot. When anybody walked up our street, there was boys playing football or cricket or whatever, and there were wee lassies playing ropes or peever wi' the Cherry Blossom tin. I never see that now. The other day we were at a christening and there was a wee girl there of seven years of age and she was dressed like a tart. She was a bonny, bonny wee lassie and she had a wee flimsy dress on with the thin straps, shoes like what the Spice Girls wear and the big earrings. I thought to mysel', 'What a beautiful kid,' but to me she looked like a wee tart. My father, who's eighty-three, said to me, 'My God, do they not dress wee girls like wee girls?' I don't mean frilly frillies but I think the kids are exploited more now. And you're at the stage now where your kids is all wanting to be the same as their friends and it's sad, it's so sad.

Sheila Your mother would've been appalled to dress you like that as a child, and I would've been with my children, but is it not something in the way that that child's mother's age group was brought up? That sees nothing wrong in turning a little girl who should be just an innocent little thing into a mini-adult?

Noreen Do you not think we're following America, where the child is becoming dominant – she dictates what things are happening in the house?

Carol I think I feel a kind of mixture, maybe because I grew up in the '60s. I ken when I was about fifteen and sixteen, I was going to discos and pubs and pretending I was older but I don't think there was the same emphasis on girls drinking. I spoke recently to some teenage girls at school and the big issue for them round assertiveness was drink: it wasn't sex, it wasn't the things that I thought it might be, it was about saying no to drink. That was a big issue. I don't really remember that being a huge issue for me as a kid. I can remember, though, going to parties; my mother was a barmaid and she would always say, 'Whatever you do, don't drink the Carlsberg Specials.' She was really obsessed by going to parties and getting drunk because then you were vulnerable and I think she was right. You would go and have a shandy or a lager but, by God, I never drank a Carlsberg Special. So I think it was a kind of mixture in the '60s in a way. Undoubtedly as I got older and was at university, some people were smoking joints but it wasn't as common as it is nowadays; it was really quite a risqué thing to be doing then.

Betty My teenage years was terrific, but as I say, listening to the young girl here, I was seventeen before I was allowed in a dance hall, and that had to be the local hall. When I was eighteen, I was allowed into the Locarno. I thought this was fantastic. Now when my daughters have a night oot with a group of girls, even though they're married, I say, 'Now watch what you're doing and do not go to the toilet all together and leave your drink in case it gets spiked,' but when I was young I felt safe. I wisnae frightened of a boy taking me down the road because I knew he wisnae gonny abuse me. I think we were more safe. A lot of bad things were going on when we were younger that we didn't know about and they're coming out of the pie now, but I enjoyed my time as a teenager. We used to go to the pictures with an orange and an apple – no cigarettes. Then we started winchin'. Nicola says 'boyfriend' but we say 'laud'. I had my first laud when I was sixteen. Oh, I thought I was the bees' knees, but then again, in our day we tried to impress the boys; the girls don't need to now. We dressed in suits and tried to be sophisticated, but anything goes noo – you go oot wi' a pair o' gutties on and it doesn't make any difference!

Sheila The teenage population was less mobile then so you tended to know the people that you were out with; you went with your pals that lived locally and you knew the local boys. Everybody knew everybody with a bad reputation then. I'll bet you can say to me all the girls of your age that had a bad reputation then. They come in now with their cars and the girls as well, they're all a lot more mobile, so you don't really know who is who, what they've done.

Betty You were talking about up in Inverness. They used to run buses from Kirkintilloch to Balfron to the dancin' and we'd go all dressed with our winkle toes and our stiletto heels, dirndl skirts, and can-can petticoats. We'd go there, and there they'd be with boots and jeans on. The Highland girls didnae like us because we were up there to take their men. Now that was the only thing that I can remember going up to Balfron or Aberfoyle – the girls who belonged to these kind of places didnae like us townies comin' up. That's the only fear we had then, in case we pinched one of their boyfriends because they let you know.

Dressing Up

Noreen At the end of the war when I was sixteen, we went into the New Look. Everyone was shocked with the New Look at first, everyone being used to uniforms – even the women wore uniforms – and suddenly these long, floaty skirts and cinched waists went to our head like whisky. First of all we were shocked, and then you had to get it. It was wonderful, it was like a release. I was lucky, I was the generation that was coming up. My sisters' generation was the generation whose boyfriends were called up, who were killed. I was the first of the happy generation. The boys I went with, there was no war, whereas girls just five years older than me were biting their nails and they were having affairs because of this 'you might never see me again', which was the biggest aphrodisiac in the world. But I was lucky, I was the new wave – the New Look, the new wave, the peace; it really was a champagne time.

At sixteen or seventeen, you didn't wear heavy make-up. Again, the war had an awful effect. There was no make-up factories, they had much more important things to make so what came on first of all would be what you'd call Number 17, just cheap make-up. But the great thing was there was no tights. They hadn't been invented. It was stockings, and when the first nylons came that was like the invention of the wheel, you know. At last you had something that was going to last you longer than one night, and people used to sell their souls and their bodies for a pair of nylons. The New Look was just a kind of long look – it was before the frou-frou petticoats came in. You got these shoes with the strap over – they were white in the summer, you blanco'd them like the way you used to do your tennis shoes. Hair suddenly was allowed to become longer, whereas before it had been cut. It was a wonderful time. But the best thing was the nylons. It was the biggest breakthrough because it lasted and that was what was the main thing.

Carol In the '60s I can remember the mini-skirt coming in, and wearing that with boots. My dad always said it looked as if the boots were holding your legs together, they were very tight laced-up boots with a very short skirt and we just thought we were wonderful. I can remember going to the Barras [market] and buying old fur jackets; they really had a horrible smell about them but I just thought I was the trendiest thing under the sun. I can remember my mother saying, 'I just don't see what's attractive about that' and I look at young kids these days who're really into sports clothes and I just don't get it. I feel like my mother: I don't get how that's attractive but I suppose people thought the same about what we were wearing.

We wore lots of black eyeliner and mascara. Then it was the white lips – you would pan-stick your lips so that you wouldn't have lips. It was a kind of Julie Christie look which is bizarre when you come across it in magazines, because nowadays people do tend to wear lipstick.

Sheila I remember very well the very first person that appeared in Inverness after the war with the New Look – it just about brought the town to a standstill. She was the daughter of fashion-shop owners, and the jacket was purple with a very nipped-in waist, black velvet trimmed, very long straight skirt, black suede stilettos and a little black velvet hat with a sort of eye veil. And everybody stopped and stared, they had never seen anything like this in their lives.

Then, of course, the next generation we all had our wide skirts and our ballerina pumps for dancing rock'n'roll. My abiding memory is this gorgeous can-can petticoat that everybody wore. They scratched your legs and got in the way but you had to have one of those, and it had to be under a black taffeta skirt. When you were jiving away in the corners, I'm sure some of us nearly had lift-off sometimes because the skirt was swirling, but that was certainly very much the thing. After the '60s came in, it changed and the hairstyles changed. I'm sure all the ladies of our age will remember back-combing your hair; you had to have this mop of back-combed hair. You spent about a week getting the knots out once you'd back-combed and lacquered it and it was pretty awful.

Betty It was very hard to get nylons with seams up the back, so you lay on your belly and your mummy got an ordinary pencil, blackleaded it on the fire and went right up the back of your leg and you were terrified in case it moved when you were dancing. Your black lead was for your eyebrows as well. But to me, the greatest thrill when I was going to my first dance. I was in Woodilee Hospital training to be a nurse at sixteen and a half, and it was the Woodilee Ball. It was ballerina dresses you got then and the shoes to match. I always remember going into my mother's display cabinet. There was a small blue bottle that sat wi' pride in Mammy's and Granny's display cabinets, and I was always dying for my first dance to get this Evening in Paris perfume. My mother said, 'Now just a small tot,' because you couldnae get Evening in Paris then, and she said, 'You know, darlin', it's only because you're my only daughter I'm giving you this'. I went out that night and I felt like Brigitte Bardot and all night everybody said, 'Oh you smell beautiful'.

Nicola I remember when I was about five or six in the early '80s, leg warmers were a big thing, and I had loads of colours of leg warmers. Nowadays, in the '90s, I think you can categorise people and it still goes by music I think. I like a lot of old '60s and '70s music, so I wear all my dad's old clothes and I go to all the second-hand shops. If you look at somebody in the street you can say they go to this club, or that club. Or if you see a girl with sort of long hair, looking very feminine, you think she goes to that club, you can categorise people. A lot of the clubs that I go to, they wear the sort of '70s clothes and play '70s music, look at the new hippies – it's quite a backward attitude I think.

Betty When you watch the fashion programmes, do you not think instead of going forward, we're going back? I've got a pair of shoes that I've had for about eighteen years and they were called Granny Shoes with the crossed straps. My granddaughter at nineteen's wearing them, because that's the in thing. Same with scarves – years ago a lady wouldn't have went oot for the messages withoot a wee scarf 'roon her neck. You wore a dirndl skirt and a sweater and a scarf around your neck. That's all coming back in now. Years ago, all you ever saw was headscarves, you never went withoot a headscarf. You never went into a church or a chapel either withoot a hat or a headscarf, that's all done away with. But now scarves are coming back.

Carol With Twiggy, there was suddenly a vogue for very, very thin women and flat-chested women and I know a lot of the men absolutely didn't like it but it was being promoted by the magazines. The thing that I think was different about the '60s and I don't think it's ever come back since, was that there was a look that everyone ultimately tried to copy. And if you pick up women's magazines from the '60s, there's these older women wearing mini-skirts and they look absolutely horrendous in them. With the black eye make-up and the pan-stick lips, there was no sense of individuality, and I think that's what's changed. They're never going to get everyone wearing mini-skirts or everyone wearing long skirts any more, I don't think people are that daft that they will follow fashion. There's about six or seven different styles, which is good and so it is easier for people nowadays to say, 'Well, I'm going to wear that 'cos it suits me.'

Betty I could never look at Twiggy and say, 'Oh my, she's beautiful, she's got a beautiful figure.' No way. When I was young the boys liked the curves. And still do.

Sheila Remember you used to stuff your bra with cotton wool or toilet paper and stockings, ripped nylons?

Betty I remember when you'd the suspender belt and your mother would say when you went to the Locarno, 'Now don't forget, don't spend your bus money.' So what we did was, if your button broke on your suspender belt you put a wee tanner, two wee tanners and that was your bus fare home. You knew if you didnae get a lumber, you went up your skirt and you were guaranteed your bus fare home.

Sheila But it was better if it was on the front one and not the back one because it was hard to sit on.

Let's (not) Talk About Sex

Carol I can remember at school we got the nurse who would come and talk to you about periods and Lil-Lets and that kind of thing. She might have said something about conception and that. I can remember my mother saying to me 'You do know about sex, don't you?' and sighing with great relief when I said yes. She really didn't want to have to tell me but she would've if, you know, I'd said no. But I can remember spending hours with girls trying to fathom out what the real story was. There was always sort of daft stories on the go: 'Babies fall into the toilet pan' or that kind of thing. I suppose you were quite old before you did actually know the proper story. It's very different nowadays.

Sheila There was never any discussion. Sex education in school comprised sitting all the boys in the back row of the hall, the girls at the front, an elderly spinster showing slides of frogs and maybe chickens, going through it very quickly and the minute you came to the human it went 'woosh' and all the boys went 'aawww'. You really did not wear Lil-Lets until you were married because... well, we don't have to go into details, but I think our opinions then were formed from a completely different source than opinions nowadays. Sex is openly in newspapers, television and all the rest of it. In those days it was the voice of the BBC and everybody believed the voice of the BBC or the ordinary press – they didn't lie. There was nothing to inform us about all these things that probably were actually going on in the world.

About twenty years ago, a relative of mine, a bachelor in his fifties, had taken his elderly widowed mother, who was about eighty, into town to their nearby village for shopping. In the street, they met an old neighbour of his mother's and his mother said to this lady, 'Oh, how is Mrs So-and-So, I believe she hasn't been well?' The lady sort of looked at him and looked at the mother, and pulled her aside and mouthed, 'Women's trouble,' so that he wouldn't hear it. Now that was the way – you couldn't speak about anything like that. Sex was just a big no-no; you either found out or you got married and you found out. I think a lot of people were still quite ignorant after having been married for a little while, having babies, probably your first spell in a maternity ward was your best reminder of what sex was all about than anything else.

Noreen I think I must be unique. I learnt all about sex at school, but not in the classroom. By the age of ten, I knew all about it and the whole school knew because we had sexual games at playtime, and it was the greatest fun out. Mind you, having said that, there was no promiscuity – you can't when you're six, seven and eight – but you do find out how things work. Older boys had books and told you and everything. Even though we didn't experience the Full Monty, it was done the way they do in Papua New Guinea, the boys of eight and nine are left with girls so that there's no embarrassment, there's no self-consciousness, it's a natural evolvement. What really shocked me was that we had to think, 'Well for heaven's sake, we'd better not say we know anything.' The guilt feeling that I have is not feeling guilty about that, it's these boys who were about ten or eleven, I think they were put on probation and things. It was a gang initiation as you would say, and there was nothing wrong with it, and I still don't think there was really anything wrong with it. It all got back to the school and there was a police raid and all this. Suddenly, it really was strange, suddenly I thought, 'What we've been doing is wrong' and it wasn't just me, I'm talking about maybe fifty kids. By the time you went to Primary Seven you knew the lot. Quite honestly, we all then had to act the innocent, and I went through a terrible spell of saying, 'No, I don't know anything about that' when I felt like saying, 'What do you want to know?' I don't think it did any harm. We couldn't understand why there was such a furore about it, you know. But there was nothing within the education system, nothing. Not my mother, not anyone. I remember the night before I married, I was terrified she was going to take me aside and I was going to say to her when she got started, 'Forget it, you know, I'm OK.'

Nicola I don't remember anything specific, I kind of feel that I always knew. Obviously I was told at some point, but I remember we had what was called

Personal Development, but it was an old teacher – he was old to me, he must've been in his fifties or sixties – and he would put on a video and just hand out leaflets through the whole hour, like 'Do You Think We Are Approaching Sex Education The Way We Should?'. But I remember I asked my mum how to French kiss when I was about ten or eleven and she says, 'You'll find out when you're older,' so I asked my dad. The thing is, I had quite an open relationship with my mum and dad, I could talk to mum about periods and my dad as well – which I think's quite common nowadays, for your mum and your dad to be talking about sex and things like that.

Betty I'm like Shirley Valentine, I'm still waiting on the orchestra. To me, sex is a myth: what you see on the television, I mean, I wonder where I went wrang. I wis thin and I wis no' bad looking but I didnae dae some o' the things that they dae.

I was a wee bit kind of green being the only girl with nine brothers. Obviously when they got taken out a bath, you always look – but my mother would never allow me to stand in the sitting room without my pants on, and the boys had to have their pants on or their 'jamas on. My mother used to say, 'Temptation's a terrible thing and you'll learn quick enough,' but I'm afraid my mother never explained sex to me and I really and truly don't think it did me any harm. Maybe I got married and my husband educated me but no' knowing about sex did me no harm. I just think the TV is the biggest education for kids nowadays. I mean, my son's thirty-six and you're sitting with your son or your grandchild … *Fatal Attraction* was on one night, and I switched it over. My granddaughter says, 'What are you doing, Granny?' I says, 'Ach, I don't like that,' and I switched it o'er. You're totally embarrassed, even in front of your husband. Especially when you see a Channel 4 programme and it's two girls; that really does my nut in – if I want to see that, I'll buy something like that.

Carol You can look back and believe that it was a much more sexually naive time, but an awful lot of it was driven underground. I mean, I was sexually abused when I was younger. It is so common for folk to talk about uncles or friends of the family, whatever, all hushed up. So behind those kind of net curtains and what seemed like a very sexless society, there was a lot going on, and I think it's actually much better nowadays, that there is more sex around to some extent because I think it's more honest, it's more open.

Noreen I think they're too acrobatic now, though.

Betty But look at it now, people think that perverts – it's acceptable. The chap that did the ▸ee girls, they're spending one million pounds a month down in London protecting him – to me the system's all wrong.

Carol I'm not saying it's not, but I think it is easier now for children to be able to say what happened to them.

Noreen But the other point is, it's terrible that now a man can't take a child on his knee. It's actually swung that way that men are terrified, like in the old days, my husband's father always said to him 'If you're travelling on a train …' – it was the trains where there was compartments with separate doors – 'If there's a woman alone, don't go into that because she'll shout rape.' You know for money, she'll say 'If you don't give me some money … ' and that's the man's side of it. It's swung to the other way, that men are afraid to show a physical affection with little girls or even little boys. I think it's a shame. It's sad that it's got to that.

Sheila It was always 'Don't talk to strangers', even when we were quite young, but in every case I ever knew about, including myself, it was never a stranger. It was a neighbour, it was somebody's grandfather, it was this elderly gentleman along the road. There was none of us at that stage, I mean we didn't understand what it was – about age ten, eleven, twelve. We knew there was something wrong, but who did you speak to? You couldn't have gone to your mother or father and said, 'This man's doing something that I don't think is right.' You didn't even have the vocabulary to explain, you didn't know what the sexual parts were called even. I mean, kids nowadays, it's just run-of-the-mill, everyday language.

Carol And you thought your parents might not even know what the words were you were talking about, or whatever.

Sheila I don't think my mother would've known, I don't think she would've believed it.

Unmarried Mothers

Sheila Up in Ross-shire, my granny got pregnant and my mother never knew till the day she died who her father was. My granny was sent to a farm where the farmer's wife took in 'fallen women' – unmarried mothers – for their confinement. They were there for three or four weeks and then taken back. Then it was my mother's granny that brought her up. But ever after, this was a stigma for the rest of her life, and that she always had this sort of chip on her shoulder that she never knew who her father was because nobody talked about it.

Betty There's many a girl got put in an institution, like Lennox Castle, because she'd a baby. I did a lot of work in these places and there was a lady there, she was institutionalised because she'd been in there for forty-odd years but she was okay. I asked the Charge Nurse what she was in for and he says, 'If you read the case notes you would die. She'd an illegitimate child and her father had her put here.'

Carol I can remember being friendly with a family in the '60s and the girl got pregnant and she disappeared. They were a Catholic family and it was a great shame in the family. She just disappeared mysteriously for six months or whatever, came back and then got pregnant again within a couple of months. It was a fairly disastrous story, even then in the swinging '60s.

Betty In my time, most of the kids that were born illegitimate were with the granny but they always called the granny 'Mammy'. They didnae know, but you'd be playing ropes and you'd say, 'There's your mammy wanting you,' and somebody would say, 'That's no' her mammy, that's her granny and you've no' to tell anybody.'

Sheila And they were brought up with aunts and uncles as siblings.

Abortion and Contraception

Noreen I never knew anything about abortion, but I think it would be there, especially in a city the size of Glasgow. But I think most girls, if they'd got into trouble, they'd heard so many terrible stories about abortion, apart from the pain, how they could die, that I think they opted for having the baby. Also, usually they had the baby because it was a love affair. This is the difference and the thought of giving away the baby of the man that they loved… I don't think abortion came into it. I think they'd rather stick it out.

Betty When I was about six or seven, I remember sitting in my granny's house and this lady came and asked 'Have you any change, Kate, for the gas?' and my granny says 'Naw, I've none.' The lady from down the stair, who was there, said,

'How did ye no' gie her it, Kate?' and she said, 'I don't like her, that's the knitting-needle woman.' I never knew what the knitting needle women was. When I got a wee bit older, I told my mother and she said, 'Aye, she was the backstreet abortionist.' If their men went to the war and they fell pregnant, they went to her and she did it with a knitting needle.

Noreen It doesn't take much imagination – I'd rather have a child naturally. And it wasn't even that, it could go into septicaemia and they could bleed to death. I think any girl who got pregnant, knew these horror stories – I think it was the option I would've taken.

Betty In every town and every village, there was always a backstreet abortionist. It was known.

Nicola Now people just go on the pill, and if they get pregnant, then it's to do with family values and stuff. I've known a few people just to go for three or four abortions, and to just walk out as if nothing's happened. Whereas me personally, I just couldn't do it, but the sense of family values has changed, that it's just so easy just to walk in and get an abortion and walk back out. I think it's pretty bad, but as I say, that's just the way I've been brought up.

Sheila There again, what they did if they realised they were pregnant was try and bring on an early miscarriage – that was the boiling bath, the bottle of gin and you sat in this water as hot as you could handle and drank gin.

Noreen There's a joke about that: gin and a hot bath and I couldn't afford enough gin to fill the bath.

Sheila I think you tried Castor Oil first, and, yes, chucking yourself downstairs. But most of them didn't really have any effect.

Betty My mother had ten kids and my granny had fourteen. In fact, the joke used to be my daddy was on night shift for thirty-odd years and they used to say, 'You'd better watch where he hings his troosers' and that was a joke in our day. But the pill to me was the sexual revolution. It's the same nowadays, you'll hear maybe you can make a mistake once but no' twice. But the point is this, yous have got more freedom than we did. You have the pill and you have contraceptives. I never knew what a contraceptive was till I was twenty-nine years of age, and I was married with three kids.

Noreen And yet there's more single parents than there was -I have my own views on this. They're doing it deliberately because they want a wee doll.

Nicola But not everybody's like that now – people still have got morals in that respect. Not everybody nowadays just has sex and has an abortion. I did say that people do, but it doesn't happen all the time.

Betty But the babies that's born don't have to be born.

Noreen You can take precautions with the pill and one thing and another, but I was reading statistics and it's going up and up and up. You just go onto the train and you see the young girls as happy as Larry with beautiful children. Now, they must've had a choice to have that, because often they don't even know who the father is, the father's away. It's not even a passionate night or something.

Carol I think for a lot of young girls very often who don't have a good job prospect or whatever, it's a chance for a bit of an independent life, they'll get their own flat or whatever.

Betty But then when they've had that kid for about two years they realise what they've missed out, so they want their grannies to watch them.

Carol I'm not saying it's the right choice, I'm just saying that I think it's often a choice that's made.

Noreen They get a lot of love from their baby but all these lovely young girls, I think, wait thirteen years and they're horrible teenagers that come in and stamp and shout and saying, 'Where's my father and why didn't you ...?', you know. It's a time-bomb.

Childbirth and Child-rearing

Betty I never wanted to have any kids – I wanted to be a mammy but I never wanted to have kids, I didnae plan it.

Noreen We were twelve years married. At the first year no-one said anything. By the fourth year there was wee jokes about 'Does he not know what to do with it?' Then it got to about the sixth year when I kind of heard, 'Poor souls, they can't have any children.' There was none of these fertility clinics. I never looked in a pram once; we were having a lovely, lovely time, and quite honestly, it never occurred to us to go to the doctor or go to a clinic or anything. That was the way it was, we were leading a normal life but I wasn't getting pregnant. Then I did but because I wasn't expecting it, I was five months' pregnant before I realised. I went to my drawer one day – we'd moved to a new house and it was all the turmoil of getting it painted, etc. – and I thought, 'I've no sanitary towels – when was the last time I bought them? Where's the chemist here anyway?' And that made me sit and think.

My husband had bought me one of these dressmaking model things that you press into – like a knight in armour – and you've got to put it on practically naked and then take it off. So that night, just to be quite sure, we did that and he pressed it all round me, put it on the stand and he looked at it and said, 'Is that really you?' He said, 'Oh, I think you should go to the doctor, there's something far wrong,' but I didn't like to say. I was five months' pregnant and it was great – I hadn't had morning sickness or anything.

Betty I'd rheumatic fever when I was young and they said it would be best to have my baby in the maternity ward, but I said no. So I had my first baby in the house and the wee midwife, Annie, would sit with the fag hanging from her mouth and my mother kept giving her tea, and I'm going, 'Oohhh, it's sore' and she'd say, 'Oh, I know it's sore, hen,' and kept smoking the fag. My mother couldnae watch me any longer and went outside, and my Aunt Rose came in and knelt at me wiping my brow. Just before Elaine was born I felt this urge to push and I went, 'Right nurse, I'm ready, you can cut my belly open noo.' She says, 'Ya silly bugger, it comes oot where it went in,' and that was my first experience of having a baby. That's how much I knew about childbirth, and I was twenty. My first baby and I thought they were going to cut me open and lift it out.

Sheila When we got married I was only eighteen so we decided we'd wait two or three years; that was a considered decision, but just the same it was, 'Anything doing yet?' because if you weren't pregnant within three months, they thought there was something wrong with you. The first one we had in hospital. The second daughter – I don't think anybody would believe the story of this birth. We couldn't get a council house because there was none and we decided we'd build our own. It was really done on the cheap, and we were living in a caravan, not a mobile home, a holiday caravan. It was the winter of 1962–63 which had been the coldest winter since 17-something. The frost had frozen the Calor Gas, and the bedcovers were frozen to the wall every morning. She was due in April and we still didn't even have the electricity in in mid-March. They came to dig a trench to get the cables in and they were lifting out three-foot wide lumps of permafrost.

I had decided that I wasn't going to go back to hospital, this was going to be a home birth. Woke up bang on the day and the house wasn't even finished, there was no wall in the kitchen, the midwife came in and she was sitting having a fag; in fact while I was having my labour pains, she was offering me one as well, and I didn't even smoke then. Eventually, they put the bed up on big wooden things and she was born at home and then the doctor turned up – 'Everything going OK?' 'Yeh, fine' and the room must've been stinking of smoke, and that was it. There was no aftercare or anything. I went to the doctor to get confirmation I was pregnant and that was it until she was born.

Betty I washed my bedroom floor and polished it the next day after she was born for visitors coming to see her.

Sheila I was actually up the ladders painting the night before. No epidurals or anything – not a bit of it.

Noreen They gave me gas and air at the end. Actually, my David was due on Hogmanay and on Hogmanay, he started to come but then decided to wait until New Year's Day and then it was January 2nd, so it went on and on. On New Year's Night, I was still in hospital and my labour had stopped. And seemingly, all the nurses had been out on Hogmanay, and the matron in these days came round and said, 'Half my staff haven't appeared, they were all out at the party last night. The night matron's coming round, I'm disgusted at this ward.' They'd put two wards into the one because there wasn't enough nurses and I was in a bed up the middle. She said to me, 'I can't have you there, you're untidying the ward. Take the pillowcase off your pillow and put all your things in it and go into the toilet and wait there till I call you.' So I went into the toilet, and she shifted the bed away and forgot all about me. I went into the last stage of labour, delivery, in the toilet on the floor. A Chinese woman came into the toilet – I was curled up in agony on the floor and she yattered in Chinese and felt my head and yattered and then shuffled out. When they came in all hell broke loose – I think he was born about five minutes after that. It was terrible.

Carol I think it was very different – Ewan was born in 1982. There was childbirth classes, visit the ward and everything like that, but I had two Caesarean sections, for medical reasons.

To Love, Honour and Obey – or Divorce

Sheila I know quite a few of my own family that were all growing up, getting married about the same time. There was two or three years when there was a wedding every two or three months. But of those marriages at that time, quite a few of them didn't last all that long, for various reasons. They had become much more materialistic. The opinions that are held now are completely different. Golly, if you had a bit of carpet square and a rug, you were a toff. A bit of lino, you were really a toff. But now a lot of the youngsters want to go into a fully furnished home with all mod cons. There's a bit of a dichotomy between the young single parents that we were talking about, and those that have got married and are sort of launching themselves on their career.

There's a bit of a fall-out, I think from the '60s parenting, that led to some of the young single parents today, because some of their parents were still trying to swing when they were long past the swinging stage. I think it was probably in an attempt to get the material surroundings, and the lifestyle and everything, that some of these young girls got pregnant because they saw their own peer groups having a fairly successful life. Others on the other hand, well, they're heading for their career but then they see this girl they were at school with and she's got this lovely baby. I think we're in a transient social time – maybe not a revolution, I think the '60s was the revolution – but I think the fall-out from the '60s is still with us and probably it'll be into the next century before there's a steadier way of life.

Betty Ah, but girls nowadays will not take the trouble. When my mother got married, it was for better or for worse. If yer daddy battered yer mammy, if yer daddy didnae work, she stood by. She took it, she kept her mouth shut. I was one of the first Catholic girls in Kirkintilloch to get divorced, and that was just in the late '60s. Now, it was my parish priest that actually told me, 'Go for it, go for it,' because my husband drank and I was brutally attacked. When he was sober, he'd say that it was me, that he was a gentleman. He was a Jekyll and Hyde. My mother was on her deathbed when she was fifty-three and she says to me, 'One day that love will turn to hate,' because I absolutely adored him. He was a fine-looking big guy and I wisnae a bad-looking lassie, we'd lovely kids, we'd a beautiful home, but the abuse I took was nobody's business. Then I woke up one day and the love had turned to hate. And I thought that couldnae happen. But my second husband – I've got a great husband but I've got a barrier up and it's sad, because he says, 'You're trying to make me a replica – I'm no' like your first husband.' But anyway I put the barrier up right away. No man'll ever hurt me again. But my granddaughters will not take what I took. Would not take the beatings I took, or the abuse.

Sheila But you didn't have a refuge.

Betty No, I had nothing.

Noreen But again I think we've swung too much the other way; as you say, 'For Better, For Worse'. There's often relationships that go on for five years and even the most passionate relationship cools. You get to the friendship plane and you have fights. Now in my day, I remember having fights, going to pack my bag and thinking, 'But what'll I do with the china, what'll I do with that, where will I go?' So you stuck it out. We had a mantelpiece with the tiles and we kept a lipstick on the top of it and I'd write, 'Sorry'. Our pride wouldn't let us say it. Or he'd write a message and that would be it and the making up was great, and you went on. Whereas if it was just a relationship and there was no contracts or anything you could've walked out and said, 'You see, it was a bad relationship,' but if you weather the storm, and it's just a storm, it gets better and better. It's too easy to walk away now.

Betty You'd to do your duty in your day, and your duty was to clean the house, cook, have everything ready for him, his clean shirt ready, and do your duty in bed. So my mother did her duty and she was a good Catholic mother so she had fourteen pregnancies, of which ten lived. But if anybody's got fourteen kids noo, they say they're either a good Catholic or a sloppy Protestant, because there's no such a thing noo as a big family.

Two to three is the most you'll get now with youngsters, and I agree with them, because it's getting harder to rear kids. It's getting expensive to rear kids. A pot of mince and a pot of stew, that would have filled the neighbours. But now, you go into a supermarket, you're buying stuff you don't really need 'cos the weans like it. The kids are no' getting the cabbage, the turnip and everything that we got. That's how you get hyperactive kids now because they didnae get the salt of the earth that we got when we were young. You either ate it or you left it, and that was it. It wisnae, 'What are you eating, what are you eating and what are you eating?'

Changed Expectations

Carol That is one thing that I'm very aware of: we think that women's lives are a lot easier these days, we've got all these mod cons and all the rest. It's not true because it used to be you'd cook one meal – Monday was mince and Tuesday was fish and whatever it was. There was a kind of ease about it, you didn't wash kids' clothes all the time. Actually, in lots of ways, women's lives are much, much harder because very often women are trying to do a job and they're trying to be the traditional wife, with these incredible high standards of being superwoman, fit, sexy, glamorous, good fun. It's completely undo-able and I think it's not surprising that women are actually feeling very tired, very stressed and very unfulfilled. At least in the old days it was do-able, you could be that good mother.

Betty Do you no' think another sad thing is keeping up with the Jones's just now? I think that to me has ruined society.

Noreen And that's your television too. I think people see on television a life that they say, 'Why don't I have that?' Whereas what you didn't see, you didn't long for. But what I'd like to ask is, what year was it when mothers started going to work en masse? In my mother's generation, if she went to work it was because she had to clean someone's house, but there was no mothers that were in an office.

Nicola Because I've just moved in with my boyfriend, we laid ground rules about exactly what I wanted to do, what he wanted to do. He's a chef so he would cook where I'd wash up, or he can't do the washing but he'd do the ironing. Whereas my mum married really young and I don't feel they got to know each other before they married. You saw somebody for six months, that's the impression I've got, and then you got married. Then they get to know each other and maybe they divorce. Whereas we've got our own independent lives as well which means I want to go where I want to go, he wants to go where he wants to go but we both kind of meet in the middle.

Betty If we'd did what you did, move in with your boyfriend, we'd be called a street whore. In our day we'd be called that.

Carol Well, it's interesting because I'm not married. I've got two kids, they're sixteen and eleven, and we have never got married. When we started living together, it was kind of risqué then – we're talking about late '70s. My mother was embarrassed and didn't really want people to know, but on the other hand I was in my early thirties and I think she thought, well what the hell, you know, I'm a big girl and I have to make up my mind. But we always thought we'd get married if I got pregnant, but didn't just because we felt it was no-one's business. Where people say marriage is the thing that holds people together, I think that we work through that. As I live longer with this person, I can see all the things that people say about you have to work hard at relationships and you've made your bed and you've got to lie in it. I believe all of that and it doesn't matter to me the fact that we are not married.

Betty When we were young, if you weren't engaged or married by the time you were twenty-one, you were an old maid. But I have never heard the word 'spinster' in the last twenty years. When we were young, say somebody went to twenty-three, you'd maybe be at a dance with your man and you'd say 'Look at her, she's twenty-three and no' even married – naeb'dy wants her.'

Nicola When I moved in with my boyfriend, he bought the flat but I pay half of everything, so everything's split down the way. But my mum's friend said, 'Oh, you've really landed on your feet', and I thought, 'I'm paying half of everything – how have I landed on my feet?' Just because I'd a nice flat and I'd a washing machine.

A Century of Change for Women

Betty I think the biggest breakthrough for women nowadays is that the men do it, can help you, whereas years ago a man wouldn't have washed a dish, hoovered or anything. Up until four years ago, my hubby just wouldn't, but noo he's brilliant, I'd rather he do it than me. Anybody that's got wee kiddies noo, they come and go better than we ever had because we had to have the dinner on the table at a certain time. Nappies oot at a certain time, everything done. Whereas noo I think everything's split down the middle. I think women have got a better deal now than we did, aye.

Carol It's true and I think that men aren't as hung up about it – even my dad, who's in his seventies, will hang out washing. Men are not embarrassed about being seen pushing a pram or getting shopping, which they wouldn't have done. But it's still a big issue in relationships – it's by no means fifty-fifty and when men and women both go out to work it can be a big bone of contention. I know, as a mother of sons, that one of the things that I very deliberately do is try and get these boys to feel that their mammy is not going to look after them all the time and that they have to take responsibility for their own washings and things. Sometimes I feel a bit of a kind of heel doing it but I actually feel this is for their future relationship. I don't think it's good for boys to be thinking that, when they've got a relationship with a girl, that she's the one that should be looking after their washing.

Sheila I would echo that sentiment, because my husband hasn't quite adopted the new man image yet, but I'm encouraging my three grandsons to follow it. But one of the things which is now, and in the future, going to make a tremendous difference to women, as the pill did, is HRT [hormone replacement therapy]. So many women now are having almost a new lease of life, instead of the misery of the menopause. I know many of my friends and my mother's friends who really went through absolute hell for years – about ten years maybe, and then suddenly became old women. Now we have something which I think is giving, speaking personally, a new lease of life. I've no doubt when the men come to talk round the table of medical discoveries it might be an interesting subject, but I think HRT has really done a lot for women of a certain age.

Noreen I think it's the mod cons. You just have to look at women's hands now. In my days it was coal fires, cleaning them out. Nowadays it's central heating. My mother used to have to put on a boiler and heat the water to do the towels. Women's hands were always callused; even in the morning, you put your foot out the bed onto cold linoleum, now it's carpet, and I think we're so lucky that it's just a push-button thing now.

Nicola I think that maybe young people have got it too easy now, they've not really experienced all that – they've just got it handed to them on a plate. I feel after listening to everybody I've just had it handed to me on a plate and I don't really appreciate it. Maybe in a couple of years' time.

Betty There's nae old grannies now. Years ago when you were fifty you were an old woman. Now, no way. But in this day and age noo, when men reach a certain age, they want a new lease of life. When men go over the forties, they get a wee bit big-headed. See the likes of a man of forty, you go to a dance, and he asks Nicola to dance and she smiles at him, she quite likes him, that's a big ego to him. There's not a woman could say, 'My husband would never, ever step astray' – that is wrong.

Noreen My husband was in showbusiness and my dentist used to say, 'The difference is if you're in showbusiness you've got all these beautiful, barely clad girls round. A woman comes to me and sits in the chair, she's terrified of me. There's no temptation so I'm never tempted, but it'd be different if someone came in with hardly anything on, and wanted to sook up to me to get a better part in a play or something.' It's dead easy to be good when there's no temptation.

Betty I've got a friend in Milngavie: Janey's a very attractive lady, she's got five sons and a daughter, and her husband all of a sudden upped and walked out with a twenty-three-year-old hairdresser, and he's fifty-eight.

Nicola I don't assume that a man goes with a woman. I wouldn't say to somebody in a work situation if we're going out for dinner, 'Are you bringing your wife?'; I'd say, 'Are you bringing your partner?' because you can't assume that everybody's straight.

Betty If I was young now, there'd be no rushing to get married, no rushing to have weans, I'd be looking for the guy that was stinking rotten with money and get me what I want.

Religion: A Search for Meaning

Carol I wouldn't say that my parents were particularly religious but we did go to Sunday School and I can remember going to Sunday School and Bible Class parties and all of that stuff. When I got to about the age of twelve, I definitely became an atheist, I don't know why. I came through a wee phase of saying to people, 'I don't believe in God' and I'd wait for that wee minute to see if I was struck down, because I had been quite religious up to that point. I'm forty-seven now and I certainly feel some kind of spiritual vacuum in my life, but any time I'm in a church, for whatever reason, I'm not surprised that they're empty because I do feel that what Christianity has to offer people these days is so limited. An awful lot of the messages and Bible readings and so on are so inappropriate to what people need. I feel in the training that I'm doing on assertiveness or team-building is actually much more relevant to people, and the sorts of things that they've got to get their heads round, than what you're getting in church a lot of the time. I think it's very sad. In a way I would love to go to church now and feel that I was getting something from it. We do need some kind of ethical guidance and some sort of spirituality, but it's no wonder people are turning to personal development and training and other things like that to get it.

Sheila The Highlands traditionally was always a centre of religion and there was various stages of disruption in the churches – the Free Church obviously still has a fairly strong hold but it is going. On the islands, it's still very much there. I feel much like Carol; my father was a church elder, my mother was in the Guild and we were always in Sunday School. Gradually it lost its meaning, its message, because I think the message was something that had never been really investigated. It was something we accepted because everybody went to church but as you got a little bit older you suddenly said, 'I don't really believe this.' I still go to church and I think there is a fundamental need in human beings – not necessarily to believe in some of the things the Bible teaches – but a general, for want of a better word, humanitarian creed to live by. We need rules which will make your life and those around you happy. It's drifting away but you can see it now moving into some of the young ones who feel the need: the happy-clappies, the evangelistic movement. To me, that is something which has a great false veneer on it and I think people are grasping onto this because there's something empty in their lives. The church isn't getting the message over in modern-day terms.

Noreen I have a friend who is an Evangelist. I had a three-hour conversation with her last night all about this because she says, 'I pray every night for your soul that I can save you.' It got to the stage that this morning she phoned me and she said 'Are we still friends?' I said yes, but I hope our friendship isn't based on the hope that I'm your victim to be saved because all you've said is true, and she gets so upset when I challenge her on things. I do agree, I think a Christian way of life is a wonderful pattern of the way to live. Everyone at one point in their life will hit tremendous pain or sadness, and it's almost that you want a mother figure, someone you can to, 'Look after me, help me,' no matter whether you're an atheist or not. If you were in agony, you'd say, 'Oh God,' and so it may not be your God, it may be the Muslim's God, but there is this need, and at the moment our church is missing it, it's missing it.

Nicola When I was younger I went to church and it was my first major decision whether to go back or not. That was my first major decision that my parents gave me, and I didn't go to church through my teenage years. Then I hit a period of depression and I had to look for something else, but I didn't really know what I was looking for. I read books on Buddhism because I thought that was more a spiritual need than a religious need – I looked for, not a person, but personal guidance and I thought maybe Buddhism or some sort of religion like that would help rather than Christian guidance.

Betty I was born a Catholic and in they days, you were either a strict Catholic or a strict Protestant. I never missed Mass, I never missed Holy Days of Obligation. When I started going oot wi' lauds, you were told to get one of your own, it was far easier to get one of your own religion. But me being me, I didnae, I got a Protestant, and the second one's a Protestant as well, and we're happy. To me, there is a God. You need someone to guide you, and how did the world start? I do believe there's a supreme being but religion – the Church of Scotland, the Catholic Church, all these churches to me they're all money-making. Now where's all this money going? To me, it should be used to solve the poverty of the world and the world's needs. These churches should be opened and their wealth, like the Queen's in the vaults going away back fae the Tudor times – what the hell use is all that lying in a vault when we've got starving kids? If all churches united and opened their assets and spread it round the world, if the powers that be, like governments, came down a peg or two, I think the world would be a better place to live in.

Sheila Things were covered up, there was a deal of hypocrisy which was brought on by depression in most cases. I think now we're able to form our own opinions and to lead our own lives and to stand up for what we believe in and what we are.

Noreen No. I think we're becoming so self-centred, in isolated pockets. It's 'I'm alright, Jack' and it's only small family units, no extended family. I think there was much more helping each other in those days, whether it was the war where it was the Dunkirk spirit as they keep saying, but I think that's gone. I think there's a hardness come into society that was never there before.

Betty Where we lived, if anybody had a death, the neighbours united with one another. Now an old man across from me died and was buried and I didnae even know nothing about it. Nobody's interested. As far as the sexual thing's concerned, I might be a bit old-fashioned. I'm no' a prude, but the way things are going, the likes of that Ibiza thing and what not, I think we're going to have another Sodom and Gomorrah. I really am frightened for my grandchildren coming up. I think sex is exploited too much and that kids are being made adults before their time and they're missing out.

Nicola I think there's a lot more pressure on teenagers and young people these days. I think it's more a personal thing you have to go through yourself; you don't go through it with your peers as such any more. You've got to find yourself and then you move on yourself. It's more a personal thing I think.

Carol I think it's a mixture. Very often we want to characterise people or things as either good or bad and usually there's a mixture. I think there's aspects of our society today that is better, I think there is probably less hypocrisy round sex and other things. There is much more desire to encourage people's self-esteem and to encourage people to think something of themselves. That's been a very typically Scottish characteristic, to put people down, to keep you in your place. I think in Scotland for a long, long time, one of the worst things you could do was think anything of yourself. Paradoxically, I think people thought that was a good thing, that if you thought nothing of yourself you would have good relationships with people. The opposite is actually true – it's only if you like yourself and you've got high self-esteem that you can have really good relationships with other people. Things like that are beginning to change so I think that all of that's good. On the other hand I agree, I think we live in a society where there is less of a community spirit, there's the breakdown of the extended family. People feel more isolated and more self-centred, but I still think it is a mixture.